# Global Pentecostal and Charismatic Healing

# Global Pentecostal and Charismatic Healing

Edited by
CANDY GUNTHER BROWN
WITH A FOREWORD
BY HARVEY COX

OXFORD
UNIVERSITY PRESS

# OXFORD
UNIVERSITY PRESS

Oxford University Press, Inc., publishes works that further
Oxford University's objective of excellence
in research, scholarship, and education.

Oxford   New York
Auckland   Cape Town   Dar es Salaam   Hong Kong   Karachi
Kuala Lumpur   Madrid   Melbourne   Mexico City   Nairobi
New Delhi   Shanghai   Taipei   Toronto

With offices in
Argentina   Austria   Brazil   Chile   Czech Republic   France   Greece
Guatemala   Hungary   Italy   Japan   Poland   Portugal   Singapore
South Korea   Switzerland   Thailand   Turkey   Ukraine   Vietnam

Copyright © 2011 by Oxford University Press, Inc.

Published by Oxford University Press, Inc.
198 Madison Avenue, New York, New York 10016

www.oup.com

Oxford is a registered trademark of Oxford University Press

Library of Congress Cataloging-in-Publication Data
Global pentecostal and charismatic healing / edited by Candy Gunther Brown;
with a foreword by Harvey Cox.
     p.   cm.
Includes bibliographical references and index.
ISBN 978-0-19-539340-8; ISBN 978-0-19-539341-5 (pbk.)
1. Spiritual healing. 2. Healing—Religious aspects—Christianity.
3. Pentecostalism. 4. Globalization. I. Brown, Candy Gunther.
BT732.5.G57   2011
234'.13109—dc22      2010013326

9  8  7  6  5  4  3  2  1
Printed in the United States of America

*For Josh, Katrina, and Sarah*

# Acknowledgments

This book developed out of collaborations with an outstanding team of scholars who graciously carved out time from their schedules to contribute chapters; I want to express my immense gratitude to each of them. The research program of which this volume is a first fruit received generous financial support from the Flame of Love Project, which is funded by the John Templeton Foundation and administered by the University of Akron and by the Institute for Research on Unlimited Love; and from Indiana University through a Lilly Endowment–funded New Frontiers in the Arts and Humanities grant, an Outstanding Junior Faculty award, and a New Frontiers traveling fellowship.

The manuscript improved through feedback from two anonymous reviewers for Oxford University Press; colleagues in the Department of Religious Studies at Indiana University, especially Nancy Levene, Richard Miller, Kevin Jaques, David Brakke, Heather Blair, Aaron Stalnaker, Richard Nance, Rebecca Manring, Lisa Sideris, and Sylvester Johnson; and auditors of an invited talk (with special thanks to Andrew Chesnut for coordinating the visit) I delivered in the Bishop Walter F. Sullivan Chair in Catholic Studies Lecture Series at Virginia Commonwealth University. I received useful counsel and encouragement from Mark Noll, John Corrigan, David Hall, David Haberman, Stephen Stein, Stephen Weitzman, Paul Gutjahr, Philip Goff, Michael McClymond, Margaret Poloma, Matthew Lee, and Stephen Post. I am especially indebted to those who have taken the time to read and comment on the entire manuscript: Amanda Porterfield, Joshua Brown, Craig Keener, and my graduate student research seminar: Kate Netzler, Sarah Dees, Dana Logan, Patrick Fritz, Jessica Rivers, Kody Steffy, Michael Metroka, LaNita Campbell, and Andrew Hatcher. My research assistant Kate Netzler helped with preparation of the manuscript. Cynthia Read and others at Oxford University Press have been tremendous resources. I am especially grateful for the love and support provided by my husband and daughters: Josh, Katrina, and Sarah.

# Contents

# Contributors

**Michael Bergunder** (Dr. habil., University of Halle) is a professor of history of religions and mission studies at the University of Heidelberg, Germany. He is the author of *The South Indian Pentecostal Movement in the Twentieth Century*.

**Rebecca Pierce Bomann** (B.A., Hamilton College) is an independent scholar trained in sociology and owns a senior service in Seattle, Washington, that integrates social work and real estate for the care of older seniors and their families. She is the author of *Faith in the Barrios: The Pentecostal Poor in Bogotá*.

**Catherine Bowler** (Ph.D., Duke University) is an assistant professor of American Christianity at Duke Divinity School. Her dissertation is entitled "Blessed: A History of the American Prosperity Gospel."

**Candy Gunther Brown** (Ph.D., Harvard University) is an associate professor of religious studies at Indiana University. She is the author of *The Word in the World: Evangelical Writing, Publishing, and Reading in America, 1789–1880*. The present book is part of a multivolume project on spiritual healing practices, pentecostalism, and globalization.

**R. Andrew Chesnut** (Ph.D., University of California, Los Angeles) is the Walter F. Sullivan Chair in Catholic Studies and a professor of religious studies at Virginia Commonwealth University. He is the author of *Competitive Spirits: Latin America's New Religious Economy;*

*Born Again in Brazil: The Pentecostal Boom and the Pathogens of Poverty*; and the forthcoming *Santa Muerte: The Mushrooming New Cult of Saint Death, the Holy Skeleton.*

**Simon Coleman** (Ph.D., Cambridge University) is an anthropologist and Jackman professor at the Department for the Study of Religion, University of Toronto. His many books include *The Globalisation of Charismatic Christianity*; *Pilgrimage Past and Present in the World Religions*, with J. Elsner; and *An Introduction to Anthropology*, with H. Watson. He is currently writing about hospital chaplaincies in the United Kingdom and about Nigerian pentecostals in the United Kingdom and Nigeria. A former editor of the *Journal of the Royal Anthropological Institute*, he is co-founder and co-editor of the journal *Religion and Society.*

**Harvey Cox** (Ph.D., Harvard University) is the Hollis Research Professor of Divinity at Harvard University. He is the author of numerous books, including *The Future of Faith*; *Fire from Heaven: The Rise of Pentecostal Spirituality and the Reshaping of Religion in the Twenty-First Century*; *The Feast of Fools: A Theological Essay on Festivity and Fantasy*, which was nominated for the National Book Prize; and *The Secular City: Secularization and Urbanization in Theological Perspective*, which became an international bestseller and was selected by the University of Marburg as one of the most influential books on Protestant theology in the twentieth century.

**Thomas J. Csordas** (Ph.D., Duke University) is a professor of anthropology at the University of California, San Diego. His books include *Transnational Transcendence: Essays on Religion and Globalization* (as the editor); *Body/Meaning/Healing*; *Language, Charisma, and Creativity: The Ritual Life of a Religious Movement*; and *The Sacred Self: A Cultural Phenomenology of Charismatic Healing.*

**Heather D. Curtis** (Th.D., Harvard University) is an assistant professor of religion at Tufts University. She received the Frank S. and Elizabeth D. Brewer Prize of the American Society of Church History for her book *Faith in the Great Physician: Suffering and Divine Healing in American Culture, 1860–1900.*

**Gastón Espinosa** (Ph.D., University of California, Santa Barbara) is the Arthur V. Stoughton Associate Professor of Religious Studies at Claremont McKenna College. His work has appeared in the *Journal of the American Academy of Religion*, the *Annals of the American Academy of Political and Social Science*, and *Pneuma: Journal of the Society for Pentecostal Studies*. He is president of La Comunidad of Hispanic Scholars of Religion, American Academy of Religion.

**Paul Gifford** (M.Litt., Oxford) is a professor of African Christianity at the School of Oriental and African Studies of the University of London. He is the author of *Christianity, Politics and Public Life in Kenya*; *Ghana's New Christianity: Pentecostalism in a Globalising African Economy*; *African Christianity: Its Public Role*; and *Christianity and Politics in Doe's Liberia*.

**Sean C. Kim** (Ph.D., Harvard University) is an associate professor of history and anthropology at the University of Central Missouri. He is the author of *The Forgotten Home Front: Photographs of Pusan, 1952–54*, with Lisa Barbash; his dissertation is entitled "Christianity in Colonial Korea: The Culture and Politics of Proselytization."

**Matthew Marostica** (Ph.D., J.D., University of California, Berkeley) is a political scientist and litigation attorney specializing in Indian law. His dissertation is entitled "Pentecostals and Politics: The Creation of the Evangelical Christian Movement in Argentina, 1983–1993."

**Gotthard Oblau** (Ph.D., Frankfurt/Main University) is a pastor in the Evangelical Church in the Rhineland (Germany) and a former staff associate of the Amity Foundation of the China Christian Council (1985–1997). His books include *Chinesische Studierende in Deutschland: Chancen Christlicher Begegnung* (Chinese Studying in Germany: Chances of Christian Meeting); *Kein Geheimnis Christ zu sein: Lebens-Bilder aus Chinas Gemeinden heute* (No Secret Christians: Life Stories from Christian Congregations in China Today), with Claudia Währisch-Oblau; and *Gotteszeit und Menschenzeit: Eschatologie in der Kirchlichen Dogmatik von Karl Barth* (God Time and People Time: Eschatology in *Church Dogmatics* by Karl Barth).

**Cephas N. Omenyo** (Ph.D., University of Utrecht; M.Ph., University of Ghana, Legon) is an associate professor, Department for the Study of Religions, University of Ghana, Legon, Ghana. He is the author of *Pentecost outside Pentecostalism: A Study of the Development of Charismatic Renewal in the Mainline Churches in Ghana*; and *The Ongoing Encounter between Christianity and African Culture: A Case Study of Girls' Nubility Rite of the Krobos*.

**Arlene Sánchez Walsh** (Ph.D., Claremont Graduate University) is an associate professor of church history and Latino church studies at Azusa Pacific University. She received the Hispanic Theological Initiative's book award for *Latino Pentecostal Identity: Evangelical Faith, Self and Society*. She is working on a book on Latina/o Word of Faith churches and a textbook, *Pentecostalism in America*.

**Angela Tarango** (Ph.D., Duke University) is an assistant professor of religions of the Americas in the Department of Religion at Trinity University in San Antonio, Texas. Her dissertation is entitled "Choosing the Jesus Way: The

Assemblies of God's Home Missions Program and the Development of a Native American Pentecostal Identity."

**Claudia Währisch-Oblau** (Ph.D., Heidelberg University) is the executive secretary for evangelism of the United Evangelical Mission, a community of churches on three continents; the former coordinator of the United Evangelical Mission's Program for Cooperation between German and Migrant Churches; and a former staff associate of the Amity Foundation of the China Christian Council. She is the author of *The Missionary Self-Perception of Pentecostal/Charismatic Church Leaders from the Global South in Europe: Bringing Back the Gospel.*

# Foreword

*Harvey Cox*

Today, Christianity is living through a reformation that will prove to be even more basic and more sweeping than the one that shook Europe during the sixteenth century. That earlier reformation, which is now endowed by the definite article and a capital letter ("*the* Reformation") was confined to one small corner of the globe. The questions in dispute then, though they seemed important to many at the time, now appear increasingly provincial. It was a European upheaval. The current reformation, however, is an earth-circling one. This is because the epicenter of Christianity is no longer in Europe (or in its North American extension) but in the "two-thirds world," the global South, which we recently referred to as "the third world." Further, the main bearers of this new reformation do not, by and large, represent the historic denominations that emerged from that sixteenth-century turmoil. Rather, they are the children of a powerful spiritual movement that appeared in its present form only at the beginning of the twentieth century, namely, the Pentecostal-Charismatic movement. This tidal wave, it is now estimated, constitutes at least one-fourth of all the Christians in the world, and it is still growing rapidly.

The old European Reformation brought several controversial issues to the surface, among them the authority of the Roman pontiff, the role of the laity, and the theology of justification—by faith or by works. The current reformation is not particularly concerned with these issues, which were more pertinent to the sixteenth century. It is more focused on the importance of experience in the Christian life, the restoration of healing as an integral part of the

gospel, and the realization of Jesus' announcement of the coming of the kingdom of God on earth, especially with its promise of justice and dignity for the
disinherited and the excluded peoples of the world. The present reformation is
shaking foundations more dramatically than its sixteenth-century predecessor,
and its results will be more far-reaching and radical.

Of course, most Christians today do not recognize either the extent or the
depth of this new reformation. But that was probably true of the sixteenth century as well. Today, we neatly classify "the" Reformation into Lutheran, Calvinist,
Anglican, and (perhaps) radical. But these categories by which we analyze that
period were not evident to people at the time, although they probably knew that
*something* was happening. Throughout the cities and towns of Europe, there
were thousands of little reformations, often incoherent, chaotic, uncoordi-
nated, and certainly not under the control of the major reformers, most of
whom thought these "enthusiasts" were going much too far. Luther's repres-
sion of Thomas Münzer and the religiously inspired peasants, and Calvin's
burning of Servetus come to mind. Likewise today, ecclesial leaders are often
apprehensive about the new currents, which seem so unpredictable, fluid, and
hard to channel—which they surely are.

Among the several facets of this new reformation, one that appears often
is healing, which is the theme of this collection of essays. Pentecostal and Charismatic groups are well known for their emotionally explicit worship and their
ecstatic utterance, which is known as "speaking in tongues" or the "prayer of
the heart." They are also often characterized by a related phenomenon that
psychologists speak of as "trance" or "dissociative behavior." But, as this book
clearly demonstrates, the practice that initially draws most people to these
groups, and the one that characterizes them more than any other, is that they
offer healing—the "making whole" of mind, body, and spirit. Healing practices
are not only integral, but they also often serve as the threshold through which
new recruits pass into other dimensions of the movement.

Most—but not all—outside observers of these movements have now
largely moved well beyond dismissing the healings that occur under their aegis
as mere trickery, self-deception, mass hypnosis, or evidence of the placebo effect. There is, of course, some of that. Charlatans find their way into all healing
practices. But the healing these new movements exemplify is increasingly
regarded more positively. Once highly skeptical, established medical schools
now offer courses in "alternative medicine," and the U.S. Department of Health
and Human Services funds many such practices. Even though the support is
quite modest, the principle is important. Of course, not all forms of alternative
healing are "religious" (what this book calls *cura divina*). Many draw on folk
resources, such as herbs and plants, or on ancient wisdom about the links
between mind and body. But, as some of the essays in this book show, the line
between divine healing and folk healing is not always a clear one. There is
much borrowing and adopting.

In any case, it is clear that some forms of healing, many of them of a religious nature, that were once uniformly rejected by the medical establishment have now gained at least a soupçon of official recognition. The camel's nose is inside the tent of the clinic. It is only a matter of time before the philosophical underpinnings of the many different forms of health care can be openly and usefully compared. These questions will include ones about the nature of illness and disease, the role of spiritual support systems in healing, the relation of individual pathogens to social dislocation and deprivation, and the manner in which a patient's belief systems need to be taken into consideration in any course of therapy. This will include the intriguing possibility—already under investigation by some experts—that such pentecostal phenomena as speaking in tongues, being "slain in the Lord," and other ecstatic expressions may release antitoxins already present in the body, thus contributing to healing.

What is now being called the "New Reformation" of the twentieth and twenty-first centuries has evoked a landslide of commentary. Some of it is well informed and instructive; some is less so. It is hard for researchers schooled in the classical categories of the Reformed tradition to come to terms with the underlying pentecostal conviction that the gifts of the Holy Spirit are ongoing, that they did not cease after the apostolic period. This belief is what gives the name "Charismatic" (*charism* means "gift") to those pentecostal tropes that have found their way into non-Pentecostal churches, both Catholic and Protestant. Some scholars also find it hard to come to terms with the sheer "materiality" (as Miroslav Volf calls it) of the pentecostal explosion.[1] Pentecostals insist that God is just as interested in our bodies here on earth, in their health and well-being, as in our salvation for the next life. This creates a common bond with the liberation theologies that have arisen in some of the same parts of the global South. Indeed, there is some evidence that pentecostals are beginning to absorb qualities once normally associated with liberation theology. The result is what Donald E. Miller and Tetsunao Yamamori call "progressive Pentecostalism."[2]

Another barrier to understanding the depth and extent of the new reformation is, of course, that so much of the activity is going on in parts of the world in which European languages are not the norm. This is why the chapters in this book on pentecostal growth in China, Korea, and Ghana are among the most fascinating. The fact that Christianity is growing most rapidly outside the old precincts of Western Christendom makes for some of the difficulty. There is also an unfortunate class division in Western countries, with pentecostals sometimes separated from their Reformed compatriots by the chasms of income, race, and social status. This class separation is diminishing in many places, but old habits die hard. Sometimes, the most intriguing pentecostal expressions are going on within mere city blocks of seminaries and university religion departments, but they are frequently overlooked or even treated with condescension. The result of this dismissiveness is that, when attempts are

made to study these recent movements by using traditional theological categories and the existing rubrics of the scholarly study of religion, they do not
always fit the new phenomena, and they often actually hinder an accurate assessment of what is going on. The scrupulously researched essays in this volume, however, demonstrate that this need not always be the case. New ways of
defining religion and of investigating the dynamics of Charismatic faith,
ecstatic prayer, and healing are finally emerging.

What are the implications of all this for the study of religion and culture in
general? One hears comments in academia about certain themes and issues
being "undertheorized." This may well be the case. But is there also such a
thing as overtheorizing? Does the academic fascination with crafting ways to
generalize, systematize, and render coherent sometimes actually obscure what
we are trying to understand? As one who has studied pentecostalism, both
sympathetically and critically, for a number of years, I would say that what we
lack is not good theory but rather something this book provides in abundance,
namely, what the anthropologist Clifford Geertz first called "thick description."[3]
Readers of these chapters will quickly find themselves immersed (in my view,
delightfully immersed) in the raw reality of Pentecostal and Charismatic healing, often in the words of those directly involved. These essays are fields ripe
unto harvest for later theorizing, but enjoyable to wander through even before
the theorizers arrive.

How does all this fit into the big picture, the unexpected revival of religion
in the twentieth and twenty-first centuries all around the world? The more I
read abut the Pentecostal-Charismatic tsunami, and the more I participate in
and observe its many manifestations, the more convinced I become that, in
addition to being a beguiling phenomenon on its own, it also provides an
invaluable lens through which to watch the whole religious resurgence. Many
of its themes stretch across the various traditions. The turn from an emphasis
on doctrine to the cultivation of a direct experience of God—as spirit, mystery,
or transcendence—can be traced in virtually all the traditions. So can the
change from hierarchical ordering to more participation. The impressive ability
of pentecostals to retrieve, absorb, and transform elements of the indigenous
religious cultures into which they move is something happening—if not quite
as well executed—in other religions as well. But the descriptions of this process
found in these pages should quickly disabuse the reader of falling back into
too-easy caricatures of "syncretism." The process is far more complex and nuanced, and it defies being reduced to a univocal category. As religions are
pushed closer and closer together by migration, popular culture, and the other
faces of globalization, more and more borrowing across once-forbidden boundaries goes on. The Peruvian villager who attends mass at least now and then,
who drops in at the local Assemblies of God temple for a healing service, and
who sometimes consults a spiritually inspired *curandera* is the rule, not an
exception. And how different is that villager from the North American who

goes to morning prayer in an Episcopal church, takes part in a tai chi class, then reads a book by the Buddhist Dalai Lama before savoring some of the Islamic mystical poetry of Rumi? Lines that used to mark thick borders are now becoming wavy and porous. And, for all their often exclusivist rhetoric, pentecostals are among the most successful borrowers.

After reading this splendid collection, one cannot help but ponder the future of Christianity, and I thought especially about the most important dialogue in which Christians are now increasingly engaged, the one with Muslims. There are over 2 billion Christians in the world, a quarter of whom are Pentecostal or Charismatic, and there are also over a billion Muslims in the same world. These two communities share a shrinking globe and now jostle elbow to elbow in many places. Sometimes, the interaction is noxious and even fatal. But there are also more neighborly efforts at cooperation and more interfaith conferences, seminars, and dialogues than ever before. The Common Word project, for example, opened new trails in Muslim-Christian relations.[4] But, one must ask, what will these interactions look like in 25 or 50 years? How will the growing preponderance of pentecostals among the world's Christians, and their presence in precisely those areas—like Africa—where tensions with Islam have been so severe, shape the form and content of the interaction? Will the relationship become uglier and more confrontational? Or is it possible to hope that the experiential, even ecstatic elements in the two movements (one thinks of the Sufi stream in Islam) and the existence of healing traditions in both might provide grounds for a more conciliatory relationship?

Whatever happens on that crucial front, there can be no doubt that Pentecostal and Charismatic healing will continue to flower all over the world. It is something no thoughtful person can afford to ignore. We need careful, accurate, empathic, and unprejudiced studies of this reality in all its multitudinous expressions, including healing. This volume provides the gold standard against which all future efforts will have to be judged.

NOTES

1 See Miroslav Volf, "Materiality of Salvation: An Investigation in the Soteriologies of Liberation and Pentecostal Theologies," *Journal of Ecumenical Studies* 26.3 (1989): 447–467.

2 Donald E. Miller and Tetsunao Yamamori, *Global Pentecostalism: The New Face of Christian Social Engagement* (Berkeley: University of California Press, 2007).

3 Clifford Geertz, "Thick Description: Toward an Interpretive Theory of Culture," in *The Interpretation of Cultures: Selected Essays* (New York: Basic, 1973), 3–30.

4 In *A Common Word between Us and You* (2007), 138 Muslim signatories issued a statement emphasizing the common ground between Christianity and Islam; see http://www.acommonword.com/index.php?lang=en&page=option1 (accessed 15 Mar. 2010).

# Global Pentecostal and
# Charismatic Healing

# Introduction: Pentecostalism and the Globalization of Illness and Healing

*Candy Gunther Brown*

Divine healing practices are an essential marker of Pentecostal and Charismatic Christianity as a global phenomenon. According to the Pew Forum on Religion and Public Life's *Spirit and Power: A 10-Country Survey of Pentecostals* (2006), more than a quarter—and in many countries two-thirds—of the world's 2 billion Christians identify themselves as Pentecostal or Charismatic.[1] The Pew survey singles out divine healing—more so than any other factor, including speaking in tongues and financial prosperity—as distinguishing Pentecostals and Charismatics from other Christians. In every country surveyed, large majorities (more than 70 percent in 8 of 10 countries) of Pentecostals reported having personally experienced or witnessed the divine healing of an illness or injury. Even in the United States, which lagged behind the curve, 62 percent of Pentecostals reported personal experience with divine healing; according to other polls, 70–80 percent of the total U.S. population believes in divine healing.[2] In the Latin American, Asian, and African countries where pentecostal growth is occurring most rapidly, as many as 80–90 percent of first-generation Christians attribute their conversions *primarily* to having received divine healing for themselves or a family member. As multidirectional processes of globalization accelerate and as Christians in the global South increasingly influence North American Christianity, divine healing will likely become even more prominent in U.S. churches in the twenty-first century.

Despite the widely acknowledged significance of divine healing to Pentecostal and Charismatic Christianity worldwide, scholars know strikingly little about how divine healing is actually practiced in specific cultural contexts or how practices reflect and shape the interplay of local and global cultural processes.[3] If we are to understand the global expansion of Christianity in particular, or to grapple with the nature of global religions, public health and epidemic disease, and other globalizing processes more generally, we must not only pay closer attention to practices surrounding illness and healing in specific contexts, but we must also begin to contextualize individual studies within a broader, cross-cultural, analytical framework. This goal can best be accomplished as a collaborative undertaking. There are few individual scholars who know enough about a sufficient range of illness and healing contexts to achieve the twin goals of thick description and comparative analysis made possible by bringing area experts into conversation with each other. This volume's distinguished, intercontinental team of contributors includes anthropologists, historians, political scientists, sociologists, theologians, and religious studies scholars from North America, Europe, and Africa writing about illness and healing on six continents. In selecting the essays for inclusion, the editor read almost everything published in the late twentieth and early twenty-first centuries on divine healing, pentecostalism, and globalization; contacted the authors of the best scholarship—that which, regardless of the widely varying personal stances of the authors, demonstrates the complexity, rather than flattening out the beliefs and practices, of their subjects—and many of these scholars graciously agreed to write chapters specifically for this book (the entirety of which then underwent anonymous external review). The essayists consulted a list of core analytical questions (see below) before and during the writing process and circulated early drafts to one another, a composition process that encouraged an unusual level of dialogue and coherence among contributions to an edited volume. The chapters have been organized by regions, and within regions chronologically and topically, in order to encourage readers to make their own cross-cultural and historical comparisons.

Throughout this volume, we capitalize the term "Pentecostal" when referring to classical Pentecostal denominations, such as the Assemblies of God, that trace their origins to the Azusa Street revivals of the early twentieth century. The lower-case term "pentecostal" functions as a shorthand way of referencing both Pentecostals and second- and third-wave Charismatics (both Protestant and Catholic) who emphasize the ongoing activity of the Holy Spirit in bestowing gifts (or *charisms*) similar to those (e.g., healing, glossolalia) described in the New Testament book of Acts.[4] The lower-case term "charismatic" is used where authors have in mind the sociologist Max Weber's influential theory of leadership.[5]

We privilege the term "divine healing" over the alternatives "faith healing" or "spiritual healing." Most practitioners prefer the term "divine healing" because it emphasizes that God's love, rather than merely human faith or an impersonal spiritual force, is the source of healing; it underscores the perceived need for supernatural intervention instead of implying that faith is a natural force that can be manufactured by human will; and it emphasizes that the object of faith, not simply the degree of faith or spirituality, matters in receiving healing. The term "faith healing" is, moreover, confusing analytically because of its negative connotations in popular parlance, evoking images—such as the flamboyant, fraudulent, money-grubbing "faith healers" of movies like *Elmer Gantry* (1960), *Leap of Faith* (1992), and *The Apostle* (1997)—that are far removed from the vast majority of religious healing practices, many of which are transacted outside large religious services and without the ministrations of prominent evangelists, many of whom are more complex figures than the stereotypes suggest. Like faith healing, the term "exorcism" is problematic because it evokes sensationalized images borrowed from films like *The Exorcist* (1973), *The Exorcism of Emily Rose* (2005), and *The Haunting in Connecticut* (2009). Although the term "exorcism" can properly be used to refer to efforts (most of which are not dramatic) to cast out evil spirits, the alternative terms "deliverance" or "liberation," borrowed from the Spanish *liberación* (Portuguese: *libertação*), underline the priority for participants of freeing individuals from oppression rather than focusing on the demons themselves.[6] For many practitioners of divine healing, the amelioration of physical or emotional illness is not perceived in isolation, but as one of many divine gifts included in "full salvation," alongside forgiveness from sin, deliverance from demonic oppression, and baptism with the Holy Spirit; healing is understood holistically as one component of the kingdom of God, which also includes prosperity, abundance, wholeness, and reconciled relationships with the human and spiritual worlds. The tendency of many scholars has been to distinguish "healing" from "cure," and thus to imply that practitioners often claim healing when they remain sick but feel reconciled to their disease or that they rationalize a failure to cure as an acceptance of death as the ultimate healing.[7] Although such is sometimes the case, we generally follow the narrower usage of the Portuguese and Spanish term *cura divina*, or divine cure, which implies that physical improvement is an essential component of what is often perceived as a more holistic healing process. In this usage, a divine cure is distinguished from a recovery that could be expected through the regular operation of natural processes. The healing may not be instantaneous or spectacular, and thus not be classified as a "miracle," but a divine healing is understood to proceed more rapidly than usual or under circumstances in which healing would not otherwise be expected.[8]

This book does not seek to answer the question of whether individuals are "really" healed or whether a divine agent is actually responsible. Although these may be significant questions for another project, the questions that compel us are how people's perceptions of seeking, experiencing, or witnessing divine healing affect their self-understandings, religious affiliations, or cultural practices. We adopt an empathetic stance that seeks to understand the perspectives and logic of our subjects as an aid to critically analyzing taken-for-granted assumptions and often unforeseen implications; methodological empathy does not imply sympathetic feelings of agreement with the subjects under study, but rather an effort to see things from the standpoint of those studied and to step outside that standpoint to analyze broader causal and contextual frameworks that sometimes complement and sometimes challenge the interpretations made by our subjects.[9] The tendency of many observers to dismiss divine healing claims as trivial or preposterous without investigating them has the unfortunate effect of increasing the suffering of those who have already suffered from illness, pain, and, in many instances, social and economic marginalization.[10] Although instances of fraud, financial exploitation, and credulousness can certainly be noted, and are indeed an important part of the story, most of the healing practitioners described in this volume are neither malicious nor naive people.[11] Narratives of divine healing are inevitably embedded in culturally specific contexts, and, at the same time, they are to participants often deeply personal and meaningful, evoking significant human emotions such as fear, hope, confusion, disappointment, courage, determination, sorrow, relief, joy, and even humor.[12] We accordingly have sought to listen and respect the struggles of people around the world to confront and make sense of painful and liberating experiences as they succeed or fail to experience healing. By describing and locating belief frameworks and devotional activities within broader interpretive contexts, we hope to contribute to an understanding of lived religious practices around the world.[13]

## Globalization, Pentecostal and Charismatic Christianity, and Healing

A broad view of divine healing practices illumines the nature of globalization, pentecostalism, and healing, and reveals how and why these topics are related. Pentecostalism is more than a religious movement that happens to emphasize healing and that happens to have spread to a number of different countries; rather, *globalization characteristically heightens the threat of disease, thereby fueling the growth of religious movements such as pentecostalism that are centrally concerned with healing.*

People define the word "globalization" in a variety of ways depending on the attributes they wish to emphasize. Most definitions share in common the idea that the world seems increasingly interconnected. As technological developments facilitate rapid, even virtually instantaneous, communication and the fluid movement of peoples, ideas, images, objects, and wealth, there is a dissolving of psychological, political, and cultural boundaries that once were maintained through spatial and temporal separation. Consequently, people in scattered locales feel increasingly conscious of their membership in an interdependent, global community, and this perception breeds an unstable combination of new hopes, fears, desires, satisfactions, and disappointments. Globalization is simultaneously a homogenizing cultural process and a process by which contributions originating in diverse, local traditions diffuse so rapidly that the distinction between cultural centers and peripheries all but disappears; particular communities—whether locally or transregionally defined—can exercise significant freedom to appropriate and modify borrowings from global cultural flows for their own distinctive purposes.[14]

One of the most frightening aspects of globalization is the increasing threat of disease, a threat that functions on two levels. First, diseases spread more rapidly in an interconnected world. In the wake of decolonization, political instability, warfare, famine, and disease have reached epidemic proportions in many countries. Because of the global marketing of agricultural and animal products and the international air travel of infected individuals, sickness can no longer be considered a local problem.[15] Diseases such as AIDS, SARS, Ebola, and mad cow disease are aggressive, encroaching, and know no geographic or national boundaries. Second, the fear of disease is potentially even stronger than the actual risk. Widespread access to information about disease, particularly through unfiltered internet sites and popular books and films that intentionally pander to fears, raises specters such as a globally catastrophic bird or swine flu pandemic.[16] Disease may in reality defy all boundaries, but it seems still more boundless in the realm of the imagination.

For the great majority of peoples living in the two-thirds world, especially in growing urban areas where high population densities and unsanitary living conditions facilitate the spread of disease, poverty and poverty-related infirmities are everyday realities that make daily survival uncertain. Globalization raises but does not always or even often satisfy hopes for the availability of new technologies, resources, and cures for diseases, poverty, hunger, and social strife.[17] Despite advances in scientific medicine and globally disseminated reports of medical miracles, even basic medical care remains unavailable or prohibitively expensive for as much as 80 percent of the world's population.[18] It is precisely in those regions of the world where poverty and sickness seem most overwhelming and where traditional religions and biomedicine alike have seemed insufficient in meeting practical, everyday needs that pentecostalism has grown the most rapidly. In contrast to the germ theory of disease foundational to scientific medicine and to the Enlightenment paradigm of uniformly operating natural law that has dominated North American and European cultures, pentecostal explanations of disease and healing resonate with many African, Asian, and Latin American cultures that envision health as depending upon right relationships with the natural and spiritual worlds. Characterizations of the Christian God as the most powerful healer, coupled with demonstrations of apparently supernatural healing power, draw people who feel overwhelmed by natural and spiritual forces that seem too powerful to overcome by other means.[19] In cultures of desperation, people are willing even to forsake their former gods, as pentecostalism demands, and to pay the high price of lifelong, exclusive allegiance in order to gain access to a source of spiritual power that promises to help them on a regular basis.[20]

Pentecostalism attracts adherents primarily through its characteristic healing practices. Secularization theories predict that, as technological solutions to human problems become more effective and accessible, religious solutions will become decreasingly relevant.[21] It is therefore striking that divine healing practices show no sign of abating even where biomedical science is the most sophisticated, convenient, and affordable. Despite technological advances, many illnesses still baffle medical doctors. Even with the best medical care, people continue to suffer lifelong, debilitating conditions and to die from disease. The promise of biomedical breakthroughs raises hopes, but disillusionment sets in when scientific medicine proves unable to cure or to halt the spread of diseases like cancer or AIDS and instead produces serious side effects while depersonalizing individuals in need of healing as biological organisms or insurance claim numbers.[22] Most pentecostals today do not reject modern medicine, but they do insist that God is able to heal even when medicine is unable to help.[23] Recognition of the limits of scientific medicine, even in industrialized nations, fuels therapeutic experimentation with divine healing—and with other alternative remedies, many of which invoke aid from personal or impersonal spiritual sources.[24] Indeed, the intermingling of naturalistic and metaphysical therapeutics is nothing new: even at the height of the age of Enlightenment, the boundaries between material and spiritual explorations often blurred. Despite the rise of scientific naturalism as a reigning paradigm in industrialized societies, most twenty-first-century people, as a reporter for *Time* magazine aptly put it, "want it all. . . . We want access to both MRIs and miracles."[25] Thus, it is not surprising that, as globalization facilitates heightened interactions among more and less developed nations, it is simply not the case that traditional societies rush to adopt strictly materialistic worldviews.[26] To the contrary, there has been a renaissance of spiritual healing practices in Europe and North America, prominently including pentecostal divine healing. As globalizing processes bring into contact conflicting assumptions about the nature of reality, people everywhere pay more attention to claims that are difficult to explain within their own worldview.[27] Indeed, the tendency to differentiate "premodern," "modern," and "postmodern" worldviews and to express surprise at the persistence of so-called premodern practices such as divine healing reflect the assumptions of naturalistically oriented observers who expect the rest of the world to evolve into their own image.[28]

The primary appeal of pentecostalism worldwide is as a religion of healing. Pentecostals envision healing as more contagious than epidemic disease. In this framework, the Holy Spirit's anointing, or the oil-like spread of divine power and love, is caught rather than taught, and it can be imparted or transferred to others—through the laying on of hands, anointing with oil, close physical proximity, objects like prayer cloths, or even contact with modern communications media.[29] Indeed, if one of the most notable characteristics of globalization is the collapsing of space and time through modern technology, then pentecostalism is characteristically a global religion. Pentecostals bring technology into the service of healing, aggressively using print, radio, satellite television, cell phones, and the internet and employing distinctly modern metaphors, such as electrical waves, to explain the invisible power of the Holy Spirit that they feel coursing through their bodies.[30] Thus, pentecostals pray for healing over cell phones, they fax prayer cloths, and they urge those listening to television, radio, or internet broadcasts to place one hand on the transmitting device and the other on their diseased body part in order better to receive the tangible anointing into their bodies through the airwaves.[31] Globalization implies freedom of movement, and pentecostals are people in motion, traveling by foot, car, or airplane to places where they hear that a healing anointing is particularly strong, in hopes of catching the anointing to receive healing or to become more effective ambassadors who carry healing to others.[32] At the same time, pentecostal mobility does not depend on physical travel, since technology links local communities and fosters a sense of membership in a global community that is full of *sanidad divina*, or divine health, and that is sharply differentiated from the corrupt, sick, and chaotic outside world.[33]

The healthful community envisioned by pentecostals, at least as an ideal, redistributes power from wealthy and socially powerful elites to those who have suffered not only physical infirmities, but also social, cultural, and economic distress.[34] Prior to the expansion of pentecostal Christianity, elite Christian theologians in Europe and North America typically devalued the human body as inferior to the spirit; taught that patient resignation was the appropriate response to sickness, which they assumed to have been sent by God to produce spiritual sanctification; denigrated female bodies as deviant from normal male bodies; and exoticized nonwhite bodies as sites of physical and moral contamination.[35] Divine healing practices, although sometimes reinscribing normative cultural assumptions or justifying the exploitative behavior of money-minded leaders, can offer a strategy for recognizing the bodily reality of poor people and for affirming the worth of female and nonwhite bodies, about whom God cares enough to heal and empower as conduits for transferring healing to others.[36] Many individuals and communities who understand themselves as recipients of divine healing interpret their experience as an expression of God's love for them. In a series of dynamic interactions termed "godly love" by scholars seeking to study the phenomenon, a healing experience often motivates individuals to seek to express greater love for God and for other people—including not only family and friends but sometimes even total strangers perhaps from another culture—by helping others to experience healing or by engaging in other forms of benevolent service.[37] One potential implication of such interactions is an increase in social capital that can enhance the health of individuals and communities.[38] Although a handful of healing evangelists have since the nineteenth century used modern communications media to establish international reputations, most pentecostals believe that God can use anyone filled by the Holy Spirit to heal the sick. Illness, according to this view, is the work of the devil, and Christians can be confident that it is God's will to heal. Pentecostals cite a variety of biblical passages to justify their belief in healing, but none is more foundational than Isaiah 53:5, which Christians interpret as prophesying Jesus' atoning death. According to many pentecostals, it is through the atonement that God in love provided not only for forgiveness from sin, but also for healing from disease, since "with his stripes we are healed."[39]

Emphasizing spiritual causes and cures for human suffering does not always produce unequivocally healthful results. Supernaturalism can obscure the pathogenic impact of political and economic globalization and deflect attention from engaging in constructive reforms of a more material nature. Divine healing practices tend, moreover, to be individualistically oriented, even if enacted as communal rituals. A fragmented, case-by-case approach to illness and healing can induce myopia concerning universalizing processes of globalization that engender diseased patterns of social relationship, symptomatic of which are recurrent cases of poverty-related infirmities. Promises that God will heal whenever sickness surfaces do not by themselves reduce the frequency with which the need for healing is experienced. At its worst, a supernaturalized model of sickness and healing encourages already-suffering individuals to internalize blame for failures that could instead be traced to systemic oppression of those very individuals by more powerful individuals, groups, and impersonal material forces, many of which are external to but act upon their local situations.

Pentecostalism has attracted the notice of many critics and curious observers, as well as adherents, and this volume seeks to provide more nuanced answers to questions asked by several audiences, including academic researchers; popular media; Pentecostals and Charismatics; and other Christians who question the authenticity of pentecostalism, or at least of certain pentecostal emphases, as a legitimate expression of Christianity. The pentecostal worldview seems strange—and troubling, especially given the rapid growth of the movement—to many religious and secular observers, particularly in Europe and North America, whose own worldviews have been shaped by the disenchanting implications of the Protestant Reformation and Catholic Counter-Reformation, Cartesian mind-body dualism, and Enlightenment and Darwinian science. In particular, charges of "syncretism" and "shamanism," which have been raised by non-pentecostal Christians and by some scholars of religion, reflect these critics' worries about maintaining a "pure" religion and their predisposition to disparage worldviews that assume the existence of a spiritual realm that is relevant to the natural world.[40] It is true that pentecostals and many indigenous healers share assumptions that conflict with understandings of the world grounded in scientific naturalism, and it also is true that there are significant resonances between the healing practices of pentecostals

and of adherents of other religions. The agenda of ferreting out phenomenological parallels and tracing cross-cultural lines of influence in order to "prove"
charges of "inappropriate" religious borrowing can have the unfortunate effect of
obscuring equally significant differences between healing traditions. Ritual performances that appear strikingly similar may be invested with fundamentally different meanings by various groups of practitioners. In some instances, pentecostals
have (sometimes strategically and sometimes unreflectively) appropriated beliefs
and practices from their local cultural contexts—as Christians have done since the
first century and as adherents of every religion have done throughout history—
but the inculturation and indigenization of Christianity are often more complex
and selective, and reflect a higher level of agency and creativity than the cliché
term "syncretism" implies. Pentecostals accept the traditional idea that spiritual
power is widely distributed, but they insist—although they are not always consistent in their reasoning—that the only legitimate way to access that power is in the
name of Jesus by the power of the Holy Spirit. Pentecostals envision Jesus as the
most powerful healer—one who can win a competition with the gods of traditional religions through a display of superior healing power.[41]

What seems most objectionable, and "shamanistic," to non-pentecostal
Christian critics and to secular critics of American self-interested consumerism
is the pentecostal concern with allegedly "lower," "selfish," "this-worldly" blessings, such as healing or financial prosperity, which are often caricatured as a
"prosperity theology" or a "health and wealth gospel" that greedy U.S. "faith
healers" have exported worldwide through their disturbingly successful use of
modern communications media.[42] There are important political valences to
such charges of shamanism that can easily be overlooked. The Korean theologian Wonsuk Ma, director of the Oxford Centre for Mission Studies, points out
that Europeans and North Americans who charge Asians with shamanism mis-
understand the politically laden connotations of the term in Asian contexts;
according to Ma, it is not that pentecostals "syncretistically" borrow shamanistic forms or practices from other religions—indeed, Christians in countries
such as Korea (a frequent target of criticism) consciously demarcate clear
boundaries between the practices of Christianity and those of other religions—
but that practical needs are devalued by Western-educated Korean evangelical
theologians as a "low-level" concern appropriate for "lower religions like shamanism or syncretistic Buddhism" rather than the "high-level" God of a ratio-
nalistic, eschatologically oriented version of Christianity. Ma advises that,
"unless one has struggled to provide three meals a day for an entire family, one
should not quickly criticize this as an egotistic religion."[43] The anthropologists
André Corten and Ruth Marshall-Fratani caution, moreover, against assuming
that health and prosperity teachings are unilaterally exported from North
America to millions of pentecostals worldwide who are "not much more than
unthinking dupes, bought over or swindled out of their pittance by scheming
global powers."[44] One of the most astute analysts of global pentecostalism,

Philip Jenkins, acknowledges that, "at its worst, the gospel of prosperity permits corrupt clergy to get away with virtually anything," including the justification of materialism, but Jenkins also emphasizes the powerlessness and dependence created by living in a very poor society and calls attention to the vested interests of prosperity's critics in defending against "successful competitors for the souls of the faithful." Rather than denying that "health and wealth are desirable goals," Jenkins notes, critics assume that "realistically, such blessings can only be obtained through secular means, through hard work, thrift, wise investment, and access to good medicine."[45]

Indeed, Christian critics have often characterized what seems—from the critics' perspective—to be an extreme emphasis on material concerns as more akin to "magic" than genuine religion.[46] For these critics, salvation is fundamentally spiritual, and undue attention to merely material concerns is dangerously distracting at best. For pentecostals (like liberation theologians), by contrast, the work of salvation begins, as Yale University's Henry B. Wright Professor of Systematic Theology, Miroslav Volf, has usefully articulated, in the material world; thus, physical redemption is an expression of and contributes meaningfully to God's ultimate redemptive purposes.[47] Scholarship on divine healing that fails to grasp this latter understanding of salvation as incorporating a material dimension can unhelpfully reduce theologically and culturally complex practices to stereotypes that diminish rather than enhance our understanding of multifaceted, diverse phenomena.

All of the chapters in this volume take into account Volf's concept of material salvation as it plays out in diverse local contexts. These studies give flesh—bruised and bleeding flesh—to pervasive human suffering and the resultant healing practices that attract so many people to pentecostalism and that symbolize the larger processes of personal and social integration that pentecostal practices facilitate. The essays also reveal that more is at stake than relief from physical suffering. Pentecostal healing envelops people's lives. It is about material reality, including economic reality, and invocations of spiritual power do not obscure that fact for the participants. Interrogating the relationship between the material and the spiritual, the essayists interact with the following topics: (1) the spirit-centered epistemology of divine healing, (2) the spirit-centered demonization of disease, (3) the body's role in a spirit-centered cosmology, and (4) Christianity's role as a medium of cross-cultural communication.[48] The essayists have, moreover, considered a broader set of core analytical questions: What do people mean (and do they always mean the same thing) when they claim to experience divine healing? What theological or empirical rationales and epistemologies are articulated? Who are the practitioners and clients? Where and when do practices occur, and who is present? Do people undertake pilgrimages to particular healing sites? What specifically happens during healing practices? What do these practices look like to the observer? What, if any, symbolic objects, modern technologies, or ritual enactments are employed? Do healing practices involve the exorcism of afflicting spirits? Are other kinds of supernatural experiences cited as accompanying healing? Do healing experiences motivate recipients to help others experience healing or to perform other kinds of benevolent service? What cultural controversies (within healing communities or between practitioners and outsiders) accompany these practices? Are some practices more controversial than others? How do practices embody or challenge local cultural norms? Are there efforts toward the inculturation of Christianity? What is the relationship between Christian healing and other local religious or healing traditions? Is "syncretism" a useful term in explaining this relationship, or is there a better alternative? How do global patterns affect local practices? Can specific lines of influence be traced (in one or more directions) between local and distant healing practitioners? Does linguistic translation mediate cultural influences? What role is played by modern communications media or itinerating evangelists? Is "health and wealth" a useful category for understanding healing practices? Does an emphasis on financial prosperity always accompany an emphasis on healing? How, precisely, does healing contribute to conversions and church growth? When healing leads to new religious affiliations, do these affiliations endure over time? What distinguishes healing in Pentecostal and Charismatic churches from prayers for healing in other Christian churches? Do Pentecostal and Charismatic churches perceive a sense of common identity among themselves or a sense of difference from other Christians? To what extent are Pentecostal and Charismatic churches networked and how does healing contribute to such networks?

Even the best scholarship often stalls at the truisms that divine healing practices are common among pentecostals, that healing testimonials claiming recovery from every condition from headaches to cancers are too numerous to count, and that healing is in many instances cited as the primary motivator for religious conversion and church affiliation. The chapters in this volume acknowledge that there is some truth to prevalent generalizations, while they paint more nuanced portraits of their subjects and their healing practices, thereby providing insight into the nature of globalization, world religions, pentecostalism, and health, illness, and healing.

## Common Themes in the Collected Essays

This volume illumines both global patterns and local variations in pentecostal healing practices. The following seven themes suggest some of the implications of this body of scholarship for several different groups of readers—offering insight into topics that have concerned academic researchers, members of the media, the interested general public, and both pentecostal and non-pentecostal Christians.

*First, these studies make a strong case that divine healing is the single most important category—more significant than glossolalia or prosperity—for understanding the global expansion of pentecostal Christianity.* Less than half of the Brazilian pentecostals studied by Andrew Chesnut spoke in tongues, while a large majority claimed to have received divine healing. Gastón Espinosa attributes the dramatic growth of Latino pentecostalism primarily to its emphasis on divine healing. Michael Bergunder, in his study of South Indian pentecostals, notes that healing and exorcism represent primary contact points for winning church members—but also emphasizes that, after the initial healings, churches must still build a lasting commitment among members through intensive pastoral care and the cultivation of an atmosphere in which members perceive themselves to experience the presence of God on a regular basis. As many as 80–90 percent of the Chinese Protestants (regardless of denomination) considered by Gotthard Oblau converted to Christianity through a personal experience of receiving divine healing for themselves or a family member. Cephas Omenyo makes a complementary argument that the success of even mainline churches in Ghana has depended upon their willingness and ability to incorporate healing and deliverance. Sean Kim's work on Korea similarly illustrates how divine healing is often the most significant growth factor for Presbyterians as well as for denominational Pentecostals. Thomas Csordas extends this insight to encompass the global spread of the Charismatic Catholic renewal. The transnational pentecostal community described by Candy Gunther Brown makes healing a fundamental element of the gospel, but places almost no emphasis on financial prosperity.

The essays in this volume define healing as often including more, but not less, than the cure of physical diseases. Rebecca Pierce Bomann and Chesnut, in their studies of Colombia and Brazil, define healing as including not only the amelioration of physical problems, but also the relief of social maladies such as unemployment, alcoholism, and domestic strife; similarly, Angela Tarango, in considering native North American Pentecostals, includes healing from racial hatred and social wrongs. Omenyo provides a broad definition of African healing as encompassing wholeness and well-being on a personal and communal level, as well as societal equilibrium and a sense of order and connection between the natural and spiritual realms.

Few of the Chinese pentecostals whom Oblau studied—and the same could be said of the Indians, Colombians, and Brazilians treated in other chapters—were "anti-medical" in the sense of rejecting modern medicine as an illegitimate or even inferior mode of receiving healing from God. But the social realities of the situations studied were such that conventional medical care was largely unavailable or unattainably expensive; seeking healing from a spiritual source did not represent a philosophical preference, but the only available option. Similarly, the anti-medical sentiments expressed by some of Heather Curtis's nineteenth-century European, North American, and Australian sources were fueled by the failures of available medical treatments to cure disease. Much more unusual on a global scale today, and reflecting an exceptionally privileged social context, is the African American pastor studied by Catherine Bowler who preaches against medicine to parishioners who do experience a philosophical tension since many of them also work at a local hospital and receive excellent medical insurance as an employment benefit. Taken as a whole, these essays suggest that the topics that preoccupy many European and North American observers, such as glossolalia, prosperity, and anti-medical teachings, are parochial when the global landscape of healing practices is considered.

*Second, divine healing practices are more diverse—and socially empowering—than what is implied by the caricatures of "faith healing" evangelists conjured by some in the media and by some scholars and religious critics of pentecostalism.* Divine healing is often sought in the context of well-attended evangelistic crusades, such as the early twentieth-century Latino revivals studied by Espinosa and the late twentieth-century Argentine revivals described by Matthew Marostica. Similarly, Csordas shows that Catholic Charismatic divine healing meetings, especially those in India, can attract enormous crowds, including substantial numbers of non-Christians. By contrast, as Oblau notes, Chinese government regulations preclude large-scale evangelistic services, and divine healing there is most often sought in the privacy of small church services or the sickroom, as one or a few lay-people—many of them poor, uneducated, and female—pray, fast, and offer physical care for the sick, persevering until the patient recovers or dies, in which case prayers are offered for resurrection. Most Chinese Protestants are first-generation Christians who converted because of a healing experience that they interpret as expressing divine love; this perception motivates converts to express love for God, family, friends, co-workers, and strangers by helping them to experience healing—either through prayer or by nursing the ill back to health. Similarly, the Ghanaian Charismatic prayer groups considered by Omenyo are small, lay-led gatherings at which everyone can participate in praying for the sick and in receiving prayers. Although Brown considers large-scale healing services in Brazil and Mozambique, she notes that American evangelists bring with them teams of dozens of "ordinary" lay Christians to pray for the sick; Brown notes, moreover, that stereotypes of faith healing aside, faith is envisioned as one, but far from the only, factor in receiving healing. More important is the anointing, or love energy, of the Holy Spirit, which is imparted through the laying on of hands, and the ministry of angels, who are envisioned as co-laboring with human prayer ministers. Bergunder observes that, following a personal healing experience, many economically poor South Indian healing evangelists and pastors give up steady incomes to devote themselves to full-time ministering to the spiritual and physical needs of others.

Several of the essayists note that divine healing practices are perceived as empowering to members of ethnic, class, gender, and geographic groups who are frequently denied social standing in other contexts. Paul Gifford, in his study of African pentecostalism, notes that Africa has tended to experience globalization as marginalization, and that pentecostalism is one of the few global phenomena in which Africa can participate as an equal. In a related vein, Bomann portrays divine healing as the only salve available to many in Colombia's working classes who have suffered as much as benefited from economic globalization; healing practices not only promise to meet physical needs, but also offer the poor a sense of self-worth and fill an important place in their emotional lives. Bergunder notes that, although a failure to receive healing can sometimes result in blaming those sick or bereaved for alleged sin or lack of faith, those who seek prayer for healing have often already tried a series of ineffective remedies, and, if once again disappointed, they will continue to hope for eventual healing; even in learning to accept inevitable death, individuals can find a sense of empowerment in their unshakeable faith that God is the Great Physician. Espinosa focuses on early twentieth-century healing evangelist Francisco Olazábal, who approved of women in ministry and attracted Mexicans, Puerto Ricans, Anglo Americans, Italians, and blacks of all classes to his services—creating an unusual context for members of these groups to interact. Espinosa notes, however, some limits to interethnic harmony, as for instance when Olazábal broke from the well-known Anglo healing evangelist Aimee Semple McPherson in reaction to her condescension toward him as a Latino. The Native Americans studied by Tarango similarly used pentecostal healing practices to forgive, resist, and overcome the racism and paternalism of white co-religionists. Chesnut points out the appeal of divine healing to poor Brazilian women who are responsible for the health care needs of their extended families. The possibilities and limits for women participants are acknowledged by Curtis in her consideration of a nineteenth-century divine healing movement that gathered momentum across Europe, North America, and Australia. Csordas similarly explores tensions in Nigerian Catholic Charismatic practices that acknowledged women's access to the charisms of the Holy Spirit, yet did so within a framework of patriarchal domination.

This book's contributors also consider the question of whether an emphasis on individual healing helps or hinders communal liberation. Oblau emphasizes the socially liberating potential of divine healing practices for Chinese pentecostals, noting that healing narratives are stories of protest against the vicious circle of illness, hunger, and debt, and illustrating how individual healing experiences can lead to social and economic betterment for entire communities. Reaching a profoundly different conclusion about the success of pentecostalism as a form of liberation theology, Arlene Sánchez Walsh depicts a Latina/o Word of Faith theology that envisions itself as liberation and is attractive to individuals who find it empowering to be told that they can overcome suffering through faith and, in some instances, that they as members of a distinctively Latina/o community have a superior solution to suffering than does the rest of the world; yet, assurances that faith inevitably results in health and prosperity indicts those who fail to extricate themselves from ongoing suffering, while turning a blind eye to socially, politically, and economically oppressive sources of poverty and poverty-related infirmities. In a connected vein, Csordas argues that the Catholic Charismatic renewal appeals to communitarian sentiment while advancing conservative values in opposition to liberation theology. Adding a further level of complexity to how we might understand the relationship between individuals and community, Simon Coleman notes that Swedish Charismatic subjects are formed not only as individual believers, but out of their engagements with others as "dividuals," or socially connected persons.

*Third, there is a significant relationship between the pursuits of health and of wealth, but the relationship is more complex than critics of a "health and wealth," or "prosperity," gospel typically acknowledge.* Although divine healing draws many people who are relatively prosperous, well educated, and upwardly mobile toward pentecostal Christianity—as with the Swedish Charismatics studied by Coleman—promises of healing have particular appeal for the poor and disenfranchised worldwide. Yet, as Chesnut notes, material deprivation per se is insufficient in accounting for pentecostalism's appeal to the poor; rather, it is the fact that illness is the most potent manifestation of poverty that drives Chesnut's Brazilian informants, generally as a last resort, to churches that practice divine healing. Coleman observes that the politically loaded label "health and wealth" may say more about commentators' assumptions concerning "proper" religion than it does about what is being described; nevertheless, Coleman explores linguistic, bodily, ideological, and theological tensions and affinities between these two concerns, which he suggests ritually complement each other. Bowler's and Sánchez Walsh's studies of the African American and Latina/o Word of Faith movements suggest that one's health and finances are related in that both function as material measures of the level of one's immaterial faith—an emphasis that can, in an effort to explain failure, lead to condemning the sick and poor as lacking faith. The Chinese Christians studied by Oblau are, however, much less concerned with using their health or wealth to prove faith than with seeking help from God to meet desperate physical and financial needs. Likewise, several essays depict African worldviews in which disease and poverty are both understood as the work of Satan and his demonic host, while health and finances are envisioned as material blessings from God that tangibly express full salvation. Whereas Omenyo considers healing to be of much greater concern than financial prosperity to African Christians, Gifford understands the defining characteristic of African pentecostalism to be a vision of "victorious living" that encompasses health while being even more concerned with the financial blessings needed for a successful life in the present world. Csordas complicates this argument by noting that Nigerian pentecostals emphasize the restitution of stolen articles in reaction against the quest for material wealth. Währisch-Oblau adds another important qualification that the efforts of African migrants to protect their material sustenance from attacks by evil spirits may appear to be materialistic, but such an assessment overlooks the foundational assumption that invisible spiritual forces determine material outcomes.

*Fourth, for most pentecostals worldwide, divine healing practices are closely connected with practices oriented toward deliverance from demonic oppression.* Several essayists evoke an "enchanted" worldview in which spiritual forces are pervasive and dominant within the physical world, making it seem self-evident that physical problems on both the individual and collective levels often demand spiritual solutions. Thus, physical healing and deliverance from demons are envisioned as two sides of the same coin. The exorcism of evil spirits often takes center stage in the healing practices of the Korean, Indian, Brazilian, Argentine, Nigerian, and African American pentecostals described in this volume—while deliverance is strikingly absent or at least invisible among the Chinese pentecostals studied by Oblau, likely because the practice is viewed as too politically dangerous. Währisch-Oblau argues that African migrant churches in Germany conceptualize evangelism not as the communication of a message, but as a spiritual battle engaged in by "prayer warriors" whose "authority" prayers of command free individuals and entire communities from bondage to the powers of evil as God's power is manifested through miracles of healing or driving out demons. She notes, moreover, that concepts of spiritual warfare among African migrants and ethnically German Charismatic churches developed in the context of globalized discourses that draw upon African traditional religions and on U.S. Word of Faith theology. In a related vein, Brown shows how North American healing evangelists have explicitly borrowed an emphasis on spiritual warfare, which involves both deliverance from demons and the welcoming of angelic assistance, from Christians in Argentina, Brazil, and Mozambique. Marostica notes the ironic reversal of North Americans intending to export spiritual warfare practices to Argentina who instead have imported new understandings of the Holy Spirit's anointing that have transformed North American healing and deliverance practices.

*Fifth, pentecostal Christianity gains adherents as people evaluate it as a more effective religion than competitors in meeting practical, everyday needs.* Curtis and Coleman each make historical arguments that show how an interest in divine healing assumes a high value on the physical body, in contrast to theological traditions that consider the body inferior to the soul and affirm that acceptance of bodily sickness is conducive to spiritual holiness. Rejecting a body-soul dualism that presents God as unconcerned with practical human needs, several essays elucidate an understanding of God as actively involved in the affairs of life and very much concerned with meeting everyday needs, including the need for healing. Many of the people described in this volume demand that, for any religion to be taken seriously as representing a God who is a true God, it must not simply provide theological explanations and hope for the afterlife, but it must also serve existential needs in the here and now. The Latin Americans, Native Americans, Africans, and Asians discussed here turn to pentecostalism not simply because of resonances with their traditional worldviews, but because pentecostal interpretations of Christianity seem more effective than other versions of Christianity or other religions in meeting their practical needs.

In promising to meet practical needs, Christianity both competes with other religions and interacts with indigenous traditions in mutually transformative ways. Csordas, in his comparative study of India, Brazil, and Nigeria, considers cross-fertilization between the healing practices of pentecostal Christianity and other religions, including Hinduism, Islam, spiritism, and African Brazilian and African religions; he finds a layering of hybridity upon syncretism upon synthesis. While likewise noting resonances between Christian healing practices and the indigenous healing traditions of Buddhism, shamanism, Hinduism, Daoism, and Confucianism, Kim, Bergunder, and Oblau all argue that Christianity competes with indigenous traditions by claiming superior healing powers; similar arguments are made by essayists writing on native North American, Latin American, and African contexts. Oblau argues, significantly, that while Daoist and Christian folk religious elements may overlap and influence each other, forming a syncretistic folk religion in many parts of the countryside, there are also instances of converts sharply distinguishing between the spirits of Daoism and the Jesus of Christianity. Bowler notes that, although hoodoo and other folk practices compete for Christians' allegiances, the African American pentecostals she studies strenuously reject all such practices as "witchcraft." Taken together, these essays push against flat renderings of pentecostalism as reducible to syncretism and shamanism and call for more robust accounts of the inculturation of Christianity in the diversity of its local contexts.

*Sixth, a common pool of divine healing beliefs and practices circulates globally through pentecostal appropriation of modern communications and travel technologies.* Curtis shows that, since the nineteenth century, participants in divine healing movements have embraced modern technology for communication and travel, allowing individuals to envision themselves as participants in a transcontinental community. A similar transdenominational, transgeographic, highly mediatized sense of community membership is exhibited by the late twentieth-century Swedish Charismatics studied by Coleman and the Latina/o churches depicted by Sánchez Walsh. The relative cheapness and ease of international air travel and the technologically mediated linguistic translation of books and music are significant in adding to global healing repertoires the contributions of the short-term North American missionaries studied by Brown and the long-term African migrants in Germany examined by Währisch-Oblau.

Gifford likewise shows that not only do Africans eagerly consume American books, broadcasts, and conference presentations, but Africans also contribute to the global marketplace by producing media offerings that are purchased and screened alongside Western transmissions. Csordas explores the complex ways that Brazilian Charismatics employ mediated representations to convey unmediated divine communications, one effect of which is to provide a revolving door between Catholicism and pentecostalism and to form a threshold between them. Although many scholars have assumed that modern developments such as scientific medicine would weaken the relevance of religious responses to illness, especially responses that are as seemingly premodern as divine healing, the collected essays instead demonstrate that, even where modernizing processes are furthest advanced, pentecostals wield modern technology to disseminate healing and deliverance practices globally.

*Seventh, divine healing practices reflect multidirectional cultural flows among diverse local contexts, no one of which exerts a dominant influence.* The situation in China described by Oblau, in which Christians have been largely cut off from foreign influences since the 1950s—and yet share characteristics with pentecostals who actively participate in global networks—is exceptional. In his comparative studies of Catholic Charismatics, Csordas notes both a universal culture and cultural fragmentation—a tension that Curtis shows to have existed since the mid-nineteenth century and to have facilitated the growth of global healing movements. Pointing out interactions among geographically separated Latino communities in the United States, Mexico, and the Caribbean that date back to the early twentieth century, Espinosa calls for a retelling of stories of globalization that trace cultural flows from South to North, from periphery to center, indeed questioning whether there are any "centers" of influence at all. Sánchez Walsh emphasizes both the theological diversity and the cultural markers of ethnic identity that exist among twenty-first-century U.S. Latina/os, as they interact with and borrow from Latina/os in Latin America and the Caribbean as well as a multiethnic, global Faith movement.

The cross-cultural interactions described in this volume encourage a more nuanced rendering of the impacts of North American missionary legacies. Tarango shows that, in borrowing from white Pentecostals, Native Americans reinterpreted the missionaries' message in light of their experiences as indigenous peoples and thus reshaped it as a gospel of not only healing physical illnesses and social illnesses like alcoholism, but also racial healing from the bitterness of past wrongs and hatred of whites as they fought the missionaries' paternalism and ethnocentrism. Währisch-Oblau describes African migrant churches in Germany not as "diaspora" churches where migrants seek a "home away from home" to preserve their cultures and original piety, but rather as missionary bridgeheads with a clear evangelistic calling toward the whole of German society. Lay migrants seek to reach out to non-Christians, engage in street preaching, and host gospel concerts that convey an evangelistic message to audiences unimpressed by public healing performances. Kim traces the origins of today's emphasis on divine healing in Korean churches, ironically, to the late nineteenth-century missionary work of Americans who did not believe in divine healing; American missionaries proclaimed the New Testament gospel, but could not control what Koreans did with it—adding an emphasis on healing that made sense in their cultural context, as they drew inspiration not only from biblical accounts, but also from indigenous healing traditions. Omenyo makes a similar argument that Africans adapted missionary-imparted Christianity along the lines of pneumatic and African traditional spiritualities that privilege healing. Marostica shows that it was in turning away from U.S. missionary models—that either neglected divine healing or restricted it to the ministrations of particularly gifted, always foreign, healing evangelists—that local healing practices developed, spread, and then returned to North America in modified forms. Victims as well as beneficiaries of globalization, the pentecostal pastors who offer prayers for healing in Colombia's *barrios*, as Bomann tells us, are not foreigners presenting an imported religion but are members of the urban poor expressing an indigenized faith. Brown demonstrates how North American missionaries today borrow directly from beliefs and practices developed in Argentina, Brazil, and Mozambique, reexporting assimilated teachings about healing and deliverance in more democratized forms to organizations within their social networks, even as countries like Brazil and Korea overtake the United States as missionary senders. Far from the dismantling of Christian practices in a postcolonial world, these essays reveal how a renewed emphasis on divine healing and deliverance characterizes the appropriation and inculturation of Christianity by peoples worldwide.[49]

We turn now to the essays for more detailed descriptions and interpretations of divine healing practices around the world. As disease and the fear of disease continue to spread in an era of globalization, pentecostalism can be expected to attract more and more adherents who need healing and hope as they struggle to survive and make sense of life on our changing planet.

NOTES

1. Luis Lugo et al., *Spirit and Power: A 10-Country Survey of Pentecostals* (Washington, D.C.: Pew Forum on Religion and Public Life, Oct. 2006). Estimates of pentecostal membership vary widely, the most conservative ranging from a quarter- to over a half-billion people; see David B. Barrett, George Thomas Kurian, and Todd M. Johnson, *World Christian Encyclopedia: A Comparative Survey of Churches and Religion in the Modern World*, 2 vols., 2nd ed. (New York: Oxford University Press, 2001); Philip Jenkins, *The Next Christendom: The Coming of Global Christianity* (New York: Oxford University Press, 2002), 2–5, 8; David Martin, *Pentecostalism: The World Their Parish* (Malden, Mass.: Blackwell, 2002), xvii.

2 A 2003 *Newsweek* poll found 72 percent of Americans believing that "praying to God can cure someone—even if science says the person doesn't stand a chance";

Claudia Kalb, "Faith and Healing," *Newsweek* (10 Nov. 2003). A 1996 Gallup poll showed 82 percent believing "in the healing power of personal prayer," and 77 percent agreeing that "God sometimes intervenes to cure people who have a serious illness." See John Cole, "Gallup Poll Again Shows Confusion," *NCSE Reports* (Spring 1996): 9; and Claudia Wallis, "Faith and Healing," *Time* (24 June 1996). 63, qtd. in Ronald L. Numbers, "Science without God: Natural Laws and Christian Beliefs," 284, in *When Science and Christianity Meet*, ed. David C. Lindberg and Ronald L. Numbers (Chicago: University of Chicago Press, 2003). Other polls suggest that 61–80 percent believe in miracles; see Robert Bruce Mullin, *Miracles and the Modern Religious Imagination* (New Haven, Conn.: Yale University Press, 1996), 262; Stephen J. Pullum, *"Foul Demons, Come Out!" The Rhetoric of Twentieth-Century American Faith Healing* (Westport, Conn.: Praeger, 1999), 150.

    3 Although globalization has become a major thrust of scholarship in fields such as American studies, economics, sociology, anthropology, and cultural and media studies, the significance of religion as an agent of globalization continues to be undervalued; see J. Macgregor Wise, *Cultural Globalization* (Malden, Mass.: Blackwell, 2008). Religious studies scholars have begun to examine particular historical and cultural contexts in which healing has been practiced and to link healing with the rapid late twentieth- and early twenty-first-century spread of pentecostalism, but they have had less to say about how local healing practices reflect, shape, and redirect broader globalizing processes; see Philip Jenkins, *The New Faces of Christianity: Believing the Bible in the Global South* (New York: Oxford University Press, 2006); Harvey Cox, *Fire from Heaven: The Rise of Pentecostal Spirituality and the Reshaping of Religion in the Twenty-First Century* (Reading, Mass.: Addison-Wesley, 1995).

    4 The term "pentecostal" references the Jewish holiday of Pentecost, which falls 50 days after Passover; according to Acts 2, Jesus' disciples received the Holy Spirit on the first Pentecost after Jesus' crucifixion. Scholars of pentecostalism often refer to three "waves" of the Holy Spirit, the first at the turn of the twentieth century with the Azusa Street revivals in Los Angeles, California, the second with the ecumenical Charismatic movement of the 1960s–1970s, and the third with the "signs and wonders" movements of the 1980s–1990s; see Paul Freston, "Brother Votes for Brother: The New Politics of Protestantism in Brazil," 68, in *Rethinking Protestantism in Latin America*, ed. Virginia Garrard-Burnett and David Stoll (Philadelphia: Temple University Press, 1993).

    5 Max Weber, "The Sociology of Charismatic Authority," in *Max Weber: Essays in Sociology*, ed. and trans. H. H. Gerth and C. Wright Mills (New York: Oxford University Press, 1946).

    6 As discussed by Marostica and Brown in this volume, a Spanish-language deliverance handbook written by the Argentine Pablo Bottari, *Libres en Cristo: La Importancia del Ministerio de Liberación*, translated into English and marketed as *Free in Christ: Your Complete Handbook on the Ministry of Deliverance* (1999; reprint, Lake Mary, Fla.: Creation House, 2000), has exerted an enormous influence on global pentecostal deliverance practices. The direct translation "liberation" is used somewhat less frequently by practitioners or scholars because of potential confusion with liberation theology—although, as suggested by Oblau and Marostica, liberation from demons and oppressive social forces are sometimes viewed as interrelated.

7  For distinctions between healing and cure, see Pamela E. Klassen, "Textual Healing: Mainstream Protestants and the Therapeutic Text, 1900–1925," *Church History* 75.4 (2006): 809–810; Linda L. Barnes and Susan S. Sered, eds., *Religion and Healing in America* (New York: Oxford University Press, 2005), 10.

8  On distinctions between healing and miracles, see Mullin, *Miracles*, 95. In practice, a rigid distinction is rarely made among the terms "healing," "cure," and "miracle"; for example, in Spanish-speaking contexts, the term *sanidad*, or healing, is often used in place of *cura*.

9  For similar scholarly stances, see Heather D. Curtis, *Faith in the Great Physician: Suffering and Divine Healing in American Culture, 1860–1900* (Baltimore, Md.: Johns Hopkins University Press, 2007), 22; R. Marie Griffith, *God's Daughters: Evangelical Women and the Power of Submission* (Berkeley: University of California Press, 1997), 23; Meredith B. McGuire and Debra Kantor, *Ritual Healing in Suburban America* (New Brunswick, N.J.: Rutgers University Press, 1988), 269; Caroline Walker Bynum, *Holy Feast and Holy Fast: The Religious Significance of Food to Medieval Women* (Berkeley: University of California Press, 1987), 8.

10  For similar critiques of this tendency, see Robert A. Orsi, *Between Heaven and Earth: The Religious Worlds People Make and the Scholars Who Study Them* (Princeton, N.J.: Princeton University Press, 2005), 28; Susan Sontag, *Illness as Metaphor and AIDS and Its Metaphors* (New York: Farrar, Straus and Giroux, 1988), 6; Elaine Scarry, *The Body in Pain: The Making and Unmaking of the World* (New York: Oxford University Press, 1985), 6.

11  André Corten and Ruth Marshall-Fratani, introduction to *Between Babel and Pentecost: Transnational Pentecostalism in Africa and Latin America* (Bloomington: Indiana University Press, 2001), 6.

12  For the cultural framing of individual experiences, see R. Marie Griffith, "Female Suffering and Religious Devotion in American Pentecostalism," 203, in *Women and Twentieth-Century Protestantism*, ed. Margaret Lamberts Bendroth and Virginia Lieson Brereton (Urbana: University of Illinois Press, 2002).

13  David D. Hall, *Lived Religion in America: Toward a History of Practice* (Princeton, N.J.: Princeton University Press, 1997); Laurie F. Maffly-Kipp, Leigh Eric Schmidt, and Mark R. Valeri, *Practicing Protestants: Histories of Christian Life in America, 1630–1965* (Baltimore, Md.: Johns Hopkins University Press, 2006).

14  For definitions of "globalization," see Roland Robertson, *Globalization: Social Theory and Global Culture* (London: Sage, 1992), 8, 184; David Martin, "Evangelical Expansion in Global Society," 273, in *Christianity Reborn: The Global Expansion of Evangelicalism in the Twentieth Century*, ed. Donald M. Lewis (Grand Rapids, Mich.: Eerdmans, 2004); Scott Lash and John Urry, *Economies of Signs and Space* (London: Sage, 1994); Martin Albrow, *The Global Age: State and Society beyond Modernity* (Cambridge: Polity, 1996), 95; Ulf Hannerz, *Transnational Connections: Culture, People, Places* (New York: Routledge, 1996), 102; Peter Geschiere and Birgit Meyer, "Globalization and Identity: Dialectics of Flow and Closure," *Development and Change* 29.4 (1998): 602; Simon Coleman, *The Globalisation of Charismatic Christianity: Spreading the Gospel of Prosperity* (Cambridge: Cambridge University Press, 2000), 55.

15  Amanda Porterfield, *Healing in the History of Christianity* (New York: Oxford University Press, 2005), 151; Sontag, *Illness as Metaphor*, 180.

16 Robert Wilson, "The Disease of Fear and the Fear of Disease: Cholera and Yellow Fever in the Mississippi Valley" (Ph.D. diss., Saint Louis University, 2007); Terence Ranger and Paul Slack, eds., *Epidemics and Ideas: Essays on the Historical Perception of Pestilence* (Cambridge: Cambridge University Press, 1992), 2–4. Popular books include Michael Crichton, *Andromeda Strain* (New York: Random House, 1969); Robin Cook, *Outbreak* (New York: Penguin Putnam, 1987); Richard Preston, *The Hot Zone* (New York: Random House, 1994); Frank Ryan, *Virus-X: Tracking the New Killer Plagues* (Boston: Little, Brown, 1997).

17 Corten and Marshall-Fratani, *Between Babel and Pentecost*, 3.

18 M. V. Gumede, *Traditional Healers: A Medical Practitioner's Perspective* (Braamfontein, South Africa: Skotaville, 1990), 38, 203.

19 Cox, *Fire from Heaven*, 256.

20 R. Andrew Chesnut, *Born Again in Brazil: The Pentecostal Boom and the Pathogens of Poverty* (New Brunswick, N.J.: Rutgers University Press, 1997), 82.

21 Donald M. Lewis, ed., introduction to *Christianity Reborn: The Global Expansion of Evangelicalism in the Twentieth Century* (Grand Rapids, Mich.: Eerdmans, 2004), 1; Martin Riesebrodt, "Religion in Global Perspective," 607, in *The Oxford Handbook of Global Religions*, ed. Mark Juergensmeyer (New York: Oxford University Press, 2006).

22 Elliot G. Mishler et al., *Social Contexts of Health, Illness, and Patient Care* (New York: Cambridge University Press, 1981), 240; Cox, *Fire from Heaven*, 104, 108.

23 For early Pentecostal resistance to medicine and the lessening of this resistance after World War II, see Grant Wacker, "The Pentecostal Tradition," in *Caring and Curing: Health and Medicine in the Western Religious Traditions*, 524–525, ed. Ronald L. Numbers and Darrel W. Amundsen (New York: Macmillan, 1986).

24 James C. Whorton, *Nature Cures: The History of Alternative Medicine in America* (New York: Oxford University Press, 2002), 246; Catherine L. Albanese, *A Republic of Mind and Spirit: A Cultural History of American Metaphysical Religion* (New Haven, Conn.: Yale University Press, 2007), 4.

25 Dan Cray, "God vs. Science," *Time* (5 Nov. 2006), http://www.time.com/time/magazine/article/0,9171,1555132,00.html (accessed 7 Dec. 2009).

26 Martin, "Evangelical Expansion in Global Society," 279, in *Christianity Reborn*, ed. Lewis.

27 Michael F. Brown, *The Channeling Zone: American Spirituality in an Anxious Age* (Cambridge, Mass.: Harvard University Press, 1997), 8.

28 Riesebrodt, "Religion in Global Perspective," 599–600; Arjun Appadurai, *Modernity at Large: Cultural Dimensions of Globalization* (Minneapolis: University of Minnesota Press, 1996), 5; Jean Comaroff and John L. Comaroff, eds., *Modernity and Its Malcontents: Ritual and Power in Postcolonial Africa* (Chicago: University of Chicago Press, 1993), xxix.

29 Griffith, "Female Suffering," 198.

30 Paul Freston, "Contours of Latin American Pentecostalism," 238, in *Christianity Reborn*, ed. Lewis; Porterfield, *Healing in the History of Christianity*, 159; Pamela Klassen, "Radio Mind: Protestant Experimentalists on the Frontiers of Healing," *Journal of the American Academy of Religion* 75.3 (2007): 651–683; Candy Gunther Brown, "Healing Words: Narratives of Spiritual Healing and Kathryn Kuhlman's Uses of Print Culture, 1947–1976," 271–297, in *Religion and the Culture of Print in Modern*

*America*, ed. Charles L. Cohen and Paul S. Boyer (Madison: University of Wisconsin Press, 2008). On the long-standing tendency of evangelicals to appropriate modern communications technology, see Mark A. Noll, David W. Bebbington, and George A. Rawlyk, eds., *Evangelicalism: Comparative Studies of Popular Protestantism in North America, the British Isles, and Beyond, 1700–1990* (New York: Oxford University Press, 1994); Candy Gunther Brown, *The Word in the World: Evangelical Writing, Publishing, and Reading in America, 1789–1880* (Chapel Hill: University of North Carolina Press, 2004); David Paul Nord, *Faith in Reading: Religious Publishing and the Birth of Mass Media in America* (New York: Oxford University Press, 2004).

31  Candy Gunther Brown, "From Tent Meetings and Store-front Healing Rooms to Walmarts and the Internet: Healing Spaces in the United States, the Americas, and the World, 1906–2006," *Church History* (Sept. 2006): 639–640.

32  On the movement-oriented nature of marking out the sacred, see Claude Lévi-Strauss, *Structural Anthropology* (Garden City, N.Y.: Doubleday, 1967), 206.

33  David Martin, *Tongues of Fire: The Explosion of Protestantism in Latin America* (Cambridge, Mass.: Blackwell, 1990), 107; A. F. Droogers, "Globalization and Pentecostal Success," in *Between Babel and Pentecost*, ed. Corten and Marshall-Fratani; Thomas A. Tweed, *Crossing and Dwelling: A Theory of Religion* (Cambridge, Mass.: Harvard University Press, 2006), 127.

34  McGuire and Kantor, *Ritual Healing in Suburban America*, 14; Gotthard Oblau, "Pentecostal by Default? Contemporary Christianity in China," 421, in *Asian and Pentecostal: The Charismatic Face of Christianity in Asia*, ed. Allan Anderson and Edmond Tang (Costa Mesa, Calif.: Regnum, 2005).

35  Darrel W. Amundsen and Gary B. Ferngren, "The Early Christian Tradition," 46; Marvin R. O'Connell, "Roman Catholic Tradition," 121; and Timothy P. Weber, "Baptist Tradition," 292, all in *Caring and Curing*, ed. Numbers and Amundsen; Bynum, *Holy Feast and Holy Fast*, 36; David J. Melling, "Suffering and Sanctification in Christianity," 47, in *Religion, Health and Suffering*, ed. John R. Hinnells and Roy Porter (New York: Kegan Paul, 1999); Bryan T. Turner, "The Body in Western Society: Social Theory and Its Perspectives," 29, in *Religion and the Body*, ed. Sarah Coakley (Cambridge: Cambridge University Press, 1997); Stacy Takacs, "Alien-Nation: Immigration, National Identity and Transnationalism," *Cultural Studies* 13.4 (1 Oct. 1999): 591–620.

36  Curtis, *Faith in the Great Physician*, 19; Walter Hollenweger, "Evangelism and Brazilian Pentecostals," *Ecumenical Review* 20 (Apr. 1968): 166; Coakley, introduction to *Religion and the Body*, 6; James W. Opp, "Healing Hands, Healthy Bodies: Protestant Women and Faith-Healing in Canada and the United States, 1880–1930," 237, in *Women and Twentieth-Century Protestantism*, ed. Bendroth and Brereton; Gastón Espinosa, "'God Made a Miracle in My Life': Latino Pentecostal Healing in the Borderlands," 124–125, in *Religion and Healing in America*, ed. Barnes and Sered; Michel Foucault, *The Birth of the Clinic: An Archaeology of Medical Perception*, trans. A. M. Sheridan Smith (New York: Vintage), xi.

37  For an example of this field of inquiry, see Matthew T. Lee and Margaret M. Poloma, *A Sociological Study of the Great Commandment in Pentecostalism: The Practice of Godly Love as Benevolent Service* (Lewiston, N.Y.: Mellen, 2009).

38  Robert D. Putnam, *Bowling Alone: The Collapse and Revival of American Community* (New York: Simon and Schuster, 2000); Stephen Post and Jill Neimark,

*Why Good Things Happen to Good People: The Exciting New Research That Proves the Link between Doing Good and Living a Longer, Healthier, Happier Life* (New York: Broadway Books, 2007).

39 Other commonly cited biblical passages include Exodus 15:26 ("I am the Lord that healeth thee"); Mark 16:18 ("they shall lay hands on the sick, and they shall recover"); Acts 10:39 ("Jesus . . . went about doing good, and healing all that were oppressed of the devil"); James 5:14–16 ("pray one for another, that ye may be healed"); Hebrews 13:8 ("Jesus Christ the same yesterday, and to day, and for ever") (AV). Not all pentecostals affirm that healing is included in the atonement; see Kimberly Ervin Alexander, *Pentecostal Healing: Models in Theology and Practice* (Blandford Forum, England: Deo, 2006), 225.

40 Lamin Sanneh, in his introduction to *The Changing Face of Christianity: Africa, the West, and the World*, ed. Lamin Sanneh and Joel A. Carpenter (New York: Oxford University Press, 2005), 7, contrasts the "stripped-down universe of a post-Enlightenment Christianity" and the "small, disinfected universe of the West" with the "larger world that Africans live in."

41 Martin, *Pentecostalism*, 6–7, 164–165; Cox, *Fire from Heaven*, 147, 222, 256.

42 For a critical interpretation of Korean pentecostal "shamanism," see Mark R. Mullins, "The Empire Strikes Back: Korean Pentecostal Mission to Japan," 92–98, in *Charismatic Christianity as a Global Culture*, ed. Karla O. Poewe (Columbia: University of South Carolina Press, 1994). For a critique of the "contemporary shamanism" of North American health and wealth movements, see Martyn Percy, "The City on a Beach: Future Prospects for Charismatic Movements at the End of the Twentieth Century," 213–222, in *Charismatic Christianity: Sociological Perspectives*, ed. Stephen Hunt, Malcolm Hamilton, and Tony Walter (New York: St. Martin's, 1997); using the Toronto Blessing as a case study, Percy characterizes promises of healing and prosperity as theologically "dubious" and "offensive," because they imply a view of God as willing to "indulge a small, Caucasian-based, international and mainly middle-class group with great blessings, whilst leaving the lot of the poor largely untouched."

43 Wonsuk Ma, "Asian (Classical) Pentecostal Theology in Context," 66, 70–72, in *Asian and Pentecostal*, ed. Anderson and Tang. Similarly, Allan Anderson, in *An Introduction to Pentecostalism: Global Charismatic Christianity* (Cambridge: Cambridge University Press, 2004), 222, defends David Yonggi Cho of the Yoido Full Gospel Church in Seoul because of the context of poverty and destitution in which his message arose, further insisting that Cho's "doctrine of 'blessings' is, however, not an individualistic 'bless me' teaching but one intended to bring 'overflowing blessings' to those people around every believer." See also Kim's essay in this volume.

44 Corten and Marshall-Fratani, introduction to *Between Babel and Pentecost*, 6.

45. Jenkins, *New Faces of Christianity*, 93–96.

46 For a theoretical discussion of "magic" and "religion," see the classic work of Emile Durkheim, *The Elementary Forms of Religious Life*, trans. and with an introduction by Karen E. Fields (New York: Simon and Schuster, 1995), 39.

47 Miroslav Volf, "Materiality of Salvation: An Investigation in the Soteriologies of Liberation and Pentecostal Theologies," *Journal of Ecumenical Studies* 26.3 (1989): 447–467.

48 I thank Amanda Porterfield for help in framing these issues.

49 Lewis, introduction to *Christianity Reborn*, 2–3.

PART I

# Europe and North America

# I

# The Global Character of Nineteenth-Century Divine Healing

*Heather D. Curtis*

On the afternoon of Wednesday, 3 June 1885, 2,000 people gathered in London's Agricultural Hall to take part in a service of anointing for divine healing. Although most participants were English, the assembly included attendees from "all quarters of the globe," including Australia, France, Germany, Holland, Ireland, Italy, North America, Scotland, Spain, and Switzerland. After explaining the biblical basis for the practices of anointing, laying on of hands, and prayer for healing in passages such as James 5, the session's chair, the Reverend William E. Boardman (1810–1896), beseeched his audience to entrust their bodies and souls to "the Lord Jesus Christ, the *real Healer*. Jesus Christ, the Lord, is the only Healer, and there is no healing but by the power of the Holy Ghost." Following an address by the Reverend A. B. Simpson (1843–1919) that affirmed the promise of "the living Christ, to manifest His personal touch of supernatural and resurrection power in the anointing of the sick," co-leader Elizabeth Baxter (1837–1926) exhorted sufferers to seek healing with confidence, conviction, and certainty. "When we pray," she proclaimed, "we shall not ask of God to heal you *if* it be His will, but *because* He has shown in His Word and in His own life, that it *is* His will." Then, Boardman prayed alongside "eight brethren and sisters, who laid on hands, anointed about 250 persons, by touching the head with oil." After the ceremony, "the crowded assembly" recited the opening lines of Psalm 103, "Bless the Lord, O my soul, and forget not all His benefits: Who forgiveth all thine iniquities; who healeth all thy diseases," and the meeting came to a close.[1]

This anointing service marked the midpoint of the International Confer-ence on Divine Healing and True Holiness, a gathering that sought to bring together "all who, in all lands" believed that "in God's thought of full salvation, the body is inseparably connected with the spirit and soul." Cognizant that they were part of a growing global movement, the conveners of the conference believed that the time was ripe, and the need "pressing," for an international discussion. In the invitation, the organizers had outlined several goals for the gathering. First, they aimed to provide an international forum for sharing insights about "the truth of His direct healing of the body through faith." Second, they acknowledged a need to deal with "difficulties" related to the doc-trines of healing and holiness. Finally, they anticipated that the meeting would help to further the revival of divine healing that had emerged in Germany a half-century earlier, spread throughout continental Europe, Great Britain, and North America, and was now beginning to expand around the world. On the opening day of the convention, Boardman set his hopes for the gathering within a broader context of prophetic expectation, interpreting the global pro-liferation of divine healing as a sign that God was "shedding forth" the power of the Holy Spirit "on a grander scale than the world has ever seen": "We are assembled here, I trust, in the opening of a new revival of Pentecost. I see in the response to the call to an International Conference, which brings so many from various lands together this evening, the preparation for God's reproduc-ing the Pentecostal fullness in the earth."[2]

The International Conference on Divine Healing and True Holiness pre-dated by several decades the Pentecostal revivals that swept through Wales, India, Korea, North America, Australia, and Chile, leading within a few years to the establishment of Pentecostal churches in some 50 countries. Yet comments like Boardman's suggest that this gathering presaged, and prompted, the worldwide expansion of divine healing through the twentieth-century pente-costal movement. This essay examines the convictions, anxieties, and expecta-tions expressed at the 1885 convention in order to shed light on how the nineteenth-century "revival of divine healing and true holiness" both reflected and contributed to the globalization of Christianity. Beginning with an analysis of how conference participants described the origins and development of divine healing practices in Europe and North America, I will show that propo-nents of this revival were intensely conscious of the movement's global charac-ter. Envisioning themselves as members of a community bound together by belief and practice, advocates of divine healing employed modern technologies of travel and communication in order to cultivate translocal connections. As they fostered this international fellowship, however, practitioners became in-creasingly aware of discrepancies in how divine healing was understood and practiced in various local contexts. Examining the debates over interpretation at the international conference highlights how leaders of the developing divine healing movement worked to maintain mutuality amid growing multiformity.

This balance—or, perhaps, tension—between unity and heterogeneity, I argue, actually contributed to the movement's vitality during the latter decades of the nineteenth century as participants from a wide range of theological, social, and regional backgrounds fashioned theologies and practices of healing that reflected both global sensibilities and particular, local conditions. As the international conference drew to a close, attendees expressed hope that their time of fellowship offered only a foretaste of a great, worldwide revival yet to come. This chapter accordingly traces the connections between the nineteenth-century divine healing movement and the emergence of Pentecostalism in the early twentieth century. The transatlantic organizational alliances, relational networks, institutional structures, and theological expectations that the international conference helped to foster, I contend, contributed to the flourishing of global, pentecostal healing, which continues to influence the worldwide expansion of Christianity in the twenty-first century.[3]

## The Origins and Development of Divine Healing in the Nineteenth Century

"About a half century ago," wrote William Boardman in the invitation to the international conference, "the Lord began to revive the truth of His direct HEALING of the body through Faith. This was in Germany, principally through the revered Pastor Blumhardt . . . and in Switzerland, through the no less revered Dorothea Trudel. At the same time, in other countries, the Lord has signally begun to revive the truth of HOLINESS through faith." Throughout the international conference, participants echoed and expanded Boardman's account of the recent revival of divine healing. According to these interpreters, healing had always been a part of the Christian tradition, but many believers had "lost faith in Christ as healer." For individuals raised within the Calvinist tradition, in particular, the idea that God actively intervened in the everyday events of individual lives jarred discordantly with one of the key teachings of Reformed theology: that Jesus had performed miracles such as healing the sick in order to demonstrate his divinity, but once the Christian church had been established, miraculous signs were no longer necessary. The age of miracles had ceased with the apostles, and although it was still permissible to pray for relief from suffering, Christians should expect God to heal them through natural agencies, or "secondary causes," rather than through a supernatural act of divine power.[4]

   In his 1881 treatise, *The Great Physician*, subtitled *Jehovah Rophi*, or "the Lord thy Healer," Boardman lamented the widespread influence of the cessationist view of miraculous healing. As a Presbyterian minister, Boardman had long believed that "healing through faith" belonged "exclusively in the category of miracles . . . one of those things for extraordinary times—not at all a continuous privilege." But Boardman's participation in the Reformed Higher Life movement that grew out of early nineteenth-century revivalism eventually led him to question this idea. In the 1830s–1840s, evangelicals from a variety of theological traditions and denominational backgrounds in both Great Britain and North America had begun to stress the necessity of "entire sanctification" through a "second blessing" or "baptism with the Holy Spirit" following conversion that endued believers with the power to conquer sin and the energy to engage in effective Christian service. After embracing a version of these teachings in the early 1850s, Boardman published *The Higher Christian Life* (1858), an exceedingly popular work that extolled the possibility of victory over sin through a "deeper work of grace" that was the source of a believer's "power for service." Boardman soon became active in promoting a "revival of Holiness" in the United States, Great Britain, and continental Europe through evangelistic campaigns and conventions.[5]

By the late 1860s, Boardman's transatlantic ministry had brought him into contact with several proponents of "Christian holiness" who pushed him to reconsider his views of miraculous healing. During a trip to Boston in 1870, Boardman visited his friend and colleague Charles Cullis (1833–1892), a homeopathic physician and fervent advocate "for the advancement of believers in the knowledge and experience of holiness." Several years earlier, Cullis had begun to wonder whether it was God's will that his ministry "should extend to the cure of disease, as well as the alleviation of the afflicted." About that time, he came across a copy of *Dorothea Trudel; or, The Prayer of Faith*, a work that recounted "the remarkable manner in which large numbers of sick persons were healed in answer to prayer" at Trudel's home in Männedorf, Switzerland. After reading the story of Trudel's divine healing ministry and ruminating on "the instructions and promises contained in the fourteenth and fifteenth verses of the fifth chapter of the Epistle of James," Cullis felt emboldened to ask Lucy Reed Drake, a young woman suffering from a brain tumor that kept her bedridden, if she would be willing to "trust the Lord" to remove the malignancy and restore her to health. Drake agreed, and Cullis proceeded to pray. Soon after, Drake rose from her sickbed and returned to her work as a city missionary. The tumor had disappeared.[6]

Boardman arrived in Boston shortly after Drake's healing. When Cullis enthusiastically recounted how God had fulfilled the promises offered in James 5, Boardman was persuaded that "healing in answer to the prayer of faith remains a permanent privilege for the people of God." In 1873, Boardman and Cullis, along with their wives, Mary and Lucretia, traveled to Trudel's home in Switzerland and to Lutheran pastor Johann Christoph Blumhardt's (1805–1880) ministry of healing at Bad Boll, Germany. After this trip, the Boardmans carried the tidings of the revival of divine healing to London, where they shared their newfound faith with friends such as Elizabeth Baxter, an evangelist and participant in the Keswick Higher Life conventions whose husband, Michael, edited the influential *Christian Herald* magazine. In 1880, Baxter and the Boardmans, along with Baxter's evangelistic co-worker Charlotte C. Murray, opened Bethshan, a "house for the healing of the sick," which quickly became the epicenter of the divine healing movement in England and, eventually, the site of the international conference.[7]

By 1885, divine healing had spread from Switzerland and Germany across Europe and to Great Britain, the United States, Australia, and India. Many participants at the international conference acknowledged the importance of Trudel or Blumhardt in their own experiences of divine healing. "It will be twenty-seven years in August next, since I set foot in that well-known house at Mannedorf in Switzerland, where that little but saintly woman, Dorothea Trudel, served the Lord," Pastor Schrenk of Bern, Switzerland, declared. "My first impression, as soon as I got there, weary and sick, was this, 'Put off thy shoes from thy feet; this is holy ground.'" Although Schrenk reverenced Trudel's role in the revival of divine healing, he also rejoiced that the movement had spread rapidly. "Mannedorf . . . used to be an international institution; but that is no longer necessary, and it will be merely a Continental institution," Schrenk proclaimed. Because Baxter and the Boardmans had developed a solid base for divine healing at Bethshan, Schrenk explained, few people would need to travel to Switzerland seeking a miraculous cure. "Faith Healing belongs to the Church," he affirmed, "and not to any Institution."[8]

Elizabeth Baxter acknowledged the centrality of Switzerland and Germany in the revival of divine healing. "I could not tell you the number of those who have corresponded with us, and told us, that thirty years, twenty years, or ten years ago, they were stirred up by reading reports of Dorothea Trudel's work in Switzerland, Pastor Blumhardt's work in Germany," she wrote.[9] Baxter's own embrace of divine healing came primarily through her interactions with Swiss pastor Otto Stockmayer (1838–1917), who had experienced healing through the ministry of Samuel Zeller (1834–1912), Dorothea Trudel's successor at Männedorf, in 1867. Several years later, Stockmayer opened his own healing home at Hauptweil, Switzerland, on the Männedorf model. During an evangelistic tour through Germany and Switzerland in the late 1870s, Baxter spent time with Stockmayer, who shared his beliefs about the scriptural basis of divine healing. Dubbed the "theologian of the doctrine of healing by faith" by a later admirer, Stockmayer was one of the earliest proponents of European divine healing to articulate systematically the biblical tenets of his healing practice. In his widely read exposition, *Sickness and the Gospel* (1878), Stockmayer argued that "Christ has redeemed us from our sickness as from our sins (Matt. viii. 16, 17)." Since Christ's atonement included both spiritual salvation and bodily healing, Stockmayer reasoned, "it is not the will of God that His children should be sick (James v. 14–18)."[10] On Christmas Day 1877, while reflecting on "the blessed truth . . . that the Lord Jesus . . . Himself took our infirmities, and bare our sicknesses," Baxter accepted the atonement theology of healing, a teaching which "brought new life into my own body, and led me ever since to look to the Lord as my physician for soul and body."[11]

Through her work at Bethshan, Baxter promoted this interpretation of divine healing—a view that spread quickly through the transatlantic Holiness and Higher Life networks to which she and Stockmayer belonged. By the time of the international conference, the idea that Christ's death on the cross atoned for both sin and sickness had become a fundamental supposition of many participants. Atonement theology offered a means for contesting a long-standing and still-pervasive Protestant devotional tradition that linked bodily suffering with spiritual holiness and valorized patient resignation as the proper Christian response to affliction. "The majority of Christians continue to believe that sickness is for their good," Baxter lamented at an evening gathering on the conference's opening day. As a result, she maintained, "there are very many people everywhere who say, I am so afraid, if I ask God to heal my body, that I should do something which is contrary to 'His will.'" Based on her reading of Jesus' life and ministry and of biblical texts such as Psalm 103:3, Isaiah 53:24, James 4:15, and Matthew 8:16–17, Baxter proposed an alternative approach to dealing with physical suffering. "There is no word of Scripture anywhere to cast a doubt on God's will to heal, and . . . sickness is never, in a single passage, spoken of as a blessing," she asserted. Jesus never told a petitioner, "It is not my Will to heal, for it is better for you to remain sick." Instead, Baxter insisted, through his healing ministry Jesus "brought soul and body near to Himself. . . . Again and again we find, in God's word, that salvation of soul and body is connected together." The appropriate response to sickness, therefore, was not acquiescent submission, but faithful prayer: "God calls us to cast *all* our care on Him, for spirit, soul, and body."[12]

Baxter's claim that God "has constituted Himself our Saviour and our Healer, that our whole being may respond to Him" was a common theme at the international conference. In their addresses to the gathered assembly, numerous speakers associated the recovery of "faith in Christ as Healer" with an anticipation that God was inaugurating a reformation in the universal church. The Reverend D. D. Smith of Wilmington, Delaware, contended that God was "reviving this truth" as a means of overcoming divisions in the Christian community. "Here, to-night," he declared, "we have unity. All denominations are here for the purpose of showing forth that Christ is a perfect redeemer—He first unifies man by making him whole, proving that He is the Redeemer of the soul and of the body, and then brings us together in that close union with Christ which brings us closer to each other." Reminding attendees that "the doctrine of healing is no new doctrine; it has been in the Church from the earliest ages," Smith listed two additional ways God was using divine healing to revitalize the church. First, instances of miraculous recovery from sickness served as a "protest against the materialism and infidelity of the age." Bewailing the growing prominence of materialist philosophy and "evolution," which explained reality without reference to a "personal God," Smith asserted that God was "reviving this precious truth" of divine healing to "show that He is a real, personal Being . . . that prayer is a power, a force, an answer—sufficient to prove that Christ is a Saviour of the body as well as the soul." A second reason for the resurgence of divine healing, Smith stated, was "because of the nearness of the return of the blessed Saviour." Like many participants at the international conference, Smith stressed the eschatological implications of divine healing. "Is not this work in the hearts, and souls, and bodies of men a preparation for this great event?" he asked. Since the second coming of Christ was rapidly approaching, Smith implied, believers had an urgent obligation to spread "the Gospel of God, the power of God manifested in the salvation of the body." "Let there go from this place," he exhorted, "an influence throughout the world which will lead thousands, yea, millions more, to take this perfect, complete Gospel of our Lord Jesus Christ."[13]

A. B. Simpson, one of the principal leaders of the divine healing movement in North America, echoed many of Smith's sentiments in his several speeches at the international conference. A former Presbyterian minister who had once accepted the cessationist view of miracles, Simpson had personally experienced divine healing while attending Charles Cullis's annual faith convention at Old Orchard Beach, Maine, in the summer of 1881. After studying the scriptures, Simpson eventually came to the conclusion that "the atonement of Christ takes away sin and the consequence of sin for every believer who accepts Him"; therefore, healing "was included in the gospel of Jesus Christ, as purchased and finished for all who accepted Jesus fully." Salvation, in Simpson's view, included both spiritual and material benefits.[14] Having determined that divine healing was a "redemption right" for believers in every era, Simpson resigned his Presbyterian pastorate to found the nondenominational Gospel Tabernacle (1882) and the Berachah Home for healing (1883) in New York City. Like Baxter and others who embraced the atonement theology of healing, Simpson challenged the conviction that "glory . . . redounds to God from our submission to His will in sickness and the happy results of sanctified affection." At the international conference, he urged attendees to come "into the very line of His will" by acknowledging Jesus as the "complete Savior for body as well as soul." God, Simpson warned, would "be grieved" if believers failed to claim the blessing of health because the need for active, energetic Christian workers in the present age was so great. "That is why the Lord wants to heal you, He wants the service of your body," Simpson remarked elsewhere. Healing, in other words, was equivalent with "the power to go forth and *minister*."[15]

Like Smith and other participants at the international conference, Simpson argued that God was reviving the doctrines of holiness and healing in

order to expand the "kingdom of our Lord Jesus Christ." "This gospel of healing is inseparably linked with the evangelizing of the world," Simpson proclaimed in his opening address to the assembly. "God has given it to us as a
testimony to the nations, and God's work wants thousands and thousands of
men and women to go to Africa, and China, and India, and live Him there."
Through the divine healing movement, God was raising up missionaries who
would manifest the "supernatural and resurrection power" of "the living
Christ" in their bodies, carrying the message of full salvation "to the uttermost
parts of the earth." Miracles of divine healing also challenged the "Skepticism"
that increasingly characterized European and North American culture. By
living out their faith, Simpson insisted, recipients of divine healing would "*be*
the gospel before the world, and before the scoffer."[16]

Part of what made the divine healing movement so powerful, Simpson
proclaimed, was the promise of renewed unity contained in the "full gospel."
There is "a brotherhood in this common faith, deeper than what we have
known hitherto," Simpson encouraged conference attendees. "So it is when we
meet here over this glorious Gospel, and when we meet in full salvation. Oh, I
tell you, dear friends, there is a bond here that nothing else has ever created in
the church of God, and I am sure one reason of the divisions of Christendom
has been, that we have only taken one part of the gospel. When we have it all,
we shall all be one."[17] In order to cultivate the "common Christian hope" in the
universal church that the divine healing movement was helping to create,
Simpson and other participants at the international conference identified a
number of strategies for spreading this "thrill of deeper kinship and oneness,"
including the need for ongoing interdenominational cooperation. Simpson
was especially instrumental in fostering partnerships among believers who
shared a common faith in holiness and divine healing. Just one year after the
conference, he outlined a plan for two new interdenominational organizations,
the Christian Alliance and the Evangelical Missionary Alliance. Officially established in 1887, these two interrelated associations incorporated many leaders of
the North American divine healing movement within a formal network that
affirmed the connection between the "full Gospel" and foreign missions.
Although these two associations formally merged in 1897 and adopted a denominational polity beginning in 1926, the founding members did not aim to
organize a separate denomination. "The Christian Alliance," Simpson
explained, was designed "to be a simple and fraternal union of all who hold in
common the fullness of Jesus in His present grace and coming glory. It is not
intended in any way to be an engine of division or antagonism in the churches,
but, on the contrary, to embrace Evangelical Christians of every name who hold
this common faith and life." The Evangelical Missionary Alliance operated in
tandem with the Christian Alliance and was also interdenominational in character. Although neither group sought to promote separatism, they did aspire to
emphasize what Simpson called the "special truths" that were "opposed by

many conservative Christians" and to "cherish and deepen" the "chords of spiritual unity" among those from different denominations who held these beliefs in common.[18]

In the years following its founding, the Christian Alliance hosted numerous conventions throughout the United States and Canada, many of which included speakers and participants from the broader transatlantic Holiness and healing networks with whom Simpson had come into contact at the international conference in 1885. In addition to encouraging these physical gatherings, advocates of divine healing like Simpson, Baxter, and Boardman continued to strengthen the "sympathy" and "harmony" among like-minded associates through publications that incorporated articles and testimonies from believers around the world. At the international conference, Simpson mentioned 40 or 50 publications "connected with Holiness" in North America and cited 4 periodicals specifically "connected with Healing." Each of these journals, including Simpson's own *Word, Work and World*, contained personal accounts of miraculous recovery, articles elucidating the doctrines of divine healing, and descriptions of how healing was helping to advance missionary work. Through these publications, editors nurtured a sense of collective identity among readers, who were encouraged to perceive themselves as part of a global Christian movement.[19]

Correspondence also facilitated translocal connections. Baxter suggested that letter writing was a principal means through which divine healing was "penetrating the whole land." Those who could not travel to Bethshan or one of the many other "Houses of Healing" that had sprung up in Great Britain during the 1880s often wrote "from their beds" to leaders who shared their requests for prayer during regularly scheduled gatherings at the healing homes. By praying at the same time as these meetings, bedridden invalids could join a community of saints that transcended geography.[20] In her periodical *Triumphs of Faith: A Monthly Journal Devoted to Faith-Healing, and to the Promotion of Christian Holiness*, U.S. leader Carrie Judd noted in an 1881 editorial the popularity of this practice at her healing home in upstate New York. "A large number of requests for prayer are received each week from fellow-Christians, and these cases are specially laid before the Lord in our meetings. Many dear believers who are separated from us by distance, are remembering the hour with us, and we all have the assurance that 'Tho sundered far, by faith we meet / Around one common Mercy Seat.'" As the divine healing movement gained prominence, Judd recounted, requests for prayer were pouring in "from suffering ones all over our land, and from those, too, in far countries beyond the sea."[21] Taking pains to cultivate this growing sense of international community, advocates of divine healing like Judd, Baxter, and Boardman frequently commented on the unity that bound them together across territorial borders and denominational barriers. As Simpson put it during the international conference, "I live in a Republic but I belong to one kingdom. I have been a Monarchist all my life, for

I believe in one kingdom, i.e., the kingdom of our Lord Jesus Christ, which is everywhere."[22]


Differences and Difficulties in Divine Healing

Promoting mutuality was a primary goal of the international conference. Yet organizers quickly realized that achieving this aim would require dealing with discrepancies and debates about how healing and holiness were interpreted and experienced in particular localities. From the start, conference leaders acknowledged the fact of diversity in the developing movement. At the opening meeting on Monday morning, Mary Boardman "spoke a helpful word to guard any against the danger of thinking that their experience must be exactly the same as another's." Although, for some, "the baptism of the Holy Ghost" might involve "rapture and emotional experience," for others sanctification would be "simple and easy"—an experience of "perfect rest in Jesus forever." The Reverend F. D. Sanford from Boston corroborated Boardman's statement during the same session. "The Lord does not lead us all in the same way," he explained. "Different people speak about this blessed work, and these blessed gifts, this marvelous life which we are convened to talk about, in different terms." Citing distinctions in the way Methodists, Congregationalists, and Baptists interpreted "entire sanctification" or "the baptism of the Holy Ghost," Sanford insisted that underlying this diversity was a scripturally grounded unity. "Every experience brings the same thing," he maintained. "It doesn't matter what you call it, so long as you have it. The blessed thing is to recognize it in another brother or sister, even though we and they may not have got into Eden by the same way."[23]

Throughout the international conference, participants celebrated the global spread of healing and holiness, while recognizing the reality of multiplicity on various levels. Although he stressed the "bond of love" that drew Christians together across boundaries and barriers to "work side by side . . . in this glorious service of Christ," even A. B. Simpson admitted that North American healing advocates were "perhaps a little behind" their brothers and sisters in Germany and England. At the conference's closing session, Pastor Schrenk confirmed Simpson's suggestion that different temporal and geographic starting points led to incongruities in how divine healing developed in diverse places. "I may say that the character of German Faith Healing is a little different from that in England; and, I think, if your English Homes had been opened 20 years ago, *they* would have had another character. They bear the stamp of the spiritual life which the Lord has given you during the last 15 years. Therefore, it is not a self-character, but it is a God-given character. And so it is in Germany, too," he declared.[24]

Although conference spokespersons regarded regional diversities as largely epiphenomenal, and therefore inconsequential, they were less inclined to accept variations in theology or practice, which threatened to undermine the movement's cohesion. The propensity of some practitioners to attribute healing powers to prominent leaders, for example, was particularly vexing to conference organizers. In his opening address, Schrenk expressed concern that "some present here to-day expected from our Conferences to get teaching by man, some deep notions from this and the other brother or sister." Simpson also worried that attendees might be ascribing too much authority to individuals rather than to the Holy Spirit. "What has impressed me in this Convention with a little fear, even amid these wonderful testimonies," he confessed, was "a fear lest we should have too much of the personal to the exclusion of God's mighty truth."[25]

Simpson admitted to this apprehension immediately after J. W. Wood of Adelaide, South Australia, spoke to the assembly. In his address, Wood described the "great and glorious work that has been done by our blessed Lord and the Holy Spirit in Australia some 12 months ago." Although Wood gave credit to "the risen Christ" for the healings that had taken place, he also claimed to have heard a voice saying: "You have healing power given to you." Wood admitted that this "part of my personal experience" had raised many questions for observers, some of whom persecuted him and "said I was a devil." Nevertheless, he felt called to his work and soon embarked on a healing campaign in South Australia. "In three weeks," he reported, "3000 people were brought under the ministry of healing."[26]

No one at the international conference directly contested Wood's claims to have been given "healing power" by the Holy Spirit, yet some participants expressed reservations about focusing on individuals as agents of divine healing. The problem with this approach, leaders like Baxter and Simpson indicated, was that people would place their faith in the "means" through which God channeled his healing power, rather than trusting in God alone. Reflecting on the conference several months later, Simpson reported that, although "the teaching and testimony of the Conference was always in the direction of honoring and exalting Christ . . . there are others, again, who claim peculiar personal gifts, and even power to communicate blessing and divine influence and healing, that lead men away from the Work and the Lord Himself, to look to the instrument." Such mislaid trust was utterly futile. "You will never be healed in that way," Baxter insisted in an 1885 article published in Simpson's *Word, Work and World.* "It is not the prayer that heals, but the answerer of prayer. . . . God is no respecter of persons."[27]

As the divine healing movement flourished and spread around the globe in the decades following the international conference, the question of whether or not specific individuals were specially anointed to serve as instruments of healing remained controversial. Indeed, this was one of the issues that ultimately would undermine the unity that conference organizers strove so diligently to cultivate, as participants in Pentecostalism were more apt to argue that particular people possessed the spiritual "gift" of healing.

Diverse understandings of leadership also arose at the international conference in connection with the position of women. No debate about this subject occurred during the sessions, apparently because Boardman, as chair, refused to "enter into discussion." At several points, however, he and other spokespersons clearly endorsed the ministry of women within the divine healing movement, justifying their position with reference to a variety of biblical texts. "Upon principal," Boardman declared, both "the sons and daughters of the Lord" were authorized to administer anointing to fellow believers. He also insisted that the Bible sanctioned women elders and indicated that "the Lord has made some of His precious daughters elders in the faith" at Bethshan. Although conceding that there were some "spheres in the church—for instance, the sphere of government" that belonged exclusively to men, Boardman contended that "much has been lost in the past by the exclusion of women from certain spheres" and urged his fellow workers to welcome women's contributions "in all departments of Christian work." Drawing primarily upon Joel 2:28–29—"Your sons and daughters shall prophecy"—Boardman celebrated women's "gifts" as a "sign of Pentecost reviving." To encourage women as leaders in the divine healing movement, he suggested, was to acknowledge and advance the "glorious work" of God's spirit "in the days that are to follow."[28]

Although Boardman evidently chose to suppress debate about women's leadership in order to maintain cohesion at the international conference, he did allow discussion of other controversial questions in the hope that instructive teaching on these subjects would alleviate "genuine difficulties" that threatened to destabilize the movement. Beginning on the second day of the convention, leaders began to address some of the "numerous questions" that participants "handed up" to the platform during sessions. The queries that organizers chose to consider focused on several key problems in the theology and practice of divine healing. One of the most prominent points of contention or puzzlement was the relationship between divine healing and medical science. Inquirers wanted to know whether trusting God for healing required them to refrain from seeking the care of physicians or to abstain from medical remedies. If so, they asked, then why did the Bible commend Luke as a "beloved Physician"? Or, "Why did God place such wonderful medicinal properties in herbs and minerals?"[29]

In his reply, Robert McKilliam, a medical doctor who was also a leading figure at the international conference, affirmed that "medicine is a boon from God, and God Himself has been pleased to use medical men over and over again in healing." Nevertheless, McKilliam maintained, "for God's people, especially in these days, when the church is being again awakened to the inheritance of a risen and glorified Christ, I find in this blessed Book 'a more excellent way.' . . . And it is a poor thing if you and I choose a *good* gift only, when we can get a *perfect* gift." Although McKilliam did not explicitly direct attendees to eschew doctors or drugs, he and other spokespersons at the conference implied that divine healing involved a disavowal of medical science in favor of "faith in Jesus Christ."[30]

While some attendees at the international conference were obviously uncomfortable with the idea of renouncing medical remedies, others testified that turning away from ineffective and expensive medical therapies made both theological and practical sense. Many participants told of futile, costly, and sometimes detrimental experiments with medical treatments that failed to cure their ailments or even increased their sufferings. After 20 years of "trying one physician, then another; one system, then another," English metalworker John Taylor "found the Lord Jesus as my Healer." Taylor had traveled from England to Australia and back—twice—on the advice of medical doctors. When a change of climate did not help, he kept trying new therapies. "The last idea was galvanism. I was clothed with magnetic appliances. What for? Oh, what will not a man do, what will he not spend, to get back his health? I spent my all," he recounted. "In twelve days," Taylor proclaimed, Jesus "did more for me than I had had done in twenty years." Although Taylor did not condemn remedies outright, he joined many others at the conference who praised faith in the Great Physician as "a more excellent way."[31]

Testimonies like Taylor's suggest that the nineteenth-century revival of divine healing was fueled in part by the failure of medical science to cure disease or alleviate afflictions. Many individuals—Taylor included—explained that they sought healing from Jesus after their physicians had deemed them incurable. For these sufferers, turning to the Great Physician was a last resort. Although critics frequently condemned practitioners of divine healing for encouraging sick persons to forgo medical interventions, proponents insisted that divine healing was their only hope for regaining health. At the international conference, advocates like McKilliam and Simpson also stressed the benefits of divine healing for the church. By seeking healing through biblical means—prayer, laying on of hands, and anointing—rather than through medical methods, faithful believers bore witness in their bodies "that there is a living Christ yet in the midst of His people" and in so doing helped the church to "gain the mighty power of God's Spirit . . . in these days of infidelity, of profession without real Christianity, of advancing evil, corruption, blasphemy, and every thing of Satan." Through the divine healing movement, in other words, God was "proving the great supernatural power in Christ" to a skeptical world and ushering in a "wondrous time of blessing" for the Christian church.[32]

How, exactly, the revival of divine healing and holiness was "blessing" participants at the convention, or was poised to transform the global Christian community, was another matter of contention at the international conference. Although many had come to London believing that "God wanted to bring about a revival of Pentecost, and that the time for this had come," by the end of the week some were wondering "why it was that we had not seen the blessing of the Holy Spirit poured out here during these meetings, as many of us have been led to expect." One respondent reasoned that petitioners had been too focused on their own needs, wants, longings, and desires rather than seeking God's glory. Another blamed "unbelief." But others took issue with the idea that the conference was not living up to expectations. "I differ with many of the friends present in regard to the blessing the Lord has given, and is giving, to us at these meetings," Pastor Schrenk declared. The problem, he suggested, was that people were clinging to their own "notions and feelings" of what "fullness of blessing" looked like rather than recognizing that God was calling them to "be partners with Himself, and not merely recipients of a blessing." "Realising this," he announced, "I shall go back to Berne [sic] with a far greater blessing than I should have if I had been feasting on wonderful impressions and feelings." Dr. Woods Smyth echoed and expanded on Schrenk's critique of "the friends who have been speaking about the poverty of blessing at these Conferences." Those who failed to see that "these meetings are bearing precious fruit," he implied, were overlooking obvious signs of the Holy Spirit's presence. "The highest forms of manifest teaching and blessing from God are furthest off from rhapsody," he asserted. Like Schrenk, Smyth suggested that the manifestation of the Holy Spirit need not be marked by ecstatic emotional experiences. In the New Testament, he argued, the power of the Holy Ghost was associated with "hard common sense, intense reasoning, and close presentations of the truth, nothing at all of the wonderful Orientalism of the Old Testament."[33]

Tensions over the roles of intellect and of emotions in experiences of holiness and healing were apparent throughout the conference. From the first day, when Mary Boardman indicated that "rapture and emotional experience" were not essential features of sanctification, to the final session in which Schrenk and Smyth censured the disappointed expectations of their peers, the question of how to assess the activity of the Holy Spirit resurfaced regularly. Leaders like Simpson urged petitioners not to "depend on any feeling" when seeking healing, but instead to seek God "not in your emotional nature, but just with your will." Sensational experiences were not to be expected even at such a momentous gathering as the anointing ceremony at the international conference. "There is no sign, there is no sound, there is no wind nor rain," he urged, "but silently amid the hush of heaven, the living Christ passes through the assembly." Despite repeated admonitions from leaders against associating the outpouring of the Holy Spirit with physical or emotional "impressions and feelings," participants continued to describe their experiences of holiness and healing in these terms and to express hopes that they were on the brink of a great revival in which the "power of the Holy Ghost" would manifest miraculously. "God is again about to send a mighty message to the world," Charlotte Murray proclaimed. "He has something much more for us . . . marvelously beyond the glory of Pentecost."[34]

When the International Conference on Divine Healing and True Holiness came to a close on Friday evening, a number of difficulties or discrepancies in the theology and practice of divine healing remained unresolved. Although conference organizers worked hard to settle controversial issues, establishing and enforcing consistency was a challenging prospect given the lack of any official governing body or formal authority structure to adjudicate theological debates or impose uniformity in practice. Although the resulting diversity may have seemed worrisome to some, leaders like A. B. Simpson expressed confidence that harmony would prevail over heterogeneity. In his retrospective report on the convention, Simpson recounted that "there was a good deal of variety of method, and even opinion on non-essential details, but when it came to the central truths and innermost life, there was blessed oneness in Him."[35]

## Conclusion

In the years following the international conference, the divine healing movement continued to attract a wide range of participants from a variety of denominational, social, and cultural backgrounds. Because the movement remained fluid and unregulated during this period, affiliates from around the world developed conceptions and modalities of healing that bore witness to their geographic and theological diversity. Over time, this multiformity challenged the mutuality that Simpson and others had celebrated at the international conference. During the 1890s, tensions over a variety of issues—including leadership and the use of medical means of healing—produced fissures that sometimes erupted into full-blown fractures in the fellowship.[36] Despite several rifts, however, divine healing remained a remarkably vibrant movement whose members envisioned themselves as participants in a global revitalization and expansion of Christianity. The organizational structures, transnational networks, and sense of universal community that the international conference cultivated provided a ready platform for the widespread diffusion of the millennial expectations that emerged so clearly at the convention. In the early decades of the twentieth century, the outbreak of Pentecostal revivals all over the globe fulfilled, for many proponents of divine healing, the fervent hope that "the fullness of Pentecost" had finally come.[37]

## NOTES

1 James 5:14–15, reads: "Is any sick among you? let him call for the elders of the church; and let them pray over him, anointing him with oil in the name of the Lord. And the prayer of faith shall save the sick, and the Lord shall raise him up; and if he have committed sins, they shall be forgiven him" (AV). See *Record of the International Conference on Divine Healing and True Holiness Held at the Agricultural Hall, London, June 1 to 5, 1885* (London: J. Snow, and Bethshan, 1885), 79–87 (hereafter abbreviated as *RIC*). For biographical accounts of Boardman, Simpson, and Baxter in relation to

divine healing, see Heather D. Curtis, *Faith in the Great Physician: Suffering and Divine Healing in American Culture, 1860–1900* (Baltimore, Md.: Johns Hopkins University Press, 2007).

2  *RIC*, iv–v, 26.

3  Ibid., iv.

4  Ibid., iv, 92; Robert Bruce Mullin, *Miracles and the Modern Religious Imagination* (New Haven, Conn.: Yale University Press, 1996), 9–30.

5  William E. Boardman, *The Great Physician: Jehovah Rophi* (Boston: Willard Tract Repository, 1881), 2; Mrs. [Mary M. Adams] Boardman, *Life and Labours of the Rev. W. E. Boardman* (New York: Appleton, 1887); Curtis, *Faith in the Great Physician*, 7–9, 59–65; Edith L. Blumhofer, *Restoring the Faith: The Assemblies of God, Pentecostalism, and American Culture* (Urbana: University of Illinois Press, 1993), 11–42; Donald W. Dayton, *Theological Roots of Pentecostalism* (Metuchen, N.J.: Scarecrow, 1987); Melvin E. Dieter, *The Holiness Revival of the Nineteenth Century*, 2nd ed. (Lanham, Md.: Scarecrow, 1996).

6  Boardman, *The Great Physician*, 13, 25, 178–180; Charles Cullis, introduction to *Dorothea Trudel; or, The Prayer of Faith*, rev. ed. (Boston: Willard Tract Repository, 1872), 5–12; Charles Cullis, *The Ninth Annual Report of the Consumptives Home, and Other Institutions Connected with a Work of Faith, to 30 September 1873* (Boston: Willard Tract Repository, 1874), 44–55; Curtis, *Faith in the Great Physician*, 1–25.

7  Boardman, *The Great Physician*, 179; Curtis, *Faith in the Great Physician*, 9–10.

8  *RIC*, 27, 159.

9  Ibid., 155.

10  Quoted in A. J. Gordon, *The Ministry of Healing; or, Miracles of Cure in All Ages* (Boston: Howard Gannett, 1882), 196–199.

11  Nathaniel Wiseman, *Elizabeth Baxter (Wife of Michael Paget Baxter): Saint, Evangelist, Preacher, Teacher, and Expositor* (London: Christian Herald, 1928), 133.

12  *RIC*, 28–32.

13  Ibid., 90–93.

14  Miroslav Volf, "Materiality of Salvation: An Investigation in the Soteriologies of Liberation and Pentecostal Theologies," *Journal of Ecumenical Studies* 26.3 (1989): 447–467.

15  *RIC*, 80–81; A. B. Simpson, "The Gospel of Healing: Common Objections," *Word, Work and World* 5.3 (Nov.–Dec. 1883): 172; A. B. Simpson, "Divine Healing," *Triumphs of Faith* 5 (Dec. 1885): 276–279.

16  *RIC*, 69.

17  Ibid., 65.

18  Ibid., 66; "A New Missionary Alliance," *Word, Work and World* 8 (June 1887): 365–368; A. B. Simpson, "Editorial Paragraphs," *Word, Work and World* 9 (Aug.–Sept. 1887): 110–111; George P. Pardington, *Twenty-Five Wonderful Years, 1889–1914: A Popular Sketch of the Christian and Missionary Alliance* (1914; reprint, New York: Garland, 1984), 34–46; Curtis, *Faith in the Great Physician*, 167–191.

19  *RIC*, 160–161; Curtis, *Faith in the Great Physician*, 167–191.

20  *RIC*, 154–156.

21  Carrie F. Judd, "Our Faith Meetings," *Triumphs of Faith* 1 (Jan. 1881): 12; Carrie F. Judd, "Faith-Rest Cottage," *Triumphs of Faith* 2 (Feb. 1882): 19–20.

22  *RIC*, 160.

23  Ibid., 14–16.

24  Ibid., 64, 158.

25  Ibid., 8, 66–67.

26  Ibid., 58–64.

27  A. B. Simpson, "The Conferences in Great Britain," *Word, Work and World* 5 (Sept. 1885): 233–240; Mrs. M. [Elizabeth] Baxter, "Questions Concerning Healing," *Word, Work and World* 5 (Nov. 1885): 297–298.

28  *RIC*, 86–87, 33.

29  Ibid., 34–37, 48–49.

30  Ibid., 34–36.

31  Ibid., 50–51, 48.

32  Ibid., 35.

33  Ibid., 135–141.

34  Ibid., 14, 84–86, 139, 136.

35  A. B. Simpson, "The Conferences in Great Britain," *Word, Work and World* 5 (Sept. 1885): 233–240.

36  Curtis, *Faith in the Great Physician*, 192–210; Jonathan R. Baer, "Perfectly Empowered Bodies: Divine Healing in Modernizing America" (Ph.D. diss., Yale University, 2002).

37  *RIC*, 26.

# 2

# Why Health *and* Wealth? Dimensions of Prosperity among Swedish Charismatics

*Simon Coleman*

## Uncomfortable Encounters?

I remember my conversation with Fredrik very well, even though it took place some years ago. We had encountered each other by chance on the hill leading up to Uppsala University's beautiful library, in the city's center. I had first met him a few months earlier, when we had both attended a meeting of Christian Student Front, a fledgling group of Charismatic students at the university who came together each week to pray, listen to lectures, and discuss how to be a good Christian. Most were Pentecostals or members of the new Charismatic ministry in town, the Word of Life (figure 2.1).[1] At one of the Front meetings, Fredrik had told me about his ambitions to become a journalist and about his efforts—both spiritual and temporal—to make a name for himself in the competitive, hostile world of the secular press. The conversation on the hill, however, seemed to be about something very different—and it has haunted me ever since. Fredrik told me that his brother, who had been ill with cancer, had recently died. The funeral had taken place a few weeks earlier. I expressed condolences, and Fredrik responded accordingly. However, he then surprised me by expressing a further thought. Perhaps, he said, his brother was not deceased, but would be resurrected in body as well as soul to rejoin his family and friends. After all, Fredrik had been praying for his brother to live, to come back, and he expected an answer to such prayers.

FIGURE 2.1. Word of Life Church, Uppsala, Sweden (1990s). Courtesy Simon Coleman.

As I am writing this, I do not recall how I responded to Fredrik's comment. I suspect I regarded the encounter as one of those occasions during my field-work when, in the midst of a conversation, I would suddenly be given a glimpse of the very different world that believers perceived to exist alongside everyday "reality." For instance, there was the dinner with a family who matter-of-factly and in some detail described the angels guarding the corners of their property. But in retrospect, it seems to me that Fredrik's attitude toward the death of his brother should not have taken me particularly by surprise. Indeed, it was of a piece with his aspirations as a budding journalist. Both of these, after all, expressed a refusal to accept conventional limits—physical, material, practical—on the Christian life. Both also had something of a political edge: success in journalism would imply not only monetary gain but also a Christian presence in a largely secular media world, just as the resurrection of his brother would defy the predictions of the irreligious medical establishment.

Unlike many of the pentecostals studied by scholars around the world, Fredrik could hardly be said to have regarded his faith as providing an eco-nomic or medical prop in a context of scarcity; after all, he was a comfortably well-off citizen of one of the most prosperous countries in the world. He was, however, openly expressing his convictions concerning the operation of "pros-perity" principles that he saw as applying to all areas of life—and death—and he was doing so in a location where such views were frequently being roundly condemned by the very newspapers with which he hoped to gain employment.

Our meeting could therefore be said to have been framed by a wider "uncomfortable encounter": between the claims of members of a growing, explicitly prosperity-oriented, Charismatic ministry, and the numerous institutions in Sweden and Uppsala—ecclesiastical, medical, educational, journalistic—that regarded the ministry and the principles it represented as a threat to society at large, indeed as something that had no right to flourish in a modern nation.[2]

The importance to Pentecostal and Charismatic Christians of health and other forms of prosperity that can confirm the reality of the kingdom of God is hardly news, as Candy Gunther Brown points out in her introduction to this volume. Furthermore, as Catherine Bowler and Arlene Sánchez Walsh affirm in their chapters, "health and wealth" theologies in particular emphasize the notion of faith as a form of agency that can produce palpable results, measured for instance in a bulging wallet or a healthy body. However, the close juxtaposition of these views, the encompassing of both within such a broad notion of prosperity, draws attention to the central claim of this volume. If divine healing practices are an essential marker of Pentecostal and Charismatic Christianity as a global phenomenon, and yet they also form part of a wider array of prosperity practices and ideologies, can they be isolated as a truly *distinct* aspect of the globalization of the faith?

My answer in this chapter, perhaps predictably, will be both yes and no. However, in asking such a question, it is worth noting that, while health and wealth ministries have received a reasonable amount of scholarly attention, relatively little has been written about why these two aspects of Charismatic practice should be highlighted and juxtaposed in the (usually external) characterizations of such believers: Why health *and* wealth? As we shall see, it may be that this politically loaded label says more about commentators' assumptions concerning "proper" religion than it does about what is being described. But at the same time, we need to ask whether there is something to be gained in analytical terms by looking at the connections between health and wealth in the religious practices of Charismatics. Doing so requires me to discuss briefly a few theoretical concepts, after which I will return to a case study approach, introducing alongside Fredrik three additional Word of Life Christians: Gudrun, Pamela, and Vera. First, we will examine several questions: What might be the linguistic, bodily, ideological, and theological tensions and affinities between health and wealth? How comfortable, indeed, is the encounter between these two concerns within prosperity ideology and practice? And how can we juxtapose academic and Charismatic understandings of physical and financial prosperity?

I want to use these questions to explore the idea that the twin searches for healing and for prosperity among the Christians I have studied—constituting what one might call their modes of physical and financial entrepreneurship—may, under certain circumstances, act as ritual complements to each other in

Charismatic lives, permitting reflection and action in relation both to the intimate self and to a wider, unbounded world whose existence is a frequent theme
in the construction of a sense of Charismatic identity and purpose. The proximate and the global are thus both powerfully thematized in actions relating to
health and wealth, and both areas, I will argue, require us to look closely at
ideological and ritualized constructions not only of the body, but also of the
person in a prominent prosperity ministry such as Word of Life.

There is also a wider argument behind these characterizations of health
and wealth Christians in Sweden. The themes of this chapter and of the volume as a whole illustrate attempts in the social sciences in the late twentieth
and early twenty-first centuries to reestablish links between the study of religion and of health, as part of larger debates over the relationship between the
body and society.[3] Anthropologists have tended to focus more on this theme
than have sociologists, and I acknowledge here the influential work of Thomas
Csordas in presenting the body as a principal point of intersection between
medical and religious definitions of human experience.[4] In these terms, the
medical and the religious become conjoined but also act as potential rivals in
the control and potential cure of the body—a point that is significant in the
context of a globalizing religious force such as pentecostalism, which encounters biomedical and other religious systems as it expands and missionizes. We
see why pentecostalism can sometimes be seen as hyper-modern in some of
the contexts it encounters, but also why it may be presented as the very image
of the anti-modern, as "faith healing" appears to challenge the assumptions of
biomedicine. As we shall see, this issue of the modernity of divine healing is
highly significant in our examination of its potential connections with wider
notions of material prosperity.

## Genealogies and Materialities

Evolutionary theories of religion have tended to assume that Christian spirituality and moral teaching could be neatly distinguished from "primitive" religions, which failed to make necessary distinctions between physical pollution
and moral sinfulness.[5] According to such views, Calvinistic Protestantism had
developed furthest in denying the power of magical cures to remove the effects
of sin, whereas Catholic sacramentalism could be seen as retaining the notion
that the cure of bodies and souls was possible through rituals of penance. At
the same time, from the eighteenth century onward, traditions of pietist asceticism merged with medical regimens of living to produce a moral code compatible with capitalism's interest in a disciplined workforce. Here, then, a link
between religious and bodily well-being reemerged but in a fundamentally
different way from that of a supposedly primitive sacramentalism, through
notions of calling and the disciplining of self and others.[6]

Whatever the validity of evolutionary understandings of Protestant asceticism, they presented a powerful ideology of self-control, and one where material prosperity provided both worldly temptation and, potentially, a sign of salvation. Arguably, one of the core problems with which the Protestant Reformation wrestled was precisely the role of material mediations in spiritual life, as the Reformation instigated efforts to transform the moral value of numerous and various semiotic forms, including ways of speaking, liturgical objects, the conscience, written texts, ecclesiastical offices, and indeed both the body and money.[7] In this view, materiality can come to be identified with external constraints on the autonomy of human agents, a threat to freedom itself. Both Calvinism and aspects of modernity seek to abstract the subject from its material entanglements in the name of freedom and authenticity, both of which offer a kind of transcendence.[8]

What does any of this have to do with healing? What is highlighted in these admittedly all-too-compressed accounts of (Protestant) materiality and modernity? The point I want to emphasize here is the ability of all of these perspectives to bring together the physical and the economic, body and money, health and wealth, as key if shifting areas of debate within Protestant discourse and self-understanding. We see how religious subjectivity may become crucially constituted in negotiations with materiality. At the same time, pentecostalism in general and its prosperity varieties in particular begin to look if not anomalous then at least located at the extreme end of a particular continuum in relation to what the theologian Miroslav Volf has termed "the materiality of salvation."[9] When agency is measured—indexed—precisely through the material, when bodily well-being and financial prosperity are celebrated as inherent aspects of the believer's identity, what does this say about how the material entanglements of semiotic forms are viewed by believers?

Intriguingly, some of the ideological roots of contemporary prosperity Christians in the West display a similar ambiguity over the role of the material. For example, there is a particular history of tensions between the flesh and the spirit in North American Christianity, including a number of key, post-Calvinist transformations of older models of bodily asceticism, which can be seen not least in the influence of nineteenth-century "new thought" metaphysics on what religious studies scholar R. Marie Griffith calls the "cheerful gospels of Health and Wealth." New thought writers and their heirs worked on linking mind and matter, with the body considered both the mirror of the soul and the elemental ground of spiritual progress and perfectibility. Significantly, the powerful ambivalence toward desire that often underlay new thought teachings existed alongside its role in the promotion of a further key shift in attitude within some evangelical circles, as penitence and sacrifice became juxtaposed with a new form of optimism and expansiveness toward the embodied self. In the latter view, the body, if properly treated, was no longer an object of disgust, but one of limitless potential.[10]

My argument is that, among Word of Life believers whom I have encountered, both health and wealth evoke issues relating to the material in particular ways that challenge ascetic ideals. The matter is, however, more complex than critics in Sweden or elsewhere would imply when they suggest that such religious adherence is merely a selfish matter of gaining a better, more beautiful body or access to untold riches. I am proposing, rather, that both provide means to act on and with the (embodied) Protestant subject. The ritualized construction of the subject depends upon, among other things, the activation of forms of materiality not only as indices of faith, but also as constitutive forces in the making of the subject as a Charismatically endowed person.

In order to make this argument, I need to introduce one final piece of theoretical apparatus: a brief comparative discussion of personhood. The anthropologist Edward LiPuma challenges the simplistic notion that the West constructs autonomous, self-contained "individuals," while societies such as those of Melanesia construct "dividuals," or relational persons.[11] His point is that in all cultures there exist both individual and dividual modalities or aspects of personhood, so that "dividualism" should be seen as involving the ways in which persons grow transactionally as the beneficiaries of other people's actions.[12]

If we see persons as somehow constituted through transactions, then the material and semiotic forms through which transactions are mediated and effected become all-important. For my purposes, both healing and the exchanges ideally leading to material prosperity (as well as other forms of Charismatic practice, such as the deployment of language) can be seen as particular negotiations between certain modalities of dividualism and individualism. Charismatic subjects are formed not only as individual believers, but also out of engagement with others through material exchanges, as filtered through a Charismatic sensibility. Self and other, as well as self and object, may become entangled, and it is notable that complaints in Sweden about groups such as the Word of Life have centered not only on their apparent valorization of health and wealth, but also on the degree to which persons lose their autonomy and distinctiveness *as* persons. Furthermore, if the person is formed out of transactions and mediations, these may occur across global and more proximate arenas of action.

## Transacting Persons through Health and Wealth

What does being a supporter of the Word of Life mean for one's Christian life? It may mean daily engagement with the group, through attending its Bible school or perhaps helping out as a volunteer in its day care for children. It may simply mean membership in the congregation and regular attendance at Sunday and midweek services. Or, for many, it implies that one attends an occasional service or reads a book by the ministry's founder, Ulf Ekman, while retaining a more regular membership in a traditional congregation. In broad terms, the group can be said to invoke and amplify pentecostal ritual tropes, as tongues are spoken with great urgency and speed, public prayer is accompanied by movements such as jumping in place or swaying, and so on. The ministry also emphasizes its global connections: not only has it established a network of its own ministries across Europe and elsewhere since the mid-1980s, it also plays host to numerous international conferences of prosperity preachers in its headquarters on the outskirts of Uppsala.

Health and wealth form significant aspects of Word of Life discourse—both public and private—and they are also part of a ritual repertoire that emphasizes their common origins in the workings of the Spirit. Testimonies concerning the achievement of miraculous cures and freedom from economic bondage are seamlessly juxtaposed in sermons and the group's literature. The touch and the speaking in tongues of the preacher during an altar call can equally well produce relief from a debt or from a physical impairment. "Negative confession"—the expression of doubt—might cause a problem in either realm of the Christian's life, just as the devil is said to attack the believer through a lack of either monetary resources or physical energy. In my experience, prosperity discourse in Sweden has little to say about a healthy lifestyle in terms of diet, other than a general disapproval of intoxicants such as alcohol or recreational drugs. At the same time, sport and the disciplining of the body—although they are viewed as being taken too far if they focus only on the body—are encouraged, just as metaphors of movement and speed permeate descriptions of the working of the Spirit.[13] Training in the principles of sports success, as in those of business success, is seen as eminently appropriate to the Christian life, with both providing measures of quantifiable achievement. The power of progressive movement as both a metaphor and a literal dimension underlying Christian practice is also clear in both aspects of the prosperous life. Wealth for Word of Life adherents must never be regarded as a static accumulation of personal resources. It is both produced and appropriately used precisely through its deployment in schemes that may seem irrational to the secular world: investment in expanding the ministry, arranging for a mortgage that seems a little too large, or starting a new business are ways of ensuring not only the flow of money, but also the blessings that money in motion can bring as it moves between both projects and people. This is an entrepreneurial view of economic activity that, for some believers, implies a rejection of more traditional Swedish values of social democracy and centralized economic redistribution. It also has parallels in assumptions concerning the use of the body. The Charismatic body is ideally mobile not only in worship, but also in mission, moving across Uppsala, Sweden, or even abroad to spread the Charismatic message. Stasis, in body or in investment, is a risk at a spiritual level: self-imposed limitation is itself a potentially demonic state.

Implicit in the foregoing remarks is that mobility depends on mediation—and often mediation through multiple semiotic forms. Thus, when Fredrik was describing his future career as well as his family bereavement to me, he was engaged in "confession" as well as description, performatively creating a state of potential prosperity within his life precisely through externalizing it in words in relation to another person (myself) and to himself. Language is thus one medium of the transactions that take place in forming the prosperous and Charismatic subject.

In the following, I will introduce three more prosperity Christians. In each case, I will argue that we see the creation of a Charismatic subject in a process that includes but goes beyond church worship, where charisma is "radicalized" into everyday life, in Csordas's term.[14] We will see how both health and wealth are involved as the products of forms of material mediation, but not materiality in an obviously "worldly" sense.

## A Child at an Older Age?

When I interviewed Gudrun, she was in her mid-60s. She was an immaculately dressed person in a home to match, who managed to be both friendly and reserved with a visiting English anthropologist. Part of her reserve may have been associated with the subject matter of our discussion, since—although she was a long-standing member of the local Pentecostal church—she was describing the impact on her life of her encounters with Word of Life figures and writings. Apparently settled and comfortable, Gudrun surprised me by telling of how in past years she had "felt bad," unable even to leave her home. Here is what happened next, as she describes her and her husband's lives:

> We read Nilsson's book *Befria Mitt Folk* [Let My People Go].[15] . . . We just read and read about the grace we have in Jesus Christ, what authority we had. . . . And we read and read. I still didn't go out. But: "No—now I'll go out in Jesus' name, simple as that." I began to praise God. I went out. I was like a child who had just begun to walk. I was happy. One Sunday morning I went to Årsta [a district of Stockholm] and was saying "Thanks, Jesus! Thanks Jesus!" I walked more and more, and each step I took I thanked Jesus. I hadn't cycled for 20 years. Then in the autumn I read God's word and it became more living through Nilsson's book, which quoted God's word all the time. . . . Then I went out, as if a whole new life had begun. . . . In September I said to my husband, "I feel I'm going to buy a bicycle." And the cycle shop had a sale—half price, the same day. My husband bought a five-gear racer. I cycled more and more. I was like a child beginning to ride. Thanking Jesus the whole time. It was a whole new life, you see.

After these experiences, Gudrun began to attend Word of Life services, to listen to Ulf Ekman's sermons and those of other preachers from his group. She felt edified (*uppbyggd*; literally, "built up") during the three hours of a typical service—not tired at all. Furthermore, although she had never gone out knocking on people's doors before, trying to convert them, she had now started to do so. All because "one takes in God's word in one's Spirit; one doesn't just listen, one takes it *in*."

Gudrun's self-description functions on many levels. It is both a response to my questioning *and* a testimony; and it is both a comment on her experiences of the Word of Life and, implicitly, a criticism of her local Pentecostal church, where she has not been able to gain such experiences. The regeneration that she has undergone has hints of being "reborn again" as her spiritual vigor goes along with an ability not only to reach out to others, but also literally to go out, to leave her home and enter public space. Her ability to cycle around Uppsala is clearly related to her ability, for the first time, to knock on the doors of its inhabitants and declare herself a Christian.

Notice, also, the complex forms of mediation that are evident here. Gudrun's regeneration seems prompted by the reading of a book, *Let My People Go*, which is associated not only with the biblical liberation from slavery but also with the father-in-law of Ulf Ekman, Sten Nilsson, a prominent if older prosperity figure in his own right. Nilsson's book blends with and helps to make more "living" the Bible itself; but Gudrun takes an active role in her liberation, not only buying the bicycle but speaking out God's word ("In Jesus' name!") while thanking Jesus for the spiritual transaction and transformation that have taken place and *are* taking place through her words. So this is a testimony about words (biblical, pastoral, self-generated) but also about the construction of a literally mobile body and a progressively more Charismatic persona.

There is little overtly about wealth here, but it is certainly not absent from the story. Notice that the bicycle shop has a sale the very day that Gudrun declares her need for one; a small financial miracle eases her passage from inward-looking to outward-oriented Christian. More generally, the movement outward and the confidence to undergo potentially embarrassing missionary trips to other inhabitants of Uppsala provide parallels to the practice of risking personal resources, trusting in God's help in financial matters that seem overly risky in the world's eyes.


Mature at a Young Age?

In Gudrun's account, Word of Life leaders act as facilitators and mediators of her freedom, but in a relatively distant way, through texts and sermons delivered to the congregation as a whole. My second account is from Pamela, a young woman in her early 20s who had a much more intimate connection with the ministry through her participation in its Bible school. As with a number of the people whom I interviewed, she also worked for a time with groups of other Word of Lifers in a telephone sales firm set up by a member of the ministry, where prayer and prosperity were believed to go hand in hand, as believers attempted to sell products over the phone to anonymous clients. Pamela's account, like Gudrun's, is not about the foundational experience of being born again, but it is about her need to free herself from a state of physical and mental depression. She says:

> Svante [the director of the Bible school] told me, "You must go now to
> Sam Whaley [a visiting U.S. preacher] for to [ask for] release
> [befrielse]"—it was, like he would cast out demons. That "you should
> now go forward for release this week." I couldn't sit and listen. And
> they took it as a sign that my demons were disturbed by listening to
> Sam Whaley. And then they said I should go forward to receive
> intercession on the last day he was there. And I went forward.
> And . . . four to five people [lay] over me, people lay on top of me.
> Stefan's [the youth pastor's] mother lay over my stomach so that her
> Spirit should work on my Spirit so that my demons should
> disappear. . . . And I lay there with a mass of people shouting in
> tongues and shouting and looking at me, looking at me. . . . Then I
> went to see Svante. He said to me: "You are free now, little girl!"

However, according to Pamela, the intercession did not fully work, so she continued to be troubled.

> I didn't want to show myself as spiritually weak again. And people
> said, "She is the new Sandy Brown" [a U.S. preacher]. Now I was a
> "hero in faith," they said. . . . [And] we felt, "Oh, they come from
> Tulsa—they are coming here to preach so that we'll become big,
> brave, spiritual masters of the fight—so now we should suck in
> everything and receive everything and in Jesus' name I'll have
> everything!"

Of course, one of the reasons that this account is intriguing is that it is much more ambivalently positioned toward prosperity ideas than was evident in Gudrun's account of her personal regeneration. Pamela's intercession does not fully "take" the first time. Mediation here is meant to occur partly through the touch and the words of a preacher from a distant place, but it takes on more dramatic and proximate physical form, as the mother of a pastor connects with Pamela's spirit through covering the girl's stomach with her own body. The nature of the transaction of spiritual power appears to work here in a single direction, alongside speaking in tongues, which is also directed at Pamela as she lies in a prone position, ready to "receive" the blessings of others (like Gudrun, she uses the imagery of listening as a kind of ingestion). One potential result of Pamela's experiences, at least as defined by other believers, is that she should become a Swedish version of a famous, global preacher, Sandy Brown—a sometime visitor to the Word of Life from the United States. This sense of a person becoming almost a copy of another is not uncommon at the Word of Life, and implies both an observation of similarity and, potentially, a form of spiritual transaction, as spiritual power is ingested and enables a person to fulfill her calling. As a kind of Swedish "Sandy Brown," Pamela should ideally convert many others to Christ. Moreover, such a mission echoes her actions before she underwent intercession, when she was a saleswoman in a Word of Life–run firm aiming to "convert" others to particular commercial products.

## A Chain of Healing?

My third account is very different from the first two. It comes from an article in a Word of Life newsletter from 1995 and is a report of what occurred in September 1991 when Ulf Ekman took part in a revival campaign in Tirana, Albania, which was also a "historic broadcast."[16] According to the report, many people were healed while watching the program on television, but the article focuses on just one of those viewers, a poor Catholic woman in her 30s called Vera Noshi. Vera explains that she had felt the impulse to go home and rest, and when she did so she happened to see Ulf Ekman appear on the screen, talking about the Bible school that was about to start in Tirana. Vera then found herself not only visiting a sick relative in the hospital, but also preaching to that relative, with the result that many people gathered around her. The next day, she came back to the hospital, and a woman who could not walk proclaimed herself healed. According to the article, Vera concludes that "the Jesus whom she received while sitting in front of the TV in September 1991 is her Provider."

On one level, this article provides a standard account of the influence of Ulf Ekman—a "worldwide man of God"—as he visits another country. The mediation of the television screen proves no barrier to the workings of the Spirit through Ekman. Yet we also see how his transforming visit to another country is also presented as a (trans)formation of the Charismatic subject at a more intimate level. Ekman's healing power is juxtaposed with that of Vera, whose metonymic link with Ekman through the screen becomes a prompt for her own career as a (now Protestant, not Catholic) healer, echoing Ekman but at a more local level. The virtual presence of Ekman via the television screen is converted by Vera into a physical presence in the ward of a hospital: transference leads to a kind of embodied mimesis. Again, finances are not to the fore but are present: Vera does not become materially rich in her new role, but Jesus provides her with the resources necessary to carry out her missionary—and mobile—calling.

Concluding Remarks

In this chapter, we have been introduced to Fredrik, Gudrun, Pamela, and Vera—all adherents of a prosperity gospel, albeit in different circumstances. These are just four people, but I have tried to use my descriptions of them and their self-descriptions as ways of reflecting on wider cultural patterns and themes. We see how practices relating to health and wealth provide a Charismatic repertoire of radicalized action that operates in church and beyond. Materiality is clearly at play here, but in particular ways: it is in motion or contributes to motion; it does not accumulate for the sake of accumulation; it is both an index and a means of spiritual progress.

Thus, even an item such as Gudrun's bicycle seems an apt container for such a spiritually charged view of seemingly worldly objects: it takes her away from her home, her comfort zone, increasing her mobility as a (spiritually and psychologically healed) Protestant subject and as an older woman rediscovering her childhood. Within this complex and often nuanced view of the power of the material, people are often the most valued mediators of spiritual power, of course, possibly through touch but also through other semiotic forms, such as spoken words, books, or even images on a television screen.

The resulting transactions between people as well as between people and other forms of materiality create dividuals as much as individuals: for instance, Pamela becomes a sometimes troubled container of the spiritual power directed at her by known and unknown others, even as she becomes an echo of a better-known advocate of the prosperity gospel. These transactions take place on local levels—in the home, on the streets of Uppsala—but also at global levels, in actuality or in the imagination.

Yet the brute physicality of the body cannot always be overcome. Fredrik's brother never did come back, and I do not know what Fredrik thought about his loss over time. The expectation that one will eventually gain the physical resources or job that one desires seems a rather more sustainable hope than that a deceased relative will return. It is also notable that, over the years, death has become a more overt theme of public Word of Life discourse. Obituaries of deceased members are now read in services, for instance, unlike the early years of the ministry, when this practice would possibly have been rejected as negative confession. At the same time, the materialities associated with health and wealth remain multifaceted and in motion, as they assist—as well as challenge—the formation of the Charismatic, prosperity-oriented subject.

NOTES

    1 For a detailed description of the founding of the Word of Life, see Simon Coleman, *The Globalisation of Charismatic Christianity: Spreading the Gospel of Prosperity*

(Cambridge: Cambridge University Press, 2000), 92–116. The ministry was started in 1983 by Ulf Ekman, then a student priest within the Swedish Church, who had attended Kenneth Hagin's Rhema Bible School in Tulsa, Oklahoma. Since its founding, the ministry has built up a congregation of around 2,000 people, a university, an international Bible school, and a network of other Bible schools and ministries across Europe and beyond. My initial fieldwork at Word of Life took place for 15 months (1986–1987), which is when I met Fredrik, and I have returned to the ministry relatively regularly ever since. In its early stages, Word of Life drew heavily on members of other congregations in Sweden, including both the Swedish Church and the pentecostal movement.

2 Coleman, *Globalisation of Charismatic Christianity*, 210–220.

3 See, e.g., David Morgan and Sue Scott, "Bodies in a Social Landscape," in *Body Matters: Essays on the Sociology of the Body*, ed. Sue Scott and David Morgan (London: Falmer, 1993), 3.

4 Thomas Csordas, "Health and the Holy in the Afro-Brazilian Candomblé," in *Cultural Bodies: Ethnography and Healing*, ed. Helen Thomas and Jamilah Ahmed (Oxford: Blackwell, 2004), 241; see also Thomas and Ahmed, "Introduction," Ibid., 1–24; and Csordas's essay in this volume.

5 Bryan Turner, *The Body and Society: Explorations in Social Theory* (1984; reprint, London: Sage, 1996), 59. Note also Turner's discussion of Weberian sociology, where he discusses Weber's argument that religious behavior originates in mundane, this-worldly interests. With time, according to Weber, the so-called routinization of charisma replaces such interests with other-worldly goals, cults of saints for prosperity, and healing in this world.

6 Turner, *Body and Society*, 59, 63, 71–74.

7 See Webb Keane, *Christian Modern: Freedom and Fetish in the Mission Encounter* (Berkeley: University of California Press, 2007), 4–5. Keane explores ambiguities over the value of materiality that he sees as key to Protestant attitudes toward modernity.

8 As Keane points out, it is precisely the religious background to ideas of modern freedom that makes sense of the impetus behind what the anthropologist Bruno Latour has famously called "purification"—the drive to draw a clear line between humans and nonhumans, between the world of agency and that of natural determinism. See Bruno Latour, *We Have Never Been Modern*, trans. Catherine Porter (Cambridge, Mass.: Harvard University Press, 1993).

9 Miroslav Volf, "Materiality of Salvation: An Investigation in the Soteriologies of Liberation and Pentecostal Theologies," *Journal of Ecumenical Studies* 26.3 (1989): 447–467.

10 R. Marie Griffith, *Born-Again Bodies: Flesh and Spirit in American Christianity* (Berkeley: University of California Press, 2004), 70, 69, 4, 16, 14, 73, traces the nineteenth-century roots of these ideas to a combination of Swedenborgianism, mesmerism, spiritualism, Holiness evangelicalism, and mind cure, a system that attributed the cures of physical illness to mental or spiritual faculties. She argues that, for Phineas Parkhurst Quimby, mind as "spiritual matter" was a process, signaling the shifting interpenetration of the movement's two strands. Ralph Waldo Trine's (1866–1958) bestselling book of 1897, *In Tune with the Infinite*, presented bodily

matters not simply as methods of bodily healing but also as signposts of spiritual progress

11  See Edward LiPuma, "Modernity and Forms of Personhood in Melanesia," in *Bodies and Persons: Comparative Perspectives from Africa and Melanesia*, ed. Michael Lambek and Andrew Strathern (Cambridge: Cambridge University Press, 1998), 56–58. While acknowledging some of the force of LiPuma's argument, we need to avoid constructing a transcultural and transhistorical notion of "the dividual," as clearly notions of personhood as well as transaction vary cross-culturally.

12  Anthropologist Janice Boddy's helpful comment on LiPuma's argument is that it espouses a broadly ecological notion of embodiment that includes the world beyond the body's edge, presenting a view of the person as composite, multiply sourced, and constituted through reciprocal engagement in a recursively meaningful world. See Boddy, "Afterword: Embodying Ethnography," in *Bodies and Persons*, ed. Lambek and Strathern, 260, 271.

13  Simon Coleman, "Of Metaphors and Muscles: Protestant 'Play' in the Disciplining of the Self," in *The Discipline of Leisure: Embodying Cultures of "Recreation,"* ed. Simon Coleman and Tamara Kohn (Oxford: Berghahn, 2007), 39–53.

14  Thomas Csordas, *Language, Charisma, and Creativity: The Ritual Life of a Religious Movement* (Berkeley: University of California Press, 1997).

15  Sten Nilsson (d. Aug. 2009) was Ulf Ekman's father-in-law. This book was published by Word of Life in 1984.

16  "83 People Healed in One Day!" *Word of Life Newsletter* (1995): 14–15.

# 3

# Material Salvation: Healing, Deliverance, and "Breakthrough" in African Migrant Churches in Germany

*Claudia Währisch-Oblau*

Three Examples

"Be Ye Revived, Oh Europe!" was the title of the weeklong revival meeting of Magnify Deliverance Ministries in Düsseldorf, western Germany, a small Charismatic church with predominantly West African members, which is headed by a woman pastor, Grace Pieper, from Nigeria. One evening, the guest preacher, Reverend Kwa Kwa from Ghana, entitled his sermon "Open Your Heavens!" He spoke about the dangers of working under a closed heaven, where people could struggle and work hard but never receive any blessings. The key to an open heaven was prayer. And once heaven was open, blessings would flow abundantly: "When your heaven is open above you, even your shadow will begin to heal! . . . Your life won't be the same . . . you will see your glory. You will see a miracle! We are in for a boat-sinking blessing!" Under the jubilant response of the assembled congregation, the pastor called forward all those who were "in need of a miracle." With a few exceptions, almost the whole congregation came forward to have the preacher lay hands on them and pray for them. A number of people fell down under the touch of the pastor; each of them was caught by assistants standing right behind them and carefully lowered to the ground. Most got up again within less than one minute. One German man started to shake as the pastor touched him, and his eyelids began to flutter. Then his eyes turned up so much that only the whites were visible, and he also fell to the ground, shaking. He got up quickly, but his head continued to shake in an unusual manner and his eyelids still fluttered for several more minutes. After these events, the woman pastor hosting the revival gave a closing prayer which ended in the Lord's Prayer. Instead of a benediction, the congregation then intoned three times: "I bear the marks of Christ on my body!" With this, the meeting ended.[1]

Holy City of God Ministries, another Nigerian-led Charismatic church in the same city, announces on its website:

> If you have any prayer request in the following areas: Salvation—
> Finance—Healing—Deliverance—Residential Permit—
> Employment—Fruit of the Womb—Wisdom—Safe Delivery—Fear—
> Holy Ghost Baptism—Peace—Depression  Demonic Dreams, e.g.,
> constant sexual dreams, etc.—Marital Problems—Others—Please
> send your request to prayers@holycityofgodministries.org.[2]

A page of testimonies follows to prove that prayer in this church is powerful. Interestingly, there is no example of healing, but two stories of residence permits granted.

The Living Water Christian Mission, led by a Nigerian, Johnson Olowookere, and based in the eastern German city of Jena, has established a "Faith Clinic," a series of regular prayer meetings in which people ask for divine healing. According to the pastor, the idea for this clinic came directly from God. A video downloadable from the mission's website shows a number of purported miracle healings: both black and white women are apparently cured from pains in the abdomen, leg, and arm, and the cut in the thumb of a small white boy disappears.[3]

These are just three examples, to which dozens more could be added. They illustrate that African-led churches in Germany, in their preaching and outreach, center on spiritual approaches to gain material blessings: health, financial prosperity, and, of especial importance for migrants, residence permits. In this chapter, the theological and epistemological bases for these practices will be analyzed, showing at their root both an "enchanted" worldview in which outcomes in the material world are determined by events in the spiritual realm, and a material understanding of salvation.[4] This epistemology is at odds with the dominant worldview in Germany, forcing migrant evangelists either to adapt or remain marginal.


African-Led Pentecostal and Charismatic Churches in Germany

Migrants from West and Central Africa began to come to Germany in significant numbers in the late 1980s. Mostly from Ghana and Nigeria, they were joined by smaller numbers of Cameroonians, Togolese, Congolese, Angolans, and Ivoirians.[5] Among the approximately 9 million people of migrant background in Germany, they constitute a small minority of probably not much more than 100,000–150,000.[6] Many of these immigrants are active Christians. As they found it difficult to integrate into existing German churches, they started churches of their own. In the Rhine-Ruhr conurbation, a triangle roughly spanning the western German cities of Dortmund, Aachen, and Bonn, about 200 African-led churches have been identified, ranging from tiny congregations of just two or three families to budding megachurches with hundreds of members.[7] There are no reliable statistics for the rest of Germany, but it can be estimated that there must be at least 700 to 800 such congregations in the country. The overwhelming majority of these churches are either independent ministries which, while clearly Charismatic in character, usually call themselves "nondenominational" and have members from diverse backgrounds, or are attached to overseas Pentecostal denominations like the Ghanaian Church of Pentecost or the Nigerian Redeemed Christian Church of God. Even though a substantial number of African immigrants originally come from a mainline Protestant background, almost all African churches in Germany are either Pentecostal or Charismatic—though most avoid the use of these identifiers.[8]

According to their pastors and leaders, these churches are not meant as "diaspora" churches where migrants can find a "home away from home" and preserve their culture and piety of origin.[9] Rather, they are conceptualized as missionary bridgeheads with a clear evangelistic calling toward the whole of German society.[10] Sunday sermons and church magazines admonish believers to reach out to non-Christians, both indigenous and migrant, around them. Most churches regularly organize evangelistic events like street preaching, gospel concerts, and "crusades" on their premises. Despite their goal to evangelize or revive "all of Europe," most African-led churches have a majority of African members, though they are usually not mono-ethnic, but rather composed of a mixture of different African nationalities and ethnicities.[11] Some larger churches have been quite successful in evangelizing other migrants, but generally African-led churches have not been able to recruit and keep large numbers of German members. Nevertheless, like Pentecostal and Charismatic churches in general, African-led churches in Germany are strongly evangelistic in character.[12]

## Immigrant Churches: Tied into a Globalized Network

African-led pentecostal churches in Germany, even if independent of any organized denomination, do not exist as unconnected islands. Rather, they are bound into dense, multiform, and flexible networks of communication, cooperation, and exchange that connect them not only to churches in the countries from which their members came originally, but also to the transnational networks that make up the global pentecostal movement.[13] Although there has been some research on the discourses that circulate within this movement, the role of migrant churches in this circulation process has received little attention.[14] This is somewhat surprising as it is likely that, in addition to satellite TV, printed materials, and international conventions and crusades, the migration of Pentecostals and Charismatics is a significant factor driving the multidirectional circulation of ideas within this globalized discourse.

African-led pentecostal churches regularly invite preachers and evangelists from the home countries or regions from which their members emigrated. Well-known preachers from Ghana and Nigeria regularly tour migrant churches all around the North Atlantic.[15] In addition, preachers from other countries are featured during special festivals or revivals. I have heard a Brazilian speak at a Francophone African festival, a Hong Kong Chinese preacher at the anniversary of a Nigerian church, and the occasional African American at crusades or revivals. In African immigrant households in Germany, Christian satellite TV networks like God TV, Trinity Broadcasting Network, and numerous others are regularly watched.[16] Those who have access to the internet also make use of the websites of internationally known Pentecostal and Charismatic leaders.[17] In terms of print media, books and magazines by U.S. Pentecostal and Word of Faith authors like Kenneth Copeland and T. D. Jakes as well as those by Bahamian Myles Munroe circulate and are read and discussed. Similarly, books and DVDs by prominent preachers and evangelists from Africa like David Oyedepo, Eastwood Anaba, Matthew Ashimolowo, and Sunday Adelaja can be found in many African immigrant households.[18]

But migrants are not only the recipients of this discourse; they are also its producers. African immigrant pentecostal pastors regularly travel to preach and evangelize, following invitations based on personal acquaintances and informal networks. Although pastors of smaller churches are usually limited to travel in Europe due to financial constraints, pastors of larger churches often engage in intercontinental travel. In a typical example, a Ghanaian pastor I know has, in recent years, preached in churches and at conventions in the United States, Colombia, Ecuador, Argentina, Guyana, Uruguay, Chile, England, Norway, the Netherlands, South Korea, Nigeria, Ghana, and the Ivory Coast. Many African immigrant pastors, particularly those with larger churches, also produce their own pamphlets and books, which are sold after Sunday services, at conventions, and when the pastors speak in other churches.[19] They likely also circulate in the writers' home countries. Pastors from larger churches also use mass media, having regular spots on private, satellite, or web-based radio; providing podcasts; or streaming their sermons on the internet.[20] Furthermore, almost every church produces its own DVDs featuring conventions, seminars, or teachings, both with their own pastors and with guest speakers.[21] Such DVDs circulate beyond the producing church through individual contacts and exchanges. In recent years, larger churches have set up websites that are also used to publish sermons and teachings.[22] This means that whatever we say about the theology and praxis of African-led churches in Germany has to take into account the interconnectedness of these churches with the globalized pentecostal movement.


## Spiritual Warfare: West African Pentecostal and Charismatic Worldviews

West African immigrant Christians firmly believe that the visible world in which they live their daily lives is enclosed in an invisible world that influences everything in the visible world.[23] This invisible world is the stage of a cosmic battle between the creator God, his son Jesus Christ, and the Holy Spirit, on one side, and the devil and evil spirits, on the other. This fight has already been won by the death and resurrection of Christ, but it is not over yet. Human beings are not just helpless victims of this conflict, but can play a part on both sides. The traditional African belief that, through means of witchcraft and magic, humans can harness evil spirits to harm other people and further their own success is seeing a powerful resurgence all over sub-Saharan Africa and is widely affirmed by African migrants in Germany.[24] On the other side, Christians can fight, expel, and subdue evil spirits and witchcraft through faith and prayer (which may be made stronger by fasting): the power of the Holy Spirit is always stronger than Satan and his minions.

Human bodies and lives are the field of this cosmic battle. Reborn Christians who have been filled with the Holy Spirit should, in their bodies and lives, constantly experience the fruits of Christ's victory. Scriptural evidence for this is avowedly found in both the Old and New Testaments: "By his stripes, we *are* healed" (emphasis mine), and "He became poor, so that by his poverty you might become rich."[25] "Victorious living" expresses itself in good health, a happy marriage, the ability to father or bear healthy children and to maintain a good relationship with them, and material prosperity, which includes a good job, sufficient finances, and legal residency in the country to which one has migrated. Salvation is material, not only spiritual: what has happened in the spiritual realm always influences the material realm and becomes tangible in it.[26] Healing and prosperity are not blessings beyond salvation and unrelated to it (as mainline Protestant theology would have it), but its expression. Consequently, if health and prosperity are lacking in a Christian's life, the influence of evil spirits is quickly suspected. Illness, marital problems, childlessness, unemployment or unsatisfactory careers, poverty, and legal problems are all interpreted as satanic attacks, and never as "crosses" that God might give someone to bear, or as God-given experiences that might serve to deepen one's faith. Such attacks may be understood as caused by witchcraft employed by relatives or acquaintances out of envy or greed, or they may be seen as simply coming from the devil, who will always try to get Christians away from Christ.[27] These problems, consequently, cannot be solved by "natural means" like scientific medicine, fertility treatments, or hard work, but only by a "supernatural breakthrough" in which the spirits or powers that have caused the problem are defeated. Only afterwards can natural solutions be applied and actually work. Consequently, pentecostal migrants will seek out a pastor to pray for their sick children before taking them to a hospital, bring their ticket and passport to be blessed before leaving from Africa for Europe, and pray and fast for a day before going to a job interview.

This enchanted worldview does not only apply to individual and family problems, but also to society as a whole. "Territorial demons" are held responsible for problems like racism, corruption, war, and drug abuse. They, too, have to be fought so that neighborhoods, cities, and even whole countries and continents can be healed and delivered. Territorial demons, like individual demons, are fought by prayer, sometimes in the form of prayer walks. Christian life, consequently, means to be constantly engaged in "spiritual warfare."[28] Although the term has been popularized in the North Atlantic by North Americans like John Wimber, C. Peter Wagner, Derek Prince, and Charles Kraft, the concept was not simply a U.S. export to Africa. Rather, as critics of the concept contend, North American theology was here influenced by two-thirds world religiosity.[29] As any visitor to the numerous Christian bookstores in Ghana and Nigeria will realize, West African Pentecostals and Charismatics are producing an enormous variety of books, manuals, videos, and DVDs on spiritual warfare topics that, even if they occasionally quote American authors, deal with such African problems as witchcraft, "water spirits," and "spirit marriage," which do not play any role whatsoever in North Atlantic spiritual warfare. The concept is clearly much more than an American import.[30]

The late Nigerian theologian Ogbu Kalu has shown that traditional African worldviews do not distinguish between the sacred and the profane, but rather claim that each space is populated by spiritual powers reaching from the Supreme Being to other deities to ancestral spirits. Kalu calls this African worldview "religious" and continues:

> Going through life is like a *spiritual warfare* [emphasis mine] and religious ardour may appear very materialistic as people strive to preserve their material sustenance in the midst of the machinations of pervasive evil forces. Behind it is a strong sense of the moral and spiritual moorings of life. It is an organic worldview in which the three dimensions of space are bound together; the visible and the invisible worlds interweave. Nothing happens in the visible world which has not been predetermined in the invisible realm. . . . The power question is ultimate.[31]

The anthropologist Birgit Meyer has shown in great detail how European pietistic missionaries impacted this worldview, and how African believers creatively appropriated and developed Christian theology.[32] Meyer explains that, while mainline Protestant theology dismissed all beliefs in spirits and witchcraft as superstition, pentecostal churches were able to integrate them dialectically by accepting the reality of the spirit world but assigning it to the realm of the devil; by offering the possibility of interpreting afflictions as caused by witchcraft and evil spirits; and by offering rituals of "deliverance" to fight such afflictions.

Prayer: The Power of the Spoken Word

Spiritual warfare is fought exclusively by prayer; it is therefore not surprising that members of prayer groups in some West African pentecostal migrant churches are called "prayer warriors." This warfare calls for a specific form of prayer, termed "authority prayer" or "prayer of command." Authority prayer significantly differs from petitionary prayer: rather than asking God to act, the speaker commands "in the name of Jesus." Typical prayer sequences begin with utterances like "I/we come against . . .," "I/we break . . .," "I/we bind . . .," "I/we declare . . ." As divine healing is understood in the framework of spiritual warfare, prayers for healing take the same syntactic form: "I break the power of this illness," "I command this illness to leave," "You are healed in Jesus' name." While many of my informants, in discussing such prayers, hold that a quiet command spoken just once should be sufficient, my observation shows that such prayers tend to be very loud and that commands are repeated over and over again. Logically, prayers for an individual's deliverance from demonic oppression or possession also do not address God, but command the demon(s): "Get out, in the name of Jesus" (figure 3.1).

In spiritual warfare, the person praying is acting in accordance with God and uses God's authority. West African pastors establish their authority by pointing to biblical passages in which Jesus commanded his disciples to heal the sick and cast out demons and in which the apostles set a precedent by healing in Jesus' name.[33] The efficacy of the prayer is ascribed to the spoken word, even if hands are laid on and oil is occasionally used in healing or deliverance prayers. But pastors tend to stress strongly that there is no special power in the oil, trying to demarcate their practices from those of traditional African Instituted Churches that they deem superstitious. "Situations can be spoken into being or out of being. *Onoma* is [a] metonym where the part represents the whole and the name of Jesus can be used to achieve effects in the physical realm."[34] Spiritual warfare prayers are spoken aloud so that the effects of God's victory over all evil powers become real and visible in people's everyday lives, manifested, among other ways, in healing from physical illness, the birth of a healthy child, the granting of a residence permit, a job, and financial success.

FIGURE 3.1a–b.  Deliverance service at Gospel Light International Church, Accra, Ghana (2001). Courtesy Claudia Währisch-Oblau. (a) One woman vomits, and others have difficulty standing during prayers for their deliverance. (b) "Prayer warrior" commanding demons to leave a woman who has fallen to the ground.

The strong sense of power ascribed to the spoken word by West African pentecostal migrants cannot be overestimated. Sermons regularly expound "the power of the tongue" and exhort believers not to bring about negative effects by speaking thoughtlessly. Words, in this context, are not conceptualized

first and foremost as carriers of information. Rather, spoken words are understood to be taken up either by evil spirits or by the Holy Spirit to generate new
realities. This is also true for authority prayer: here, spoken words are meant to
create a new spiritual reality that in turn will effect changes in the visible world.
They are creative words like those reported in Genesis 1. When God speaks, or
when humans speak "in Jesus' name" (i.e., with God's authority), the words
will be turned into action.[35]

At first glance, the practice of ascribing so much power to the spoken word
may lead one to think that West African immigrants basically follow the U.S.-
authored Word of Faith theology,[36] but such reasoning seems simplistic. The
spoken word carries great powers in traditional West African understanding,
and it is likely that, on this basis, Word of Faith theology was heard as expressing a truth already known, and has for this reason become so popular among
West African immigrants. Spiritual warfare theology and the praxis of authority
prayer among West African migrants in Germany must be understood as a
bricolage in which elements taken from traditional African thinking, pietistic
missionary theology, classical Pentecostal theology, international neo-pentecostal preaching, and intercultural and interdenominational insights are reworked
into a creative, new theology.

Evangelism and Healing in the Context
of Spiritual Warfare: West Africa

In the context of spiritual warfare, evangelism takes on special significance.
Rather than being understood as the communication of a message to be
accepted as true, evangelism is seen as a spiritual battle by which individuals
are freed from bondage to the powers of evil and brought into the realm of the
living God. From its beginnings, Pentecostal evangelism has emphasized the
"full gospel": Christ did not only come into the world to save people from sin,
but also as the healer of their illnesses.[37] Consequently, evangelism can be
staged as a "power encounter"[38] in which the power of God is manifested
through miracles like the spontaneous healing of illnesses or the driving out of
demons. This means that healing and deliverance have a place not only within
the life of a Christian congregation, but also they belong first and foremost to
its missionary outreach toward non-Christians. Prosperity, while also being
preached in evangelistic sermons, cannot be as easily and quickly demonstrated as a miraculous healing and therefore plays less of a role when it comes
to evangelistic power encounters.

The importance of healing in evangelism becomes obvious when, as one
travels through West African cities like Accra, Kumasi, and Lagos, one is
struck by the ubiquity of posters and banners advertising all kinds of "miracle crusades." Private radio and TV stations in Ghana and Nigeria regularly

broadcast worship services and evangelistic conventions during which miracle healings are featured. Both local church leaders and visiting evangelists
from the North Atlantic engage in such healing evangelism, and crusades by
well-known evangelists can draw enormous crowds. For example, the evangelistic ministry, combining preaching and healing, of the German Reinhard
Bonnke draws hundreds of thousands all over Africa.[39] The style of such crusades follows a stock pattern, regardless of whether an unknown preacher
speaks to a few dozen people sitting in plastic chairs on a roadside, or whether
a celebrity evangelist fills a huge stadium. There is rousing gospel music, a
sermon that stresses the breakthroughs to be had right now, an altar call for
those "who want to give their life to Jesus," and a further altar call for those
"who need a miracle." In a smaller setting, people will come forward to have
the evangelist lay hands on them individually, while in the case of very large
crowds, the evangelist may simply ask people to lay a hand on the body part
that needs healing while he (there are women evangelists, but the celebrity
evangelists are almost all male) prays for all of them simultaneously from the
stage. Immediately afterward, those who have experienced miraculous healing are asked to come forward to give testimony. (Usually, screeners will pre-
check to make sure people have a consistent story before they go to the
rostrum.) Such testimonies often include a demonstration of healing:
formerly blind people have to count the fingers the evangelist holds up in
front of their faces, deaf people have to repeat words whispered behind their
backs, and those who could not walk have to walk or even run along the stage
for all to see. Although the altar call usually comes before the healing, evangelists expect that the evidence of miracles will lead people to convert; power
evangelism means that God's power becomes so evident that people cannot
but believe.

Such evangelism patterns are becoming globalized through mass media,
particularly satellite television and the internet. While the influence of American televangelists can hardly be denied, West African pentecostal healing evangelists have long been producers of such media, saturating some private TV
and radio stations in countries like Nigeria or Ghana with back-to-back programming, particularly during weekends. Larger healing evangelistic ministries also run websites with reports and videos, making their materials
accessible around the world. To provide just one example: Dag Heward-Mills
(the grandson of a Protestant missionary from Switzerland who also has a
black African heritage), the "doctor-turned-healer" and the founder and general
overseer of Lighthouse Chapel International, a Ghanaian megachurch with numerous branches in Africa and Europe, has set up an organization named the
Jesus Healing Crusade, "a ministry that carries the gospel of Jesus Christ to the
world through massive evangelistic crusades accompanied by healing miracles,
signs and wonders." The ministry website claims that "these crusades present
the full gospel in powerful preaching, divine healing, free medical outreaches,

distribution of clothes to the poor and the free distribution of books to all converts and local pastors," transforming "multitudes wherever they go with the
power of the blood of Jesus."[40] Several such crusades are held every year, mostly
in Ghana, but also in neighboring countries.[41]

## The Pastor as Healer and Mediator of Divine Power

My long-term observation of West African migrant churches in Germany
and of pentecostal churches and ministries in West Africa shows that, when it
comes to authority prayer, pastors are usually perceived as more powerful than
ordinary congregation members, and visiting pastors and evangelists even
more so. Although churches, with few exceptions, have active prayer groups,
people seek out their pastors when they have problems, and public displays of
authority prayer center on a pastor as the "anointed" man or woman of God.
In interviews, pastors talk about having to be available around the clock for
such prayers, not switching their mobile phones off even when they go to
sleep.

My extensive interviews with migrant pastors show that their theological
perspectives on their role are rather contradictory.[42] On one hand, most deny
that they have special spiritual gifts that would set them apart from their
congregation, and they stress the pentecostal belief that the Holy Spirit can
operate through every believer, empowering everyone in the same way. On
the other hand, pastors claim a special authority grounded in their calling as
pastors and the anointing they have received, describing themselves as mediators of divine power who stand between God and their congregation.[43] To
maintain and strengthen this anointing, pastors have to lead intensive spiritual lives, engaging in long times of prayer and regular periods of fasting.
Fasting in particular is seen as spiritually empowering, and few pastors would
engage in a deliverance session without having forgone food for a day or two
before. Pastoral authority is legitimized by miracles: "His ministry is blessed
with signs and wonders following" or "his ministry was accompanied by
signs and wonders, as it is taught in the Bible" are typical phrases found in
the introduction of pastors.[44] In turn, congregation members expect from
their pastors particular spiritual authority and efficacy of prayer, even though
they are taught to pray authoritatively by and for themselves. This inherent
contradiction between a democratic understanding of spiritual giftedness
and the authoritarian perception of pastoral anointing is a major cause of the
many splits in pentecostal migrant churches that can be observed.[45] Talking
with pastors and witnessing the relocation of members between churches
also suggest that West African migrants will join a church and stay with it due
to healing or breakthrough experiences, though quantitative research on this
is sadly lacking.

It is not surprising, therefore, that in more than nine years of fieldwork among immigrant churches in Germany, I have never witnessed an African immigrant pastor pray for healing in a supplicating manner. Authority prayer is employed without exception and healing pronounced even when it is not visible. This can happen in very casual ways: a pastor, in the midst of a conversation with someone else, may lay his right hand on the forehead of a sick person asking for his prayer from the side, murmuring "You are healed in Jesus' name!" and turn back to his original conversation. In other cases, extreme efforts are made: a Ghanaian pastor once related that a member of his congregation died in a hospital despite the pastor's firm conviction that God would heal this person. Rather than admitting defeat, the pastor called several members of his congregation, who stayed with the corpse for a whole night, without interruption calling on the body to rise up again "in the name of Jesus," though without success.[46]

Such failures, though, are rarely discussed. When asked about cases where healing did not happen, pastors' reactions range from "Everybody gets healed!" to "God is free to do what he wants." Blaming a lack of faith or hidden sins in the life of the sick person seems to be rare. On the other hand, someone who is sick and not healed by a pastor's prayer tends to seek someone "more powerful."

## Contextualization I: The German Situation

After all that has been said, it should be expected that miracle crusades are a preferred form of evangelism by West African pentecostal immigrants in Germany. But interestingly, this is not the case. When asked about their evangelistic work in Germany, two Ghanaian immigrant pastors had this to say:

> The approach is different. . . . If I want to do a strong campaign of evangelization . . . get on a Gospel Concert, make a program: Gospel Concert, everybody is going to come! European, Western, German, they're going to come to a concert, and that's an open door. The place is packed! . . . For Africans, you just come and say, "This is a Gospel Crusade, there will be prayer and deliverance"—they will come in their numbers, the place is packed, you see the response. . . . So there's a difference. But the message will be the same. The message will be the same! Jesus is Lord, Jesus will save you.[47]
>
> Basically, the message is the same, whether Germans or Ghanaians or Americans, the message is the same. But . . . there are times you need to change the method. In Ghana, even because of problems, because of poverty, when you tell people that Jesus is the solution to your problems, they will come. When they see some miracles, they will come. But when you go to some place[s], miracles

only won't bring the people. . . . There are some places, like, maybe, Germany, when you want to attract the people, you need to develop maybe your music ministry, because people are attracted by music. . . . You have to study the situation and to allow the Holy Spirit to teach you what to use.[48]

Both speakers are clearly aware of the fact that, in Germany, evangelism through miracles has little appeal. To understand the reasons for this, a short look at the German situation is in order.

Germany is a welfare state where everybody is guaranteed a basic livelihood and where access to quality medical care is universal. Consequently, religious faith has become dematerialized, highly spiritualized, and private. Mainstream Christianity in Germany is strongly influenced by Enlightenment philosophy, which expects the solution of material problems through social action rather than through prayer, and is consequently strongly engaged in diaconal work. Pentecostal and Charismatic Christianity has remained very small and marginal overall, and is diverse and splintered into many groups that are often hostile to each other. There are classical Pentecostals in denominational churches, Charismatic renewal movements within the sizable Roman Catholic and German Protestant churches as well as within the (very small) Baptist and Methodist churches, and a growing number of newly founded, independent churches and ministries that can be broadly classified as pentecostal.[49] Although divine healing plays an important role in all these groups, only a few pentecostals also preach material blessings, though some of the largest and most prominent new churches are tied to the Word of Faith movement.[50]

German society is, overall, highly secularized. Since the mid-1980s, however, a trend toward a new, particularly esoteric religiosity can also be observed.[51] Modern health care is often experienced as "soulless," and a longing for "holistic" healing expresses itself in growing numbers of people who seek metaphysical healers or ask for healing prayers. Charismatic churches and groups have reacted to this openness by establishing a growing number of "healing rooms" and offering prayers for healing in connection with worship services;[52] and in the German Protestant Church, more and more congregations are offering "anointing/blessing services," usually following a strict liturgy, which tend to be far better frequented than normal Sunday services.

## Contextualization II: West African Healing Evangelism in Germany

In a situation where people are materially secure and where religion is highly privatized and spiritualized, miracle crusades will obviously hold little attraction, and West African migrant pastors quickly learn that they are not a valuable tool of evangelism in Germany. Germans need a different kind of material salvation than do African immigrants, such as a solution for their psychological problems. Consequently, West African evangelists in Germany tailor their evangelistic methods according to the people whom they want to convert. If they engage in miracle crusades at all, the leaflets are usually in English or French, signaling that the target group is other sub-Saharan immigrants and not Germans. My observations of evangelistic gatherings bear out this assumption. If a West African immigrant church announces a gospel concert, many white faces can be seen in the church, and pastors preach a message that does not use any spiritual warfare imagery. If a church does a miracle crusade, the audiences are overwhelmingly black and the message centers on spiritual warfare.

Nevertheless, West African–led churches do engage in healing evangelism toward Germans. Most churches have a small number of German members (usually no more than three or four) who tend to come from the margins of society, being former drug addicts, unemployed, homeless, or suffering from long-term psychiatric problems—people who are rarely found in a mainline, middle-class congregation. Anecdotal evidence suggests that many of them were led by healing or other material blessing experiences to join a migrant church, though my observation also has been that such Germans tend to leave again after a year or two.[53]

Until the twenty-first century, German churches paid little attention to migrant churches and tended to completely ignore West African pentecostal congregations. But while Catholic and mainline Protestant church leaders are highly critical of West African spiritual warfare evangelism—the Protestant Church in the Rhineland issued an internal paper in 2007 outlawing the performance of deliverance rituals by migrant churches using Protestant premises—pentecostal churches have started to open up to the migrants. The Federation of Free Pentecostal Churches now has, among its 600-plus member churches, almost 70 African-led congregations.[54] In Charismatic and Pentecostal circles in Germany, the conviction is growing that the African immigration to Germany is actually a missionary movement of the Holy Spirit, that the African evangelists bring with them a spiritual power that is lacking in Germany, and that this power is particularly expressed in the ability to heal and deliver.[55] For example, a 2008 issue of the German magazine *Charisma/Come Holy Spirit*, which is widely read in Charismatic circles, is entitled "The Blessing Is Coming Back" and centers on African-led churches in Germany.[56] Here, the reader finds the testimony of a woman who describes how she was healed from depression and addiction to several medications due to prayers and counseling by a Ghanaian immigrant pastor. It is not by accident, though, that this woman was not healed instantly and publicly during a crusade, but rather in a longer-term process conducted in a private setting; German sensibilities have clearly been taken into account.

Conversely, only a few mostly smaller German-led Charismatic churches have, in recent years, invited West African healing evangelists for evangelistic campaigns particularly aimed at Germans and styled in the manner of international healing evangelism crusades. In the broader public as well as in the German Protestant Church, such campaigns are usually met with strong criticism or even ridicule, and even many pentecostals remain skeptical when it comes to healing evangelists like Charles Ndifon, who claims outrageous successes and states: "I do not pray for the sick, I heal them."[57] While a growing number of Germans might allow for the possibility of the miraculous healing of illnesses as the answer to petitionary prayers, even many Pentecostals and Charismatics would reject authority prayer, sensing that such prayer implies a claim to be in command and in control of miraculous powers, and feeling uncomfortable about the showy character of a public healing service. This means that West African migrant pentecostals will have to adapt their theology and practice to become more palatable to the Germans around them, or else remain marginalized in Germany even if they are tied into strong global networks.

NOTES

1  Field notes, 12 Oct. 2004.

2  See http://www.holycityofgodministries.org/prayer_req.htm (accessed 23 Feb. 2009).

3  See http://www.faithclinic.de/EN_zeugnisse.htm (accessed 23 Feb. 2009).

4  For a discussion of "enchanted" worldviews, see Michael Saler, "Modernity and Enchantment: A Historiographic Review," *American Historical Review* 111.3 (June 2006): 692–716.

5  For official statistics, see https://www-ec.destatis.de/csp/shop/sfg/bpm.html.cms.cBroker.cls?cmspath=struktur,vollanzeige.csp&ID=1019121 (accessed 23 Feb. 2009).

6  Exact figures are unavailable as migrants who take German citizenship are no longer counted in the Central Register of Aliens. Moreover, there may be a large number of undocumented immigrants from these countries.

7  Unpublished database of the United Evangelical Mission in personal collection of Claudia Währisch-Oblau, last updated Apr. 2008.

8  "Mainline Protestant" here denotes classical Reformation churches, e.g., Lutheran or Reformed, as well as evangelical churches like Baptist or Methodist.

9  See Afe Adogame, "Mapping Globalization with the Lens of Religion: African Migrant Churches in Germany," in *New Religions and Globalization: Empirical, Theoretical and Methodological Perspectives*, ed. Armin W. Geertz and Margit Warburg (Aarhus, Denmark: Aarhus University Press, 2008).

10  For an in-depth analysis, see Claudia Währisch-Oblau, *The Missionary Self-Perception of Pentecostal/Charismatic Church Leaders from the Global South in Europe: Bringing Back the Gospel* (Leiden: Brill, 2009).

11  Afe Adogame, "Raising Champions, Taking Territories: African Churches and the Mapping of New Religious Landscapes in Diaspora," in *The African Diaspora and the Study of Religion*, ed. Theodore Louis Trost (New York: Palgrave Macmillan, 2007), 17–34, calls African diaspora churches "transnationalized."

12  Allan Anderson, *Spreading Fires: The Missionary Nature of Early Pentecostalism* (London: SCM, 2007).

13  Afe Adogame, "The Quest for Space in the Global Spiritual Marketplace," *International Review of Mission* 89.354 (July 2000): 400–409.

14  See, e.g., André Corten and Ruth Marshall-Fratani, *Between Babel and Pentecost: Transnational Pentecostalism in Africa and Latin America* (Bloomington: Indiana University Press, 2001); and Murray W. Dempster, Byron D. Klau, and Douglas Petersen, eds., *The Globalization of Pentecostalism: A Religion Made to Travel* (Irvine, Calif.: Regnum, 1999).

15  See, e.g., the listing of Patrick Anwuzia's speaking appointments at htttp://www.zoeministriesworldwide.org/conventions.html (accessed 23 Feb. 2009); in 2007, Anwuzia addressed African-led churches in the United States, the Netherlands, Belgium, Germany, Spain, and England; in March 2009, he was back in Germany.

16  See http://www.god.tv; http://www.tbneurope.org; and, for a listing of stations receivable in Germany, see http://www.christtv.de (all accessed 22 June 2007).

17  See, e.g., the link list on http://www.icf-aachen.org/events. php?item=breakingnews (accessed 23 Feb. 2009), which includes, among others, the websites of Benny Hinn, Ulf Ekman, and Frederick K. C. Price.

18  For products by Oyedepo, see http://www.davidabioye.org/bookstore.php; for Anaba, see http://www.believersbookshop.co.uk/product_info.php?products_id=2015; for Ashimolowo, see http://www.goodreads.com/author/show/736825.Matthew_Ashimolowo; for Adelaja, see http://www.sundayadelaja.com/order-int.html (all accessed 23 Feb. 2009).

19  Two examples from my collection are Sarpong Osei-Assibey, *Going the Extra Mile: The Secret to Your Blessing* (privately published, 2007); and Bosun Ajayi, *Return to the Narrow Path* (Lagos, Nigeria: Ibunkun Alafia, 2006). See http://www.houseofsolution.org/bookstore.html for the book list of another Ghanaian pastor in Germany.

20  E.g., a Nigerian pastor based in Oberhausen has a weekly sermon hour on Reborn Radio (the "station for African diaspora"): http://www.rebornradio.com/pastorjeremiah.asp (accessed 6 Aug. 2007); see also http://www.houseofsolution.org/index.html (accessed 23 Feb. 2009).

21  A number of such DVDs are in my collection, including footage of deliverance and healing sessions, preaching, Bible studies, and teachings on issues like "successful marriage."

22  See, e.g., http://www.houseofsolution.org (featuring video); http://www.faithcentre.de; http://www.wolic.de (all accessed 6 Aug. 2007).

23  This argument is laid out in more depth in Währisch-Oblau, *Missionary Self-Perception*, ch. 5.

24  Personal communications to the author by informants from churches in Cameroon, Ghana, Nigeria, Congo, and Tanzania. As examples, see the

growing number of children abandoned in Kinshasa because their parents believe them to be wizards and witches, or the spate of albino killings in Tanzania in 2008/2009.

25  Isaiah 53:5; 2 Corinthians 8:9.

26  See the important article by Miroslav Volf, "Materiality of Salvation: An Investigation in the Soteriologies of Liberation and Pentecostal Theologies," *Journal of Ecumenical Studies* 26.3 (1989): 447–467.

27  Immigrant West Africans live in constant fear of such attacks, particularly when they travel to visit their home countries. To stave off spiritual assaults, many enter a period of fasting and prayer before traveling in order to strengthen their spiritual "armor."

28  For an introduction to the concept, see Charles H. Kraft, "Spiritual Warfare: A Neocharismatic Perspective," in *New International Dictionary of Pentecostal and Charismatic Movements*, ed. Stanley M. Burgess and Ed M. Van der Maas (Grand Rapids, Mich.: Zondervan, 2002), 1091–1096.

29  See, e.g., Scott Moreau, "Religious Borrowing as a Two-Way Street: An Introduction to Animistic Tendencies in the Euro–North American Context," in *Christianity and the Religions*, ed. Edward Rommen and Harold Netland (Pasadena, Calif.: Carey Library, 1995), 166–183; and Robert J. Priest, Thomas Campbell, and Bradford A. Mullen, "Missiological Syncretism: The New Animistic Paradigm," in *Spiritual Power and Missions: Raising the Issues*, ed. Edward Rommen (Pasadena, Calif.: Carey Library, 1995), 143–168.

30  G. F. Oyor, *Who Needs Deliverance? Revised and Enlarged Edition (with 500 Powerful Breakthrough Prayer Points)*, 3rd ed. (Ibadan, Nigeria: Freedom Press, 2000), bought at a Catholic bookstore in Kumasi, Ghana, is a typical example of using spiritual warfare to overcome individual problems. Water spirits are revered in traditional African religions as givers of wealth and fertility; see Kofi A. Opoku, *West African Traditional Religion* (Accra: FEP International, 1978), 60–65. In pentecostalism, water spirits are seen as particularly dangerous because they enslave people with false promises; D. K. Olukoya, *Violent Prayers to Disgrace Stubborn Problems* (Lagos, Nigeria: Battle Cry Ministries, 1999), 123–125; Oyor, *Who Needs Deliverance?* 139–154. Many West African pentecostals blame their inability to find a marriage partner on conscious or unconscious, but "legally binding," marriages to a spirit. If such marriages are revoked during a deliverance session, the person will be free to marry a human being; Olukoya, *Violent Prayers to Disgrace Stubborn Problems*, 104–109.

31  Ogbu Kalu, "The Pentecostal Model in Africa," in *Uniquely African? African Christian Identity from Cultural and Historical Perspectives*, ed. James L. Cox and Gerrie ter Haar (Trenton, N.J.: Africa World Press, 2003), 230.

32  Birgit Meyer, *Translating the Devil: Religion and Modernity among the Ewe in Ghana* (Trenton, N.J.: Africa World Press, 1999).

33  Biblical precedents cited include John 14:12 and Acts 3:6, 9:40, and 14:10.

34  Kalu, "Pentecostal Model," 232.

35  Such speech acts cannot be understood as "performative" in the sense of J. L. Austin, *How to Do Things with Words* (Oxford: Clarendon, 1962). Anthropological research has shown that linguistic categories do not suffice to analyze "magical"

speaking; see D. S. Gardener, "Performativity in Ritual: The Mianmin Case," *Man*, n.s., 18.2 (June 1983): 346–360; John McCreery, "Negotiating with Demons: The Uses of Magical Language," *American Ethnologist* 22.1 (Feb. 1995): 144–164; Yuval Harari, "How to Do Things with Words: Philosophical Theory and Magical Deeds," in *Jerusalem Studies in Jewish Folklore*, ed. Tamar Alexander, Galit Hasan-Rokem, and Shalom Sabar (Jerusalem: Magnes Press of the Hebrew University of Jerusalem, 1998) (English summary of an article originally in Hebrew), http://www.folklore.org.il/JSIJF/jsijf19-20.html (accessed 9 Aug. 2007); Stephen Hunt, "Dramatising the 'Health and Wealth Gospel': Belief and Practice of a Neo-Pentecostal 'Faith' Ministry," *Journal of Beliefs and Values: Studies in Religion and Education* 21.1 (2000): 73–86.

36  See Gifford's, Sánchez Walsh's, and Bowler's essays in this volume. For an introduction to Word of Faith theology, see L. Lovett, "Positive Confession Theology," in *New International Dictionary*, ed. Burgess and Van der Maas, 992–994. For further reading, see Kenneth E. Hagin, *Right and Wrong Thinking for Christians* (Tulsa, Okla.: Kenneth Hagin Ministries, 1966); Kenneth Copeland, *The Laws of Prosperity* (Fort Worth, Tex.: Kenneth Copeland Publications, 1996). A critical study is D. R. McConnell, *A Different Gospel: A Historical and Biblical Analysis of the Modern Faith Movement* (Peabody, Mass.: Hendrickson, 1988).

37  Anderson, *Spreading Fires*, 35.

38  This term, coined by C. Peter Wagner, is rarely used by West African evangelists.

39  See "Bonnke, Reinhard Willi Gottfried," in *New International Dictionary*, ed. Burgess and Van der Maas, 438–439, and http://www.cfan.org (accessed 26 Feb. 2009); see also Marostica's essay in this volume for an example of Bonnke's global influence.

40  See http://www.daghewardmills.org/about_evi.html (accessed 26 Feb. 2009); http://www.lighthousechapel.org (accessed 28 Feb. 2009). It should be noted that, in general, West African healing evangelists are not opposed to medical care.

41  See http://www.healingjesuscrusade.org/reports.html (accessed 26 Feb. 2009).

42  These are analyzed in greater depth in Währisch-Oblau, *Missionary Self-Perception*, ch. 3.

43  If pressed for a systematic statement, most would probably distinguish between the baptism of the Holy Spirit, which every believer can receive, and the anointing which is special to a ministry. But there is no systematic reflection on such issues. The view that pastors mediate between God and congregants is shared by pentecostal migrant pastors from Asia and Latin America.

44  See, e.g., http://www.houseofsolution.org/our_pastors.html; http://www.livingwater-missions.de/EN_index.htm (both accessed 27 Feb. 2009).

45  An extensive analysis of this contradiction can be found in Währisch-Oblau, *Missionary Self-Perception*, ch. 3.

46  In very private conversations, West African pastors sometimes confide their fear that, if their "authority prayer" does not lead to at least partial healing or success, members might leave their congregation to look for another pastor with a "stronger anointing."

47  Interview with R. N. from Ghana, 16 Nov. 2005.

48  Interview with A. O. from Ghana, 12 Apr. 2005.

49  In 2008, the Roman Catholic Church had 25.1 million members, the Evangelische Kirche (here translated as German Protestant Church rather than Evangelical Church to avoid confusion with "evangelical" churches, which differ in significant ways in character and theology) 24.8 million, and pentecostal churches (including migrant churches) approximately 100,000 members; http://www.remid. de/remid_info_zahlen.htm (accessed 25 Sept. 2009). The Charismatic renewal movements in the mainline churches do not publish membership figures, but can be estimated at several hundred thousand at most. See also Peter Zimmerling, *Die Charismatischen Bewegungen: Theologie, Spiritualität, Anstöße zum Gespräch* [The Charismatic Movement: Theology, Spirituality, Impulses for Conversation] (Göttingen: Vandenhoeck and Ruprecht, 2001), 50–54, 258–294.

50  See the article on the Word of Faith movement, "Glaubensbewegung," in *Handbuch der evangelistisch-missionarischen Werke, Einrichtungen und Gemeinden: Deutschland-Österreich-Schweiz* [Handbook of Evangelist Missionary Work, Institutions, and Communities: Germany, Austria, Switzerland] (Stuttgart: Evangelisches Verlagshaus, 1997).

51  See Reinhard Hempelmann et al., eds., *Panorama der neuen Religiosität: Sinnsuche und Heilsversprechen zu Beginn des 21. Jahrhunderts* [Panorama of the New Religiosity: Search for Meaning and Promise of Salvation at the Beginning of the Twenty-First Century] (Gütersloh: GVH, 2001), 210–309; Sören Asmus, "Das Evangelium im westlichen Kontext" [The Gospel in the Western Context], in *Das universelle Wort spricht nur Dialekt: Einführung in kontextuelle Theologie Vorlesung an der Kirchlichen Hochschule Wuppertal im WS 2003/2004 in Zusammenarbeit mit der Ökumenischen Werkstatt Wuppertal* [The Universal Word Speaks Only Dialect: Introduction to Contextual Theology: Lectures at the Wuppertal Theological Seminary in the Winter Term 2003–2004 in Cooperation with the Ecumenical Workshop at Wuppertal], by Sören Asmus, Jutta Beldermann, and Friedrich Huber (Wuppertal, Germany: Vereinte Evangelische Mission, 2004), 205–244.

52  See http://www.healingrooms.de (accessed 25 Sept. 2009).

53  There is no way of knowing whether they leave the church completely, or whether they move on to other churches.

54  See http://www.bfp.de/arbeitszweige-des-bfp/arbeitsgemeinschaften/ arbeitsgem-internationaler-gem-aig.html (accessed 25 Sept. 2009).

55  This view is quite similar to ideas expressed by the African evangelists themselves; see Währisch-Oblau, *Missionary Self-Perception*, ch. 4.

56  "The Blessing Is Coming Back," *Charisma/Come Holy Spirit* 146.4 (2008).

57  For typical criticisms, see "Warning against Miracle Healer" (2 Nov. 2009), http://www.rp-online.de/public/article/duesseldorf-stadt/485424/Warnung-vor-Wunderprediger.html; "First Donations, then the Miracle: A Spectacle" (9 Nov. 2007), http://www.wz-newsline.de/?redid=183323; "Expert on Sects Advises against Visit of 'Healing Conference'" (5 Nov. 2007), http://www.epd.de/west/west_ index_52707.html (all websites accessed 27 Feb. 2009). For a representative claim, see http://www.youtube.com/watch?v=7VaHQaW1Ctc (accessed 27 Feb. 2009); and see Henri Nissen, "Ein Gott, der Wunder tut: Ein Journalist untersucht die

Heilungen im Dienst von Charles Ndifon" [A God Who Does Miracles: A Journalist
Examines the Healings in the Services of Charles Ndifon], *Materialien der
Evangelischen Zentralstelle für Weltanschauungsfragen* [Materials of the Protestant
Central Office for Worldview Questions] (Nov. 2004): 436–438. The quotation from
Ndifon is translated from German, "Faszinierend: Wunder und Heilungen heute"
[Fascinating: Miracles and Healings Today], http://www.jesus.ch/index.php/D/
article/15-People/17465-Faszinierend:_Wunder_und_Heilungen_heute (accessed
25 Sept. 2009).

# 4

# Blessed Bodies: Healing within the African American Faith Movement

*Catherine Bowler*

The Victorious Faith Center (VFC) was lit up like a jack-o'-lantern, its orange-tinted fluorescent lights illuminating the bustling sanctuary through the tall panes of glass that formed the church's street-facing wall. Sandwiched between a nail salon and a payday loan office in a Durham, North Carolina, mini mall, the storefront church warmed the dim streets with shouts of praise and prayer on this and every Wednesday night (figure 4.1). A dozen or so women—elders, deacons, and mothers of the church—bantered and laughed as they prepared for the service. The din of chatter ceased when a woman stumbled through the doors, her thin figure shifting awkwardly as she struggled to put one foot in front of the other. She teetered at the entrance, her eyes scanning the room and her expression twisting from some unseen ailment. A mother of the church sprang from her seat, crossed the room, and pulled the newcomer into a long, tight hug. "Praise God!" Shouts of encouragement erupted from all corners. The woman's slack face smiled and ran with tears as people clustered around her in a spontaneous praise circle.

"I'm going to praise his name!" sang the church mother, beginning the familiar tune of a VFC favorite. "Each day is just the same!" joined another. The clapping and the soft thud of tennis shoes stomping on the beige-carpeted floor anchored the chorus.

> Look what the Lord has done
> Look what the Lord has done
> He healed my body, He touched my mind
> He saved me JUST IN TIME.[1]

FIGURE 4.1. Victorious Faith Center, Durham, North Carolina (2009). Courtesy Maria Bowler. (a) A storefront church door makes its statement of faith known even at the entryway.

The woman, whose name was Essence, I soon learned, had just taken her first unaided steps after a sudden illness had left her paralyzed. The VFC members celebrated her healing as a triumph over Satan, who robs believers of the health, prosperity, and abundant life that God grants to all the faithful.

As one of thousands of U.S. congregations belonging to the Faith movement, the Victorious Faith Center practices healing as part of a broader prosperity theology. The Faith movement, known alternatively as the "health and wealth" or "prosperity" gospel, claims membership in the millions and promises to imbue believers with spiritual, physical, and financial mastery over their lives.[2] Although the prosperity gospel draws from various theological

FIGURE 4.1.*(continued)*  (b) A cross illuminates the façade of the storefront.

and cultural streams, courses through different denominational channels, and animates black, white, and Latino churches in the United States and worldwide, these American expressions of Christian abundance can be understood as a single movement that stems from a coherent set of shared understandings.[3] First, the movement conceives of faith as an "activator," a power given to believers that binds and looses spiritual forces, turning the spoken word into reality. Second, the movement envisions faith as palpable.[4] This faith is measured in the wallet, in one's personal finances, and in the body, in one's personal health, making material reality the measure of the success of immaterial faith. In this way, Faith believers have accepted what theologian Miroslav Volf called the "materiality of salvation," seeing, as Candy Gunther Brown argues in this volume's introduction, that the "work of salvation begins . . . in the material world; thus, physical redemption is an expression of and contributes meaningfully to God's ultimate redemptive purposes." Third, the movement expects faith to be victorious. This chapter will examine part of the second aspect of faith—faith as measurable health— by drawing upon 18 months of ethnographic observation, participation, and interviews with African American Faith churchgoers from a Durham, North Carolina, congregation.[5]

This chapter argues that the drama of health and healing serves as one of the defining features of the American Faith movement, as believers use their bodies, alongside their finances, as the testing ground for their faith. While most black prosperity teachers share their white counterparts' largely positive assessment of medicine, African American adherents have adopted a stronger focus on the instrumentality of faith to effect divine healing. Whether they accept or, like VFC, reject biomedical solutions, African American believers ultimately put their confidence in the power of a divine prescription: faith.

## African Americans in the Faith Movement

In the last third of the twentieth century, prosperity theology made a comfortable home within black Protestantism, a tradition commonly associated with social protest, civil rights, and stalwart congregations of Baptists and Methodists. What seemed to adherents like a new discovery, however, can be viewed as a historical recapitulation in African American Protestantism, as it drew upon persistent metaphysical and pentecostal combinations that appeared throughout twentieth-century African American religious history.[6]

In the 1920s and 1930s, as the Great Migration pressed black folks into northern urban landscapes, a groundswell of alternative religious communities promised religious—and often metaphysical—solutions to pressing social and economic problems. A small but noticeable number of African Americans drew from the metaphysical well of "new thought." Originating in the 1880s, new thought, a cluster of thinkers and metaphysical ideas, popularized the notion that people shape their own worlds by their thinking and speaking. By the first decades of the twentieth century, new thought ideas had become a popular religious force that married a gospel of success with the power of the mind, offering believers a path to prosperity through positive thought.[7] These newly uprooted African American communities, like many others in the wider American culture, latched onto its articulation and spiritualization of American self-perceptions. New thought uncovered hidden truths that Americans longed to hear: that divinity was lodged somewhere in their beings and that their secret powers demanded expression.

Metaphysical gospels spread in the urban North, as leaders like Sweet Daddy Grace, Prophet James Jones, Father Divine, and, later, Reverend Ike promised to smooth the rough edges of capitalism and industrialism with theologies that countered poverty, disease, and despair.[8] These early prosperity gospels explicitly combined metaphysical religion, pentecostalism, and African-derived traditions (hoodoo, voodoo), a cross-pollination that resulted in world-affirming black theologies. They asserted the importance of materiality, prosperity, and religious access to the good life. Although these metaphysical gospels remained but a small part of African American Protestant traditions, they helped lay the groundwork for African American participation in the Faith movement.[9] After World War II, when pentecostals heralded the righteous acquisition of health and finances, African American followers found precedent for their vision of material salvation in the echoes of the black metaphysical religions of the interwar period.

The Faith movement took shape in the early 1950s when a generation of white pentecostal preachers embraced money as the primary "miracle" of their ministries.[10] With a healing revival in full swing and many itinerants still working the preaching circuit, Kenneth Hagin, Oral Roberts, and others folded up their tents in favor of established ministries, a focus on finances, and using the new television and radio media to promulgate their message. Kenneth Hagin, credited as the father of the Faith movement, gave the burgeoning revival an institutional home at Rhema Bible Institute in Tulsa, Oklahoma, and molded a theology of abundance into a popular religious force. His theology, drawn from the metaphysically inflected Christianity of thinker Essek William Kenyon (1867–1948), infused pentecostalism with confidence in the power of positive speech to heal, finance, and enliven the Christian life.[11] Although Hagin's message won widespread support, it was the empire building of Oral Roberts that gave the Faith movement solid footing. Their messages combined a Christological framework with the instrumentality of metaphysical religion, guaranteeing believers the ability to change their circumstances by tapping into new spiritual powers.[12] In so doing, the Faith movement, unlike the black prosperity gospels of the interwar period, appropriated metaphysical religion indirectly as an amplification of pentecostal notions of power.

The Reverend Frederick J. Eikerenkoetter (1935–2009), known to the world as Reverend Ike, gave the African American prosperity gospel its first national platform. A southerner who migrated to the black urban North and who blended pentecostal and spiritualist traditions, Reverend Ike's ministry echoed many of the metaphysical prosperity theologies of the first half of the twentieth century. But Reverend Ike also patterned his ministry and message after Oral Roberts, whose denominational independence, financial focus, and creative fundraising techniques he admired. Reverend Ike's prioritization of faith's instrumentality likely resulted from the stronger measure of metaphysical religion he injected into the prosperity gospel. Although the later faith teachers, black and white, rejected any metaphysical legacy and distanced themselves from the flamboyant Reverend Ike, no one forgot his fiery promises of material wealth for the right-thinking Christian. Reverend Ike's popular message served as a sturdy bridge across which subsequent preachers and participants would carry a black metaphysical—and heavily instrumental—Christianity into the future.[13]

Since the late 1970s, prosperity theology has risen with new vitality within African American religion.[14] Frederick K. C. Price, who counted himself the theological heir of Kenneth Hagin and Oral Roberts, became the preeminent African American prosperity preacher. His crusades, publications, sprawling megachurch, and nationwide television program advanced the Charismatic renewal that captivated black churches in the 1980s and 1990s. Price, alongside Keith Butler, Leroy Thompson, Eddie Long, Creflo Dollar, T. D. Jakes, and an emerging generation of black prosperity preachers, reflected the optimism of a rising black middle class, who thirsted for a gospel that made sense of their newfound economic gains. In so doing, they became prophets of what historian Scott Billingsley has termed a "second wave" of the neo-pentecostal movement.[15] This second wave washed black congregations—Pentecostal and historically black denominations alike—with an ideology of upward mobility dominated by Hagin's Word of Faith theology.[16]

By the 1990s, prosperity theology dominated African American popular religion. It saturated the programming of Black Entertainment Television, the covers of *Essence* magazine, and the gospel tunes of Shirley Caesar, accenting the upbeat over the blues. The "new black charismatics," as Billingsley called them, unlike their white counterparts, flourished inside as well as outside of denominational structures. Much to the consternation of denominational boards, many Faith pastors capitalized on the autonomy imbedded in Baptist and Pentecostal ecclesiology and preached their controversial prosperity gospel from denominational pulpits. Some even climbed to the highest ranks of leadership.[17] The fearless ones forged new paths. In 1994, Paul Morton and like-minded Charismatic Baptists formed the Full Gospel Baptist Church Fellowship, a denomination stacked with teaching on prosperity and the gifts of the Spirit. Although some famous black preachers had been educated and promoted by Rhema Bible Institute and Oral Roberts University, the African American Faith movement drew strength from multiple sources. Independent African American churches and leaders proved adept at supporting, educating, and promoting one another. A decade into the new millennium, black megachurches and itinerant preachers towered over the urban spiritual landscape.[18] Megachurches, bursting with almost half of American churchgoers, were disproportionately led by African American prosperity teachers. Their inflating churches predictably centered in urban black centers like Chicago, Detroit, Los Angeles, and Atlanta, home to the highest number of megachurches and African Americans.

The Victorious Faith Center was one of hundreds of small African American congregations swept up in the heterogeneous Faith movement. Locally, like many small, independent African American churches, it loosely associated with other like-minded churches, sharing ministers, church programs, worship events, and healing services.[19] Healing practices were largely shaped within the confines of these densely networked, immediate interactions and took place primarily in homes and churches. Electronic and printed religious media and itinerant preachers supplemented the spiritual practices of these local church bodies, as prosperity theology coursed through popular television, radio, books, seminars, and the rallies of traveling preachers.[20] These outside influences remained spiritual constants, religious resources that connected believers to the wider Faith movement as they offered the saints a host of solutions for their particular spiritual and physical needs.

## Spiritual Promises and the Laws of Faith

Pastor John Walton, the senior pastor of the Victorious Faith Center, relished the memory of his realization that "traditional" Christianity was dead. Reared in a black Baptist church in Durham, North Carolina, he had known nothing of miracles and spiritual gifts—just lively preaching and the boisterous praise of the assembled. One Sunday, a man interrupted the Baptist service, approaching the altar with the shrill repetition of "Praise Jesus! Praise Jesus!" Walton, though a layperson at the time, approached the pastor with a warning from God. "God said, 'That's not my spirit in him,'" Walton told the pastor. The Baptist pastor, Walton remembered, turned to him sharply.[21] "*You* do something!" he retorted.

"I ran up to the man, put my hands on him, and I declared 'In the name of the Lord Jesus, come OUT of this man!'" The man dropped to the ground, shrieking, and moved across the floor. Walton's eyes widened in the telling. "He moved across the floor like a snake. Like he had not a bone in his body." Walton grabbed the slithering demoniac by the leg as the man vomited up the spirit, which lay like a green, glistening sac on the church floor. In the chaos of the altar scene, Walton glanced back at his pastor. There he was, Walton continued, hiding behind the pulpit. Traditional Christianity, for all its Bible reading, praising, and community support, had failed. It was dead without the one thing Walton claimed that day, a word he repeated in his deep baritone: power.

Prosperity theology claims a power rooted in the operation of faith. Believers conceptualize faith as a causal agent, a power that actualizes events and objects in the real world. Faith acts as a force that reaches through the boundaries of materiality and into the spiritual realm, as if plucking objects from there and drawing them back into space and time. As Kenneth Hagin explained, "It is already real in the spirit realm. But we want it to become real in this physical realm where we live in the flesh."[22] Faith makes things "real," transcending the separation between two universes for the sake of each believer.

Faith is inextricably bound to the spoken word. Confession, the words people say, overcome circumstance, Hagin insisted. According to Mark 11:23, "whosoever shall say . . . and shall not doubt in his heart, but shall believe that those things which he saith shall come to pass; he shall have whatsoever he saith." Hagin's Bible brimmed with promises, and Jesus' comment that "you shall have what you say" offered a guarantee. Faith became the force that would actuate believers' very words. Speaking positive things out loud, called "positive confession," became a spiritual discipline. Believers expect their affirmations to release power (faith) to bring these assertions into reality.

Prosperity theology heralds divine health as a fundamental demonstration of the power of faith. Grounded in the thought of E. W. Kenyon and following well-established pentecostal precedents, the Faith movement promises divine health as a provision of the atonement, connecting Jesus' crucifixion with believers' physical healing. Using Isaiah 53:3–5, Faith teachers, though varying widely in interpretation and focus, agree on three fundamental ideas.[23] First, healing is God's divine intention for humanity. Second, Jesus' work on the cross effected not only redemption but also deliverance from the penalties of sin, namely, poverty, demonic interference, and sickness.[24] Third, God set up the laws of faith so that believers can access the power of the cross.[25] Believers' primary task is to live in the power of the resurrected Christ by applying faith to their circumstances, measuring their lives and bodies for evidence of spiritual power.[26]

Leaders perform divine health in its idealized form every Sunday. Many Faith celebrities have made their own healing into the centerpieces of their ministries, embodying God's healing power and the ability of believers to tap into that power. Oral Roberts, David Yonggi Cho, and Benny Hinn are but a few examples.[27] As the founder of the contemporary Faith movement, Kenneth Hagin's own healing became the standard for all subsequent healing narratives. An ill and bedridden teenager, stricken with tuberculosis, Hagin believed he was no longer sick after reading Mark 11:24: "Therefore I say unto you, What things soever ye desire, when ye pray, believe that ye receive them, and ye shall have them." As a result of Hagin's faith, he eschewed the devil's work in causing the illness and as a result: "I have not had one sick day in 45 years. I did not say that the devil hasn't attacked me. But before the day is out, I am healed."[28] Prosperity televangelists and megachurch pastors frequently cite their own divine health as the gold standard of faith, encouraging congregants to reflect prosperous living in their own bodies, minds, and circumstances.[29] From prosperity pulpits, television screens, and countless books guaranteeing the abundant life, Faith teachers embolden believers to put the laws of faith to physical use.

## Practices of Healing

"Does anyone need healing today?" Pastor Walton called out to the 80 assembled, just before the close of the service. During my time at VFC, I had seen dozens of people respond to his call for healing. A middle-aged man I recognized as new to the congregation approached the altar and the two quietly discussed his symptoms. "Get this man a chair." Walton said. "Sit down!" The congregation sat expectantly as Walton knelt before the seated man, holding one outstretched leg in his hands. He diagnosed the problem easily. "One leg is shorter than the other!" he exclaimed, and implored God to lengthen the other leg to match. "Oooh!" Walton exclaimed in surprise. "It jumped when I touched it just now!" We waited. Some moved quickly into prayer, both for the pastor and the patient. Pastor Walton prayed heartily, as he asked for God's healing touch. When he finished, the brief expected show of agility followed, as Pastor Walton asked the man to touch his toes several times, like an athlete warming up for a sprint. Everyone burst into applause. Walton smiled. "Praise Jesus!" someone called out.

From the pulpit, VFC preached a clear route to healing. Right standing with the divine focused on sacred alignment, a mystical interconnection that harmonized the believer with God. Prosperity theology posits that people share in God's healing power by activating their faith and tapping into God's spiritual laws. For the sick congregants of the Victorious Faith Center, healing restored mental and physical wholeness, aligning believers with God's divine intentions. These public acts of healing exhibited a moment of spiritual stasis, as believers reinvigorated their spiritual authority over the demonic causes of their illnesses. Psychological, social, behavioral, emotional, and physical causes could be rooted out and identified as spiritual realities: a spirit of cancer, a spirit of laziness, a spirit of jealousy, etc. As Pastor Walton argued, "It's all spiritual! It's all spiritual. It is! Because it deals with spirits." What outsiders categorized as distinct etiologies, Faith believers attributed to a single spiritual cause subject to an epistemic cure.

Within this Holy Spirit-centered framework, healing required belief and practice to mutually reinforce one another. Rather than accepting illness with passive resignation, prosperity believers understand the will as the master of the body.[30] As VFC believers understood their senses to be deceptive, ruled by what E. W. Kenyon called "sense knowledge," they did not simply wait for their bodies to assure them that healing had occurred. They *acted as if*—not only believed—they were well. A few examples, taken together, will illustrate the centrality of performances of faith. A respected elder taught Sunday school, where he urged believers to avoid negative confession by keeping their troubles to themselves. "If anyone asks," he said, mimicking a hobbled walk with a crutch, "just say 'I'm blessed! I'm going on in Christ!'" Rather than asking for prayer again and again, the believer must ignore "sense knowledge" and trust that God has already healed. Enacted faith would not be limited by circumstances. As he argued further: "On your deathbed you'd better be saying 'By his stripes, I am healed!'" The elder's instruction to mimic health was not hypocrisy, but rather, it imitated the desired outcome, entwining action and belief. Going through the motions of divine health, a practice known to late nineteenth-century faith cure advocates as "acting faith," it put performance on an equal footing with reality. Take the common occurrence of a VFC believer who, in receiving a revelation from Pastor Walton that he or she is healed, begins a shout (an ecstatic dance of praise). Or, to return to the case of the VFC member's public healing from a stunted leg, the man was not asked how he *felt* but rather to perform exercises, enacting a healed body. Performance and belief were linked so that believers acted out their healing before they identified symptoms to confirm it.

Believers expected to counteract even the most intractable foes. Demonic forces, manifested in any state of mental or physical distress, such as anxiety, cancer, or paralysis, were no match for the spiritual weapons prosperity believers had at hand. "Deliverance," the process of expelling demons, was chief among them. Although the church drew techniques for deliverance from a variety of sources, VFC members largely practiced methods popularized by Charismatics within Word of Faith circles in the early 1990s. Using a popular deliverance manual as a guide, the church began a ministry that earned it a local reputation as a deliverance specialist.[31] The deliverance team, men and women trained for spiritual warfare, would first privately question the participant about his or her past sins, asking a comprehensive list of questions designed to inventory the person's spiritual past. In what often took hours, the participant pored through the past and present to shine a light on all demonic manifestations embedded in habits, generational curses, and emotional distress. The team, through prayer and laying on of hands, commanded the devils, in Jesus' name, to be gone. In a spiritual practice referred to as "purging," the believer was coached through the act of coughing up the demons by vomiting.[32] This preliminary deliverance required total disclosure by the patient and sincere repentance, as an incomplete deliverance yielded the return of multiplied demonic forces. Once delivered, believers were encouraged to "take themselves through deliverance," purging the spirits in their bathrooms at home and praying the blood of Christ upon themselves (to invoke Jesus' atonement as salvation and protection.)

Good health required full participation in the liturgical and sacramental life of the church. Devout believers used the week as spiritual preparation for their corporate worship, often fasting, praying, and preparing themselves for what God might have in store. A heightened sense of spiritual intensity electrified Sunday mornings, particularly for those waiting to hear answers to their prayers. Suspended confirmation, a healing believed but not yet experienced, required believers to position themselves to be blessed. Although God's provision was frequently described as a direct channel, some language suggested a circuitous route between the waiting believer and his or her personal miracle. When bodies refused to be healed, the saints left room for answers to prayers that did not always arrive on schedule. "Some lessons can't be taught," so the saying went, "they can only be caught." Often, believers held out for a word of revelation from the pastor or a visiting evangelist. Prophetic revelations frequently manifested as visual cues; one visiting pastor, for example, described seeing clouds above the heads of those for whom he had a message. Angels, doves, dragons, and clouds of light leapt out of the realm of metaphor and danced around the sanctuary, showing God's anointed the spiritual climate. Pastor Walton's acute spiritual sensitivities allowed him to see and hear things "in the spirit," an ability that allowed him to monitor his congregants' faith lives.[33]

Those with chronic pain or problems did not revisit the altar again and again. As healing had been given once and for all, church life did not make liturgical space for those whose prayers had not yet manifested. Ruth, a pillar of VFC, lived in the not-yet. She did not yet experience the benefits of her faith, and she struggled with an ailment she would not speak aloud. Although Ruth had become one of my closest consultants and someone I considered a friend, she avoided being interviewed. Concerned, I asked Ruth's best friend and another close consultant, Anita. "Is she worried about having to talk about the fact that she—," I stumbled, looking for words, "hasn't been healed?" "No. No," Anita countered quickly. "She has been healed. She is just claiming her healing. No, I think she's worried about negatively confessing." Saints who had "claimed their healing" must maintain their faith until the physical evidence corresponded to the mind's assent, a process known as "keeping their healing." Spiritual vigilance characterized this period, as believers must be careful not to speak or act in any way that might hinder their blessing.

## Spiritual Competitors: Hoodoo and Medical Science

Hoodoo and other African American folk practices contended for the saints' allegiances. Although largely invisible to outside observers, hoodoo (known also as "conjure" or, in Georgia and South Carolina, "rootwork") has survived as a viable religious tradition in African American communities in the Anglo Protestant South. Church members at the Victorious Faith Center spoke openly about its unwelcome presence, either as a supplement to Christianity or as an alternative religious practice.

Hoodoo persisted as a religion of utility. It came to the Anglo Protestant South through African slaves who, despite large-scale conversion to Christianity during the Great Awakening, retained elements of their indigenous

religious traditions.[34] The African-based tradition that endured the Christian-
ization of slaves bore few of the markers of an "organized religion" found in
its Catholic voodoo or African Caribbean Santeria counterparts. Hoodoo
boasted no priests or priestesses, sacrificial offerings, gathered community,
or even devotion to ancestral spirits and deities.[35] Instead, hoodoo functioned
as a healing practice, rather than a cosmology. By definition, hoodoo referred
to "a system of magic by which individual 'workers' serve their clients." Most
often, believers who hired a hoodoo "doctor" or "worker" sought to protect
themselves from harm, particularly the evil intentions of others. Charms,
composed of symbolic ingredients (such as hair, roots, bones) acted as potent
spiritual agents. Clients sought charms capable of working for them, as in the
case of a woman who purchased a love charm to induce a cool bachelor to
marry. Clients also turned to hoodoo doctors to diagnose spiritual maladies.
Hoodoo workers discerned which illnesses were "unnatural," caused by the
"hex" or "trick" of a human enemy. For example, a hoodoo worker might have
identified a charm buried near someone's house as the origin of a patient's
disease. Although some concluded that the specialists' abilities came from
Satan, and others believed they came from God, most churchgoers agreed
that hoodoo held the power to heal or harm.[36]

For the sanctified believers of the Victorious Faith Center, hoodoo could be
called only one thing: witchcraft.[37] Although people joked about desperate
women who put "roots" in a man's food, an equivalent to love potions, the
matter evoked deadly seriousness. The African American Faith movement's
emphasis on the instrumentality of faith evoked a strong parallelism between
faith's and hoodoo's power to effect change, causing believers to draw thick
theological lines between them. In the prosperity gospel, negative circumstances visit those who fail to live by faith. Believers expertly sought out the
causes of any personal misfortune, from small matters like the common cold
to large matters like cancer or a car accident. In doing so, they often settled
upon two answers. First, in most cases, they assumed that their own actions
had failed them in some way. The cause and effect were generally parallel, as
small mistakes warranted small difficulties. For example, a negative word spoken at home may have led to a headache. Second, believers frequently concluded that Satan launched a direct attack on their lives. A car accident on the
way home from church, for example, could be interpreted to mean that the
devil hated faithful worship. In interpreting misfortune as an answer to either
sin or righteousness, believers exhibited the flexibility of interpretation, as the
seeming rigidity and certainty of prosperity theology was molded to meet the
spiritual needs of individual believers. Many of the larger and more enduring
problems believers faced were understood as evil forces. In this light, hoodoo
workers' use of hidden charms, secret attacks, and defenses exemplified Satan's
clandestine attacks. God's faithful must be alert to the spiritual forces working
against them. Believers exchanged stories of men who fell under the spell of

witches and married them, unaware of Satan's shadow over their lives. Pastor Walton warned them about "roots" secretly placed in their food or drink.

Although Satan's attacks may come from anywhere, hoodoo influences do not. Churchgoers pointed the finger at South Carolina. As several members reported, North Carolinians drove down to South Carolina to do rootwork or buy charms. But as hoodoo historian Carolyn Long, author of *Spiritual Merchants*, described, hoodoo flourished as a centuries-old healing tradition up and down the southeastern coast, from northern Florida to southern North Carolina.[38]

Hoodoo formed a dark counterpart to the Victorious Faith Center's triumphant faith. On a community level, it served as an ugly reminder of past pain. Pastor Walton, during a Sunday school lesson to committed members, recounted their collective African religious past, "the religion of our ancestors," as one of witchcraft and satanic worship.[39] Believing that circumstances must bend to the will of every believer, Pastor Walton interpreted African American history as one not only of hardship, but also of failure. Slavery, poverty, and suffering must be, in part, God's response to their African witchcraft. Although this interpretation may seem shocking to outsiders, Walton's conclusion that black Americans merited the horrors of slavery must be tempered by his belief that all suffering is temporary. God could have and would have rescued all who called out for him.

Hoodoo workers and VFC believers share a faith in the power of religious objects to prevent, diagnose, and cure illness. Hoodoo workers' reliance upon symbolic agents—objects representative of or invested with proximate spiritual power—resembles the widespread pentecostal use of handkerchiefs, cloths, or ribbons to facilitate healing.[40] Many Faith teachers, black and white, borrow freely from this pentecostal heritage in the sacred use of commonplace objects, particularly handkerchiefs, as one divine healing practice among many. In so doing, hoodoo and the prosperity gospel write with an overlapping spiritual grammar, ruled by unseen forces, spiritual power, and supernatural beings and expressed by ritual objects.[41]

For example, famous pentecostal healers like Oral Roberts and William Branham made such "points of contact" a staple of divine healing, asking believers to place the blessed object on the afflicted area. At times, preachers invested the objects with symbolic as well as spiritual value. Prosperity pastor Creflo Dollar advised the saints to cure poverty with dollar bills hidden in their shoes.[42] An anointed ribbon clutched during prayer or a handkerchief mailed by a famous evangelist was not simply a reminder of faith, but a vehicle for it. Resting on Acts 19:12, African American saints had long used symbolic agents, called "contacts," in healing services, as a special transference of God's power to the afflicted.[43] Victorious Faith Center churchgoers fondly remembered Pastor Walton's former use of an anointed handkerchief as a powerful spiritual era. But Walton had set aside the handkerchief so as not to seem reliant on it.[44]

The Holy Spirit can be channeled through objects or visit without them, the saints reminded me.

In short, hoodoo promised people revelation, a clear view of the hidden magic working for or against them. And God's anointed preachers, who claimed their own revelatory sight, formed the perfect heroes to overcome the feared conjurers. As a whole, those who relied on hoodoo and those who did not concluded similarly: evil attacks linger everywhere. Secret sources of spiritual evil must be ferreted out to restore emotional and physical well-being.

Within many African American prosperity congregations, medical science has proved to be a common and no less insidious threat to faith. This has by no means been a consensus opinion. The Faith movement mirrored the wider pentecostal acceptance of medicine, holistic remedies, and, to a limited degree, psychology as methods of divine healing.[45] Most teachers, black and white, displayed an increasing comfort with medicine as *part* of God's divine plan for human health.[46] A thick minority strand of African American prosperity teachers, however, railed against medical science as the panacea for sick bodies.

Spiritual healing, for many African Americans, may have been the only available treatment. As theologian Tammy Williams observed, "[I]n a country in which forty-two million persons lack health insurance, twenty percent of whom are African American, Jesus may be the only doctor that some African Americans encounter on a regular basis."[47] But not so in Durham, known as the City of Medicine. Unlike many underinsured African American communities, VFC exhibited a high level of familiarity, knowledge, and access to the health care system. Many of the members worked for Duke University Hospital as health care providers—nurses, laboratory technicians, phlebotomists, pharmacy assistants, etc.—and knew the medical solutions available to them during a time of illness. Their critique of the health care system stemmed from broader cultural sources, including the past and present failures of the health care system to provide African Americans with color-blind treatment. Racism dressed as impartial science, seen clearly in intelligence theories, Social Darwinism, and eugenics, has cataloged the supposed biological, social, and intellectual inferiority of the black population.[48] The majority of African Americans, unlike their white counterparts, distrust both biological and social explanations for the causes of mental illness; the former implies black genetic inferiority, while the latter characterizes the black family as dysfunctional.[49] In this way, African American Faith churches reflect a popular mistrust of biomedical treatment and the categorization of disease, denying the authority of the health care system to restore black bodies to health.

Theological differences further refine these broader cultural sources of alienation from the medical establishment. Believers protest that doctors, hospitals, and pharmaceutical companies promise materialistic solutions to what the Faith movement deems to be a spiritual problem. Unlike Christian

Scientists, Faith believers do not deny the physical reality of illness. Yet, prosperity theology, drawing on its metaphysical (particularly new thought) heritage, does deny that the causes of illness originate outside the spiritual mind. Victoria, a head nurse at a major Duke medical facility, explained the distinction during our discussion of how to live by faith while simultaneously working as a medical professional. I wondered aloud how she and others could diagnose illness without negatively confessing, since labeling the disease *as such* would speak it into existence (or confirm its reality to the believer). Instead of saying "This is what it *is*," she explained, a believing doctor could say "This is what we *found.*" Illness, as material reality, is not an illusion or the mind's projection. It is, Faith believers posit, a physical manifestation of a spiritual problem. To VFC members, illness took on a different ontological status. They did not contest biomedical accounts of its symptoms, but disagreed on the nature of its causes and cure.

Members of VFC accepted medical intervention at different levels. At the level of diagnosis, most accepted biomedical science's authority to name the disease. Although they were warned by the pastor not to repeat it and to whisper it only in prayer, no one questioned its effects. Most believers accepted medical treatment as a supplement to divine healing, known as practicing "according to your faith." This provision allowed the saints to accept treatment for more complicated illnesses while leaving smaller problems to the power of faith. From the pulpit, VFC churchgoers were encouraged to start with a small ailment—a headache—and have faith commensurate to overcome. Walton himself had overcome his reliance on eyeglasses that way, as he fought through initial headaches and blurred eyesight before gradually regaining clear vision. Members frequently reminded each other to "start with a headache," using positive confession and the efficacy of faith to overcome small tests before moving on to larger ones. The testimony of one VFC member provides a helpful illustration. In being advised that her gallbladder was about to burst, the believer underwent an ultrasound, but leapt off the examination table once the preliminary screening seemed positive. She counted it a success that she did not have to undergo surgery, though occasional pain continued to bother her. Medicine, for many saints, was diagnostic but not curative. Most VFC believers accepted some health care intervention as an unwanted necessity, as vaccinations were prerequisites for children to attend school and for anyone to travel abroad. As the processes of globalization heightened the threat of disease, these Faith believers, if they recognized these processes, did not blink. Preventive medicine, such as flu shots or regular doctor visits, were avoided as a marker of spiritual honor. Armed with excellent health care if they wanted it, believers argued that they already had true "preventive medicine" in a spiritual bottle, through fasting, tithing, prayer, and worship.

Medical healing posed the most direct threat to the logic of faith. Medicine relies upon the diagnosis of symptoms, signs that believers called "lying symptoms" because they rely upon "sense knowledge" over "revelation." Head-aches were a useful and frequently cited example. Just as Tylenol does not cure a headache but simply numbs the pain, believers indicted medicine as inca-pable of treating the root of the problem. Medical certainty in materialistic so-lutions would contribute to believers' ultimate demise, the saints argued, as people, overcome by their sense knowledge, would not develop the faith required to subdue their disease. As Pastor Walton preached, most believers with advanced illnesses did not recover because their symptoms grew stronger than their faith. Medical science bolstered confidence in the material over the spiritual realm, doing harm to true faith.

## Explanations for Suffering

How did believers within the Faith movement reconcile their beliefs with the persistence of disease or, worst of all, death? Funerals served as a perpetual reminder to believers of the limitations of faith. For the duration of an illness, however intractable, congregants and leaders traded testimonies of sudden recoveries, miraculous cures, and God's persistent interventions. Expectations ran high. Pastor Walton, like most contemporary prosperity teachers, fre-quently reminded believers that God promised them 70–80 years of divine health.[50] Although church members would protest that it happened less fre-quently in their midst than in other communities, tragedy visited the Victo-rious Faith Center. Spouses passed away unexpectedly, children were lost to diseases, members perished in accidents. Although hardship could later be deemed a test, the finality of death revoked any license for retrospective blessing. In a spiritual cosmos dominated by possibility thinking, funerals marked a true ending.

During my time at VFC, Judy, a long-time member in her 60s, suffered from a brain tumor, failed to respond to chemotherapy, and passed away. Her participation in church life had grown increasingly limited, and as her health waned, her visibility also diminished. Privately, the church rallied around Judy's grieving widower, providing him with meals, assistance, and comfort. Publicly—in sermon, song, tithing, and prayer requests—the church passed over her illness and subsequent death in silence. While sick-ness and death, in general, proved to be constant topics, her death, other than an announcement of her funeral, received neither positive nor negative acknowledgment.[51]

Four categories of interpreting "failure" emerged from my interviews with members and my ethnographic observation that may contextualize the silence surrounding Judy's death. First, and most commonly discussed among believers, was suspension of judgment. Believers frequently declared themselves unable or unwilling to draw conclusions from another person's difficult circumstances. Although the physical evidence appeared to confirm a member's spiritual distress, observers chose not to, in their words, "judge." When a soloist's congested voice cracked on the high notes, or a speaker sniffled into the microphone, shouts of encouragement only could be heard in the pews. In all cases, believers continued to cite their unfailing certainty in God's blessings and refused to apply their conclusions to their neighbor's plight. For example, Victoria, a medical professional in her 50s, described seeing another church member exiting a discount department store with purchases. The member, embarrassed by having bought cold medication, immediately confessed to Victoria. Victoria remembered thinking, "I don't care what you have in the bag! I can't [even] see what you have in the bag!" But she replied to the parishioner: "I'm not God!" Victoria's silence over a fellow believer's spiritual misstep was rooted in a cultivated humility. As she explained:

> I've learned not to judge people. When I see people prostituting, drug
> addicts, I see it like this: there but for the grace of God go I. It could
> be me. So I don't judge people. I don't judge people when they're
> sick. If they're in the hospital, I wouldn't say, "OH, YOU DON'T
> HAVE ANY FAITH." I always say, you don't know what you're going
> to do if you're put in that person's position.

Although Victoria's career in the medical field frequently allowed her to see fellow churchgoers as they sought out medical (and therefore less spiritual solutions), she declared herself unable, as "not God," to pronounce a critical verdict. In the difficult months that followed the congregation's loss of Judy, silence may have been mixed with charity and a suspension of judgment.[52]

Second, silence may have carried lingering condemnation. In this spirit-centered demonization of disease, bodies charted a spiritual territory. Preachers encouraged the saints to examine their own bodies for signs of Satan's triumph over divine health. Any other conclusion appeared to mitigate death's harsh lessons. "A baby dies and a pastor says 'God has a plan,'" Walton said, shaking his head. "No! That baby was stolen [by Satan]."[53] Death meant failure, the failure on the part of the believer to win the spiritual battle against illness. "Your biggest enemy is not Satan! It's yourself," Walton preached weekly.[54] Further, as Faith theology teaches that healing is granted once and for all, some ill saints avoided or were discouraged from asking for continued help, as it might identify them as faithless. For example, members typically asked for public prayer for others, or waited until a triumphant testimony before acknowledging an illness (and subsequent healing). In contrast to the black church's historic position of solidarity with a suffering Christ, VFC believers chose a once-and-for-all savior and an ensuing silent illness over public shame.[55]

Third, contrary to church teaching, some believers quietly concluded that illness could portend righteous suffering. Although the saints expected that their faith would be measured in their bodies—their personal health—making material reality the evidence of immaterial faith, some would not blame themselves for what they experienced. Suffering believers referred often to the book of Job, where they found a righteous man who suffered without blame. Ruth, who taught Sunday school from a wheelchair, described her predicament as a "Job moment." Setting aside the hard causality between faith and health, Ruth argued confidently, though not publicly, that her suffering was a difficult test of faithfulness. As her reference to Job implied, her misfortune would dissolve to reveal only empty accusations and a righteous sufferer.

Fourth, some members of VFC questioned the church's teachings that tragedy implied any individual failure. In whispers, mutters, and private conversations, some believers struggled with the theodicy implied by any personal loss. How could a good God allow suffering? Or, in this case, how could any church heap condemnation on tragedy? The public silence muted public grief, creating friction between some churchgoers and the church itself. As an ethnographer, I often heard these complaints framed as an example of overcoming the negative confession of others, as members recalled their dealings with fellow believers who expressed doubt, anger, or frustration. In an environment where speech acts were closely monitored and controlled, parishioners rarely disagreed openly with the church's teachings.

Within African American Faith communities, the multiple interpretations of the meaning of suffering often yielded silence. The silence may have reflected a breakdown in spiritual vocabulary to express the inexpressible: that God had somehow failed or that a loved one had. In the intimate and totalizing spiritual environment of a Faith church, where each member's health, wealth, and circumstances stood on display, the ambivalent silence might simply have allowed for a deep breath, a little space that mitigated the anxiety of revealing both the good and bad that unfolded in each person's life.

Sitting between the grieving widower and Ruth's wheelchair on a Sunday morning, I listened to Pastor Walton preach against resigning oneself to death. As the sermon detailed God's promises to provide perpetual health, Pastor Walton did not seem convinced that believers could ever meet the same end as nonbelievers. Famous healers like A. A. Allen and Smith Wigglesworth, Walton reminded listeners, raised the faithful from the dead.[56] In the everyday healing practices of the African American Faith movement, faith operated as a spiritual guarantee, drawing health and prosperity into the lives of people willing to suspend naturalistic explanations for supernatural, pneumatological causality. From where I sat, divine healing did not always seem plausible. But through God, the saints reminded me, all things were possible.

NOTES

1 Mark David Hanby, "Look What the Lord Has Done" (Exaltation Music, 1974).

2 Believers debate vigorously among themselves about the preferred term for this movement. Insiders reject the label "health and wealth" as derogatory. The term "prosperity" garners a mixed reaction, as some worry that it evokes a materialistic framework. I interchange the term "prosperity gospel," preferred by many scholars, with the more inclusive phrase "Faith movement," as it is both comfortably used by insiders and it encompasses a broader denominational scope than simply "Word of Faith," which refers to the theology of Kenneth E. Hagin. For sociological and historical treatments of Faith churches, see Milmon Harrison, *Righteous Riches: The Word of Faith Movement in Contemporary African American Religion* (New York: Oxford University Press, 2005); Gerardo Marti, *Hollywood Faith: Holiness, Prosperity, and Ambition in a Los Angeles Church* (New Brunswick, N.J.: Rutgers University Press, 2008).

3 Many members would protest the term "movement" as they frequently deny influences from one another and from institutional and theological sources. While this speaks to the denominational and theological diversity among pastors, the originality of each teacher also serves a practical function. Pastors' health, wealth, and charmed lives serve as the bedrock of their ministries, as they offer themselves as living examples of how prosperity theology works. As such, teachers tender their biographies as revelation, and this is not conducive to the acknowledgment of shared influences. Without overstating the unity of this fractured assembly, this chapter assumes theological and lived continuities among black prosperity churches.

4 Miroslav Volf, "Materiality of Salvation: An Investigation in the Soteriologies of Liberation and Pentecostal Theologies," *Journal of Ecumenical Studies* 26.3 (1989): 447–467; Brown, introduction to this volume.

5 The "Victorious Faith Center," a pseudonym I have assigned to the church, consists of approximately 80 members. In January 2007, I began my ethnography at this church as a graduate student in Professor Glenn Hinson's class "The Art of Ethnography" at the University of North Carolina, Chapel Hill. I continued to attend as a participant-observer and researcher until the summer of 2008. After 18 months of regular Sunday attendance (and, often, attendance at the Wednesday evening services), I completed a dozen interviews, though many more informal conversations took place over lunch, coffee, and email. Initially, I adopted a collaborative ethnographic model, attempting to involve consultants in a shared interviewing, writing, and editing process. I soon realized that, for many participants, this method might be prohibitive and possibly harmful. Their theology commands positive speech, and some consultants saw being interviewed as tantamount to "negative confession," the proclamation of disease or misfortune that *causes* these circumstances to be actualized. My commitment to them and my moral responsibility dictated that I switch to a less interactive model, which still aimed for the honesty, vulnerability, and accessibility that mark collaborative ethnography. I solicited feedback from those interviewees for whom negative confession would not be an issue, either because what they said was positive or because they did not rigorously monitor their speech practices.

6 Following Catherine Albanese, American metaphysical religion replaces "occultism," "gnosticism," or "harmonialism" as the umbrella term for European

magico-religious traditions (e.g., spiritualism, new thought) that center on individual and communal pursuits of spiritual power. Metaphysical religion is primarily magic, wielded to manipulate material and spiritual realms and drawing believers to a personal restoration and connection to a greater spiritual plane. See Catherine Albanese, *A Republic of Mind and Spirit: A Cultural History of American Metaphysical Religion* (New Haven, Conn.: Yale University Press, 2007).

7 See R. Marie Griffith, *Born Again Bodies* (Berkeley: University of California Press, 2004).

8 For accounts of alternative black prosperity theologies, see Jill Watts, *God, Harlem U.S.A.: The Father Divine Story* (Berkeley: University of California Press, 1995); Jonathan L. Walton, *Watch This! The Ethics and Aesthetics of Black Televangelism* (New York: New York University Press, 2009), 47–74; Marie Dallam, *Daddy Grace: A Celebrity Preacher and His House of Prayer* (New York: New York University Press, 2007).

9 A vivid example of this combinatory impulse can be seen in black spiritualism, a fluid assemblage of Catholicism, voodoo, hoodoo, metaphysical spiritualism, and African American Protestantism. Newborn congregations of spiritualists sprang up across the black urban North, and, by the 1930s, black spiritualists were the fastest growing religious communities among African Americans. To be sure, black spiritualism remained a modest movement, a tiny fraction of the African American Protestant majority. Albanese, *Republic of Mind and Spirit*, 474. For a history of black spiritualism, see Hans Baer and Merrill Singer, *African-American Religion in the Twentieth Century: Varieties of Protest and Accommodation*, 2nd ed. (Knoxville: University of Tennessee Press, 2002), 183–215. For a discussion of the interaction of new thought with black spiritualism, see Darnise C. Martin, *Beyond Christianity: African Americans in a New Thought Church* (New York: New York University Press, 2005), 37–59.

10 Healing remained a vital aspect of the Faith movement; it had been a persistent theme from pentecostalism's inception. For the most comprehensive historical account of the revivals that gave way to the Faith movement, see David Edwin Harrell, *All Things Are Possible: The Healing and Charismatic Revivals in Modern America* (Bloomington: Indiana University Press, 1975), 135–239; for the movement's major figures since World War II, see Scott Billingsley, *It's a New Day: Race and Gender in the Modern Charismatic Movement* (Tuscaloosa: University of Alabama Press, 2008).

11 There is considerable debate about the sources of E. W. Kenyon's theology. Although there is persuasive evidence that Hagin plagiarized Kenyon's work, I find Dale Simmons and Geir Lie compelling in their contention that Kenyon appropriated metaphysical religion much more selectively and "evangelically" than McConnell and others have detailed. See D. R. McConnell, *A Different Gospel* (Peabody, Mass.: Hendrickson, 1988); Dale H. Simmons, *E. W. Kenyon and the Postbellum Pursuit of Peace, Power, and Plenty* (London: Scarecrow, 1997); Geir Lie, *E. W. Kenyon: Cult Founder or Evangelical Minister?* (Oslo: Refleks, 2003).

12 Catherine Bowler, "Positive Thinking," in *The Encyclopedia of Religion in America*, ed. by Charles H. Lippy and Peter W. Williams (Washington, D.C.: CQ, 2010), 1734–1737.

13 Here, I am indebted to Jonathan Walton, *Watch This!* 73, who argues that Reverend Ike served as a "connectional" figure between the interwar and

contemporary black media forms, namely contemporary televangelism and religious race records and radio of the interwar era. I suggest that prosperity preachers, in drawing from Ike, taught a prosperity gospel once-removed from his explicitly metaphysical sources.

14  Billingsley, *It's a New Day*, 104–129.

15  Ibid., 13.

16  Here I follow Shayne Lee in his cautious inclusion of T. D. Jakes among prosperity preachers. See Shayne Lee, *T. D. Jakes: America's New Preacher* (New York: NYU, 2005), 98–122. See also Lee's examination of how Jakes simultaneously distances himself from the extremes of prosperity teaching in Shayne Lee and Phillip Luke Sinitiere, *Holy Mavericks: Evangelical Innovators and the Spiritual Marketplace* (New York: New York University, 2009), 53–75. African American churches seem to have discovered prosperity theology at the same time as Arlene Sánchez Walsh's Latina/o Faith churches did.

17  Among Pentecostals, Charles Ellis III, pastor of the Detroit megachurch Greater Grace Temple, serves as the assistant presiding bishop of the Pentecostal Assemblies of the World; in 2009, the Church of God in Christ appointed Bob Jackson, pastor of Acts Full Gospel Church, as the jurisdictional bishop for Mexico. Kenneth Marcus's Turner Chapel AME Church and Jamal Harrison-Bryant's Empowerment Temple AME Church championed a gentle prosperity gospel among Methodists.

18  Walton, *Watch This!* 106–107.

19  For an excellent treatment of the Holy Spirit in sanctified churches in North Carolina, see Glenn Hinson, *Fire in my Bones: Transcendence and the Holy Spirit in African American Gospel* (Philadelphia: University of Pennsylvania Press, 2000).

20  For a helpful summary of black televangelism and megachurch preachers, see Walton, *Watch This!* 2–4.

21  Pastor John Walton, interview by author, Durham, North Carolina, 3 Feb. 2007.

22  Kenneth E. Hagin, *In Him*, 42nd ed. (Tulsa, Okla.: Kenneth Hagin Ministries, 1980), 11.

23  Isaiah 53:5: "But he was wounded for our transgressions, he was bruised for our iniquities: the chastisement of our peace was upon him; and with his stripes we are healed" (AV).

24  Freedom from demonic influences was not automatic, as believers had to cast out any demons that still resided within them. The power of faith can be guaranteed, but believers must put it to work.

25  There was some debate within the Faith movement about the degree to which anyone could access the power of faith, regardless of holiness. Lydia Walton, the First Lady of VFC, argued that anyone could see its power without personal faith, as she had begun "naming it and claiming it" before she understood its implications.

26  Prosperity theology's obsession with "evidence" stems from its amplified pentecostal understanding of "signs and wonders." Authentic Christianity must bear witness to itself, not simply in the truth of its teachings but by the supernatural trail following it.

27  Both Oral Roberts and David Yonggi Cho claimed healing from tuberculosis, and Benny Hinn from stuttering.

28  Robert Bowman quoting Kenneth Hagin, *The Name of Jesus* (Tulsa, Okla.: Kenneth Hagin Ministries, 1979), 133. Claims to perfect health also affect the way that prosperity teachers narrate the deaths of the significant expositors of their message. Faith celebrity Kenneth Copeland, for instance, claimed that E. W. Kenyon and Smith Wigglesworth announced their own deaths and passed away on their own terms. As Copeland wrote in *Walking in the Realm of the Miraculous* (Fort Worth, Tex.: KCP, 1979), 72–73, "when the time comes for you to depart from this life, you will leave your physical body *on purpose* instead of being driven out of it by sickness or disease" (original emphasis). Contrary to Kenyon's daughter's eyewitness account that Kenyon died from cancer, teachers continue to re-narrate his death as resulting merely from old age, thereby further evidencing his faith. Similarly, Hagin is described as dying peacefully at age 86, having simply put his head down one morning after eating breakfast; critics note that Hagin claimed to have been healed of heart problems at age 16, yet he was repeatedly hospitalized for cardiovascular failures—including on the day of his death.

29  One of the most influential prosperity teachers of the 1980s, Jim Bakker, retreated from prosperity theology after he was imprisoned for fraud. Just as upwardly mobility and prosperity theology go hand in hand, so too rapid downward mobility may loosen the theological connection between circumstances and God's favor.

30  The Faith movement inherited its negative view of suffering from the divine healing movement of the late nineteenth century, which, as Heather Curtis demonstrates in her essay in this volume, contested "a long-standing and still-pervasive Protestant devotional tradition that linked bodily suffering with spiritual holiness and valorized patient resignation as the proper Christian response to affliction." Faith believers similarly rejected the notion that God might send sickness for the good of the patient.

31  The church used this Baptist handbook as a deliverance manual: Frank Hammond and Ida Mae Hammond, *Pigs in the Parlor: A Practical Guide to Deliverance* (Kirkwood, Mo.: Impact, 1973).

32  This understanding of purging was based on early Charismatic leaders Don Basham and Derek Prince's teachings that Christians could be targets for demonic activity and that "in most cases the spirits seem to leave through the mouth." Don Basham, *Deliver Us from Evil* (Washington Depot, Conn.: Chosen, 1972), 206–207; Derek Prince, *They Shall Expel Demons: What You Need to Know about Demons—Your Invisible Enemies* (Washington Depot, Conn.: Chosen, 1998), 212–214.

33  Laypeople infrequently offer revelations or claim to sense things in the spirit that take on larger meaning for the church as a whole. Lay revelations may inspire individuals, but leaders are expected to provide the more dramatic gifts and anointings.

34  Following Melville Herskovits's *The Myth of the Negro Path* (New York: Harper, 1941) and Albert Raboteau's *Slave Religion* (New York: Oxford University Press, 1978), most scholars agree that African religions as systems collapsed, but that fragments ("survivals") of an African spiritual heritage remain. For an excellent historiographical summary, see Paul Harvey, "Black Protestantism: A Historiographical Appraisal," in

*American Denominational History: Perspectives on the Past, Prospects for the Future*, ed.
Keith Harper (Tuscaloosa: University of Alabama Press, 2008), 120–146. I am
persuaded by Yvonne P. Chireau's argument in *Black Magic: Religion and the African
American Conjuring Tradition* (Berkeley: University of California Press, 2003), 151, that
the African American conjure ("supernaturalism") tradition is one such African-
derived tradition, which "coexists with Christianity as an alternative strategy for
interacting with the spiritual realm."

35 Carolyn Long, *Spiritual Merchants: Religion, Magic, and Commerce* (Knoxville:
University of Tennessee Press, 2001), 74.

36 Ibid., 75.

37 "Witchcraft" itself was an inclusive category. Besides hoodoo and voodoo, it
included a variety of "alternative" therapies, such as yoga, acupuncture, and
meditation. Pastor Walton preached vigorously against practices like yoga, though it
did not surface in any interviews with congregants as a concern. In addressing hoodoo
and voodoo, however, it may be difficult for scholars to access the lived religion of the
participants. As Long addressed in her introduction to *Spiritual Merchants*, these folk
practices, if not castigated as demonic, are perceived to be an embarrassment to the
African American community. At VFC, if participants dabbled in these practices, they
did not say so. Regardless of whether VFC congregants ever encountered hoodoo
directly, I draw here on their familiarity with it as a spiritual alternative.

38 In these Low Country black communities, African religion survived, in part,
because of the greater autonomy afforded to slaves. See Long, *Spiritual Merchants*,
71–96.

39 Although he did not in this particular instance, Walton taught that all must
repent and break the generational curses that bind people to a demonic past. All
people need to free themselves from the demonic heritage, which people pass on to
their children.

40 The Faith movement has borrowed many devotional practices from its
pentecostal heritage. In particular, many Faith teachers, black and white, continue the
sacred use of commonplace objects, particularly handkerchiefs, as one divine healing
practice among many. Historian R. Marie Griffith, in her investigation of pentecostal
prayer cloths, documented their widespread use from pentecostalism's inception
through the 1950s and 1960s, when Oral Roberts made them a staple of his ministry.
Roberts, one of the pioneers of the Faith movement, effectively reaffirmed their use as
a "manifestation of mediated grace." See Griffith, "Material Devotion: Pentecostal
Prayer Cloths," interview in the Material History of American Religion Project
*Newsletter* (Spring 1997): 1–3, http://www.materialreligion.org/journal/handkerchief.
html (accessed 13 July 2009).

41 The overlapping influences of pentecostalism, conjure (including hoodoo and
voodoo), and black spiritualism have infused a minority of black Protestant traditions
with strong doses of pentecostal, African, and metaphysical magic. For instance,
Bishop Charles Mason, the founder of the Church of God in Christ, the largest black
Pentecostal denomination, moved between conjure and pentecostalism to gain
spiritual guidance. Mason divined spiritual direction from his collection of sacred
objects, including "roots, branches, and vegetables that he consulted as 'sources for
spiritual revelations,' revisiting the tradition of conjuring charms"; Chireau, *Black*

*Magic*, 109–111. As mentioned earlier, black spiritualism added metaphysical categories to black supernaturalism; see Martin, *Beyond Christianity*, 37–59.

42  Stephanie Y. Mitchem, *Name It and Claim It? Prosperity Preaching in the Black Church* (Cleveland, Ohio: Pilgrim, 2007), 76–77.

43  Chireau, *Black Magic*, 110.

44  That Pastor Walton stopped using the handkerchief points to the ongoing tension between sacred and profane uses of objects. The ritual use of the handkerchief stands in tension with an emphasis on the sufficiency of positive confession, as prosperity theology teaches that the spiritual requires no material medium. However, it might also signal that congregants, drawing on voodoo, hoodoo, or black spiritualist ideas of sacred relics, began to see the object as invested with its own power. The term "contact" itself reflects an intentional distancing from undesirable spiritual corollaries—icon, relic, sacrament—all of which point to Catholicism and perceived superstitions.

45  See Joseph Williams, "The Transformation of Pentecostal Healing 1906–2006" (Ph.D. diss., Florida State University, 2008).

46  A few examples serve to illustrate Faith teachers' acceptance of "naturalistic" remedies: Benny Hinn's ongoing partnership with Eric R. Braverman, M.D.; Joel Osteen's *Healthy Living* DVD series; Paula White's co-authored book with her fitness trainer, *The Ten Commandments of Health and Wellness* (Tampa, Fla.: Paula White Enterprises, 2007).

47  Tammy R. Williams, "Is There a Doctor in the House? Reflections on the Practice of Healing in African American Churches," in *Practicing Theology: Beliefs and Practices in Christian Life*, ed. Miroslav Volf and Dorothy C. Bass (Grand Rapids, Mich.: Eerdmans, 2002), 97.

48  W. Michael Byrd and Linda A. Clayton, *An American Health Dilemma*, 2 vols. (New York: Routledge, 2000–2002).

49  Brittany S. Carlton, "Mental Illness in the African American Community," unpublished paper, submitted for course on Religion, Illness, and Healing taught by Candy Gunther Brown, Indiana University, 20 April 2009.

50  Psalm 90:10: "As for the days of our life, they contain seventy years, or if due to strength, eighty years." For a theological examination of long life in Word of Faith theology, see Paul L. King, *Only Believe: Examining the Origin and Development of Classic and Contemporary "Word of Faith" Theologies* (Tulsa, Okla.: Word and Spirit Press, 2008), 300–308.

51  Healing practices vary widely among African Americans who participate in the Faith movement. For a comparison of traditional and Word of Faith black healing practices, see Williams, "Is There a Doctor in the House?"

52  Cf. similar arguments made by certain South Indian pentecostals in Bergunder's essay in this volume.

53  Congregational visit (4 Feb. 2007).

54  Congregational visit (3 Feb. 2008).

55  Other theological explorations of the Faith movement have made similar critiques. As D. R. McConnell argues in *A Different Gospel* (Peabody, Mass.: Hendrickson, 1988), 166, "The time when a dying believer needs his faith the most is when he is told that he has it the least. . . . Perhaps the most inhuman fact revealed

about the Faith movement is this: when its members die, they die alone." See also
King, *Only Believe*, 301; Hank Hanegraaff, *Christianity in Crisis* (Eugene, Ore.: Harvest
House, 1993), 259–60. As Arlene Sánchez Walsh argues in this volume, the liberating
qualities of this theology should not be overlooked. African American Faith teachers
like T. D. Jakes and Frederick Price reject the sacralization of suffering for similar
reasons as Sánchez Walsh's Latina/o believers.

56  Smith Wigglesworth, *Smith Wigglesworth on Healing* (New Kensington, Pa.:
Whitaker House, 1999).

# 5

# Jesus as the Great Physician: Pentecostal Native North Americans within the Assemblies of God and New Understandings of Pentecostal Healing

*Angela Tarango*

Eight days after being "saved" at a New Year's Eve service in the mid-1930s in Montreal, Quebec, Rodger Cree, a 17-year-old Mohawk, experienced baptism in the Holy Spirit. He recalled, "I saw a ball of fire that was lodged in the ceiling—when that ball of fire touched my head, I began to speak in a different language, altogether. Supernatural."[1] A desire to go into the ministry seized Cree, and he enrolled at a French Canadian Bible college. While growing up on a small reserve outside Montreal, Cree had experienced racial prejudice at a young age, which gave him cause to distrust and dislike French Canadians. Upon entering Bible college, he was tested: "I remember going to school and walking and I heard someone say (in French) 'the savage has come.' The Holy Spirit kept me from turning around—I learned how to deal with those people."[2] For Cree, learning to heal from and overcome his own prejudices defined his religious experience as both a Pentecostal and an indigenous person. Even though Cree experienced physical healing later in life during a bout with rheumatic fever, it was the emotional and mental healing from hatred and mistrust that stayed with him. During the middle decades of the twentieth century, Cree was one of a handful of North

American native Pentecostal leaders who began to speak of pentecostal healing in terms different from those of their white counterparts; for native believers, pentecostal healing went beyond the physical; encompassed healing from hatred, mistrust of white North Americans, and broken promises and treaties; and focused on reconciliation and divine judgment.[3]

Pentecostalism offered a distinct religious experience for Native American believers, which differed greatly from other forms of Christianity. Christian missionary work to native peoples in the Americas has a long and painful history, and Protestant evangelical, mainline, and Catholic groups created a multitude of problems when they confronted native cultures during the classical missionary period (the eighteenth and nineteenth centuries). Historian William McLoughlin succinctly sums up these problems: "The three great stumbling blocks in accepting Christianity were its failure to address the basic issues of corporate harmony, bountiful harvests, and sacred healing."[4] By the time Assemblies of God (AG) missionaries began evangelizing indigenous peoples in the 1920s, centuries of colonization had wrecked traditional native life. The ideal of corporate harmony, or balance, was gone; native peoples lived on lands that no longer supported their traditional way of life; and the ills, both physical and mental, that needed healing were numerous. It is in regard to this last issue, sacred healing, that Pentecostalism offered native Christians the most unique experience in comparison with other Christian groups. Physical healing has long been a part of traditional native religions, and although Pentecostals were not the first Christian missionaries to preach divine healing, they heavily emphasized its embodied, miraculous form and made it a centerpiece of their belief. Other experiences that Pentecostalism encouraged, such as prophecy, direct connection with God, and visions, were also common to a majority of traditional native religions. Loud, boisterous music, singing, and ecstatic dance marked native modes of worship in traditional religions and in Pentecostalism. The indigenous peoples who chose to become Pentecostal entered a new world of belief, but in terms of bodily experience—singing, dancing, divine healing—they blended native and Pentecostal experiences.

The Pentecostal emphasis on sacred healing appealed to many native peoples and drew native believers to the movement. It also encouraged those believers to expand their definitions of healing. Indigenous Pentecostals believed in divine physical healing, but the early native leadership also emphasized a different kind of healing: mental and emotional healing rooted in reconciliation and divine judgment. Jesus became the Great Physician who healed hearts, bodies, and minds.[5] This chapter will explore how native Pentecostals expressed their views on healing and redefined pentecostal healing to meet their particular needs as colonized peoples—as indigenous Americans. In this sense, they were not so different from other minority groups that embraced pentecostalism, yet they defined their healing within a native worldview, using native terms and native forms of understanding. In so doing, indigenous Pentecostals pushed the flexible boundaries of pentecostalism, worked out their own religious identities—identities that embraced their Pentecostal and native aspects—and, in the process, laid the groundwork for the racial reconciliation movement within the Christian Right, which gained prominence at the turn of the twenty-first century.

The history of native Pentecostals within the AG is a complicated one, and in order to explore the various themes of healing, this essay is divided into three parts. I begin with an overview of early AG missions to Native Americans. Then, I focus on white AG missionaries and their approach to pentecostal healing in order to highlight how they viewed healing differently from their indigenous counterparts. I continue by examining native AG missionaries who served their own people and explore the various types of healing that they experienced. I consider a wide range of healing experiences—from the healing of alcoholism to racial reconciliation. I close the chapter with a comparison to the racial reconciliation movement among twenty-first-century Charismatics and other evangelicals. The main goal is to broaden how scholars treat both native Pentecostalism and modern native religious identities as a whole.

It is crucial to note that most of my source material comes from Pentecostal archives—and therefore must be filtered carefully. Because of the paucity of sources on early native Pentecostals, and because the entire first generation of leaders is now dead (with the exception of Rodger Cree), I have striven to capture their voices where I can. The main source cited is the *Pentecostal Evangel* (*PE*), the weekly periodical of the AG. This source is problematic because it remained under white AG control throughout the twentieth century; therefore, it is biased toward portraying the AG in a favorable light. I have done my best to interpret with this bias in mind, and I have also utilized as many other sources as possible to capture the thoughts of indigenous Pentecostals outside the *PE*—mainly missionary tracts, a handful of personal writings, and interviews. At times, the sources have been infuriating in their bias and lack of detail, yet they are the only sources that give historians any glimpse of native Pentecostal life in the early decades of the movement.

## Home Missions

The Assemblies of God began its missionary work to native peoples in 1918.[6] As part of the AG's home missions program, white missionaries spearheaded Pentecostal evangelistic work among indigenous peoples. Missionary work to Native Americans never became as popular as foreign missions in the early years, yet a small subset of white Pentecostals embarked on missions to various tribes or served native peoples in urban areas. The actual numbers are unknown, but in the first decades (1930s–1940s), there were probably no more than 50 missionaries, judging from articles in the *PE*. Home missions became more popular by the 1950s (probably due to the end of World War II), and larger numbers of home missionaries set off to minister to native groups in the western and southwestern parts of the United States. The majority of the missionaries were married, white men, while some were single women, who typically worked in pairs. They tended to be simply educated, and most of the early missionaries had little ministerial training.[7] These early white missionaries were self-selecting and self-directed, and always entered the ministry to native peoples because they were "called." (Testimonies from this period emphasized a supernatural moment when a believer experienced a message from God, telling him or her to go spread the gospel among native peoples.) The AG's Department of Home Missions did not exist until 1937, and even then, it mainly served to fundraise; it did not coordinate where missionaries chose to evangelize.[8] Even with the support of the Department of Home Missions, most missionaries had to raise their own money from supporters or from fundraising pleas in the *PE*. Thus, white AG missionaries often set off to reservations with little money, no language skills, and, probably, little idea of what they would encounter there.

White Pentecostal missionaries did make converts on the reservations during the earliest decades of evangelization (1930–1950), and many of those early converts formed the first generation of early indigenous leadership within the AG. In 1937, the *PE* notes, George Effman and his wife Lilian were conducting mission work among a tribe in La Push, Washington.[9] What the *PE* does not say is that Effman was of the Klamath nation, from the area near the border of California and Oregon, and he was probably evangelized by the earliest AG missionaries who worked in this region.[10] Effman is not the only influential native leader who emerged in this period. In April 1948, the *PE* recorded the first "Indian Convention," a gathering of missionaries and indigenous Pentecostals on the San Carlos Apache reservation. One of the speakers was a young Navajo, Charlie Lee, who had been converted at an Apache revival and who, according to the *PE*, was "blessed with a fine voice to sing the gospel."[11] The young Navajo student eventually became an influential leader, but at that time, Lee was simply a young Pentecostal exhorter. Another early leader was Andrew Maracle, a young Mohawk who became a missionary to his own people and was the uncle of John Maracle, the first Native American to hold a seat on the AG's Executive Presbytery.[12] John McPherson, a mixed-blood Cherokee evangelist rose to prominence in the AG, and in 1979 he became the first national Indian representative.[13] Rodger Cree, the Mohawk mentioned earlier, was the only known member of the first generation of indigenous missionaries alive as of 2009, and he was still active in evangelistic work with his people.[14] Cree's family was evangelized by a Canadian disciple of Aimee Semple McPherson during Pentecostalism's early decades. Effman, Lee, Maracle, Cree, and McPherson were all in the vanguard of indigenous leadership.

## The Indigenous Principle and the Miracle Model Contrasted

The native Pentecostal experience remained different from the white Pentecostal experience in a multitude of ways. Indigenous Pentecostals found themselves within a large, mainly white denomination where they often had to fight fiercely to have their voices heard. In their struggle for autonomy, native Pentecostal leaders tried to live out and implement the "indigenous principle"—the idea that Christianity and thus Pentecostalism should be wholly rooted within one's own culture.[15] Native leaders latched onto the indigenous principle after hearing about its success among AG missionaries in Latin America. Their century-long battle resulted in a native Pentecostal identity that was rooted in the struggle for the indigenous principle and autonomy for native believers within the AG. Despite decades of struggle, native Pentecostals remained a part of the AG and did not abandon Pentecostal Christianity. Instead, they established indigenous churches, helped to train fellow native missionaries, built and supported their own all-native Bible college, and gained national leadership roles within the AG (figure 5.1).[16] Despite roadblocks, pain, and difficulties, native Pentecostals carved out a place within the AG.[17]

White Pentecostals approached healing in a manner that was markedly different from their indigenous counterparts. For white Pentecostal missionaries, healings were essential to Pentecostal evangelization because they demonstrated the Holy Spirit's active power in a believer's life. They were dramatic and tangible evidence of God. White missionaries put much emphasis on dramatic and miraculous healings, much more so than their native counterparts. They felt that they had to "prove" the miraculous power of Jesus and the Holy Spirit in order to convert indigenous people to the "Jesus way." Spurred by reports of miraculous healings and revivals among the white population, especially during the Voice of Healing revivals of the 1940s–1950s, white missionaries fanned out across the reservations and reported back their own miracles.

Pentecostals believe that the era of miracles did not end with Jesus' death, but that true believers can perform miracles as vessels of the Holy Spirit.

FIGURE 5.1.  Native American leaders at an Assemblies of God General Council meeting (1949). Courtesy Flower Pentecostal Heritage Center.

The beginning of white missionary Alta Washburn's mission work coincided with the "great revival" of healing within American pentecostalism in the 1940s–1950s. According to historian David Harrell, "the common heartbeat of every service was the miracle—the hypnotic moment when the Spirit moved to heal the sick and raise the dead."[18] In the greater American pentecostal culture, believers flocked to these revivals and avowedly witnessed miraculous healings. The AG missionaries read of these events and prayed that the Holy Spirit would send great acts of healing to the reservations.

White missionaries often wrote of miraculous transformations that led skeptics into the Pentecostal fold. Early in her initial missionary posting on the Apache reservation in White River, Washburn experienced her first "great miracle" as a Pentecostal missionary. In the middle of a sermon on God's miraculous nature, an Apache woman ran in carrying a baby.

> She literally threw the baby into my arms. The baby's little body was cold and stiff in death. She had just taken it from the hospital morgue and was on her way to the cemetery for its burial. Reckless faith, however, directed her to the church. She wanted us to pray her baby would live again! There I stood holding that little corpse. This had to be possibly the greatest challenge of my ministry. . . . As I prayed, I began to feel warmth return to that little body and the rigid little limbs became limp and moveable, I handed that baby restored to life into its mother's arms. All of us in that Sunday service were overcome with the knowledge that we had actually beheld the resurrection power of the Lord.[19]

According to Washburn, her congregants were awed, and she was unable to finish her sermon. After word spread among the Apaches, they showed up at the mission, and her ministry began to grow. Eighteen years later, a young man and his mother visited Washburn's parsonage in Phoenix, where she was serving the All Tribes Church. He asked for her blessing before his departure for Vietnam. The young man—Washburn claimed in her autobiography—identified himself as the Apache baby whom she had healed, and Washburn prayed over him that he might come back from Vietnam alive. A few years later, she heard that he had returned safely to the reservation without any battle injuries.[20] Washburn's autobiography is filled with reported miracles and the blessings of the Holy Spirit that she avowedly witnessed in her many years in the ministry. From her commentary on each incident, it appears that not only were the miracles affirmations of God's power but they also reminded Washburn of God's call in her own life. They affirmed the importance of her work.

Most of the reported miracles were not as dramatic as Washburn's "resurrection," and most usually involved accidents and physical infirmities. For example, a Navajo infant was burned badly by boiling water. The PE reported, "The skin had slipped several places and water was running from her body where there was no skin. Little Marian was in great pain."²¹ According to the doctors, the child would be in the hospital for four weeks for skin grafting, but instead of waiting for modern medicine to work, the missionaries implored their congregation to pray for the child's healing. According to the *PE*, she was healed within two weeks. In another case of healing, missionaries prayed over a young, disabled Apache woman. A week later, they returned to visit the woman and found that "Ardella had not had to use her crutches since the last time we prayed for her. She had been cutting wood and even had walked about one-half mile to a friend's home." The missionaries concluded, "God definitely healed this young lady and she has been able to remain true to the Lord."²² One of the main themes of healing testimonials was the limitation of modern medicine and the medical profession. Miraculous healings often were sought and seemed to occur when medical care could not completely fix the physical ailment.

According to *PE* reports, many of those who were healed "stayed true to the church," as might be expected since they had, in their view, received a tangible experience of God's power, showing that God's salvation was material as well as spiritual.²³ In one case reported to the *PE*, a group of Christ's Ambassadors, teenage evangelists from the All Tribes Mission in Phoenix, visited with a young indigenous couple who was expecting a child. They had been told that the baby would not survive its birth. "The CA's told them of God's power to heal and prayed for the lady with her permission—at the same time that the Christians were praying for the woman, a fine, healthy baby was born to her." The father of the child was reportedly amazed at the miracle, and realized that it was "God who gave us our child."²⁴

Healings proved crucial for successful missionary work, because the experience of healing appeared to reveal God's power to both the missionaries and those to whom they preached. Often, white missionaries did not speak the language of the people on the reservation, which led to a heavy reliance on native interpreters, but an apparently miraculous healing could speak to those witnessing it despite the language barrier. Yet, in spite of this mutual understanding, white missionaries and the white-run *PE* regarded healing differently from many of the native missionaries who came after them. For white missionaries, divine healing focused on the healing of physical bodies. Indigenous missionaries expanded the idea to include healing that encompassed righting not only physical and spiritual wrongs, but also mental and cultural ones in order to address their specific experiences as Native Americans.

Native missionaries, like their white contemporaries, emphasized the New Testament's message of the death and resurrection of Jesus in their religious work. But unlike their white counterparts, they interpreted the gospel according to their needs as natives. They reshaped it as a gospel of healing—not just from illness and alcoholism, but also from the bitterness of past wrongs and breaches of trust by white people in general and also by white missionaries. Native missionaries attempted to alleviate stereotypes and misconceptions of indigenous people through articles and pamphlets that they distributed to the greater AG public. By interpreting the gospel for their own purposes and by disseminating to white Pentecostals information about their history and culture, native missionaries used their autonomy to fight long-held misconceptions of natives. In so doing, they subtly fought the use of racist language in the *PE*; demanded the development of indigenous pastors and leaders; pushed the AG to recognize that native-run indigenous churches were central to the evangelization of native peoples; and forced the AG to face its sometimes racist, often paternalistic history of missionary work. Native missionaries offered up a "performance of reconciliation" to their white counterparts and in so doing, "offer[ed] striking critiques of both past and present-day colonial practices."[25]

Native Conversion Narratives

Healings often featured prominently within native conversion narratives. This section will explore the conversion narratives of indigenous leaders Jimmie Dann, Andrew Maracle, and John McPherson, who presented conversion as the major turning point of their lives. This is indicative of the importance that Pentecostals place upon conversion and the personal testimonial. The stylized nature of Pentecostal conversion narratives presents certain problems for the historian, however. As Grant Wacker has observed, all conversion narratives take the form of a "relentlessly stylized, three-step sequence": the initial problem, the event of conversion, and the benefits that occurred after conversion. Because believers recount testimonials as a reflection of a spiritual journey, the authors, as Wacker puts it, "cast their words in a dramatic before-and-after framework in which the Pentecostal experience marked a transition from darkness into light. We simply never find an admission that things might have been the same, let alone better, before the transition." Another major problem for the historian is that testimonials in print are invariably "shorn of their real-life context."[26] Although the testimonial offers a narrative of a particular life and emphasizes specific events that fit into this narrative, there is no way of knowing the full context in which conversion occurred. Only the memory of the convert, a suspect memory that has reconstructed the event to make it fit into the language of Pentecostalism, survives. Even with these problems, conversion narratives are important sources for how Pentecostals have experienced episodes of divine healing.

Jimmie Dann grew up on the Shoshone reservation in Fort Hall, Idaho. A Sun Dancer in his youth, he sought spiritual power so that he might heal and lead his people from their poverty and troubles. Stationed in the Pacific theater during World War II, Dann worried about death. He asked himself, "If I am killed, will the Great Spirit take me to the Happy Hunting Ground?" Dann struggled in his attempt to find answers to his questions. Throughout the war, he claimed that he kept practicing the Sun Dance to protect himself—it is likely that he just continued reciting his sacred prayers and songs—as the Sun Dance as traditionally practiced by the Plains tribes is always a communal, not an individual event. As he explains it, "On the islands where our unit was stationed I often slipped away alone and sang the songs of our tribal dances, begging the Great Spirit to keep me from harm."[27]

Although Dann survived the war unscathed, he grew more disillusioned with the Sun Dance and, after returning home, turned to liquor. Prior to World War II, Dann had felt a calling to be a medicine man or a tribal leader, but now, unsure of what he believed, he turned away from all religion. In 1946, white AG missionaries appeared on the Fort Hall reservation. Angry that the "White man's religion" had arrived, Dann did all he could to drive out the missionaries, physically threatening them and disturbing worship services. Twice, Dann faced the authorities for his actions. Three years later, a now-married Dann was out one evening with his wife, when for lack of anything else to do, she suggested that they visit the AG mission. He noted that "hate for the missionary still burned in my heart. But when we reached the church, a great desire for cleansing from sin came over me and in spite of myself I turned my car into the churchyard." That evening, Dann converted to Pentecostalism and was baptized in the Holy Spirit. He wrote that God had placed a "burden" on him: "Now for the first time I could do something for my people. I could tell them of Jesus." Dann later attended Southwestern Bible Institute and became a prominent traveling evangelist.[28]

Born in 1914, Andrew Maracle faced a harsh life on the Six Nations reserve in Ontario, Canada. His mother died in childbirth along with the baby. Because his father was a logger who traveled often, Maracle and his seven siblings were separated and sent to live with friends and relatives. In a childhood that lacked stability, Maracle moved frequently among family, friends, and strangers. At his first long-term foster home, Maracle became acquainted with the traditionalist longhouse religion and became an avid practitioner. Maracle recounts how the longhouse religion gave his life meaning: "Traditional dances were a form of worship and expression of thanksgiving for the seasons and their first fruits. To waste was wrong! Each individual was taught 'he was a way or law unto himself.' We were told to 'Listen very, very carefully.' I became infused with spiritual, cultural and political knowledge. I also clung tenaciously to my Mohawk language." For Maracle, his Mohawk identity imposed an obligation to embrace and defend his nation's traditional religion and language. He became, in his words, an adamant "defender of the faith" whenever he encountered Christianity. He antagonized the missionaries on the reservation until one day he wandered into an AG mission looking for a meal. By the end of the evening, he had converted and found himself "cleansed of sin."[29]

Conversion did not immediately change Maracle's life in the clear-cut way it changed Dann's. Rather than becoming a missionary, he continued working as a day laborer while testifying at church in the evenings. The major turning point for Maracle was a near-fatal accident in upstate New York (ca. mid-1930s). A large metal roller he was hauling with a horse team broke loose, spooked the horses, and landed on him. When Maracle awoke, he found himself in a hospital, paralyzed from the neck down. The doctors told him he would never move again. Determined that God would help him, Maracle lay in the hospital for six weeks praying. Then, his cousin Lansing Maracle and his pastor came from Canada to visit.

> The pastor said: "Brother Maracle, we are going to pray for you. Do you believe that God is going to heal you?" My answer came without any hesitation. "I don't believe only God can but I believe He will heal me!" Pastor Freez reached out to place his hand on my head to pray, but before he made contact, another hand touched me and was gone! Praise "His" wonderful name. I was instantly healed by the power of God.

Maracle's doctor came to check on him the next morning and attributed his unexpected recovery to a miracle. After experiencing this healing, Maracle found a new purpose in life. He enrolled in the local Zion Bible College so that he could become an AG missionary.[30]

Dann recovered from alcoholism and the mental scars of the war. Maracle experienced physical healing from the injuries inflicted on him during his logging accident. Physical healing and healing from alcoholism or violence were common motifs in Pentecostal conversion narratives, for both whites and natives. Many indigenous leaders reported physical healings during their lifetimes, but for some native Pentecostals, healing went well beyond the physical. Consider the conversion narrative of John McPherson, a Cherokee. In McPherson's narrative, with conversion came a sense of reconciliation from racism and self-hatred.

Late one evening in 1943, McPherson, a young soldier, went out drinking with his wife Naomi. As he stumbled from one bar to the next, he spied a Pentecostal preacher on the street corner exhorting sinners to come to Christ. Although McPherson grew up in a Salvation Army home and his wife was the daughter of a Pentecostal preacher, neither had converted to Christianity. McPherson recounted: "We heard the melodic refrain of a song, and recognizing it to be religious in nature, stopped to listen for a moment. This time, I heard more then [sic] just a melody, I listened to the words of the preacher."[31] Despite his wife's dismay, McPherson knelt down on the street and prayed the "sinner's prayer" and, at that moment, a realization washed over him.

> All my life I had labored under the stigma of being born an Indian. I had always been made to feel I wasn't quite as good as people with White skin. I was amazed after laboring under that stigma all my life

to find the One who so loved me that He died upon the cross for me. He wasn't ashamed of me or my copper skin. He wasn't ashamed of my humble beginnings or ancestry.[32]

From that moment on, John McPherson became Brother McPherson and, after the end of World War II, he embarked on a long career as a traveling evangelist and AG missionary.

For McPherson, with conversion came the realization that belief in Jesus offered healing. Even though there were times when McPherson encountered racism after his conversion, he believed that Jesus loved him. Divine love did not come with any conditions, and it was attainable for all who believed. For McPherson, his conversion experience was a powerful marker in his life because not only did his experience affirm his belief, but his perception of divine love helped him to cultivate a rhetoric of divine judgment and reconciliation that appears in writings from the later years of his ministry.

### Addressing Misconceptions

Native missionaries knew that most white Americans, including their own AG brothers and sisters, held misconceptions about indigenous peoples, and they set out to address them. Their main venue was the *PE*, which native missionaries used to their advantage. First, they educated the greater Pentecostal public on the wrongs done to Native Americans, particularly the wrongs of the U.S. government. With the exception of a handful of outspoken early white missionaries, white Pentecostals rarely offered public criticism of the U.S. government for its Indian policies. Most white Americans did not know what life was like on the reservations and did not really understand the intricacies of Indian policy, so it was left to native missionaries to explain how badly the government had wronged them.

The two events that indigenous missionaries used to gain the public's attention were the Cherokee Trail of Tears and the Navajo Long Walk, events that showed the cruelty and indifference of the U.S. government. Notably, the two authors who were responsible for the articles in the *PE* and subsequent tracts were not only significant evangelists, but one came from the Cherokee tribe and the other married into the Navajo tribe.

John McPherson developed "The Trail of Tears" (first preached ca. 1950) article and tract from a popular sermon he often used while evangelizing. The tract contains both a creative retelling of life on the trail and the historical facts of the forced march. McPherson boldly asserted that the Cherokees removed by the government from their homelands in North Carolina and Georgia were a civilized people and included many Christians. He also noted that the nation had aided the U.S. government in its battles against the Creeks. McPherson described the removal as especially brutal: "Men were seized in the fields; women were taken from their hearths; children were taken from their play and always if they looked back, the victims saw their homes in flames."[33] He continued by vividly describing the forced march, undertaken in harsh winter weather, and he emphasized the large numbers of women and children who died in the ordeal. McPherson's retelling is accurate according to eyewitness accounts written by a Baptist missionary who observed the violence.[34]

McPherson hoped that, by vividly retelling the injustices the government had inflicted, he would arouse the sympathy of his white readers and inspire them to become missionaries to natives. But the most informative part of the article, for my purposes in this chapter, is the closing paragraph, where McPherson presented the gospel as a means of reconciliation.

> But I, as a descendant of one who walked the death march, can hold
> no malice against my fellow man. For what has happened to my
> people I can harbor no ill in my heart because I have been born again
> and washed in Calvary's flow. God, the perfect Judge, in His own
> hour will settle the account and His judgment will be swift and sure
> and just. The "Trail of Tears" of the Cherokee is history. It has been
> duly recorded in eternity's archives awaiting the position of the
> Almighty. Let the judge of all the world weigh the action and the
> actors who must explain more than four thousand silent graves.[35]

McPherson attested that, by becoming a Christian, he could move forward and leave behind his anger at the government and at the men who had inflicted so much pain on his people. In essence, Pentecostal Christianity had healed him from the wrongs of the past and allowed him to overcome his feelings of hatred. Note that McPherson strongly emphasized divine judgment—so while it may seem that the U.S. government and President Andrew Jackson escaped punishment for their misdeeds, he believed they would have to face God and answer for their actions. McPherson's tract serves as an example of an accessible account (in the mid-twentieth-century United States, the story of the Trail of Tears had mainly been relegated to history books) of the injustices the government committed against the indigenous peoples of the continent, as well as illustrating how McPherson and his native brothers reshaped the gospel.

Coralie Lee, the white wife of Navajo missionary Charlie Lee, wrote "The Long Walk" tract (ca. 1960s). Like "The Trail of Tears," it was published as both a *PE* article and as a pamphlet for fellow Pentecostals. Coralie was likely inspired by the stories that her husband Charlie Lee and his family passed down—because Charlie Lee came from a traditional sheep-herding family and his ancestors had been prisoners on the Long Walk. Also like "The Trail of Tears," "The Long Walk" emphasized the injustices of the federal government toward the Navajos, a piece of history that is less well known to the U.S. public. The tract described how the U.S. government, through its agent Kit Carson, starved Navajos who resisted removal from their homeland. Lee painted a vivid picture of Carson and his men slaughtering Navajo sheep herds and cutting down fruit trees in order to break the spirit of the Navajos who were opposing their forced removal. Eventually, most Navajos surrendered and gathered at Fort Defiance. Next, they were forced to walk to Fort Sumner, where the government imposed an experiment on them.[36] The government forced the Navajos to become farmers and live in settled towns like the Pueblo peoples, and the experiment failed. Farming for a living was anathema to the semi-nomadic Navajos, who had long subsisted on a combination of sheep, goat, and horse herding and the fruits of their orchards. Eventually, the U.S. government allowed them to return to their homeland to herd sheep.[37]

Lee's purpose in writing her article was twofold. First, she hoped to educate Pentecostal readers about a major event in Navajo history. Second, she addressed the need for educated, indigenous missionaries and for money to support them. She stated: "The great need is for the Indians themselves to go to Bible schools and come back as missionaries, especially to those who are unreached as yet due to the language barrier. But most Navajos are not wealthy enough to pay for schooling and families are large."[38] Sister Lee, as the wife of Charlie Lee, understood that the most effective way to reach natives with the message of Christianity was by training native missionaries. Like her husband, she had fully embraced the "indigenous principle" and was willing to take the risk of asking the *PE* readership for support and money to implement an idea that the white AG leadership did not completely accept—an idea that Charlie Lee pioneered on the Navajo reservation and that was not widely practiced by white missionaries.

Besides educating the general Pentecostal readership on indigenous history, native evangelists used their writings to make their fellow natives seem less an exotic other and to clarify for their readers the special difficulties of reservation life. One article written by McPherson and Paul Kinel tried to dispel long-held stereotypes regarding natives. "Often the published material about Indians is either sentimentally unrealistic or brutally untrue. Indians were and are neither ignorant and blood-thirsty savages, nor misunderstood heroes. Indians are human beings, living interesting lives in accordance with customs and beliefs which, though ancient in origin, are greatly modified by several hundred years of contact with white people."[39] Unlike their white missionary colleagues, who generally emphasized the exotic or savage nature of the people they were evangelizing, native missionaries wrote about the essential humanity of the people they served. In the great majority of *PE* articles on home missions, white missionaries used now-troubling language to describe native peoples; they emphasized their "darkness," "heathen ways," and how they "savagely" danced in front of fires during traditional ceremonies while beating "tom-toms." Indigenous women were occasionally referred to as "squaws" and natives' "poverty" was continually emphasized.

White Pentecostals made no allowances for the significant differences in tribal cultures or customs, deeming them all to be "heathen." It is worth noting, however, that such language was commonly used in reference to other missionized groups; Native Americans were not the only "heathens," according to the AG. Any non-Christians were similarly portrayed.

In contrast to other *PE* authors, McPherson and Kinel pointed out the diversity of the indigenous peoples in North America, including differences of language and customs. They noted this in order to point out how difficult it was to evangelize natives without skilled missionaries who could speak the languages or money with which to develop such a clergy. In addition, the authors emphasized the terrible condition of the infrastructure of the reservations, and noted that it was a result of failed U.S. Indian policy (rather than implying that natives were poor through faults of their own). Money for repairs and building would aid in the spread of the gospel and make life better for people. Although the article ended with a plea for donations to the AG's Indian Home Missions Department, McPherson and Kinel succeeded to a great extent (demonstrated by the fact that they managed to get their critical article published in the *PE*) in confronting old stereotypes—stereotypes that their white counterparts played upon in the same periodical.[40]

## Reframing Healing as Reconciliation

At the very heart of pentecostalism is its restorationist/primitivistic impulse, which allows believers to frame the gospel in terms of healing, miraculous events, and prophecy. For native missionaries, however, the focus on healing tended also to be internal, and more collective. They framed healing in terms of healing from the pains of racism or from the injustices of history. Several early native leaders reported healings they felt gave them power to navigate a new path in becoming a Pentecostal native. Both McPherson and Cree felt that the Holy Spirit healed them of their personal prejudices. This idea of healing was not an anomaly, but rather the norm among native Pentecostals; for them, the most important sort of healing was of the heart and spirit, in addition to the healing of the body.

Indigenous missionaries sometimes gave hints of their own view of healing in the articles they wrote for the *PE*. Klamath George Effman elegantly summed up native missionaries' approach: "When Christ enters the life He gives a new heart. This removes from the Indian all the former hatred and mistrust for the White man. Christ is the Great Physician and He can meet both the physical and spiritual needs of the heartsick Indian."[41] Even though Christ can "give a new heart," as the majority of native evangelists believed, it was still hard to give up old prejudices, a point that Cree was careful to make.[42] Although he credited the Holy Spirit with helping him to overcome his hatred of the French, it was at times painful and difficult, especially when the French did little to convince him that they were deserving of his love and forgiveness.[43]

Native evangelists were open about the pain of the past and the atrocities their people had suffered. Even though most embraced reconciliation, they always held those who "sinned" against their people to account. McPherson made this point strongly in his "Trail of Tears" sermon, which stressed divine judgment, and offered a way of turning the deep anger of his fellow natives into more productive feelings.

> In recounting the migration into exile of the Cherokee in 1838, with
> its atrocities, its blood and death, we are appalled and rise up to
> protest the way the Cherokee were treated by fellow men. But I ask
> you, how have you treated the Christ, who left heaven and adorned in
> the robes of flesh, was born in a manger and later suffered and died
> that you might have life and have life more abundantly? He too
> walked a trail of tears, a journey of sorrows.[44]

At the end of his sermon, McPherson challenged his fellow natives to understand that Christ was someone like themselves. A poor man, despised by many, Jesus was eventually beaten and killed by his detractors. In others words, Christ was like the indigenous people, and because he was like them, he could truly understand and address the difficulties of their lives and history. McPherson believed that accepting Christ would change the harshness of native life and give his people hope, something he felt many were lacking on the reservation.

In advocating reconciliation and forgiveness, native Pentecostals' interpretation of the gospel moved beyond the idea of spiritual salvation. For indigenous evangelists, salvation from sin and gifts of the Holy Spirit were not enough to solve the ongoing problem of being a native under a government that over the centuries had stolen their land and destroyed their way of life. Cree and McPherson understood that their fellow natives had to move beyond the wrongs of the past. Becoming a Pentecostal and embracing a gospel of healing and reconciliation was one way for indigenous people to do that.

The use of pentecostal healing as reconciliation did not end with the mid-twentieth-century AG native pastors. At the turn of the twenty-first century, the language of racial reconciliation began to appear prominently among indigenous members of new Charismatic and more broadly evangelical groups such as the Promise Keepers. Cherokee scholar Andrea Smith has written extensively on this phenomenon in her book *Native Americans and the Christian Right: The Gendered Politics of Unlikely Alliances* (2008). Smith demonstrates that native members of the Promise Keepers tend primarily to come from Charismatic Christian groups, many from the Vineyard Christian Fellowship.[45] The racial reconciliation movement among native members of the Promise Keepers did not appear out of nowhere. Twenty-first-century Charismatic native believers may have moved beyond the original denominations that gave birth to Pentecostalism, but they have not moved beyond the earlier ideas of healing. The native push for the indigenous principle, as it was known in the AG, is what allowed a modern native leadership to emerge within the new Charismatic movement, because indigenous AG pastors modeled how natives could carve out an autonomous space in a white organization. The AG's missionary work to native peoples is what planted the seed of pentecostal beliefs on many reservations in the first place.

The first generation of AG native evangelists, by reworking their understanding of pentecostal healing, sowed the seeds for the later twenty-first-century racial reconciliation movement among groups such as the Promise Keepers. Consider one of the many examples that Smith uses in her work: native Promise Keeper Jeff King. "He calls on all American Indian men to model Christ by forgiving and reconciling with their white Christian brothers and to let go of the bitterness incurred by five hundred years of genocide."[46] King's words, and the words of other native members of the Promise Keepers movement, such as Tom Claus, Ross Maracle, and Tom Bee, echo the language initially used by mid-century AG native evangelists such as Rodger Cree, John McPherson, and George Effman. The main difference between modern native Charismatics and first-generation AG native pastors is that indigenous Charismatics have moved beyond carving out a space within a denomination (the AG) to engaging evangelical and pentecostal Christianity at large.

The first generation of twentieth-century native AG missionaries and pastors set the standard for the native Pentecostal and Charismatic believers who followed them in the twenty-first century. As the first group of converts to pentecostal Christianity, it was they who began to define Jesus as the Great Physician—the one who could heal native Pentecostals of racial hatred and the bitterness of the past, as well as of physical infirmities. As this chapter has shown, these native Pentecostal leaders expanded the traditional pentecostal understanding of healing that white missionaries brought with them. Moving beyond physical healing, indigenous Pentecostals stressed that the Holy Spirit and Jesus could wipe away hatred, mistrust, and anger. For many native Pentecostals, this healing was fundamental to their ongoing engagement with the AG, where they continually ran into problems caused by the paternalism of their white colleagues. Without their focus on this new kind of pentecostal healing and racial reconciliation, it is doubtful that they could have stayed within a denomination that often put up roadblocks to indigenous advancement and leadership within the AG power structure. Knowing that the Great Physician could tend to their needs and pain buoyed many native Pentecostal believers as they fought the AG for official leadership positions and to implement the indigenous principle in its missionary work. Finally, the words of AG believers such as Cree, Maracle, McPherson, Effman, Lee, and Dann show how they inspired, directly and indirectly, the new generation of native leadership in the new Charismatic and evangelical groups, and laid the foundation for the modern racial reconciliation movement.


NOTES

1 Rodger Cree, interview, Springfield, Mo., 8 Aug. 2006; Cree does not give the date of his conversion, but judging by other events in his narrative, it likely occurred in the mid-1930s.

2 Ibid.

3 Although Cree is Canadian by birth and nationality, he became a missionary to several southwestern U.S. tribes and to the Lumbee of North Carolina after a bout with rheumatic fever during a missionary posting among the Cree people of the Hudson Bay. Weakened by his illness, but devoted to working among indigenous people, he found a second home among U.S. tribes in warmer climates. Cree speaks Mohawk, French, and English fluently; he also made it a point to learn to sing hymns in Pima when he was among that tribe. Cree is typical of most AG native missionaries; they ended up (at one time or another) ministering to tribal groups that were not their own (the main exception being the Navajo missionary Charlie Lee). This points to the modern development of a pan-Indian identity in general, which extends to Pentecostal Native Americans. Because they are such a small group within the AG, indigenous Pentecostals have tended to emphasize their cultural similarities as natives, not their tribal differences.

4 William G. McLoughlin, *The Cherokees and Christianity, 1794–1870: Essays on Acculturation and Cultural Persistence* (Athens: University of Georgia Press, 1994), 15.

5 White Pentecostals and Charismatics have demonstrated increasing interest in mental and emotional healing since the second half of the twentieth century, but the emphasis has been on personal traumas rather than social wrongs.

6 "Amongst the Indians," *Christian Evangel* (27 July 1918): 5.

7 Information such as education, age, and marital status was gleaned from the "Deceased Missionary Files" that the AG holds on past missionaries. However, not every missionary has a DMF, sometimes the files lack basic information, and they are not filed by type of missionary work (that is, home and foreign missionaries are all filed together). Therefore, I had to rely on the *PE* to gather the names of missionaries to Native Americans, and then tried to track down every missionary's DMF. A DMF could not be located for about half the missionaries listed in the *PE* from the early period.

8 For more on the structure of the AG's Department of Home Missions, see Gary McGee, *This Gospel Shall Be Preached: A History and Theology of Assemblies of God Foreign Missions to 1959* (Springfield, Mo.: Gospel Publishing House, 2003).

9 "A Forward Step to Reach the Navajo Indian," *PE* (11 July 1937): 9.

10 "George Effman," DMF, Application for Ordination, RG 8-27, shelf loc. 75/5/1, Flower Pentecostal Heritage Center, Assemblies of God Headquarters, Springfield, Missouri (hereafter FPHC).

11 "First Indian Convention," *PE* (10 Apr. 1948): 11.

12 "Andrew Maracle," DMF, Application for Ordination, RG 8-27, shelf loc. 76/5/3, FPHC.

13  John T. McPherson with Phil Taylor, *Chief: My Story* (Tulsa, Okla.: Carbondale Assembly of God, 1995).

14  Rodger Cree, interview, Springfield, Mo., 8 Aug. 2006.

15  Gary McGee, "Assemblies of God Mission Theology: A Historical Perspective," *International Bulletin of Missionary Research* 10.4 (Oct. 1986) 166–169. The most famous proponent of the indigenous principle (the person who gave the term its specific name), who was also Charlie Lee's teacher at Central Bible Institute, was Latin American missiologist Melvin Hodges, the author of *The Indigenous Church* (Springfield, Mo.: Gospel Publishing House, 1953), *The Indigenous Church and the Missionary: A Sequel to the Indigenous Church* (South Pasadena, Calif.: Carey Library, 1978), and *A Theology of the Church and Its Mission: A Pentecostal Perspective* (Springfield, Mo.: Gospel Publishing House, 1997). Charlie Lee (Navajo) took Hodges' ideas and popularized them among indigenous Pentecostals. Lee also founded his own mission in Shiprock, New Mexico, among the Navajo and created the first all-native, self-supporting, General Council–affiliated Native American Assemblies of God church (recognized by the AG in 1976).

16  The AG's first all-indigenous Bible college was originally founded by white missionary Alta Washburn in 1957. Washburn (one white missionary of whom native Pentecostals speak with deep fondness and affection) defied the AG hierarchy in establishing the Bible school, because the white leadership did not believe it was needed. Washburn's school was formally taken over by the AG in 1967. It is now called the American Indian College of the Assemblies of God (Phoenix, Arizona). The position of national Indian representative for the AG was created in 1979 to satisfy native demands for greater national visibility and was filled by John McPherson. Currently, the position is held by John Maracle (nephew of Andrew Maracle), who has also become the first indigenous member of the AG's Executive Presbytery. (Maracle was voted into the position in 2008.)

17  Miroslav Volf's "Materiality of Salvation: An Investigation in the Soteriologies of Liberation and Pentecostal Theologies," *Journal of Ecumenical Studies* 26.3 (1989): 461, notes, "Thus, whereas Pentecostalists are eager to help individuals in need, they are virtually blind to the need for changing the structures of their societal life." This quote succinctly sums up how white Pentecostals treated native Pentecostals within the AG. Although white Pentecostals were concerned for their indigenous counterparts, they did not understand how the white-controlled structure of the AG kept native leaders from assuming any sort of control over ministry to Native Americans. Native ministers sought to change the structure that oversaw missions to native peoples (they wanted more education for indigenous missionaries and a greater emphasis on native-run churches), but the AG did not feel that such change was warranted. That was when the native missionaries turned to the indigenous principle in order to show that the unwillingness of the AG to foster indigenous churches was not just problematic, but un-Pentecostal. In this way, native Pentecostals are radically different from white Pentecostals in that they have long used their pentecostal beliefs to attempt to change societal and ecclesial structures.

18  David Harrell, *All Things Are Possible: The Healing and Charismatic Revivals in Modern America* (Bloomington: Indiana University Press, 1975), 5–6.

19 Alta Washburn, *Trail to the Tribes* (Springfield, Mo.: self-published, n.d.), FPHC, 21–22.

20 Ibid.

21 "Healings Reported on American Indian Field," *PE* (27 June 1965): 27.

22 Lemy Pike and Hazel Pike, "Jicarilla Apaches Build a New Church," *PE* (17 July 1960): 16.

23 Volf, "Materiality of Salvation," 447–467.

24 "Phoenix Indian CA's Believe They Are Saved to Serve," *PE* (17 July 1960): 21.

25 Andrea Smith, *Native Americans and the Christian Right: The Gendered Politics of Unlikely Alliances* (Durham, N.C.: Duke University Press, 2008), 102.

26 Grant Wacker, *Heaven Below: Early Pentecostals and American Culture* (Cambridge, Mass.: Harvard University Press, 2003), 58.

27 Jimmie Dann, "I Received No Peace from the Shoshoni Sun Dance," *PE* (18 July 1954): 10.

28 Ibid., 10–11.

29 Andrew Maracle, "From a Log Cabin: An Autobiography of the Life and Ministry of Rev. Andrew Clifford Maracle," RG 17, shelf loc. 2/3/8, FPHC, n.d.

30 Ibid., 4, 7.

31 McPherson with Taylor, *Chief*, 48.

32 Ibid.

33 John McPherson, "The Trail of Tears," distributed by AG Home Missions, shelf loc. 9/3/6, RG 11-56, FPHC, n.d., n.p.

34 For Baptist missionary accounts of the Trail of Tears, see William G. McLoughlin, *Champions of the Cherokee: Evan and John B. Jones* (Princeton, N.J.: Princeton University Press, 1990).

35 McPherson, "Trail of Tears," last page.

36 The majority of Navajos who went to Fort Defiance were elderly men, women, and children. Most young warriors were killed in skirmishes with Carson's men, and those who survived hid in Canyon de Chelly with the few sheep herds that escaped government detection. For a readable history of Carson and his battle with the Navajos, see Hampton Sides, *Blood and Thunder: An Epic of the American West* (Garden City, N.Y.: Doubleday, 2006).

37 Coralie Lee, "The Long Walk," distributed by AG Home Missions, uncataloged, FPHC, n.d., n.p.

38 Ibid.

39 John McPherson and Paul Kinel, "The First Americans," *PE* (31 Aug. 1958): 14.

40 Ibid.

41 George Effman, "The First Are Last," *PE* (25 Feb. 1962): 12.

42 The language of Christ giving a "new, clean heart" is a striking foreshadowing of similar language that native Charismatics and other evangelical leaders would use in the twenty-first century during their affiliation with the Promise Keepers. This shows the continuity between the modern native leaders who joined the Christian Right and the early AG leaders, who predated them by almost a half-century. Smith, *Native Americans*, 99, calls this trend "performing reconciliations" and points out how it shows that indigenous peoples continue to defy

categorization when it comes to how they employ conservative Christianity for their own uses.

43 Cree interview.

44 McPherson with Taylor, *Chief*, 96.

45 Smith, *Native Americans*, 79.

46 Ibid., 92.

# PART II

# Latin America, the Caribbean, and the Borderlands

# 6

# Latino Pentecostal Healing in the North American Borderlands

*Gastón Espinosa*

This chapter argues that the U.S. Latino pentecostal movement has engaged in divine healing practices for almost 100 years, and that the tremendous emphasis given divine healing is one of the major reasons that there are now 9 million Latino Protestants in the United States, two-thirds of whom self-identify as Pentecostal or Charismatic. The key to this movement's growth has been its tradition of blending evangelism and healing. Latino pentecostal evangelists like Francisco Olazábal (1886–1937) conducted large-scale healing services in urban *barrios* and *colonias* in order to attract and convert the masses. After participants were converted, Olazábal used them to help plant new churches and missions, which institutionalized and spread the practice of mixing healing and evangelism. This religious practice might have been kept localized and marginalized had it not been for Olazábal's emphasis on planting indigenous and autonomous Latino churches in almost every location where he conducted large-scale (two weeks in duration or longer) evangelistic services.[1]

Latino pentecostals like Olazábal created indigenous and autonomous Protestant churches as early as the 1920s that institutionalized and transmitted their message and practice of divine healing. Olazábal and A. C. Valdez, Roberto Fiero, Aurora Chávez, Matilde Vargas, Juan Lugo, Carlos Sepúlveda, Leoncia Rosado Rosseau, and countless others tapped into preexisting belief in divine healing. Their emphasis on healing was important because of the direct connection between health and economic survival as sick or injured persons could not work and thus could not support their families due to the high costs of medical treatment. In many respects, the Latino pentecostal community provided a faith based form of alternative healing that addressed physical, spiritual, social, and emotional issues. In a word, their healing practices tended to be "holistic." This essay explores the role of healing through the life and ministry of Olazábal, one of the Latino community's most prominent healing evangelists.

Latino Pentecostal Healing at the Azusa Street Revivals

Francisco Olazábal's decision to mix evangelism and healing was a direct by-product of the Azusa Street revivals in Los Angeles. In 1916, his wife, Macrina, experienced healing of a physical ailment after George and Carrie Judd Montgomery prayed for her. This traumatic event prompted Olazábal, then an itinerant Methodist minister in San Francisco, to leave the Methodist Church and join the Pentecostal movement. In 1917, he joined the Assemblies of God, the tradition with which the Montgomerys were most associated. In 1906, the Montgomerys had joined the Pentecostal movement after George had visited William J. Seymour and the Azusa Street revival. There, he witnessed the revival's practice of mixing healing and evangelism. By the time Olazábal joined the Pentecostal movement, a number of other Latinos were already engaging in evangelistic healing work. Olazábal was thus grafted into a movement that placed a high premium on mixing healing and evangelism at Azusa Street and beyond.[2]

It is significant that almost every major reference to Mexicans at the Azusa Street revival involves healing. The first person allegedly healed at the revival was not an Anglo nor an African American, but a Mexican. Shortly after the Apostolic Faith Mission opened, Arthur G. Osterberg, an Azusa Street participant and eyewitness, reported that a Mexican man with a clubfoot was the first person healed at the revival. He described the event as follows:

> All at once a man who had come in walking haltingly with a clubfoot, got up and went out into the aisle and he was clapping his hands and his face was uplifted. His wife looked at him and pretty soon she followed him. They walked toward the back and then toward the front [of the mission], and by this time they were walking arm in arm and he [was] clapping his hands and his face [was] uplifted. That must have taken place for four or five minutes, then it quieted down, then he came down with his wife. I noticed when he came up the aisle . . . he wasn't stumbling like he was when he walked into the meeting. I knew something had happened to his foot. . . . For the first time he noticed—he stood there [in the mission] moving it and then started to walk—then he started to shout "Hallelujah."[3]

The healing left an indelible impression in Osterberg's mind.[4] This apparent miracle convinced him that there was "something different" at Azusa than "any other work" he had ever attended.[5]

Similarly, the Mexican American evangelist Adolfo C. Valdez reportedly witnessed "many healings" at the mission, including that of his father.[6] Likewise, Abundio and Rosa López attested that divine healing was part and parcel of their ministry at the Azusa Street Mission and in their evangelistic work.[7] In a classic example of mixing evangelism and healing, Abundio and Rosa López wrote in 1906:

> We testify to the power of the Holy Spirit in forgiveness, sanctification, and the baptism with the Holy Ghost and fire. We give thanks to God for this wonderful gift, which we have received from Him, according to the promise. Thanks be to God for the Spirit, which brought us to the Azusa Street Mission, the Apostolic Faith, old-time religion. I [and] my wife, on the 29th of last May . . . came for sanctification . . . and [we] thank God for the baptism with the Holy Spirit and fire which I received on the 5th of June, 190[6]. We cannot express the gratitude and thanksgiving which we feel moment by moment for what He has done for us, so we want to be used for the salvation and *healing of both soul and body*. I am a witness of His wonderful promise and *marvelous miracles* by the Holy Ghost, by faith in the Lord Jesus Christ. May God bless you all.[8]

Before his death, Abundio joined Olazábal's Latin American Council of Christian Churches, no doubt in part due to its openness to healing.

The Lópezes' blending of healing and evangelism was evident not only at the Azusa Street revival, but also at other Pentecostal and Charismatic missions in Los Angeles, like the Pisgah Mission.[9] In January 1909, the Pisgah movement, which placed a heavy emphasis on divine healing, claimed that its work was "spreading rapidly among . . . Spanish and Mexican" Catholics due to "immemorial traditions and belief in divine healing." Pisgah leaders claimed that one-fourth of the congregation at one of their missions in southern California was made up of "Spaniards and Mexicans, among whom are many cripples and deformed."[10] One Pisgah writer reported, "We went among Spanish, French, and colored people, and were rejected but once. We prayed for one lame person . . . and she was healed."[11] At one service in January 1909, 14 Mexicans came forward for healing. The writer stated that many Mexicans were "afflicted with fearful visitations." Exactly what these "fearful visitations" were is uncertain. Perhaps they refer to the hexes and spells they believed could be cast upon them by *brujas* (witches), *diableras* (satanic witches), and *espiritualistas* (spiritualists). If this is true, then perhaps some Mexicans sought to use pentecostalism's emphasis on divine healing and spiritual warfare to restore their health by breaking the power of hexes and other fearful afflictions they believed had been cast upon them by malevolent spirits, thus making pentecostalism doubly attractive.[12]

Mexican interest in divine healing was neither unique nor transitory. It is the key to understanding the power and attraction of pentecostalism. Latino pentecostals from the beginning intuitively understood salvation as both material and spiritual.[13] Pentecostal evangelistic healing services are one of the main reasons that tens of thousands of Catholics left the church to join the Pentecostal movement in the 1920s–1930s. This kind of physical healing and spiritual power offered hope to people unable to pay for proper medical care or the fees that many spiritualists and *curanderas* charged to perform healing ceremonies, *limpias* (cleansings), or counterspells. Furthermore, many Mexicans and Mexican Americans were reluctant to go to an "American" doctor because they were used to going to village or local healers.

Many preferred to take their medical problems to a Mexican Catholic folk healer or *curandero/a* like Don Pedrito Jaramillo, El Niño Fidencio, María Teresa Urrea, and others. For example, in her 1923 study of social attitudes among Mexican immigrants in Los Angeles, Evangeline Hymer found that 42 percent of Mexicans surveyed preferred to take their medical problems to a Mexican healer rather than to an American doctor (20 percent) and almost one-third (28 percent) reported that they preferred to use Mexican herbs rather than "drug store medicine." Echoing what early pentecostal leaders also said, she observed that among "members of the lower caste . . . faith in divine healing is still unshaken."[14] Many sought out healers because they believed that bodily healing and the spirit world were intimately related. In the minds of many, there were no accidents in life. All blessings and misfortunes were tied to the supernatural world—for better or worse. Furthermore, there were sicknesses and diseases that a modern "American" doctor could simply never heal. Some people believed that sickness and disease were caused by hexes, curses, spells, and malevolent spirits, not natural ailments. They believed that, in order to break a curse or spell of a witch, a satanic witch, or a spiritualist, one had to invoke a more powerful spirit. Pentecostal evangelists boldly declared that the Holy Spirit *was* that more powerful spirit.

Francisco Olazábal and other pentecostal evangelists offered Latinos a new alternative way to break spells and cultural prohibitions in society while at the same time empowering them to transition into a largely Protestant society. For although Pentecostals were often viewed as a sect by mainline Protestant churches, they nonetheless embraced and promoted a largely Protestant world-view, theology, and way of life. This worldview along with the spiritual and material power it brought them was especially attractive to the poor, who could often not afford to pay someone to break spells. It was also attractive to women seeking ways to transcend machismo. While Latino converts transformed the symbols, source of power, and meaning behind divine healing, they left intact its cultural and spiritual importance, necessity, and regularity in the Latino consciousness. Although other Latino Protestant traditions acknowledged that divine healing was possible, only pentecostalism made it a central tenet of faith.

Healing in the Mexican imagination was connected not only to the spirit world, but also to practical, on-the-ground material and economic needs. It was not just a pie-in-the-sky religion, but offered direct psychological, spiritual, and material benefits. The material benefits of healing—whether physical, psychological, or psychosomatic—were all the more important because illness left up to one-forth of immigrants in poverty, due largely to their inability to work. One major study of the Mexican population in Los Angeles in 1920 found that, although Mexicans made up only one-twentieth (probably an underestimate) of the population of Los Angeles, they made up one-fourth of all the poverty cases handled by L.A. county charities. Significantly, the top two reasons that they were in poverty were health related—"acute illness" and "chronic physical disability," which together left fully one-third (33 percent) of all Mexicans poverty-stricken.[15] In light of this fact, it is not difficult to see why thousands converted to pentecostalism—a religion that promised physical healing and, indirectly, economic hope as well as spiritual benefits.

## Birth of Charisma

Francisco Olazábal was born into a traditional, pious Catholic family in El Verano, Sinaloa, Mexico, on 12 October 1886 (figure 6.1). Although little is known about his father, we do know that his mother was a devout Catholic who nurtured Francisco in the rich and vibrant world of Mexican popular Catholicism. From her, he learned to pray the rosary and to the saints, venerate Our Lady of Guadalupe, light colorful prayer candles at their home altar, and honor the local priest. Popular Mexican Catholicism taught that sickness and disease

FIGURE 6.1. Francisco Olazábal (1886–1937). Courtesy Gastón Espinosa.

were not caused by chance or microbes but rather by evil spirits and spells cast by witches, spiritualists, and angry village saints. Olazábal grew up in a world where the supernatural was alive and divine healing was an accepted part of everyday life.[16] He no doubt heard stories about Mexican folk healers like María Teresa Urrea from his home state of Sinaloa and of Don Pedrito Jaramillo from the nearby state of San Luis Postosí, where he would later attend seminary.[17]

Olazábal's spiritual world took a dramatic turn away from popular Mexican Catholicism when in 1898 his mother converted to evangelical Protestantism in Mazatlán, Mexico. Her conversion changed her life—and his. After receiving what seemed a divine calling to the lay ministry, she left home to hit the itinerant evangelistic trail. She took Francisco on her evangelistic journeys throughout the rugged Sierra Madre of central Mexico, carrying a Bible in one hand and a rifle in the other. They spread their newfound faith from village to isolated village. While on occasion they stayed with hospitable guests, more often than not due to anti-Protestant sentiments they lived off the land and camped just outside of town.[18]

Around 1903, the restless teenager set out on his own. He turned away from his mother's evangelistic ministry and traveled north to visit his relatives in San Francisco, California. Caught up in the fantastic stories he read about faraway exotic places and seeking a chance to earn some silver, he planned to sail the world as a mariner. His plans dramatically shifted after he rededicated his life to Jesus Christ in 1904 through the evangelistic work of George Montgomery, a member of the Christian and Missionary Alliance. After his rededication, he decided to answer a divine calling to the ministry. He returned to the Methodist Church of his youth and attended the Wesleyan School of Theology in San Luis Potosí, Mexico, from 1908 to 1910. During this time, he conducted small-scale evangelistic and revival campaigns in the Mexican states of Durango, San Luis Potosí, and Zacatecas, and across the U.S. border in Texas. As the fires of the Mexican Revolution (1910–1917) engulfed the nation, hundreds of thousands of Mexicans, including Olazábal, fled across the U.S. border. He assumed the pastorate of a small Mexican Methodist church in El Paso, Texas, in 1911.[19]

While in Texas, Olazábal met a Euro American Methodist woman who encouraged him to study at the Moody Bible Institute. At Moody, he was profoundly influenced by Dwight L. Moody's revival strategies, R. A. Torrey's *How to Pray*, and especially Charles Finney's *Lectures on Revivals of Religion*. When Torrey left Moody for a pastorate in Los Angeles, he asked Olazábal to minister to the growing Mexican population in Los Angeles. He accepted the offer but soon parted company with Torrey over differences in belief concerning Spirit baptism. Olazábal joined the Methodist Episcopal Church in California and was ordained in 1916.[20] Drawing on Moody's and Finney's strategies, Olazábal held evangelistic meetings throughout the greater Los Angeles and Pasadena area and built a massive new mission-style church in Pasadena to minister to his growing flock of converts. Shortly thereafter, Olazábal was transferred north, where he was a circuit preacher for two Spanish Methodist churches in San Francisco and Sacramento. His evangelistic, revivalistic, and fundraising work caught the attention of the Anglo American Methodist bishops, who began to whisper about his one day becoming a bishop.[21]

After moving to San Francisco, Olazábal ran into George and Carrie Montgomery. To Olazábal's surprise, they had become Pentecostals, a group he often criticized from the pulpit. After initially rejecting the Montgomerys' newfound message, Olazábal was persuaded that baptism with the Holy Spirit was a second definite experience and a necessary part of the Christian life. He also became convinced that divine healing was available to all who asked in faith. Olazábal's belief was put to the test and confirmed when he, the Montgomerys, and a few other people laid hands on and prayed for his wife, who was suffering from a physical ailment—and she recovered after prayer. He quickly realized that the combination of practicing the spiritual sign gifts (speaking in tongues, healing, Spirit baptism, etc.) and his newfound belief in divine healing placed him at odds with some of his Methodist colleagues, who saw Pentecostals as largely uneducated if well-intentioned schismatics. He decided to leave the Methodist Church in order to preach the "full Gospel."[22]

Soon after Olazábal left the Methodist Church, he joined the Assemblies of God (AG) and received ministerial credentials in 1917. He traveled south to Los Angeles, where he conducted an evangelistic campaign for Alice E. Luce, an emerging leader in the Spanish-speaking AG. After the campaign, he returned to El Paso and opened a Mexican mission to reach the thousands of immigrants streaming across the U.S.–Mexico border. There, he conducted a number of evangelistic, healing, and revival services. By 1921, his charismatic personality, ability to heal, and rhetorical gifts had reportedly led to the conversion of over 400 Mexicans along the border. As Olazábal's popularity continued to grow, he ran into conflict with Alice Luce and H. C. Ball, a Euro American AG leader. Reflecting the well-intentioned pious paternalism of his day, Ball tried to take control of the second Latino AG convention in Victoria, Texas, and dictate its agenda and outcome. Olazábal recognized the racialized politics he now faced and, with nine cents in his pocket, resigned in December 1922. When later asked why he resigned, Olazábal gave as his answer: "The gringos have control."[23]

## Aimee Semple McPherson and the Mexican Billy Sunday

On 14 March 1923, the Interdenominational Mexican Council of Christian Churches (Pentecostal) was legally incorporated in the state of Texas, and the first completely independent and autonomous Latino Protestant denomination in the United States was born. Olazábal was quickly elected president of the council. By 1924, the group had over 30 churches in California, Texas, Arizona, New Mexico, Kansas, Illinois, Michigan, Ohio, Indiana, and Mexico.[24] Although Olazábal conducted evangelistic healing crusades in the Mexican Assemblies of God, it was not until after he left that his healing ministry began to take on genuinely national proportions. His national healing ministry was ignited by the reported healing of the 12-year-old deaf-and-dumb daughter of Guadalupe Gómez. Olazábal had never before performed what was, in the minds of his followers, such a "great" and obvious "miracle." Church of God leader Homer Tomlinson, one of Olazábal's closest Anglo American friends, wrote that "from this new beginning his faith for healing and the salvation of souls seemed to take on new proportions."[25] Empowered by a newfound confidence in God's ability to heal, throughout the 1920s Olazábal crisscrossed the nation preaching evangelism, healing, and revival to thousands of Mexicans in migrant farm labor camps, factories, and inner-city barrios. He conducted large-scale, evangelistic healing services in El Paso, San Antonio, East Los Angeles, Boyle Heights, Watts, Brownsville, Nogales, San Fernando, and Houston. In Los Angeles, his campaigns caught the eye of another former AG evangelist, Aimee Semple McPherson.

In 1927, the glamorous McPherson was fascinated by the reports she heard from some of her Mexican American parishioners about Olazábal's healing crusades in Los Angeles and especially Watts. After personally attending his evangelistic healing services in Watts, she dubbed Olazábal the "Mexican Billy Sunday"—after the foremost evangelist of their day. Shortly afterward, McPherson invited Olazábal and his two Mexican congregations to her 5,000-seat Angelus Temple in Los Angeles. Olazábal's church members attended evening services there for months. At one historic meeting in 1927, she and Olazábal went to the podium, where Olazábal translated McPherson's sermon into Spanish. The Mexican congregation was emotionally moved not only by McPherson's characteristic theatrics and hospitality but also by her public blessing of "our Mexican brethren."[26]

The familial emphasis on "our" brethren was not merely rhetorical. McPherson asked Olazábal and his movement to merge with her Foursquare Gospel denomination. Flattered by the offer, he said the decision had to be made by the entire council. He took the idea to the next national convention, where his Mexican compatriots soundly defeated the proposal. They did not want to submit to Euro American control and, in effect, replace one set of Euro American leaders for another. Olazábal related the council's decision to McPherson. She was indignant at what she considered the rejection of a very generous offer to a Mexican denomination made up of migrant farm laborers, maids, ditch diggers, and the like. She excoriated Olazábal and demanded that he return the more than $100 "love offering" she had raised for him at Angelus Temple. Defiant, Olazábal told McPherson that "love offerings" are never returned. Angry, McPherson told Olazábal to get out of her office. Sometime thereafter, she persuaded one of his leaders, the music director Anthony Gamboa, to defect to the Foursquare Gospel denomination and start a rival ministry just blocks away from Olazábal's Bethel Temple. This conflict helped to give birth to Foursquare's Spanish-speaking work in the United States.[27] Despite this break, one cannot overestimate the symbolic impact of Olazábal preaching onstage with McPherson in Angelus Temple. He stood on the platform of one of the largest churches with one of the most famous evangelists in America. In an era when Mexicans were segregated and considered cheap labor, her public praise of Olazábal's ministry convinced many of his followers that he was indeed "anointed of God."

As word of Olazábal's healing campaigns spread across the United States, he was invited by a Latino AG minister to speak at the Palace Opera House in Chicago. Although he broke fellowship with Ball and Luce, he still had many friends and standing invitations from people in the Assemblies of God to hold services in their churches—both Latino and Euro American. His evangelistic healing and revival campaigns attracted thousands for weeks. The traffic was so great that police had to be called out to control the crowds. He used this as a base of operations to preach in other places, including Joliet, Illinois, and Indiana Harbor, Indiana. He went on to hold evangelistic healing crusades in Houston; Modesto, California; Laredo, Texas; and Mexico City, the latter at the request of David Ruesga, who pioneered the AG work in Mexico before eventually starting his own independent denomination in 1931.[28]

## The Spanish Harlem Revival of 1931

Word of Olazábal's massive evangelistic healing crusade in Chicago spread rapidly to New York City. After Francisco Paz, an AG minister, attended one of Olazábal's healing services in Chicago, he asked him to conduct a campaign in New York City. In the summer of 1931, Olazábal traveled north and east from his base in East Los Angeles for what would become the most important chapter of his life and the birth of his transnational ministry. "Probably not less than 100,000 different people have attended the Olazábal meetings in New York City since he inaugurated his meetings in New York in August, 1931," one periodical reported.[29] Despite the humidity and sweltering summer heat, eyewitnesses claimed that vast throngs attended his services (figure 6.2). The large crowds were no accident. Olazábal and his small team of followers distributed 30,000 flyers announcing the healing and revival campaign. The flyers promised marvelous miracles and divine healing for the sick.

Olazábal's services blazed with drama and power. Despite the grinding poverty the Great Depression was wreaking on the Puerto Rican and Latino community outside the church, inside the church some people claimed to find relief for their aching souls. The dramatic services followed the same pattern

FIGURE 6.2. Francisco Olazábal, New York City revival (1931). Courtesy Gastón Espinosa.

nightly. Olazábal walked to center stage, led the congregation in some rousing singing, preached a 25-minute evangelistic sermon—often in a conversational style—and then lifted his arms in the air and asked those in the balcony to come down to the front of the church, repent of their sins, and become born-again Christians. Thousands streamed down the aisles to answer his call. Afterward, Olazábal began what many, perhaps most, of the people came for—divine healing. While many turned to vaudeville or a *curandera* or spiritualist to relieve their aching souls, others turned to El Azteca, or the Mighty Aztec, as Olazábal's followers called him.

Olazábal Jr. stated that his father saw healing as a means to an end. He believed God gave him the ability to heal in order to attract and convert the masses to Protestant Christianity, a faith rooted in heartfelt belief, intellectual assent, and a transformed life. It was important that people first hear the gospel before they came forward for prayer. For this reason, he required anyone seeking healing to fill out a prayer card and have it hole-punched five to seven times (depending upon the duration of the revival and representing the number of nights attended) before he or she could come forward for healing, although exceptions were regularly made for the deathly ill, the elderly, and children. This evangelistic strategy forced those seeking healing to hear the "message of salvation." Olazábal required this because he claimed onstage that he would only agree with the sick in faith that God could heal them. He prayed *with* people, not *for* them. They too had to exercise faith. Requiring them to attend multiple services not only allowed them to learn how to become a born-again Christian, but also encouraged them to exercise their faith based on the miracles they witnessed every night. While Catholics did not have to convert to his personal Protestant Pentecostal brand of Christianity in order to be prayed for, they did have to agree with him in faith that God could heal before he would pray for them. Why? Because he was not—as he often said—a miracle worker or a faith healer, just another believer agreeing with them in prayer.[30]

Olazábal and his followers reported that countless people were healed of major illnesses and medical conditions, such as blindness, tuberculosis, deformity, tumors, heart conditions, rheumatism, and deafness. As at the Azusa Street revival in Los Angeles more than 20 years earlier, the "relics" of their former life—rosaries, amulets, canes, and crutches—were thrown into a large pile onstage as symbols of God's power. The testimonies of those who were healed were published every month in his denominational periodical, *El Mensajero Cristiano*. The revival converted thousands to pentecostalism and prompted Olazábal to move the mother church of his movement from Bethel Temple in East Los Angeles to the new Bethel Temple in New York City. This church, an enormous former synagogue, had grown from just a handful of members in August 1931 to over 1,500 members by 1932, making it one of the largest churches in New York City. The vast majority of his parishioners were Puerto Ricans, former Catholics, spiritists, and self-proclaimed socialists. Some also came from Presbyterian and Baptist churches.[31]

One famous healing that seized the attention of the masses was that of María Teresa Sapia. Famous in the Puerto Rican underworld, she was reportedly a notorious gambler and rumrunner during Prohibition. Yet asthma and other ailments had whittled her body down to a scant 75 pounds. Hopeless, she turned to Olazábal for healing and redemption. At one of his services, Sapia reported that she was healed after he prayed for her. Immediately, she converted and gave up her lifestyle. She soon became heralded as the "Mary Magdalene" of Puerto Rico. After her conversion, she became a loyal supporter and preacher, and assisted Olazábal at his crusades.[32]

Sapia was not alone. Thousands of women flocked to the movement because it afforded them the chance to go into the ministry and exercise a prophetic voice in the Latino community. No doubt influenced by his mother, Refugio Olazábal, and Carrie Judd Montgomery, Maria Woodworth-Etter, and even Alice Luce and Aimee Semple McPherson, Olazábal credentialed women to go into the ministry. They could preach from the pulpit and organize, pastor, and administer churches. Many also served as evangelists and missionaries. Women were not, however, normally allowed to serve communion, perform baptisms, or conduct weddings without a male elder or pastor present, although exceptions were regularly made. This was in part due to machismo, but more practically to Latino and Euro American social conventions and gender restrictions. Despite these limitations, the council produced a number of famous women pastors, evangelists, and revivalists, such as María Jiménez, who pastored large churches in Chicago and El Paso. It also produced a number of converts who conducted evangelistic healing ministries. Matilde Vargas led evangelistic services in Latino communities across the United States. Leoncia Rosado Rosseau founded the Damascus Christian Church and then in 1957 the Damascus Youth Crusade, one of the first faith-based drug and alcohol rehabilitation ministries in the Latino community and in New York City. Although there were limits, he gave Latinas more freedom to engage in ministry than did virtually any other Christian denomination in the United States.[33]

Word of Olazábal's healing services raced not only through Depression era Spanish Harlem, but also through New York's Italian and Euro American boroughs. It was not long before a growing number of Italians and Euro Americans began attending regularly and coming forward for spiritual encouragement and bodily healing. The number of non–Spanish speakers attending Olazábal's services was so large that he began holding English-language services on Monday nights and Italian-language services on Thursday evenings and Sunday mornings. Olazábal also regularly ministered in black Pentecostal churches in Harlem and throughout New York City. His ministry had now crossed linguistic and racial boundaries in a day when white supremacy and segregation dominated the racial and social imagination of

many in Euro American society and even in the Christian church.[34] After
Homer Tomlinson, the pastor of Jamaica Tabernacle Church of God, heard
about the "miracles" taking place at Brooklyn Temple, he invited Olazábal to
conduct revival and healing services in his Euro American church. Surprised
by the offer and eager to make connections with other leaders in New York,
Olazábal accepted. Tomlinson proclaimed the campaign an "overwhelming
success," as over 800 people converted and "hundreds were healed," including
a 24-year-old who had been paralyzed since his youth.[35]

## Olazábal and His Critics

Olazábal was accused, among other things, of not healing everyone he prayed
for. He openly acknowledged this fact. Indeed, Frank Olazábal Jr. stated in an
interview that his father only claimed to heal about 80 percent of those he
prayed for. Puerto Ricans like Roberto Domínguez and at least one Anglo
American member of Homer Tomlinson's congregation claimed that, despite
Olazábal's prayers for healing, they had not been healed. Olazábal responded to
these charges and others like them by stating that it was God's prerogative to
heal. He simply agreed with them in faith and prayer that God could heal. He
was nothing more than a vessel through which God manifested his healing
power, nothing more. From a critical reading of the healing testimonies published in Olazábal's *El Mensajero Cristiano* magazine, it is clear that a majority
of those who claimed healing were women. Furthermore, most of the healings
were for minor ailments, although a number of people did claim to be healed
of major ailments like tuberculosis, cancer, tumors, blindness, deafness, and
terminal diseases. Most doctors would probably categorize many attested cures
as examples of psychosomatic healings brought about by the power of positive
suggestion. Regardless, that the Latino community has a long tradition of folk
healing and that most people could not afford a doctor helps to explain how
Olazábal attracted thousands of people to campaigns across the United States,
Mexico, and Puerto Rico.[36]

## Puerto Rico para Cristo: The Mexican Billy Sunday in Puerto Rico

Despite protests from critics, news of Olazábal's evangelistic healing crusades
spread to Puerto Rico. In 1934, he conducted the first mass pentecostal island-
wide evangelistic healing and revival crusade in Puerto Rican history. He held
services in tents, churches, civic auditoriums, and sports arenas. *El Mundo*, the
largest secular newspaper on the island, dubbed Olazábal the "Mexican Billy
Sunday" and claimed that 20,000 converted.[37] He quickly realized that the key
to his success was his ability to garner interdenominational support across the

island. While at first some denominations opposed his work, by the end of his Puerto Rican campaign, most had been won over by the overwhelmingly positive response of both the press and the masses. Many Protestant ministers, such as Daniel Echeverria (Baptist) and Carlos Sepúlveda (Presbyterian), both of whom had attended the Evangelical Seminary of Puerto Rico, decided to join Olazábal's new Latin American Council of Christian Churches. The more inclusive name was not accidental; it recognized that a once largely Mexican work had blossomed across the United States and Puerto Rico into a truly transnational Latin American ministry.

By 1936, Francisco Olazábal stood at the height of his popularity. He conducted large evangelistic healing services in Puerto Rico, New York City, Chicago, El Paso, and Edinburg, Texas. Letters arrived from all over the United States, Latin America, and Spain asking him to conduct crusades. He began sketching plans to conduct services in Latin America and Spain. By that year, he had already sent or had plans to send missionaries and revivalists to Puerto Rico, Cuba, the Dominican Republic, Mexico, Chile, Argentina, Venezuela, Ecuador, and Spain. This was in part facilitated by the fact that members of his Spanish Harlem church, which numbered about 1,500 during its heyday, included members from every Spanish and Portuguese country in Latin America. These converts became the beachhead for missionary work throughout Latin America. They also stand in sharp contrast to the message of books like David Stoll's otherwise outstanding study *Is Latin America Turning Protestant?* (1990), which has a 1970s picture of Jimmy Swaggart on the cover, implying that the origins of the movement were Euro American.[38] Olazábal's story points to the indigenous origin of Latin American pentecostalism.

The Euro American Christian community picked up on Olazábal's revivals and plans to convert U.S. Latinos and people in Latin America to Protestantism. In 1936, the *Christian Herald* magazine published a flattering lead article on his ministry. Writing for the *Christian Herald*, Spencer Duryee described Olazábal as "The Great Aztec," whose transnational ministry was "one of the most startling stories . . . in modern religious history." He went on to compare Olazábal to the apostle Paul, John Wesley, David Livingstone, and William Booth.[39]

Although Pentecostal in creed, ritual, and practice, Olazábal recognized that his interdenominational evangelistic healing message transcended denominational boundaries and also put him at odds with those suspicious of the pentecostal experience. Rather than push his brand of Christianity on people, he simply invited them to receive the baptism of the Holy Spirit and spiritual gifts when they were ready. He invited non-Spirit-baptized ministers like Carlos Sepúlveda, Frank Hernández, Daniel Echeverria, Miguel Díaz, and Felipe Sabater, all of whom came from mainline or evangelical denominations, not only to join his movement, but even to pastor churches. While in private Olazábal often said that speaking in tongues was the key to his healing ministry, publicly he stated that he was not a sectarian Pentecostal. He was simply "a Christian." This kind of ecumenical-sounding discourse attracted the attention of influential mainline Protestant leaders like Robert E. Speer, who agreed publicly to support Olazábal's next Puerto Rican campaign in the spring of 1936—the year in which Olazábal's transnational ministry took a dramatic turn. Just days before his departure to Puerto Rico, however, he received devastating news: Speer had decided to withdraw his support. Shocked and disheartened, Olazábal asked his trusted friend Homer Tomlinson why Speer had removed his backing. "Tongues," Tomlinson quietly said. Speer had telephoned Tomlinson and stated that he had just learned that Olazábal "belonged to the 'tongues' people" and therefore had to withdraw his support immediately.[40]

Disappointed but not demoralized by the loss of Speer's support, Olazábal arrived in Puerto Rico in the spring of 1936 ready to repeat his 1934 campaign. Yet the setback with Speer was nothing compared to what he experienced on the island. Roman Catholic leaders looked at Olazábal as farmers look at an oncoming plague of locusts. They reportedly used their influence with the newspapers to criticize Olazábal and to persuade them not to announce his campaign or even his arrival on the island. More devastating than this opposition, however, was the resistance he faced from his Pentecostal and evangelical brethren, who felt threatened by his growing popularity and denied him access to meeting spaces. Olazábal wired his wife in New York and asked her to send his large evangelistic tent to protect visitors from the drenching tropical rain and scorching sun.[41] At every turn, his advance was checked. Even before his tent arrived, he boarded a ship and steamed home for New York City, arriving unannounced and without fanfare. According to one report, on the porch of his home, in front of close friend Tomlinson, Olazábal wept. With tears streaming down his face, he confided that he had never been so discouraged in his life. Rejection by the Anglo establishment was difficult, but to find Latino Protestant leaders also aligned against him had caught him by surprise. The 1936 Puerto Rico para Cristo campaign and the issues it brought to the fore marked a sharp turning point in Olazábal's vision. Prior to that campaign, he saw his healing ministry as bridging the racial and denominational divides that fragmented American Protestantism. He now realized that such bridging would be very difficult, if not impossible.

## Pentecostal–Roman Catholic Tensions and the Healing of Southern White Bodies

Although Olazábal's pride and image had been tarnished, he soon hit the road for a new campaign in El Paso, Texas, the place he had begun his transborder ministry in the United States 25 years earlier, in 1911. Securing the enormous city auditorium, Olazábal attracted thousands of Catholics to his services, and countless numbers came forward for salvation and divine healing.[42] Olazábal next headed for Cleveland, Tennessee, having realized that if he was going to have an international and multiracial ministry, he needed major financial support and the freedom to travel unrestrained by the cares of administering his council. On 10 September 1936, before an audience of 6,000 white southern members of the Church of God's Annual Assembly, Tomlinson invited him to join their denomination. Caught off guard and as a sign of courtesy, the somewhat reluctant Olazábal placed his hand on a Bible and swore allegiance to the Church of God. Although no formal legal documents had been signed and Olazábal made it clear that the invitation had to be decided by the entire leadership of the council, it was a symbolic gesture of what the Church of God hoped would be considered an inevitable union.[43] Reignited by his recent campaigns, Olazábal confidently led 2,000 Latinos in a planned march down New York's Fifth Avenue. Standing six abreast, shouting, praising God, and singing, they boldly waved colorful banners and gathered for a rally. The parade was a powerful symbol that Olazábal, the pentecostal movement, and Latin American immigrants were here in Spanish Harlem—and, by inference, the United States—to stay.[44]


"A Great Oak Has Fallen upon the Mountain":
The Death of Charisma


"Rev. F. Olazábal . . . Dies of Injuries Suffered in Auto Accident" read the *New York Times* obituary on 12 June 1937.[45] Near Alice Springs, Texas, on his way to an ordination service in Mexico, his car had skidded off the slippery blacktop surface and turned over on 1 June. Critically injured, he was taken to a hospital where he appeared to recover. Then, on 9 June, Olazábal died from internal hemorrhaging. He had seemed to know that death was imminent and reportedly dictated a message to his followers. In it, he admonished them to continue the work he had started and to keep the Holy Spirit at the center of their ministry. In the minds of his followers, a giant had fallen.

In a scene reminiscent of the funerals of presidents and other national figures, Olazábal's body was placed in a $2,000 gas vapor–filled casket and taken for display to Houston, New York, Chicago, El Paso, and finally Los Angeles. His lifeless body was placed on public display in his great temple in the heart of Spanish Harlem for three days. Some estimate that not fewer than 50,000 Latin Americans, Puerto Ricans, Anglo Americans, and African Americans paid their last respects in Harlem. Homer Tomlinson eulogized Olazábal, stating that "a mighty man of God has fallen in the midst of his labors. . . . A great oak has fallen upon the mountain."[46]

The Significance and Legacy of Francisco Olazábal

Olazábal left a lasting mark on Latino Christianity in the United States. He did more to shape the early Latino pentecostal movement in North America than did any other single Latino leader in the United States. Called the "Apostle Paul to the Latin Americans," Olazábal contributed to the origins or development of at least 14 denominations. By the time of his death, he claimed 150 churches and 50,000 followers throughout North America and the Latin Caribbean.[47] The work of Mexican American evangelists like Olazábal helped to lay the foundation for the religious reformation taking place in the twenty-first century in the Latino community in the United States and Puerto Rico. It also helps to explain why there are more than 9 million Latino Protestants in the United States today, 64 percent of whom are Pentecostal or Charismatic.[48] Supporting this seismic shift in Latino religiosity, scholar Andrew Greeley estimates that as many as 600,000 U.S. Latinos may be leaving the Roman Catholic Church every year for evangelical/pentecostal Christianity. He argues that almost a million U.S. Latinos "defected" from the Roman Catholic Church to evangelical/ pentecostal Christianity between 1973 and 1989. He calls this "mass defection" "an ecclesiastical failure of an unprecedented proportion."[49] Almost all the scholarship on this shift in Latino religiosity has argued that it is a relatively new post-1960 phenomenon, but actually this seismic shift began in the early twentieth century. The Latino pentecostal movement in general and the ministry of Francisco Olazábal in particular served as one stream in the growth of the first nationwide mass conversions from Roman Catholicism to Protestantism throughout the United States, Mexico, and Puerto Rico.

Olazábal was a Latino pentecostal evangelist and healer whose popularity can be attributed to his leadership, charisma, and reputed gift of healing. The fact that he stood up against Euro American leaders and seized control over his own life and movement in Jim Crow America was remarkable in the 1920s–1930s. He was the Protestant version of famous Catholic folk healers like El Niño Fidencio, Don Pedrito Jaramillo, and María Teresa Urrea. His ministry tapped into the tremendous emphasis on healing in Latino spirituality and culture. His healing ministry along with his emphasis on church planting, women in ministry, personal evangelism, citywide crusades, and mass-marketing techniques help to explain his ability to attract the masses. All of these factors helped to give birth to one of the first completely transnational Latino movements in North America and the Latin Caribbean, which in turn helped to spread the movement throughout Latin America.

Olazábal's prophetic rejection of Anglo American racism and pious paternalism created a message that would rise again during the Chicano movement (1965–1975) in another pentecostal leader, Reies López Tijerina, who also had an AG background, but later left to start his own ministry.[50] Olazábal's story

challenges the still widespread view that Latino Protestants in general and
Pentecostals in particular were controlled and manipulated by Euro American
denominations and leaders. Although this was true for some Latino Protestants, it was not true for all  There is also a long tradition of indigenous, independent, and autonomous Latino Protestant churches that are completely run
by and for Latinos. These traditions have created an alternative self-affirming
Latino Protestant subculture in the borderlands that emphasizes healing and
cultural empowerment. Olazábal's story also demonstrates that the Latino
community was more denominationally pluralistic than has hitherto been
recognized. Pentecostalism was able to enter the marrow of Latino culture and
society precisely because it reimagined and resymbolized the supernatural
worldview of Latino popular Catholicism and metaphysical traditions. It began
to transform the Latino religious marketplace by offering a hybrid *via media*
that affirmed selected ritual (though not necessarily theological) aspects of
Latino Catholicism, metaphysical traditions, and Protestantism. Olazábal's story
shatters the biracial view of early Pentecostalism as essentially a black-and-white
story. It also demonstrates that the present growth of pentecostal healing in
the Latino community actually traces its roots back to the early twentieth
century, and not to the 1960s–1970s as is often believed. Francisco Olazábal's
legacy is evident in the thousands of indigenous, independent, and autonomous Latino pentecostal churches and missions scattered throughout the
Americas, which continue to blend healing, evangelism, and sociocultural
empowerment.

NOTES

I wish to thank Catherine Albanese, Mario T. García, Mike McClymond, Candy
Gunther Brown, Sarah Cline, Colin Calloway, John Watanabe, Robert Gundry, and Rick
Pointer for their critical feedback on early drafts of this chapter. It is the basis for a
critical biography that I am currently writing for Oxford University Press.

    1 Gastón Espinosa, "Obama Threaded the Moral Needle of Latino Evangelicals
in '08," *Religion Dispatches* (28 June 2009), http://www.religiondispatches.org/
archive/politics/1591/obama_threaded_the_moral_needle_of_latino_evangelicals_
in_';o8 (accessed 15 Jan. 2010). This development of an independent, indigenous,
autonomous Latino Protestant church counters an argument by Barry Kosmin and
Seymour Lachman, *One Nation under God: Religion in Contemporary Society* (New York:
Harmony, 1993), 138, that, by contrast to African Americans, "There is no tradition of
a separatist or autonomous Hispanic church" in the United States.

    2 A. C. Valdez with James F. Scheer, *Fire on Azusa Street* (Costa Mesa, Calif.: Gift
Publications, 1980); Abundio L. López and Rosa López, "Spanish Receive the Pente-
cost," *Apostolic Faith* (Oct. 1906); Arthur G. Osterberg, "Oral History of the Life of
Arthur G. Osterberg and the Azusa Street Revival," transcribed interview by Jerry
Jensen and Jonathan Perkins, 1966, Flower Pentecostal Heritage Center, Assemblies
of God Headquarters, Springfield, Missouri.

3  Osterberg, "Oral History," 12; also see Thomas R. Nickel, *Azusa Street Outpouring: As Told to Me by Those Who Were There* 3rd. ed. (1956; Hanford, Calif.: Great Commission International, 1986), 13.

4  Mrs. Knapp [*sic*], untitled article, *Apostolic Faith* (Sept. 1906): 2; *Apostolic Faith* (Sept. 1906): 3.

5  Richard Crayne, *Pentecostal Handbook*, 3rd. ed. (1963; Morristown, Tenn.: Richard Crayne, 1990), 228.

6  Valdez with Scheer, *Fire on Azusa Street*, 27, 34, esp. 39.

7  López and López, "Spanish Receive the Pentecost," 4.

8  Ibid., emphasis mine.

9  Charismatics differed from Pentecostals in that they tended to work within their existing Christian traditions to promote the spiritual gifts and they did not dogmatically affirm the initial evidence theory that the baptism with the Holy Spirit must be evidenced by speaking in unknown tongues.

10  "Work among Spanish," *Pisgah* (Jan. 1909): 11–12.

11  "A Revival in Los Angeles," *Pisgah* (Dec. 1910): 13.

12  "Work among Spanish," 11–12.

13  Miroslav Volf, "Materiality of Salvation: An Investigation in the Soteriologies of Liberation and Pentecostal Theologies," *Journal of Ecumenical Studies* 26.3 (1989): 447–467.

14  Evangeline Hymer, "A Study of the Social Attitudes of Adult Mexican Immigrants in Los Angeles and Vicinity" (M.A. thesis, University of Southern California, 1923).

15  G. Bromley Oxnam, *The Mexican in Los Angeles: Los Angeles City Survey* (Los Angeles, Calif.: InterChurch World Movement of North America, 1920), 6, 10, 15.

16  For more on Mexican popular Catholicism and folk healing, see Robert T. Trotter II and Juan Antonio Chavira, *Curanderismo: Mexican American Folk Healing*, 2nd. ed. (Athens: University of Georgia Press, 1997); Ari Kiev, *Curanderismo: Mexican American Folk Psychiatry* (New York: Free Press, 1968); William Madsen and Claudia Madsen, *A Guide to Mexican Witchcraft* (Mexico City: Minutiea Mexicana, 1972); June Macklin, "*Curanderismo* and *Espiritismo*: Complementary Approaches to Traditional Health Services," in *The Chicano Experience*, ed. Stanley A. West and June Macklin (Boulder, Colo.: Westview, 1979), 207–226.

17  Juarez Cano, "El Rev. Francisco Olazábal: Datos Biográficos," *El Mensajero Cristiano* (June 1938): 6–8, 12–13; Roberto Domínguez, *Pioneros de Pentecostés: Norteamerica y Las Antillas*, 3rd ed. (Barcelona, Spain: Clie, 1990), 1:41–42; Luís Villaronga, "¿Quién es Olazábal?" *El Mundo* (1934): 31; Luís Villaronga, "Datos para la Biografía del Rvdo F. Olazábal," *El Mensajero Cristiano* (Oct. 1938): 5–6; Frank Olazábal Jr., Latino Pentecostal Oral History Project (LPOHP), telephone interview, May 1998, Hanover, New Hampshire.

18  Cano, "El Rev. Francisco Olazábal," 6–8, 12–13; Domínguez, *Pioneros de Pentecostés*, 41–42; Villaronga, "¿Quién es Olazábal?" 31; Villaronga, "Datos para la Biografía," 5–6.

19  Homer A. Tomlinson, *Miracles of Healing in the Ministry of Rev. Francisco Olazábal* (Queens, N.Y.: Tomlinson, 1938), 6; Domínguez, *Pioneros de Pentecostés*, 32–35.

20  Domínguez, *Pioneros de Pentecostés*, 36.

21  Methodist Episcopal Church, *Official Minutes of the Sixty-Fourth Session of the California Conference of the Methodist Episcopal Church* (Santa Cruz, Calif.: Methodist Episcopal Church, 1916), 26, 34; Methodist Episcopal Church, *Official Minutes of the Sixty-Fifth Session of the California Conference of the Methodist Episcopal Church* (Santa Cruz, Calif.: Methodist Episcopal Church, 1917), 185.

22  Tomlinson, *Miracles of Healing*, 6–7; Domínguez, *Pioneros de Pentecostés*, 32, 35; Francisco Olazábal, "A Mexican Witness," *Pentecostal Evangel* (16 Oct. 1920).

23  H. C. Ball, "A Report of the Spanish Pentecostal Convention," *Christian Evangel* (28 Dec. 1918): 7; Francisco Olazábal, "God Is Blessing on the Mexican Border," *Weekly Evangel* (1 Oct. 1921): 10; Victor De León, *The Silent Pentecostals: A Biographical History of the Pentecostal Movement among the Hispanics in the Twentieth Century* (Taylors, S.C.: Faith Printing Company, 1979), 28–29, 99; H. C. Ball, letter to Pastor J. R. Kline in personal collection of Gastón Espinosa, 7 Feb. 1933, 1–2; Tomlinson, *Miracles of Healing*, 7.

24  Miguel Guillén, *La Historia del Concilio Latino Americano de Iglesias Cristianas* (Brownsville, Tex.: Latin American Council of Christian Churches, 1991), 93–114.

25  Tomlinson, *Miracles of Healing*, 7–8.

26  "La Hermana McPherson en la Carpa de Watts y el Hno. Francisco Olazábal en 'Angelus Temple' de Los Angeles," *El Mensajero Cristiano* (Oct. 1927): 6–8; J. T. A., "Un Servicio Evangelio para Los Mexicanos," *El Mensajero Cristiano* (Nov. 1927): 7–8.

27  "La Hermana," 6–8; Frank Olazábal Jr., *Revive Us Again!* (Eagle Rock, Calif.: Frank Olazábal, ca. 1986), 81.

28  "Primera Sesion de la Iglesia Interdenominacional de Chicago," *El Mensajero Cristiano* (Sept. 1929): 8–9; "Iglesia de Chicago, Ill." and "Testimonios de Sanidad Divina," *El Mensajero Cristiano* (Sept. 1930): 12–16; Tomlinson, *Miracles of Healing*, 11.

29  "Cuatro Meses con el Rev. Francisco Olazábal en la Ciudad de Nueva York," *El Mensajero Cristiano* (Jan. 1932): 11–12.

30  Tomlinson, *Miracles of Healing*, 1–2.

31  Ibid.

32  Olazábal Jr., *Revive Us Again!* 123; Tomlinson, *Miracles of Healing*, 12.

33  Gastón Espinosa, "'Your Daughters Shall Prophesy': A History of Women in Ministry in the Latino Pentecostal Movement in the United States," in *Women and Twentieth-Century Protestantism*, ed. Margaret Lamberts Bendroth and Virginia Lieson Brereton (Urbana: University of Illinois Press, 2002), 25–48.

34  "Cuatro Meses," 11–12.

35  Homer A. Tomlinson, "Letter to the *Pentecostal Evangel*," *Pentecostal Evangel* (13 Oct. 1931).

36  Domínguez, *Pioneros de Pentecostés*, 18.

37  Luís Villaronga, "El Evangelista Olazábal en Rio Piedras," *El Mundo* [San Juan, Puerto Rico] (5 May 1934); Guillén, *La Historia*, 122–131; Spencer Duryee, "The Great Aztec," *Christian Herald* (Aug. 1936): 6.

38  David Stoll, *Is Latin America Turning Protestant? The Politics of Evangelical Growth* (Berkeley: University of California Press, 1990).

39  Ernest Gordon, "Revival among Spanish-Speaking," *Sunday School Times* (24 Aug. 1935): 550–551; Duryee, "Great Aztec," 5–7; Tomlinson, *Miracles of Healing*, 12, 17, 24.

40  Tomlinson, *Miracles of Healing*, 16–17; Domínguez, *Pioneros de Pentecostés*, 18, 44.

41  Tomlinson, *Miracles of Healing*, 18–19; Domínguez, *Pioneros de Pentecostés*, 45–46; "La Campaña Olazábal en Puerto Rico," *El Mensajero Cristiano* (Apr. 1936): 3.

42  "Campaña Olazábal de El Paso, Texas," and Carlos Sepúlveda, "La Campaña Olazábal en El Paso, Texas," and "Glorioso Servicio de Despedida," *El Mensajero Cristiano* (Aug. 1936): 6–7, 15; Tomlinson, *Miracles of Healing*, 19–20.

43  Olazábal Jr., LPOHP; Travis Hedrick, untitled article, *Chattanooga Times* (12 Sept. 1936): 1, 7; Tomlinson, *Miracles of Healing*, 16.

44  Homer Tomlinson, "Big Parade of 2,000 Lead Down Fifth Avenue New York City," *White Wing Messenger* (7 Nov. 1936): 1, 4.

45  "Rev. F. Olazábal, Evangelist Here," *New York Times* (12 June 1937).

46  A. D. Evans, "Brother Olazábal Killed in Auto Accident," *White Wing Messenger* (19 June 1937): 1; "A Mighty Man of God Has Fallen in the Midst of His Labors," *The White Wing Messenger* (3 July 1937): 4; Tomlinson, *Miracles of Healing*, 23–25; Domínguez, *Pioneros de Pentecostés*, 50–56.

47  Villaronga, "¿Quién es Olazábal?" 31; Duryee, "Great Aztec," 5–8; Cano, "El Rev. Francisco Olazábal," 6–8, 12–13; Domínguez, *Pioneros de Pentecostés*, 41–42.

48  Gastón Espinosa, *Hispanic Churches in American Public Life: Summary of Findings* (Notre Dame, Ind.: Institute for Latino Studies at the University of Notre Dame, 2003), 14; Espinosa, "Demographic Shifts in Latino Religions in the United States," *Social Compass* (Sept. 2004). For a comparison of demographic trends taking place in the United States, Mexico, and Latin America, see Espinosa, "The Impact of Pluralism on Trends in Latin American and U.S. Latino Religions and Society," *Perspectivas* (Fall 2003): 9–55.

49  Andrew M. Greeley, "Defections among Hispanics," *America* (30 July 1988): 61–62; Greeley, "Defections among Hispanics (Updated)," *America* 27 (Sept. 1997): 12–13.

50  Rudy L. Busto, *King Tiger: The Religious Vision of Reies López Tijerina* (Albuquerque: University of New Mexico Press, 2005); Carlos Muñoz Jr., *Youth, Identity, and Power: The Chicano Movement* (New York: Verso, 1992).

# 7

# Santidad, Salvación, Sanidad, Liberación: The Word of Faith Movement among Twenty-First-Century Latina/o Pentecostals

*Arlene Sánchez Walsh*

The Maranatha denomination's mother church in Chicago is in an older industrial section of the city, tucked away in a largely Puerto Rican and Mexican neighborhood. I began studying this group in 2005 because of something I heard Pastor Nahum Rosario say at one of his services. Up until the end of the gathering, it seemed like a typical pentecostal service. Worship was enthusiastic and lengthy; the preaching was animated and lengthy. Before dismissing the congregation, Rosario led those gathered in a series of confessions, but the one that caught my attention was this: "In the name of Jesus, I am a money magnet, finances come to me now."[1] Wondering if such an affirmation was part of the normative worship process—and probably wondering if it worked—those confessions put me on a quest that I am still on: trying to understand the totality of the Word of Faith message in a variety of social, cultural, and theological contexts.

I grew increasingly puzzled when I began an email exchange with another Latino pastor, Greg Marquez, in Los Angeles, California, who described the Word of Faith message as the "true" liberation theology.[2] Although my own biases led me to dismiss this statement largely because of the spokesperson's self-described neo-conservative politics, his further explanation made sense: Word of Faith theology promises that anyone can "activate" his or her faith to receive health and finances. For members of marginalized communities for whom political action offers little hope of ending the endless cycles of poverty, undereducation, chronic sickness, and political marginalization, the Faith message promises a unique solution. Marquez described his global vision as including the use of weekly radio broadcasts to Mexico with the goal of opening sister churches in order to liberate Mexicans from poverty and poverty-related infirmities: "They don't have to live that way, God wants to financially provide for them."[3]

Through such interactions, a number of questions arose to drive this research. Why, if the Word of Faith seemingly offers no concrete answers to the day-to-day problems of many Latina/os, does the Faith message seem an attractive option to many?[4] If the Faith teaching is truly liberation theology, then what, if any, are its consequences for a historically marginalized community? The problem of ongoing suffering, physical and otherwise, seemed the most incongruous piece of the claim that the Faith message produces liberation. If people should be healthy and prosperous all the time, and if all one needs is faith to activate the healing and other material blessings that are already part of God's eternal plan, then why do Latina/os who embrace the Word of Faith message continue to suffer? And how does embracing an Anglo-authored Faith message affect Latina/o experiences and identities as Latina/os?

This chapter examines selected varieties of religious expression found in the Word of Faith movement as it has become grafted onto Latina/o pentecostalism, paying particular attention to how cross-culturally mediated divine healing beliefs and practices have shaped, reflected, and transformed global Faith and pentecostal traditions. I will construct working typologies of healing practices within the Latina/o Word of Faith movement in an effort to move beyond flat notions of assimilation versus acculturation in discussions of Latina/o identity. Since ethnicity and ethnic identity are fluid and not easy notions to categorize, this project considers more stable indicators of identity formation, such as geographic location; the age, gender, and social location of congregants; and the theological education and political affiliations of pastors. I will use these indicators to establish a typology based on the strength or weakness of adherence to "orthodox" Word of Faith teachings on healing and prosperity proffered by the late Kenneth E. Hagin, principal architect of the global Faith movement.[5] Based on my ethnographic fieldwork, including observations of services, interviews with pastors and congregants during which questions probed levels of agreement with Hagin's teachings, and media analyses (tracking church websites for a period of six months, watching over 100 hours of videotaped sermons, and collecting printed materials from church offices), this project categorizes specific congregations as "orthodox" Haginite, "moderate," or "reformer," and uses these classifications as one means of gauging levels of demonstrated interest in maintaining, modifying, or even rejecting Latina/o identity.[6]

In developing and testing these typologies, I selected for in-depth study three congregations that represent significant markers in the Latina/o church community: two churches in Los Angeles, California—El Centro Christian Center (ELCC) in El Centro, and San Gabriel Valley Family Center (VFC) in Glendora—both of which belong to Kenneth Hagin's multiethnic Rhema movement, and the predominantly Latina/o Maranatha World Revival Ministries in Chicago, Illinois, which is the headquarters for a global, independent Latina/o denomination. The ELCC is a multicultural church in the poorest county of southern California; its politically conservative Latino pastor is a well-educated former lawyer and Rhema Bible Training Center graduate whose desire is not only to build his existing congregation, but also to develop Spanish-speaking sister churches in the United States and Mexico. The VFC is pastored by a U.S.–born Latino who does not speak Spanish, prefers not to discuss issues of race or ethnicity, and seems comfortable with the high levels of assimilation he has attained for himself and his church. Maranatha is an indigenous Word of Faith church founded by Latina/os (Puerto Rican) and is composed largely of immigrants. The chapter also draws on research at other Latina/o congregations in Reno, Nevada; Azusa, California; Waukegan, Illinois; and Bayamón and Ponce, Puerto Rico. Although this method does not offer sufficient data to make many definitive statements about the overall nature of such a diverse movement as Latina/o Word of Faith churches, it does provide a fresh angle for considering healing practices in relation to ethnic identity, and it allows consideration of the question of whether the Faith message is in any meaningful sense for Latina/os a form of liberation theology.

To apply the typologies developed by this study, ELCC can best be described as orthodox Hagin. Interviews with the pastor, church staff, and congregants reveal strong adherence to Hagin's ideas about illness, prayer, and activating the Word of Faith in every instance that there is sickness or financial need; when theological questions arise, leaders refer congregants directly to Hagin's writings. The VFC, by contrast, can best be described as moderate. In fieldwork conducted at the church, no healing services were observed; sermons were generically evangelical in tone and content; there was little discussion of spiritual gifts and no discussion of Word of Faith essentials such as "activating faith" or "speaking faith into action"; neither were there confessions or prayer time for healing. One of the only markers of Hagin's influence was that the pastor and his wife had graduated from the Rhema Training Center, and they were sending their son to seminary at Joel Osteen's Bible institute in Houston, Texas. Finally, Maranatha falls under the last category: reformer. This denomination has appropriated an amalgam of Word of Faith and pentecostal teachings, adapting and remaking them as their own. As a Latina/o-founded, Spanish-language church, efforts to support a distinctly Latina/o communal identity are most evident among this group; yet, Maranatha's emphasis on individual revelations and confessions of faith have led this denomination to discount the merely material and social contexts of oppression that some commentators would consider essential to enacting a meaningful form of Latina/o liberation theology.

The Word of Faith movement began as an outgrowth of U.S. Pentecostalism. By the 1940s–1950s, many in the Pentecostal movement had grown tired of what they viewed as "dead" denominationalism and an overall "quenching of the Spirit."[7] Leaders such as Kenneth E. Hagin began to preach a message that expanded on the traditional pentecostal idea of spiritual gifts to include a new revelation that one could receive, called the revelation of the Word of Faith.[8] "Word of Faith" means that humans control their destiny through how much faith they generate to fulfill the promises that God has already given to them.[9] Such churches emphasize a distinction between the "logos" word, that which God speaks generally, and the "rhema" word, that which God speaks to the believer now backed by creative power. For example, in Word of Faith churches, it is common to pray for healing, believing that the healing has already occurred, and to ask persons to simply accept by faith that they have received their healing as a rhema word; there is no need to pray for the same physical, emotional, or financial issues over and over again if one agrees that God has already given what one has asked for by faith.

By the early 2000s, Hagin's Rhema Bible Training Centers operated in 14 countries around the world, including 4 in Latin America. Latina/os began to move out of classical Pentecostal denominations into Charismatic and Word of Faith churches beginning in the 1970s.[10] Those initial Word of Faith expressions, however, did not include much in the way of cultural markers that allowed Latina/os to maintain their ethnic identity; therefore, the next movement within the Word of Faith was toward autonomous, independent churches. Some of these church movements, like Maranatha, were exported from Latin America and the Caribbean to the United States and still bear strong marks of Latina/o identity. Others, like those that affiliated with Hagin's Rhema network, draw from the wells of classical Pentecostalism and Haginite Word of Faith teachings and tend to be assimilationist in their attitudes toward ethnicity—because they envision their adopted theologies as expressing a biblical standard of faith that supersedes secular conventions of identity politics. In this chapter, I will consider the similarities and differences among healing practices and their contextualizations in several Latina/o Word of Faith churches in order to develop and test my typologies of orthodox, moderate, and reformer Haginite theologies and practices; assess the cross-cultural, transnational, and theological negotiations that have animated ongoing conversations and controversies, focusing particularly on the question of whether the Faith message functions as a Latina/o liberation theology for these church communities; and illumine more broadly the interrelated subjects of divine healing, global Faith movements, and Latina/o pentecostalism.

## Rhema Churches, Southern California

This study begins with two Rhema churches in southern California: El Centro Christian Center (ELCC) and San Gabriel Valley Family Center (VFC). Both were founded in the early 1980s and are today pastored by Mexican American Rhema graduates. The former can be classified as orthodox Haginite and the latter as more moderate.

The ELCC is characterized by strict adherence to Hagin's core doctrines related to activating one's faith in order to achieve blessings, especially healing, from God.[11] On the first Sunday morning when I visited to conduct fieldwork, ELCC met for its first time at a local high school, where it still meets, attracting 50–75 attendees weekly to its English-language services.[12] Greg Marquez had been leading the church for the previous 13 years. The service began with worship through song, which lasted around 25 minutes. After that, Pastor Marquez asked if anyone had a prayer request; those who did were asked to come to the front so Marquez could pray for them. There was nothing out of the ordinary for this type of prayer ritual except that afterward, when there was another prayer session and the pastor asked people to come for a host of reasons—healing, finances, conversion, Spirit baptism—a woman went up again for prayer, as she had done at the start of the service. Marquez knew the woman and, calling her by her first name, he asked if she was coming for the same prayer request as last time; when she answered affirmatively, he asked her to go back and sit down. She did not protest, but simply returned to her seat. Marquez continued to pray for people as I moved to the back of the sanctuary to interview members of the congregation as they were leaving the service.

Such a display as rebuffing a woman coming for prayer, especially by a pastor to one of his congregants, might shock those unaccustomed to the idea behind this action. Word of Faith pastors teach that faith is an active, almost tangible thing, and if faith is interrupted from working in a person's life by doubt and disbelief or by sin in the person's life, then the promises of God will not be fulfilled. Therefore, to pray for this woman again for the same thing would have constituted an open display of not accepting the core teachings of Hagin regarding healing: that it is available to everyone who asks in faith, and that once one asks for something in faith, one should not ask for it again, since that would display a lack of faith.[13]

The healing portion of this service yielded no dramatic incidents beyond the woman being asked to sit down. At least on the surface, there was no direct evidence of any healing. Outside the service, and during later interviews, congregants typically answered my questions about healing by affirming their belief that healing was going to happen; they had already claimed it, now they were required to continue in faith until the healing physically manifested itself, because in the spiritual realm, the healing had already occurred. Marquez explained this reasoning later using classic Hagin theology.[14] When people are not healed, physically or otherwise, it is because they do not exercise a sufficient amount of faith; if people simply exercised faith, they would have their prayers answered. Orthodox Haginite churches tend to be biblical literalists; therefore, disease of any kind is demonized as having some kind of satanic influence, or it could be that the person has not stayed faithful to trusting in God's intent to always heal. Regardless, congregants often described their concern for those who do not continue to affirm their faith for healing: they are unwittingly becoming weaker in faith and can become subject to demonic influences. All of this sounds typically Haginite.

This raises the question of whether ELCC's embrace of an orthodox Haginite Word of Faith position indicates that, more broadly, the church's Latino leader and members have abandoned their ethnic identities and assimilated to U.S. theological and cultural values. Countering this conclusion, beginning in the summer of 2007, Marquez began a Spanish service that drew roughly a dozen people; he has been televising a program in Spanish across the Mexican border since the late 1990s. Marquez appears to be quite aware of his ethnicity and aware of the public image of Mexican Americans, particularly around the question of undocumented people. Writing in his internet blog in 2007, Marquez took issue with his fellow political conservatives, whose anti-Mexican sentiments could not be unwound from the anti–illegal immigration policies that conservatives like Marquez supported. Marquez concluded his blog with oft-cited biblical quotations that plea for justice for the alien.[15] In an interview with Marquez, his understanding and sympathy for the large Mexican population of the Imperial Valley was clear.[16] I picked up on a statement he had made to me via email regarding the Word of Faith being the true source of liberation theology for Latina/os and asked him to expound on that; as he did, he launched into a passionate plea for Latina/os to not be wed to ideologies that make them victims; they have the power, through faith, to obtain things that have eluded them through secular means. This seems a very important point. Even in adopting an Anglo-authored theology, Marquez turned it in a distinctively Latina/o-oriented direction.

The other Rhema church studied for this project would not be considered as orthodox Haginite as ELCC. The pastor, Ray Almaguer, also prefers not to highlight his ethnicity. During interviews, Almaguer seemed uncomfortable talking about the issue of ethnicity, and during services, he seemed not terribly interested in correcting the mispronunciation of his name by non-Latina/o congregants, who spoke fondly of him.[17] There is a different and more complex relationship with Word of Faith theology and with ethnicity at Marquez's church, which can be classified as moderate Haginite.

The VFC meets in an affluent suburb of Los Angeles, in the hills above the San Gabriel Valley.[18] The multiethnic congregation consists of around 50 people who meet in their own building. Services differ from ELCC's in that

they are much more traditionally and generically evangelical rather than pentecostal or Word of Faith. After the 20 minutes or so of worship in one observed
service, there was no altar call, no request for prayer, no time for healing.[19]
From worship, the service transitioned to announcements and then to a sermon, which was notable for its insistence that women be viewed as equals in
ministry. The service concluded with corporate prayer time. Sermons during
other observed services focused on topics such as building faith and family.
There was during some services prayer for healing, but it was a rare occurrence. Rather than include a weekly healing prayer time, what VFC seemed to
do was to invite speakers, all of whom were part of the Word of Faith tradition,
to preside over special sessions at the church, when a more focused time of
prayer for healing, as well as prophecy, glossolalia, and teaching on how to
"grow your faith" for finances, more typically occurred. It may be that VFC has
not abandoned the Word of Faith teachings its pastor learned in Bible college
but that, like many evangelical and pentecostal churches, the church leadership
has chosen to conduct more generic Sunday morning services that appeal to a
broad constituency, while restricting the more distinctive and supernaturalist
elements of its spiritual identity to certain services only attended by those who
are truly interested in the Word of Faith message.

What can be said about the two totally different services described for
ELCC and VFC? For one, they are snapshots; they are not indicative of the
totality of these churches, but each is relatively typical of other services
observed in these churches. Speculating on why healing is central to ELCC and
not VFC would be easy if one were simply to take into account their geographic
differences. The ELCC is located in the Imperial Valley, the poorest county in
southern California, while VFC is located in Glendora, California, a wealthy
upper-middle-class suburb. However, ELCC's congregation is not composed of
the vast numbers of immigrant agricultural workers that mostly populate the
Imperial Valley. Most ELCC attendees are working class or middle class, and
have access to health care through their jobs. Both churches are ostensibly
"Latina/o," yet neither Marquez nor Almaguer discussed their ethnicity at any
great length during interviews or in their services.

The discrepancy in the relative emphasis on healing between ELCC and
VFC seems to stem primarily from differences between the two pastors. Like
many pentecostal churches, these two (like Maranatha, discussed below) are
mirror images of their pastors' theological and cultural worldviews. The ELCC
is more orthodox, it seems, partly because Marquez really admired "Daddy"
Hagin; Marquez is an articulate, well-versed spokesperson for Hagin's teachings, and he teared up on several occasions just talking about him. Almaguer
did not convey the same kind of personal attachment to Hagin or his teachings;
he seemed more willing to draw upon diverse theological and cultural elements,
and more comfortable with generic U.S. evangelical themes such as salvation,
discipleship, and church growth. For Almaguer, the Hagin influences are

there, but they seem to have been filtered through a variety of guest speakers, conferences, and the occasional special church service. Almaguer's Word of Faith proclivities seamlessly weave into his larger U.S.–oriented evangelical theological sympathies to such an extent that little, if any, direct Hagin-like emphasis—or, for that matter, more typically Latin American emphases—on healing is discernible.[20]

The moderate or blended stance represented by VFC's Almaguer might be critiqued by more orthodox Haginites as capitulating to the "dead formalism" of U.S. evangelical Christianity—a critique raised by ELCC's Marquez against evangelicals generally although not pointed specifically against moderate Latina/o Word of Faith churches like VFC. Indeed, Marquez prognosticated in his internet blog in 2009 that the death of American evangelicalism could not come too soon: "If the leaders of American evangelical Christianity were alive in Elijah's day they'd be the ones trying to explain away, in extremely erudite and scholarly language, the fact that their God had not answered by fire."[21] For Marquez and other orthodox Haginites, Word of Faith is the antidote to a docile and superficial evangelical Christianity that long ago abandoned the notion that God is active, powerful, and willing to do anything Christians ask as long as they ask in faith. This more immediate expectation of faith producing tangible material results in ELCC as compared with VFC may help to account for why healing is treated so differently in these two churches.

Healing is one of Marquez's central topics for sermons (as is prosperity) because, for him, healing and prosperity are empirically verifiable and thus function as divine signs that the revelation of the Word of Faith is authentic. There is no intellectual parsing of terms in this church; one is either healed, receives it, and believes that it will happen, or one does not; there is little, if any, public discussion of the kinds of secondary and tertiary—or more spiritual, emotional, and psychological claims of—healing that are sometimes expounded upon in Faith churches. It seems that there is at ELCC, as at many other pentecostal churches, a defined, if implicit, script for approaching healing prayer. Physical healing is overwhelmingly the first choice for pastors or prayer teams to address; after that comes emotional and psychological healing. Thus, if someone asking prayer for a bad back is not apparently healed, Marquez moves on to praying for emotional or psychological healing. But physical healing has particular evidentiary value in demonstrating that ELCC is an authentic first-century pentecostal church where faith sets the Holy Spirit in motion to work in miraculous ways.

## Maranatha World Revival Ministries, Chicago, Illinois

In seeking to recapture authentic pentecostalism, orthodox Haginite churches closely resemble the Maranatha churches that are here classified as reformers.

Maranatha, a denomination based in Chicago which was founded by a Puerto Rican native, Nahum Rosario, shortly after immigrating in 1978, differs from Haginite Word of Faith churches in part because it is deeply grounded in its ethnic roots as a Puerto Rican import and, as such, maintains ethnicity as a crucial component of self-identification. Maranatha also, although tenuously, reveres not only Hagin and other Word of Faith teachers but also certain Anglo pentecostal pioneers, notably Smith Wigglesworth (1859–1947) and A. A. Allen (1911–1970), both of whose anti-denominationalism and faith for healing or prosperity make them appealing mentors to adopt cross-culturally—although they are not venerated to the degree that Hagin is in orthodox Word of Faith churches.[22] Indeed, Maranatha disavows the extent of its borrowings from non-Latina/o sources, in part, it seems, to emphasize the authority that comes from Rosario's claim to have received a revelation from God to start Maranatha as a distinctly Latina/o church movement.

Maranatha is populated mostly by Latina/os and is geographically representative depending on the part of the country in which congregations are located. In the churches of southern California, Nevada, and the Southwest, Maranatha is distinctly Mexican and Central American; churches in the Midwest and along the East Coast are Puerto Rican and Dominican. By offering Latina/os an apparently authentic pentecostal experience untethered to classical Pentecostal denominations and their associations with bureaucracy and dead traditions, while also offering ethnic solidarity that is more difficult to maintain in Anglo-authored movements like the Word of Faith, Maranatha competes with ethnically specific Pentecostal denominations like Asamblea Apostólica (Oneness Pentecostal, which is predominantly Mexican) and Iglesia de Dios Pentecostal (Puerto Rican). Maranatha churches are located in urban areas, where Spanish-speaking Latina/os are demographically dominant. The dominant language used in Maranatha services is Spanish, and there is little desire for change. Rather, there is a desire to help non–Spanish speaking attendees with translation during services.

Maranatha's theological emphasis is God's desire for his people to prosper and be in good health; thus, what sets Maranatha apart as a reformer congregation is not so much a distinctive theological agenda as an emphasis on incorporating Anglo-authored Word of Faith and pentecostal teachings within a thoroughly Latina/o cultural context. The humble Chicago location of Maranatha's headquarters church denotes more of the social reality of Latina/o life in Chicago than the appearance of prosperity that the church covets. Maranatha is in a tough neighborhood on the northwest side of Chicago; housed in a former factory building, the church is nondescript from the outside, and there is no parking lot. This is a cause of great consternation to Rosario, who asked the congregation to pray specifically for the $18,000 it will take to buy the lot and build on it. Entering the building, the church is rather plain. The sanctuary, though it could seat close to 1,000, was never during our fieldwork more than one-third full and usually held only about 150–200 people.[23] The cameras that taped every service for purchase later at the church bookstore were focused on the front of the church, seemingly in an attempt to portray a fuller church.

Congregants dressed impressively for church; men wore suits, and women wore dresses and went into the bathroom frequently to fix their hair and makeup. If one were to note anecdotally the professional status of the crowd, it would have been working class to middle class, with a few people who introduced themselves with titles like "Dr."[24] In comparison to the heavily working-class ELCC and the upper-middle-class VFC, Maranatha congregants dressed better. In terms of attendance, the two Rhema churches were smaller, never more than 50–100 people on any given Sunday. Maranatha's website, updated frequently and visually appealing, presents its message to anyone who wishes to read about its history, download sermons, listen to sermons on internet radio, or buy any number of products. It greets visitors with the church's motto: "Santidad, Salvación, Sanidad, Liberación" (Holiness, Salvation, Healing, Deliverance). "Apostle" Nahum Rosario's welcome message boasts of over 300 churches globally that are affiliated with Maranatha (the website lists a dozen churches that have direct web links; other affiliations are noted via pinpoints on a world map, but were difficult to verify).[25] Maranatha's in-house and online bookstores sell books by former heroes of pentecostalism, like Wigglesworth and Allen, as well as by nearly every prominent Word of Faith teacher, including Kenneth Hagin, Kenneth Copeland, Jerry Savelle, and Charles Capps. Indeed, Maranatha, like other Faith churches, participates in the consumption and production of globally marketed health- and prosperity-related books, sermons, and CDs. Maranatha illustrates the more general insight drawn by anthropologist Simon Coleman that Faith teachings originating in the United States are constantly "re-packaged and re-disseminated into the transnational realm" as health and prosperity are sold in different ways to diverse cultural audiences.[26]

Despite Rosario's protestations to the contrary, it appears that the chief reason people attend Maranatha is the charismatic personality of—and sense of ethnic affinity cultivated by—the church's founder and self-titled apostle; likewise, people are attracted to the church's affirming prosperity message— although Maranatha, like several of its affiliates (notably the churches in Waukegan and Puerto Rico) reject being labeled as "prosperity churches." Efforts to interview Rosario were fruitless; I never got past the myriad of gatekeepers the church had prepared to insulate Rosario from researchers. The church website presents a great quantity of personal information about Rosario, centering on the revelation he believes God gave him to begin a church in the late 1970s. Acting upon this vision, Rosario managed to create a sense of community—solidified by shared use of the Spanish language and Rosario's explicit elevation of Spanish above English—by cultivating a sensibility that the congregation understood something that the larger world did not. Often, Rosario referred directly to the Latina/o community. For instance, he commented, "Spanish don't develop things—we reveal things. That's why the language is so superior."[27] Although he was making a joke, there was an aspect of seriousness to it that created an overall sense of specialness within the community. Such comments not only unite the mostly bilingual members of the church but also affirm the 10 percent of the congregation who wear headphones every Sunday during the English service (which attracts an average of 40 attendees, compared with the 150–200 people who typically attend the church's Spanish services) in order to listen to the proceedings translated into Spanish.

Rosario is not the only one to create an environment for churchgoers to be comfortable with being Latina/o; similarly, other Maranatha churches express the same desire to promote their message primarily in Spanish. Websites from Maranatha churches in Columbia, South Carolina; Reno, Nevada; San Diego, California; and Waukegan, Illinois are nearly all in Spanish. These churches are small, with average attendance between 25 and 75. All copy the Maranatha statement of faith, promote prosperity and healing, and prominently display their affiliation with, or acquiescence to be under, the covering of Apostle Rosario's mother church in Chicago. Only one church, Maranatha in Waukegan, featured a curious deviation from the other Maranatha churches that had connections to the Chicago church. The Waukegan church had a link in the website to its food pantry, Pan y Peces (Bread and Fishes), and intimated that though it believed in God's provisions, it felt that the congregation was called to provide some more substantial programs for outreach to the Latina/o community.[28] In the churches studied for the larger project, I did not find any others that had communal ministries such as food pantries—a point to keep in mind when considering the implications of Word of Faith theology for liberation.

Doctrinally, Maranatha's emphasis on the certainty of healing emanates from Haginite Word of Faith and classical Pentecostal teachings, but these teachings are reformed, or recontextualized, for the Latina/o community. The Maranatha website proclaims in its doctrinal statement that "the perfect will of God is the physical healing of every believer and is received by faith and through the laying on of hands (Isaiah 53:4–5, 1 Peter 2:24–25, James 5:14–15)."[29] Therefore, being in the perfect will of God means that healing is assured, if it is asked for in faith. The power of believers to move themselves into this perfect will is assumed to be immense. People can use a list of confessions—that formally sound strikingly similar to Catholic liturgical prayers, which are familiar to many participants—to bring about the promised blessing. Of the half-dozen teachings that Rosario has on the church website at any given time, confessions take up approximately six pages of short paragraphs that one should speak in order for that dimension of faith to become activated. There are paragraphs for healing, church growth, finances, family, and generally strengthening one's faith. In these confessions, there are a few parenthetical citations that refer to the Bible, but they are not like typical statements of faith, where Bible verses follow nearly every sentence. The website explains the purpose of confessions: "[Y]ou have the power to bring blessing or cursing upon your life depending on what you confess daily; these confessions will help you have a victorious life. Repeat them with a loud voice and you will begin to experience the abundance of life that Jesus has promised those who have faith."[30] Because the victorious life is one of abundance, spiritually and materially, living a cursed life then necessarily means that one does not have enough faith, or one has failed to activate faith by speaking blessings into existence.

The blessed life prominently includes the material provision of physical health and financial prosperity. Confessions attest that "sin, death, sickness, and poverty have no power over me because the Spirit of life in Christ Jesus has set me free from the law of sin and death. . . . In the name of Jesus I cast out devils. In the name of Jesus, nothing I eat harms me, and in the name of Jesus I lay hands on the sick and the sick do recover."[31] At the same time that Maranatha emphasizes healing through prayer, it does not proscribe taking medicines and there are medical doctors who attend the church. Similarly for finances as for health:

> Christ has redeemed me from poverty. . . . I know the grace of my
> Lord Jesus Christ, that though He was rich, yet for my sake He
> became poor, that I, through His poverty, might become rich. I
> always remember the Lord my God for He gives me the power to
> make wealth that He may establish His covenant with me. Since I am
> a faithful tither, I am not cursed. God sends overabundant blessing
> upon me and rebukes the devourer of my finances. For this reason, I
> am a money magnate [sic] and the wealth of the wicked cometh to
> me. Money cometh to me now. Increase cometh to me now. Promo-
> tion cometh to me now. Abundance cometh to me now. In the name
> of Jesus, the favor of God is upon me now.[32]

The poverty one may face in this life has been abrogated by Jesus' birth into poverty; by this reasoning—which draws heavily upon the prominent Anglo pentecostal healing evangelist Oral Roberts's (1918–2009) teachings on "blessing pacts" and "seed faith"—there is no excuse to remain poor, provided that one exercises faith and behaves faithfully through tithing.[33] One's physical and financial condition is thus intimately tied to—and can provide evidence concerning—the state of one's faith. Yet, in tension with this idea, Rosario chastises his congregation for undue materialism and charges them to give things that they do not need away: "There are so many things we don't want to wear any more—but they don't give it to the Salvation Army. They're going to bring it with them to their caskets—they're going to need three caskets. If you have things you don't need—give it away."[34] Aside from Rosario's occasional pronouncements, there is little systematic expression of this latter idea in this theological framework, which places great emphasis on prosperity as a sign of faith rather than of materialism.

Alongside confessions that believers can use to create the conditions for their own blessings, Rosario also emphasizes the idea that individual believers must receive revelations of their blessed status directly from God. Rosario's sermons typically focus on spiritual experiences that offer believers revelatory encounters with God.[35] Rosario is relatively vague about the nature of the requisite revelation, but it seems that he is loosely following the African American Word of Faith preacher Frederick Price's teaching that there is a distinct and necessary spiritual gift called the "revelation of the Word of Faith."[36] People are asked to pray for a revelation and often do claim to receive one; for those who have not received a revelation, they are to pray that God will give them one. During one service that I visited, a person in the congregation stood up during a break in worship when Rosario asked the congregation to pray for revelation and noted that God had given him a new revelation of praying for a person who was nearby standing in the same line; the congregant reported that the person had a heart attack shortly thereafter but recovered because of his revelatory prayers. Rosario's focus on revelation is doubtless appealing in part because it is personal, experiential, and democratic, since anyone can receive one. The focus also minimizes the need to understand the particulars of faith since, as Rosario tells his audience: "What you don't understand, you don't have to understand, let it slide."[37] As long as one has revelations, there is no need to "struggle so much" to try to activate the faith that God has already given in the revelatory realm.[38] The radical alteration of one's perspective on God intertwines people's faith lives with divine presence so that receiving continual revelations from God creates a reciprocal bond of God giving material blessings to his people in return for financial giving from his people.

## Latina/o Word of Faith *as* Liberation Theology?

All three congregations in this study—whether classified as orthodox, moderate, or reformer Word of Faith—like the broader swath of Latina/o pentecostal churches I have studied since the late 1990s, defined faith primarily as a matter of individual rather than communal responsibility. This is not to suggest that there is no concern for the community, but Latina/o pentecostalism (like U.S. pentecostalism generally) is rooted in individualistic notions of piety and morality. This tendency has led the Latino Protestant theologian Harold Recinos to call for the expulsion of the privatized notion of God from Latina/o churches.[39] Reaching a somewhat more optimistic conclusion about the implications of a focus on individual faith, the Latino theologian Orlando Espín notes that the "symbols of popular religion have historically proven themselves quite capable of promoting explicit and often socially effective responses to evil. Instead of utter powerlessness, through popular religion's symbols, the people can define themselves as empowered. In doing so, popular religion is thereby granting meaning and hope."[40] Rather than supporting the collective empowerment of Latina/os to rid their communities of suffering, these alternative forms of meaning and hope support the individual empowerment of Latina/os to take their material circumstances under their own control.

In a theology that emphasizes the inevitability that a life of faith leads to material blessings such as health and prosperity, ongoing suffering—whether on an individual or communal level—has no value or meaning. The ELCC's Marquez explicitly discounted the idea expressed by many evangelicals that suffering can be virtuous: "Try to make virtue out of the suffering church they have merited for failing to follow after God. They excuse the suffering they endure for failing to walk in the spirit by attributing it to the service of God."[41] In Faith thinking, there is no room for the idealizing of physical, emotional, financial, or any other kind of suffering. If a person is suffering, the condition should be temporary; it can be overcome through faith; there is no framework for understanding suffering as having collective causes or as being rooted in oppression so that individuals lack the social, economic, and political power to overcome regardless of the levels of their faith. Suffering, when understood as existing outside the will of God, becomes very unattractive, and its ongoing presence necessarily either indicts God's power and goodness, or indicts the faith levels of Christians.

Both Rhema congregations that I have considered tended toward cultural and linguistic assimilation to U.S. Word of Faith or more broadly evangelical Christianity. Orlando Espín worries that making Jesus a victor without extending that victory to the existential realities of vanquished Latina/os imposes a "deculturized evangelism" on still-marginalized peoples. Historically, religious conversion has often implied cultural conversion, which has robbed Latina/os of their language and ethnic identity.[42] The ELCC's Marquez, to a greater extent than the VFC's Almaguer—whose moderate Word of Faith position has diffused into a generically evangelical church identity—seemed aware of the realities of the immigrant population that surrounds him. Marquez used the Spanish language to broadcast Faith teachings into Mexico and defended Mexican Americans against racist stereotypes when speaking to his fellow, non-Latina/o political conservatives. Yet Marquez displayed little theological framing outside the general lens of individual "liberation" to deal with systemic issues; these issues just never came up. As a political conservative, Marquez was loath to support government intervention for nearly any systemic problem, and nearly always deferred to an uncontextualized language of the free market. As the Latino theologian Arturo Banuelos frames the issue, "Hispanic theologians do not ask the church to join the struggle against an evil pagan world, but rather against oppressors."[43] In Banuelos's view, a genuinely liberating theology requires a more intentional systematic expression against oppression, not just an affirmation of the individual's power to create the conditions of blessing through faith.

To a greater extent than either Rhema congregation, Maranatha cultivates a communal sense of identity as Spanish-speaking Latina/os. Individuals participate in the communal recitation of confessions during services or virtually by reading and listening to church teachings on the internet or through books and CDs, and they seek to receive and act on revelations of the Word of Faith communally by praying and speaking prophetically over one another. Rosario claims that there are communal benefits to individuals activating their faith—for instance, by giving enough money to build a "prayer mountain" retreat modeled on the Pentecostal David Yonggi Cho's Prayer Mountain in Korea. More often than not, the benefits of faith pertain to individuals, but when communicated through testimonies and songs, they become communally significant since they bolster the continued evolution of church members into a communal experience of accessing by faith the unbridled power of the Holy Spirit to sanctify, save, heal, deliver, and provide abundant life. The Faith message democratically promises to individuals that they can harness God's power without mediation by any hierarchy or external authority as long as they speak blessings into reality by faith. Despite its emphasis on Latina/o community, Maranatha eschews merely material and societal explanations and solutions for the marginalized status of Latina/os in favor of spiritual explanations that are manifested in the exorcism of generational curses and in individuals sowing many seeds of faith in order to release God's blessings. In this respect, the reformer stance might be viewed as the least conducive to taking seriously the social and political causes of oppression, which so often manifests in poverty, illness, and other suffering. Yet, the individual sense of empowerment endued by the Faith message, coupled with the sense of membership in a distinctly Latina/o Faith community proffered by reformer churches like Maranatha, helps to make sense of how a theology not specifically tied to easing the communal vanquishment of Latina/os would be, for many, the faith of choice.

There exist few places where the realities of Latina/o life can receive a theological prescription for liberation in pentecostalism. Those prescriptions emanate almost wholly from the supernatural work of the Spirit, the transformative faith of Christianity, and in Faith churches—the alleviation of social ills through the confession that a believer with enough faith simply should not be suffering at the hands of these ills. In a critical reading of Latina/o Word of Faith movements, individual certainty, comfort, ease, abundance, and health constitute imperfect alternatives to the five foci of the wounds of Christ that so captured the devotional life of the Christian church for centuries. It is this radical refraction that deserves further study and a serious examination of its implications for Latina/o evangelicals in the United States and in Latin America.

    1  Field notes (January 2005).

    2  See Miroslav Volf, "Materiality of Salvation: An Investigation in the Soteriologies of Liberation and Pentecostal Theologies," *Journal of Ecumenical Studies* 26.3 (1989): 447–467.

    3  Email communication (14 Feb. 2007).

    4  The term "Latina/o" refers to Latinos and Latinas together, thereby calling attention to the fact that Latina experiences cannot in all instances be submerged into Latino-dominated narratives.

    5  Hagin has been charged (convincingly) with plagiarizing many of his ideas from the earlier pentecostal Essek William Kenyon, but Hagin won for Kenyon's ideas unprecedented popularity; see Bowler's essay in this volume. There is also much debate about the extent to which Hagin is the author of a global Faith movement, given the largely independent emergence of similar groups, such as David Yonggi Cho's Yoido Full Gospel Church in Korea; see Kim's essay in this volume.

    6  The literature on Latina/o ethnic identity in disciplines such as ethnic studies, sociology, religious studies, and history is vast and contested. I draw on the sociologist Rubén G. Rumbaut's ideas in "The Crucible Within: Ethnic Identity, Self-Esteem, and Segmented Assimilation among Children of Immigrants," in *The New Second Generation*, ed. Alejandro Portes (New York: Russell Sage Foundation, 1996), on segmented assimilation. Latina/os occupy a variety of spaces ethnically, pick and choose based on multiple factors, and assimilate into the majority culture in a fragmented method that does not abrogate most Latina/o ties to things such as family, language, or religion (a majority of Latina/os, upward of 65–70 percent, are Catholic).

    7  See William L. De Arteaga, *Quenching the Spirit: Examining Centuries of Opposition to the Moving of the Holy Spirit* (Lake Mary, Fla.: Creation House, 1992).

    8  The traditional pentecostal repertoire of spiritual gifts is based primarily on 1 Corinthians 12.

    9  Hagin taught that believers who activated faith were capable of living well into their 90s without health ailments. Hagin died in 2003, at age 86; see Bowler's essay for controversies surrounding the cause of Hagin's death—because of its implications as an empirical test of the Faith message.

    10  For the role of Latina/os in early pentecostalism, see Espinosa's essay in this volume.

    11  This position differs from other versions of the Word of Faith, such as the innovation of Frederick Price (founder of Crenshaw Christian Center), which was embraced by Maranatha, that one should strive to receive a distinct revelation of the Word of Faith, the same way one seeks to receive Spirit baptism.

    12  I conducted fieldwork at ELCC between March and June 2007.

    13  Other (less orthodox, according to the typologies herein developed) Latina/o Word of Faith churches that I studied did pray repeatedly for people, and did not view this as contrary to the spirit of Hagin's teachings; for example, a church in Azusa,

California, adhered more to the teachings of Kenneth Copeland and Charles Capps, both of whom have Hagin's imprint on their ministries, but they do not teach exactly the same thing regarding prayer for healing.

14  Interview (15 Mar. 2007).

15  Greg Marquez, "Anti-Amnesty or Just Anti-Mexican" (21 May 2007), http://www.ivchristiancenter.com (accessed 27 Apr. 2009).

16  Interview (15 Mar. 2007).

17  Interview (15 Mar. 2007).

18  I conducted fieldwork at VFC between June and August 2007.

19  Field notes (Aug. 2007).

20  For the emphasis given to spiritual healing by many Latin Americans, see Espinosa's essay in this volume.

21  Greg Marquez, "The Coming Evangelical Collapse Sounds Right to Me" (10 Mar. 2009), http://www.ivchristiancenter.org (accessed 15 Oct. 2009).

22  Allen is a curious choice of mentor in that he struggled all his life with alcoholism and died from cirrhosis of the liver; he did, though, have a sizable outreach to Latina/os in the Southwest, and his ministry still sells Spanish editions of his books, for instance, *El Precio del Poder de Dios para Hacer Milagros* [The Price of God's Miracle-Working Power] (Miracle Valley, Ariz.: A. A. Allen Revival, n.d.), which can be purchased from Maranatha's website.

23  I owe a great debt to my research assistant, Michelle Krejci, University of Sheffield, who conducted fieldwork at Maranatha, Chicago, May–June 2005, extending upon fieldwork that I began in Jan. 2005.

24  Krejci field notes (1 May 2005).

25  See http://www.maranathausa.com/english_links.htm (accessed 15 Oct. 2009).

26  Simon Coleman, *The Globalisation of Charismatic Christianity* (Cambridge: Cambridge University Press, 2000), 36.

27  Krejci field notes (11 May 2005).

28  See http://www.maranatharevival.com/panes (accessed 15 Oct 2009).

29  "Doctrinal Declaration of Maranatha World Revival Ministries," http://www.maranathausa.com/english_whatwebelieve.htm (accessed 15 Oct. 2009).

30  "Confessions for a Life of Victory," http://www.maranathausa.com/confessionseng (accessed 15 Oct 2009).

31  "My Position and Victory in Christ," http://www.maranathausa.com/confessionseng (accessed 15 October 2009).

32  "My Prosperity and Daily Provision," http://www.maranathausa.com/confessionseng (accessed 15 October 2009).

33  See, for example, Oral Roberts, *God's Formula for Success and Prosperity* (Tulsa, Okla.: Abundant Life, 1956), and Roberts, *Miracle of Seed Faith* (Tulsa, Okla.: Oral Roberts Evangelistic Association, 1970). The blessing pact idea was that God blesses those who give (specifically, in the original context, to Roberts's television ministry). The seed faith concept built on blessing pacts to offer a powerful agricultural image (that has since been picked up by innumerable ministries as an extremely effective fundraising strategy) of how God provides blessings in a reciprocal fashion: there is a spiritual law parallel to natural law by which those who sow into a particular ministry

will later reap a harvest (that includes not only money but other forms of material and spiritual blessings, such as healing and salvation—not only for oneself but also for others for whom one prays) in return.

34  Krejci field notes (15 May 2005).

35  We examined all 30 sermons that Rosario posted on the Maranatha website during the spring and summer of 2005 and compared them with the website's comprehensive sermon index; the content was remarkably consistent.

36  Krejci field notes (12 May 2005).

37  Krejci field notes (15 May 2005).

38  Krejci field notes (9 May 2005).

39  Harold J. Recinos, *Good News from the Barrio* (Louisville, Ky.: Westminster John Knox, 2006).

40  Orlando Espín, *A Fé do Povo: Reflexões Teológicas sobre o Catolicismo Popular* [The Faith of the People: Theological Reflections on Popular Catholicism] (São Paulo, Brazil: Paulinas, 2000), 169; although Espín's work focuses on Latina/o Catholic popular religion, his insights are applicable to Latina/o pentecostals.

41  Marquez, "Walking in Love," http://www.ivchristiancenter.com (accessed 10 Mar. 2009).

42  Espín, *Fé do Povo*, 169.

43  Arturo J. Banuelos, "U.S. Hispanic Theology: An Initial Assessment," in *Mestizo Christianity*, ed. Arturo J. Banuelos, 55–82 (Maryknoll, N.Y.: Orbis, 1999), 76. Like Espín, Banuelos is addressing Latina/o Catholics, but his arguments are applicable to Latina/o pentecostals.

# 8

# Exorcising the Demons of Deprivation: Divine Healing and Conversion in Brazilian Pentecostalism

*R. Andrew Chesnut*

As pentecostals, poor Brazilians are able to reclaim their health because their religion, unlike its major religious rivals, conceptualizes religious affiliation as conversion. Religious affiliation conceived as a "positive transformation of the nature and value of a person" makes sense to individuals and groups who have been negatively evaluated by society.[1] Affiliation is rarely conceived of as conversion among those occupying the apex of the social pyramid, because such people already enjoy a positive social evaluation. A Brazilian industrialist, for instance, seeks religious continuity with his secular status. He asks God to affirm his earthly status, not to transform it. In contrast, the poor individual seeks to turn away (*convertere*) from the contagions of the diseased social body. In turning away from alcoholism, domestic strife, and deficient medical "care," the convert begins to recover her health, to restore her social, physical, and spiritual integrity.[2]

The disease of poverty in its multifarious forms predisposes the dispossessed of Brazil and Latin America to accept the pentecostal practice of *cura divina* (divine cure or faith healing). Nevertheless, illness itself is only a necessary, not a sufficient, condition for conversion to pentecostalism. If the maladies of material deprivation were the sole engines propelling pentecostal expansion, then this popular expression of Protestantism would claim most Brazilians as members. Before an individual accepts the preacher's *chamada*, or call, to conversion and walks to the front of the church to publicly "accept Jesus," a series of interrelated events has taken place that has brought the individual to worship in the spartan pentecostal temple. No two persons follow the exact same path to the doors of a pentecostal house of worship, but the life histories of my informants evidence a common road traveled by the great majority who have adhered to the faith. A closer inspection of this path and its milestones will shed new light on the dynamics of the meteoric pentecostal growth in Brazil and throughout Latin America.

Health Crisis

Illness, like hunger, is a permanent fixture of the urban periphery and rural areas, and its mere presence does not alarm people. When, however, a lingering but apparently benign condition worsens, or a sudden and virulent pathogen attacks, the crisis impels the afflicted or her family to action. Whatever the nature of the illness, people first tend to seek to defuse the crisis through secular channels. The gods, as sociologists of religion Rodney Stark and William Bainbridge postulate, are only implored after a cheaper or easier way of remedying the situation has come to naught.[3]

In the case of physical illness, Belenenses (residents of Belém, the capital of the state of Pará where I conducted most of my research), like most Amazonians and particularly the economically disadvantaged, will normally draw on their vast pharmacopoeia of medicinal plants, herbs, and roots before visiting a health clinic or attempting to scrape together enough cash to purchase pharmaceuticals.[4] The colorful Ver-o-Peso market spilling beyond Belém's historic riverfront is an open-air pharmacy stocking everything from basil (not for pesto but for medicinal baths) to cinchona bark from which quinine is extracted. Affordable prices make these organic drugs the remedy of choice, regardless of religious affiliation, in the *baixadas* (the local term for *favela*) and even in many middle-class homes. When, over 40 years ago, terminally ill Fidelis Coelho decided he would not leave his then-pregnant young wife, Lucia, with another mouth to feed, he concocted a three-liter batch of abortifacient. Although she had six children already, Lucia refused her dying husband's home "remedy."

The failure of a home remedy to cure an illness sends the afflicted or her kin out of the *casa* and into the *rua*, or street, in search of succor. In the case of physical infirmity, the quest for medical aid usually begins at either the municipal health clinic or the local pharmacy. Likewise, alcoholics seeking treatment often go to Alcoholics Anonymous.[5] Sufferers of domestic strife, unable to resolve conflict on their own, typically do not knock on institutional doors in search of relief but seek solace from an empathetic family member, neighbor, or friend. At this intermediary stage of the quest for health, those able to remedy their situation through secular intervention give thanks and continue the daily struggle to survive, not knowing when the next health crisis will erupt.

For the other *desenganados* (those whose medical condition has been pronounced incurable), battered wives, and alcoholics, the failure of secular or worldly solutions leaves the supernatural as the only remaining source of health. Only a miracle performed by the gods can save the afflicted at this point. The fulfillment of a *promessa* by the Virgin of Nazaré or a miraculous cure performed by the queen of Belenense Umbanda healers, the Cabocla Mariana, renews supplicants' faith in the restorative powers of their familiar deities and ends the arduous path to recovery.[6] However, the Catholic saints and the spirits of Umbanda, because they blur the line dividing the sacred from the profane, do not possess the healing power of the pentecostal Jesus and Holy Spirit. Rosilea Garcia found the Catholic saints unable to grant her the transformative power she needed to resolve her alcohol problem: "Yeah, I used to go to the Catholic church but only out of tradition. I would sit and kneel like everybody else. I used to go to the Church of Nazaré. I would remain there kneeling and looking at those images [saints]. I would talk to them about what I was feeling, and nothing would happen. I would leave feeling the same as I had when I came, you understand?"

Many sufferers of the afflictions of poverty never even have the opportunity to beseech their traditional deities for aid; in their moment of crisis, a pentecostal evangelist, *visitadora*, or lay missionary arrives at their home or hospital bed, bringing the message of divine healing for the body and soul and salvation from the sinful (i.e., sick) world. Unlike Umbanda and Catholicism, which customarily require supplicants to come to the sanctuary or *terreiro* to access the means of religious production, pentecostalism, via its zealous evangelists, brings its healing services out of the temple and into the public and private realms of street, home, and hospital. For example, José Vergolino was trying to drown his problems in drink, but a young missionary from the Foursquare Gospel Church, a friend of his sister, kept after him.

> When she would come visit me, I would say, "I don't want to have anything to do with that church stuff. You're just talking bull. What you're saying has nothing to do with me." She would say, "OK, no problem" and leave. But she came back to my house every week, asking how I was. She was worried about me. I would say, "Look, I'm not interested in that church stuff. I have a good time going to parties and fooling around." She would say, "Oh, José, you don't have any peace in your life. You're not happy. You know only hardship. It breaks your mother and father's heart." And I would say, "Odete, get out of here. I'm not interested in that. I want to enjoy my life." But she wouldn't give up. She kept on talking and talking to me about Jesus. And the day arrived when I really had to accept. I said, "Fine, I'll go to your church."

Thus, it is the coalescence of the patient, the spiritual medic, and her medicine at the critical moment of crisis that sets the stage for conversion to pentecostalism. An analysis of each factor will aid in understanding the paramount importance of divine healing in conversion to this branch of Charismatic Protestantism.

## Familiar Contact

The afflicted, having reached the point of despair at the "closed doors" (*portas fechadas*) of secular and possibly sacred institutions, listen intently to the pentecostal proselytizers, who offer an immediate and comprehensive solution to the sufferers' physical, psychological, social, or spiritual illnesses. The agent bearing the pentecostal message of healing most often is a relative, friend, or neighbor (someone such as Odete, who proselytized José Vergolino), a part of the afflicted's preexisting network of kin, work, and neighborhood relationships.

Pentecostalism in Latin America recruits primarily along family lines. A plurality (43.3 percent) of my informants made their initial contact with the pentecostal faith through a family member. A family member who has undergone a positive transformation in the Assembly of God or Foursquare Gospel Church, among other denominations, is living testament to the healing powers of his Charismatic religion. At the very least, the individual in crisis is more likely to accept prayers or an invitation to worship at a new church from a spouse or sibling than from a stranger.

Church recruitment in Belém does not occur principally along spousal lines, but pentecostal women had much greater success than men in drafting their spouses into the fold. While only 4.3 percent of married women had been introduced to a pentecostal church by their husband, 25 percent of my male informants had been led to the faith by their wives. The gender gap in which women outnumber men by a two-to-one ratio partly accounts for the striking difference. Put simply, wives are statistically more likely to be believers in the first place than are their husbands.

But the gender gap does not explain all. Even more crucial are the dichotomous social realms in which the two sexes operate. Men work, play, and die in the street. Many are more attuned to the drama unfolding outside their front door than to the scene inside their home.[7] Hence, friends and colleagues, companions of the street, more than wives or family members, are the primary recruiters of men into pentecostalism. Nearly one-third (30 percent) of my male interviewees had been evangelized by friends or co-workers. Women, by contrast, were proselytized in the culturally constructed female domain of the household. Whereas pentecostal kin ranked below friends and wives in recruiting men to the faith, relatives were the principal disseminators of the gospel of health among women. A slight majority (53.2 percent) of sisters-in-faith cited a family member (excluding husbands) as the person responsible for first introducing them to Charismatic Protestantism.

Some pentecostal women in the Belenense *bairros* of Guamá, Terra Firme, Sacramenta, Jurunas, and Condor also "accepted Jesus" through the influence of friends or neighbors but many more did so through kin relationships. Twenty-eight-year-old Quadrangular (Foursquare Gospel member) and homemaker Teresina Lima typifies the female pattern of conversion. Teresina's older brother and parents became converts after her younger brother's apparently miraculous cure. Doctors at the military hospital in Rio de Janeiro had told Teresina and her family that only a kidney transplant would save the life of her younger brother. Fearing for his life, Teresina decided to donate one of her kidneys to her critically ill brother. In an attempt to enlist divine aid, her older brother vowed to accept Jesus if the complicated surgery proved successful. The older brother fulfilled his vow after watching his younger brother make a full recovery. Certain that Jesus had guided the surgeons' hands in transplanting her vital organ, Teresina, her younger brother, and her parents followed her elder brother into the Foursquare Gospel.

The success of low-intensity proselytization among preexisting social networks does not preclude the churches from organizing the faithful into mission brigades that, depending on the groups and the occasion, evangelize both in public plazas and door to door. *Visitadoras* are by far the largest and most dynamic missionary brigade. In pairs, they trudge along the fetid mud paths of the inundated shantytowns to bring the good news of health and salvation to those stricken by the diseases of deprivation. Once, when I was in the middle of an interview with a wizened, tubercular informant, I had the opportunity to witness a pair of *visitadoras* in action. Perhaps forewarned by my interviewee or his family, the *Assembleiana* duo had come to proselytize me. Noticing my persistent cough, they inquired as to the state of my health. I explained that my cough was nothing more than a cold that a little rest would cure. Not satisfied with my answer, the two *servas de Deus* (servants of God) shot up from their makeshift seats and launched into a rousing hymn that recalled the healing powers of Jesus, the Great Physician. In case that was not enough to exorcise my cold, the hymn segued into a powerful prayer for my health that joined everyone in the house in a circle of interlocking hands. Although not a pentecostal, I perceived the therapeutic value of a roomful of believers focusing their spiritual energy on me.

Beyond the intimacy of a small prayer circle in a believer's home, pentecostal pastors recruit collectively during the *culto*, or worship service. At the smaller houses of worship in the *baixadas*, the preacher asks all visitors to stand while the entire congregation welcomes them with a melodic hymn. The pastor then mentions the presence of any distinguished visitors, such as an evangelist from the central temple or a North American researcher. Thus, within the first 15 minutes of the service, the visitor has lost his anonymity. For the researcher who finds himself often participating more than observing, the loss of anonymity can be a source of frustration. However, recognition is received gratefully by the visitor who has led an anonymous and often invisible life as one of the millions of João or Maria da Silvas.[8]

The message delivered to visitors in diverse liturgical forms presumes affliction. Evangelistic flyers handed out at the Universal Church of the Kingdom of God (Igreja Universal do Reino de Deus, or IURD) in Belém ask in boldface, "What is your problem? Vices, finances, unemployment, illness, nervousness, depression, or family fights?" Pentecostals presume that potential converts want a salvation that is, to adopt theologian Miroslav Volf's term, material and spiritual, addressing their practical, day-to-day needs, as well as promising a carefree afterlife.[9] Despite the near-exclusive emphasis given by some scholars to "prosperity" teachings, in the cited flyer—typical of many similar flyers distributed by other pentecostal denominations—financial lack is one in a list of several categories of need that drive the imagined convert to the door of a pentecostal church. Pastors, often *favelados* themselves, know the misery of the shantytowns and assume that the visitor has entered the temple seeking relief. Also cognizant of the visitor's attempts to remedy her situation through secular and possibly sacred channels, the preacher underscores the futility of seeking a solution that does not involve Jesus and the Holy Spirit. "You who were given no hope by doctors, you who received a false cure from the demons of Macumba, there is a solution," proclaimed a preacher at the Foursquare Gospel Church in the *bairro* of Guamá.

One of the most effective evangelistic techniques is the conversion testimonial. The following anonymous narrative, published in the *Estandarte Evangélico* in 1990, contains the key elements constituting a pentecostal testimonial.

> When doctors here on earth tell us that the illness a person is
> suffering has no cure, that the only thing left to do is to die, I want to
> say that there is a greater doctor than earthly doctors, who does not
> give up and who is ready to offer healing, salvation, liberty, new life,
> and all that we need. Just accept Him as savior, doctor, teacher,
> advocate, and master of your life. . . . I was dying of uterine cancer. I
> spent ten years suffering when I wasn't a believer. But I knew
> someone in the prayer circles was interceding for cancer patients. I
> then vowed to serve Jesus for the rest of my life if he cured me. He
> healed me immediately without needing an operation.

The individual's preconversion life was full of pain and affliction, in this case "ten years of suffering." The attempt to relieve the pain through institutional health care failed miserably. The physician's prognosis was grim, "the only thing left to do is to die." Desperate due to the exhaustion of secular resources, the woman turns to the supernatural, gratefully accepting the prayers offered in the *círculo de oração* (prayer circle) for cancer patients. To invoke the healing powers of Jesus, the woman, drawing on her past relationships with the

Catholic saints, enters into a contractual agreement, a kind of *promessa* with the Doctor of Doctors.

As part of the worship service, conversion testimonials are followed by spirited hymn singing and fervent praying. The preacher then invariably leads the service to a climax with the *chamada*, or altar call. Non-pentecostal visitors, *desviados* (apostates), and believers feeling "weak in the faith" are invited to come to the front of the church. Overcome by their own emotions, many sob plaintively as the pastor lays his hands on their head and asks them if they are ready to accept Jesus as their Lord and savior.

## The Cure

The patient and the healing agent have brought the ailing visitor to the altar, where she has decided to accept Jesus and become a member of the Assembly of God, for example. But before she commits to follow Jesus before the pastor and congregation, the third integer of the conversion equation, the cure, must be factored in. That the patient and healing agent have come together at a critical juncture in the patient's affliction is a necessary but insufficient condition for conversion to occur. The healing agent, such as a family member, a *visitadora*, or a pastor, can extol the myriad virtues of surrendering oneself to Jesus. But until a cure, a miracle demonstrating God's omnipotence, takes place, the equation remains incomplete. An analysis of divine healing, the powerful engine driving pentecostal growth in Brazil and much of Latin America, will aid in solving the conversion equation.

Divine healing, even more than glossolalia, is the most universal and potent gift of the Spirit in Latin American pentecostalism. While less than half (46.8 percent) of all my pentecostal informants in Belém regularly spoke in tongues, the great majority (86.4 percent) claimed that Jesus or the Holy Spirit had cured them of some type of physical or psychological ailment. From 1970, the year the Assembly of God in Belém began to register the incidence of divine healing in its annual reports, to 1990, the number of recorded cases of *cura divina* skyrocketed 3,733 percent. Demand for healing surged particularly in the "lost decade" of the 1980s, when financial shocks to impoverished households were severest.[10] Interestingly, the authors of the annual reports did not, by contrast—even during the lost decade—chart the incidence of divinely mediated financial prosperity.

On the other side of the continent, sociologists Christian Lalive d'Epinay and Hans Tennekes, in separate studies of pentecostals in Chile, highlight the universality of divine healing. Lalive D'Epinay, a pioneering researcher of Latin American pentecostalism, discovered that 98 percent of Chilean pastors surveyed had been used by the Holy Spirit to heal a believer, but only 57 percent had ever spoken in the "tongue of angels."[11] Similarly, 56 percent of Tennekes'

Chilean *crente* informants alluded to a divine cure in their conversion stories.[12] Some Toba Indians of the northern Argentine Chaco also came to pentecostalism through illness.[13] According to theologian Harvey Cox, who has researched pentecostal growth across the globe, Africans typically visit a church for the first time seeking relief from an illness that has proved resistant to folk or modern medicine.[14]

*Cura divina* in its most elementary and common form is the curing of a physical malady through direct or indirect intervention of one of the three persons of the Trinity. Jesus, owing to his evangelical role as a thaumaturge, and the Holy Spirit, charged with miraculous power, are the principal healers in pentecostalism. God the Father is a powerful but less tangible figure. As the biblical Jesus bestowed the gift of healing on his disciples, who cured the sick in his name, Jesus and the Holy Spirit, operating in pentecostal churches, typically use believers, both clergy and laity, as human conductors to restore the health of the infirm. Yet, while the great majority (86.4 percent) of my informants had experienced divine healing, only 11.4 percent claimed to have served as healing agents in the cure of another person. The gift of healing appears to be limited to pastors and exceptionally devout believers, usually female.

At some point during nearly every pentecostal church service I attended in Belém, Rio de Janeiro, and São Paulo, the preacher called the afflicted forward to be divinely cured. The pastor and his assistant(s) would lay their hands on, or cup them around, the patient's head while leading the congregation in impassioned prayer for the Holy Spirit to flood (*derramar*) the house of prayer with a current of healing power. If the sickly petitioners were too numerous and the pastor was unable to lay his hands on each person, he would extend his arms toward the group, functioning as a conduit for the supernatural serum unleashed by the Holy Spirit. Supplicants were also able to direct the divine healing power beyond the walls of the temple to afflicted family members and friends not present at the service. In continuity with Catholic tradition and Umbanda practice, the faithful at *cultos de cura divina* place photographs of the ill, bottles of water, cooking oil, work cards, flour, and salt at the altar to be blessed. Charged with prayer, these objects function as spiritual conductors, facilitating healing in absentia.[15]

In some churches, divine healing so dominates the liturgy that the sanctuary resembles a hospital. The stern *obreiras* (ushers) who patrol the pews of the Universal Church of the Kingdom of God, Foursquare Gospel, and God Is Love (Deus e Amor) wear celestial blue or off-white nurse's uniforms. As spiritual nurses, the *obreiras* perform triage on the patients in the pews. An *obreira* attends to the mildly afflicted with a vice-grip maneuver in which her hands, positioned at the front and back of the patient's head, force out the demon(s). Those tormented by stronger fiends are sent, sometimes dragged, to the altar where the spiritual medic, the pastor, operates. Dramatizing his role as healer, the head pastor at the mother church of God Is Love in Belém often led the service dressed in a bleached doctor's smock. The crude wooden canes and crutches adorning the back wall of the small foyer add to the medical imagery. Finally, the bare white walls and the harsh electric light recall the aseptic corridors of a hospital. Visitor and believer alike have entered a spiritual emergency ward.

Although they frequently employ human agents in the business of healing, Jesus and the Holy Ghost need no mediators to operate on the sick, as the following testimony graphically illustrates.

> For four years I was suffering from a disease of the liver and was getting sicker each day despite the treatment and medication. Then I made a vow to serve Jesus for the rest of my life if He would extend his healing hand over me. One night a few days later I received a visit. Two young men dressed in white spoke to me saying, "Your illness is serious but don't worry. The Lord said He will heal you." The following night, in bed, I felt the Lord touch me and remove my liver. I saw that it was swollen, and then He burned it with a white flame which made a loud noise, and all of a sudden it was restored to its normal and perfect state.[16]

The supernatural surgery on the patient's possibly cirrhotic liver was not performed without a price. In exchange for a restored organ, the long-suffering patient first vowed to dedicate his life to Jesus, in other words to become a member of the Assembléia de Deus. The English term "faith healing" captures the dialectic between the two components: the ailing supplicant first must have faith, must believe, that Jesus indeed possesses the power to heal the mind, body, and soul.[17] No matter how fervently the petitioner prays, only genuine faith will spur the Supreme Physician to action.

The most efficacious manner of expressing one's faith, in accord with the mechanics of Brazilian popular religiosity, is through a vow or, in Catholic parlance, a *promessa*. The type of vow made by the aforementioned liver patient recurs with such frequency on the pages dedicated to *testemunhos* in the *Estandarte Evangélico* that I have denominated it "the standard vow." Failed by traditional and modern medicine and perhaps the deities of Umbanda and Catholicism, the afflicted promises to accept Jesus and to become a pentecostal in exchange for the cure of her own malady or a family member's.

The act of divine healing, in turn, inspires faith. The desperate individual seeks a supernatural cure not only because all other resources have been exhausted, but also because she has either personally witnessed an act of faith healing or heard about it through pentecostal preaching or her network of social relationships. Moreover, the healing rituals of Catholicism and Umbanda are part of her religious formation. That the pentecostal Jesus cures believers of their earthly and spiritual afflictions is nothing new. The novelty, rather, consists in the price and potency of the remedy. Whereas the Virgin of Nazaré and her fellow saints demand an act of ritual sacrifice for the granting of a miracle, and the Cabocla Mariana requests that her medium, the mother or father of the saint, be compensated for her healing services, the pentecostal Jesus orders the patient to convert, to be born again and become a *nova criatura* (new creature).

Since they require little of their human supplicants beyond ritualistic payment, the saints and spirits cannot provide the kind of comprehensive health coverage that the pentecostal Jesus can. The pentecostal convert must repent, rejecting the sinful (sick) world of "men" in favor of the righteous (healthy) world of God and his saints.[18] Adopting the ascetic moral code of classical and modern pentecostalism, the neophyte renounces the sins of the world, manifested as the pathogens of poverty. The believer still inhabits an impoverished world but now, through an ascetic lifestyle, has the power to resist many of the contagions spawned by poverty. Conversion to pentecostalism is no panacea for the multiple viruses caused by material deprivation, but it does immunize its followers against some of poverty's more malignant strains.

## Exorcising the Demons of Deprivation

Another type of divine healing has become increasingly popular since the emergence of neo-pentecostalism in the early 1980s.[19] Interviews with clergy and laity, in addition to my own observation-participation in *cultos*, confirm the fact that after Tuesdays, the day of *cultos de cura divina* at the Universal Church of the Kingdom of God in Belém and throughout the country, the church attracts the greatest number of worshipers on Fridays, when services focus on *libertação* (exorcism or deliverance). This method of faith healing has had such success in the IURD that most Brazilian pentecostal denominations have incorporated it into their liturgy. Even the Assembly of God, which has traditionally preferred to keep the demons at bay rather than conjure them up to then be exorcised, adopted the practice of Friday exorcisms in 1988.[20]

The fundamental difference between traditional faith healing and *libertação* lies in folk etiology. Despite regional variations, the way Amazonian *caboclos* (mestizo inhabitants of the rural interior) classify illness captures the duality of popular etiological conceptions in Brazil. On the one hand is "normal" illness or sickness. The common cold, fever, malaria, cuts, allergies, tuberculosis, nasal congestion, among other ailments, can be treated successfully by home remedies, pharmaceuticals, and doctors. "Abnormal" illnesses, on the other hand, also known as *pajé* afflictions (*sofrimentos de pajé*), are maladies cultivated by evil. Only a *pajé* (Amazonian healer) can treat evil eye, *susto* (soul shock), spirit attack, *boto* (magic related to the enchanted river dolphin of Amazonian folklore), and the arrow of the beast (*flecha de bicho*).[21] Where traditional and modern medicine fail to cure normal illnesses, traditional pentecostal faith healing can prove a potent remedy. Likewise, *libertação* can free those suffering from abnormal sicknesses caused by the evil spirits that have resisted the healing powers of the *pajé*, the mother of the saint, or the *curandeira* (folk healer).[22] In short, *cura divina* heals the pathogens of the soma, and *libertação* expels the demons of the psyche.

Regardless of the particular type of evil spirits that worshipers blame for their distress prior to entering the austere warehouse that serves as the mother church (*sede*) of the IURD in Belém, pastors expose the demons as the familiar *exús* (trickster spirits) of Umbanda. As offensive as it is to many Umbandistas, the demonization of the pantheon of African Brazilian deities strikes a resonant chord in Brazilian popular religiosity. Who in the *favelas* of the urban periphery has not feared the malevolence of a *coisa feita*, a work of sorcery intended to block the path (*trancar a rua*) of a rival or enemy through sickness or injury? Through faith in both the pastor and the Holy Spirit, the possessed is liberated from the yoke of the Cabocla Mariana or Tranca Rua (Road Closer, a popular *exú*). But only conversion and affiliation with the IURD will bring lasting and comprehensive protection from the *espirítos malignos*. And, like other forms of divine healing, *libertação* often is the first step in the conversion process (figure 8.1).

FIGURE 8.1. "Miracles!!! A cockroach! A spider! A lock of hair! Vomited up by a woman! A work of *macumberia* [witchcraft], came out of a man's foot! Power of God" (1994). Courtesy Andrew Chesnut.

Fake Healing?

Because pentecostal healing is ascribed to God and requires faith, many nonbelievers dismiss it as religious fakery or superstition. Pentecostal preachers are
denounced as the latest vendors of holy snake oil to the ignorant masses.
Indeed, certain churches in Brazil have deceived congregants through practices
related to divine healing. The IURD, in particular, has been denounced in the
national press for marketing "holy oil," supposedly from the Mount of Olives
in Israel, and Dead Sea salt. Laboratory analysis of the two "sacred" substances
exposed the unguent as common Brazilian soybean oil and the salt as the same
sodium chloride with which Brazilians liberally season their food.[23] Paradoxi-
cally, such stories of fraudulent faith healing in print and electronic media
probably do more to bolster pentecostalism than weaken it. Pentecostals who
are aware of denunciations in the press are likely to dismiss them as Catholic
propaganda aimed at discrediting their dynamic religion. Many potential pentecostal converts cannot afford to buy magazines or newspapers, and even if
they have heard rumors of charlatanism in pentecostal churches, the urgency
of their illnesses overrides any doubts.

Medical malpractice, misdiagnosis, and a general disregard for the health
of the poor—more than fraud—may account for a significant amount of what
pentecostals present as divine healing. Like Nizila da Silva, who skeptical
interpreters might conclude was misdiagnosed with ovarian cancer and then
attributed negative test results to divine intervention, many of the *desenganados* who have vowed to become believers in exchange for a supernatural cure
can see only the healing hand of Jesus in the resolution of their health crises.
In the following account, Joanna Macedo, a 33-year-old manicurist and member of the IURD, saw the awesome power of God, and not extreme medical
incompetence: "The other day in the church I heard about a man who had died
of a heart operation, and his family called the pastor there to the wake. The
pastor went and said a prayer, and they started to shut the doors. The pastor
put holy oil on the body, and that man who was in the coffin got up, and everybody was hugging him." Once a supplicant has enlisted divine aid through a
·vow, she will invariably point to Jesus or the Holy Spirit as the source of her
recovery. A miraculous cure from the Holy Spirit is more comforting than the
possibility of medical malpractice.

Extramural suspicion of the mundane sources of many instances of pentecostal faith healing in no way diminishes the power of the religion's most
universal experience. Regardless of the opinions of skeptics and nonbelievers,
the fact that millions of pentecostals believe that Jesus and the Holy Spirit heal
on the basis of faith alone makes *cura divina* a subjective reality. Like the patient
whose health improves because of her faith in the curative properties of the
little white capsule she takes three times a day, though it is merely a placebo,

pentecostals create the possibility of divine healing through belief. But unlike the placebo patient, who has only her pills, the pentecostal has recourse to an entire community of spiritual medics, her *irmãos na fé* (brothers and sisters in faith), who are ready to pray for her health and provide social support. The scope of this chapter precludes an in-depth consideration of this community. Here it suffices to say that even medical science is beginning to recognize the therapeutic value of prayer. According to research, ritual acts, such as prayer, might actually activate the human immune and endocrine systems. Medical researchers are also investigating the potential medical benefits of dissociated states of consciousness, such as those that may be experienced in the baptism of the Holy Spirit.[24]

## Fulfilling the Vow

Having invoked the healing power of the Doctor of Doctors for an ill family member or on her own behalf, the new convert must seal her vow by publicly declaring her commitment to serve Jesus. The pastor of a small Assembly of God congregation in the *baixada* of Sacramenta, 47-year-old José Araujo, rushed to the nearest church to publicly proclaim his devotion to Jesus after his wife's cure. His voice competing with the din of hammers and saws raising the roof of his unfinished church, José explained to me how he had become a member of the Assembly of God.

> The doors began to close; things were bad. My wife got sick and couldn't do anything at home. She suffered a lot with the swelling of her face. The swelling just got worse and worse. It was then that I had a revelation, when I was working at the hospital for minimum wage. And the Lord spoke to me saying this: "Your wife's cure depends on you." I said, "What do you mean, Lord?" It was a Sunday, the second Sunday of April 1981. It was around six in the afternoon, there at the maternity wing. That was when He said, "Your wife's cure depends on you." I heard the voice, and I looked outside and didn't see anybody. I said, "Is that really you, Lord, speaking to me? If it is you, and you are the master of truth, if you are the savior of the world like people say and you heal, I want you to take me to the place where your truth exists, and there I will accept you as my savior."
>
> On that day, the second Sunday of April of 1981, at six in the afternoon, I saw that being dressed all in white, and He was saying, "Let's go." And He went ahead, with me following. I arrived home, and my wife was lying in the hammock. That was when I told her I was going to church to accept Jesus Christ as my savior, and she said,

"I'll go with you." I said, "You're sick, you can't" and she said, "No, I'm going."

So I arrived here [in the church], and when I went in they were singing that hymn number 15. Then the whole congregation stood up, and I said, "I want to accept Jesus as my savior." They all knew that I was a very hardened man when it came to the gospel. I had a bad reputation. And so the whole church stood up and the pastor said, "Let us pray for this citizen who wants to accept Jesus as savior." At that moment great power filled the church, but I didn't recognize it. Today I know how to discern what it was. The whole church was taken by the power of God, and that night I devoted myself to Jesus, and my name was written in the book of heaven. A week later my wife's face had returned to normal.

Most converts, unlike José, do not customarily march into the church and assertively declare their desire to accept Jesus. More typical is the manner in which Hezio Nazareno, a 21-year-old Quadrangular, responded to the preacher's *chamada* (figure 8.2).

It was a Saturday youth service, and the church was full. I had already been participating for about three months, and that Saturday, when the pastor was preaching the message for young people, God touched me through the pastor's message. God touched me, and I got up. I got up, the pastor launched [*lançou*] the invitation, and I stood up from the pew and went to the front, and when I got there in front I felt something, something different. God was calling me to come to Him. I always remember that touch. God was calling me. And I accepted Jesus, and it was a very good thing, like this great happiness had taken over my heart and my life.

Hezio, José, and their co-religionists have poignantly illustrated the relationship between divine healing and conversion to pentecostalism in Brazil. A health crisis, typically physical illness, leads the afflicted individual to accept Jesus in exchange for a cure. Brazilian pentecostals, of course, do not conceptualize the *voto* (vow) as an exchange, but the contractual agreement, according to the mechanics of popular religion in Brazil, is the most effective way to implore the gods for something. The pentecostal God, however, demands a higher price from his supplicants than a pilgrimage or some other act of ritual self-sacrifice. The pentecostal God commands the petitioner to convert, to turn away from the old world of sin (sickness) and commence her spiritual and physical renewal. The *Deus todo poderoso* (omnipotent God) of the *crentes* does not transform the world but, through conversion, restores the health of his believers and inoculates them against the most common pathogens of poverty.

FIGURE 8.2.  Participation in a Foursquare Gospel Church service, Belém, Pará, Brazil (2004). Courtesy Candy Gunther Brown.

NOTES

1 Rodney Stark and William Bainbridge, *A Theory of Religion* (New York: Lang, 1987), 197.

2 I privilege the feminine pronoun over the masculine, since women constitute approximately two-thirds of the pentecostal population in Brazil.

3 Stark and Bainbridge, *Theory of Religion*, 85.

4 R. Andrew Chesnut, *Born Again in Brazil: The Pentecostal Boom and the Pathogens of Poverty* (New Brunswick, N.J.: Rutgers University Press, 1997). Based on ethnographic and historical research, this book argues that the dialectic between poverty-related illness and faith healing is propelling pentecostal growth in Brazil and throughout Latin America.

5 In Belém (capital of the state of Pará, in northern Brazil), a metropolitan area of a million and a half people, about 20 different AA groups meet each weekday; *Portal dos Alcoólicos Anônimos no Pará*, http://www.aapara.com.br (accessed 30 July 2009).

6 The saints and their devotees are bound by a contractual agreement called the *promessa*. In exchange for divine intervention, or a miracle, supplicants promise to "pay" for the aid by performing a ritual act of sacrifice, normally a procession or pilgrimage; John Burdick, *Looking for God in Brazil* (Berkeley: University of California Press, 1993), 169.

7 *Favelado* men's proclivity to gravitate toward the street was particularly striking during the matches of the World Cup soccer tournament. Before halftime had even

started, the men at the non-pentecostal homes where I was invited to root for Brazil had already rushed into the street. A few would remain there, watching the game through the window.

8  The surname da Silva is so common among the Brazilian poor that I had to order my informants' life histories by their middle names.

9  Miroslav Volf, "Materiality of Salvation: An Investigation in the Soteriologies of Liberation and Pentecostal Theologies," *Journal of Ecumenical Studies* 26.3 (1989): 447–467.

10  *Relatorio Anual* [Annual Reports] *da Assembleia de Deus em Belém*, 1968–1993, housed at the mother church of the Assembleia de Deus, Belém, Brazil.

11  Peter Wagner, *Porque Crescem os Pentecostais?* [Look Out! The Pentecostals Are Coming] (Miami, Fla.: Vida, 1987), 122.

12  Hans Tennekes, *El Movimiento Pentecostal en la Sociedad Chilena* (Iquique, Chile: Centro de Investigación de la Realidad del Norte, 1985), 34.

13  Bryan Wilson, *Magic and the Millennium* (London: Heinemann, 1973), 123.

14  Harvey Cox, *Fire from Heaven: The Rise of Pentecostal Spirituality and the Reshaping of Religion in the Twenty-First Century* (Reading, Mass.: Addison-Wesley, 1995), 247.

15  I never observed spiritual conductors, such as photographs of the infirm, at any Assembly of God service. Reacting to the rich visual imagery of Brazilian Catholicism, the denomination banished what it saw as "idols" from the sanctuary. The result is temples devoid of almost any visual symbols, including the cross.

16  Anonymous, *O Estandarte Evangélico: Orgao official da Assembleia de Deus em Belém* (Aug. 1982).

17  In the common scenario in which the supplicant requests a cure for someone else, such as a sick child, the divine remedy depends on the faith of the supplicant, not on the faith of the child. Thus, one way a nonbeliever can be cured is through the faith of a believer.

18  The word "saint" in pentecostal terminology denotes not self-sacrificial virgins or pious Good Samaritans but the common believer.

19  "Neo-pentecostalism" refers to the latest generation of churches founded mostly in the late 1970s–1980s. Best represented by the Universal Church of the Kingdom of God, these denominations greatly relax the strict moral codes of classical Pentecostalism, put exorcism and prosperity theology at center stage, and incorporate elements of folk Catholicism and African Brazilian religions into their practices. Further research might prove otherwise, but I hypothesize that the relaxed moral code of neo-pentecostalism attenuates the churches' healing power.

20  *Atas do culto administrativo da Assembleia de Deus em Belém* [Administrative Acts], 1930–1993, Assembleia de Deus, Belém.

21  Raymundo Heraldo Maues, "Catolicismo Popular e Controle Eclesiastico" (Ph.D. diss., Universidade Federal do Rio de Janeiro, Museu Nacional, 1987), 1:217–218.

22  The experience of urban poverty has changed the nature of spiritual malaise. Residents of the *baixadas* no longer fear the spell of the *boto* but are attacked by what Bishop Macedo of the IURD calls "unclean spirits" (*espíritos imundos*). Unclean spirits, according to the bishop, cause constant headaches, fainting spells, suicidal feelings,

nervousness, undefined illnesses, fear, loneliness, insecurity, vice, failure, visions, and voices; Edir Macedo, *O Espirito Santo* (Rio de Janeiro, Brazil: Grafica, 1993), 27.

23  "O bispo não é santo," *Veja* (17 July 1991): 58–60.

24  Cox, *Fire from Heaven*, 109; Jeffrey Kluger, "The Biology of Belief," *Time* (12 Feb. 2009), http://www.time.com/time/health/article/0,8599,1879016,00.html (accessed 30 July 2009).

# 9

# The Salve of Divine Healing: Essential Rituals for Survival among Working-Class Pentecostals in Bogotá, Colombia

*Rebecca Pierce Bomann*

The bus lurches forward suddenly, startling the weary passengers, who instinctively grab the nearest handrail to keep from toppling over. Ten minutes of waiting in stalled traffic in rainy, dark Bogotá after a day of hard labor, in the warmth of a crowded bus, had lulled many passengers to relax their grip and lean against the nearest seat or pole. The heavy jerking motion of acceleration quickly rouses them to hang on once again, white knuckled, murmuring protests to the bus driver. He yells back a profanity, punishing everyone with an extra harsh brake, as if he were hauling convicted felons to prison. Each seat on the bus holds one passenger and his or her bags, but those who are standing are pressed together, four across the aisle, in tight rows the entire length of the bus. It is impossible to walk to the back—one has to squeeze, push, with "perdón, señor" and "perdón, señora." A dozen people crowd the front and back steps, two hang out the front door in the rain, and three more hang out the back door. In the most violent motion of the bus, screeching to a sudden stop, more than 100 bodies swing forward. They are packed tightly, painfully, and still there is another hour to get home.

Indignity, injustice, and harsh conditions are all familiar to the passengers of this bus. They are among thousands who live in the marginalized *barrios* on the far south of sprawling Bogotá, who labor

10- to 12-hour days in the city as maids, brick makers, factory workers, and construction workers. Impersonal globalizing processes had, on one hand, created many of the jobs at which working-class Bogotános labored, but these same global engines had also produced economic pressures that kept wages low and working conditions deplorable. The workers' industriousness is rewarded with a long, exhausting commute. Once they have arrived after dusk to their hand-built, makeshift homes, there will be laundry to wash by hand, water to heat for baths, and hungry children to feed. The security and survival of these laboring poor are frequently jeopardized by Colombia's struggling economy, long history of terrible violence and civil strife, and stark social inequalities.[1] For these people, no life is safe, no job is secure, no meal is taken for granted, and no medical care is guaranteed. They share a raw, determined will that drives them forward to survive each week.

Finally, the bus finishes its climb into the steep hills that surround Bogotá, lurching as it arrives at the barrio of Nuevo Progreso (figure 9.1). All over the steep hillside that is the barrio, one sees hundreds of single bulbs hanging in doorways, powered by tenuously rigged wires. Scrawny dogs forage in the piles of garbage in alleyways. Muddy rainwater is flowing in streams on the unpaved streets, and weary passengers reluctantly step into it as they get off the bus and begin their trek home. Smells of cooked meat, fried *buñuelos*, and fresh bread waft from tiny open storefronts, mixed with the cool evening air and choking bus exhaust. The lilt of salsa music is heard from a small, lit *panadería*, where men relax with a few bottles of *cerveza*.

FIGURE 9.1. Nuevo Progreso, Bogotá, Colombia (1993). Courtesy Rebecca Pierce Bomann.

A few doorways up, a different kind of music penetrates the barrio air. It is loud, joyous, with tambourines and earnest singing voices. Barrio residents walking home look in with curiosity as they pass the tiny pentecostal church with its double doors propped wide open (figure 9.2). The bouncing tempo of an accordion finishes the last few measures and then trills while the believers clap and shout praises to God. "Who lives?" shouts the pastor into the microphone, his voice clearly heard halfway down the block. "Christ!" responds the congregation. "Who saves?" the pastor shouts. "Christ!" they shout back. "Who heals?" "Christ!" "Alabado sea al Señor" (Praise the Lord), the pastor proclaims, and the believers applaud. With the accordion still trilling behind him, the pastor paces back and forth in front of the believers, holding out his Bible toward them. "Do you know that the same Lord Jesus Christ who healed people in the Bible is here today with us?" "Amén, gloria a Dios!" (Amen, glory to God), cries an elderly woman, her hands clasped in front of her. "I feel his presence," the pastor affirms. "And he can heal today like he did in the Bible. Did you know that the demons tremble when Jesus is here? Praise God, we have the presence of the Lord. For those who believe, everything is possible. Jesus can heal you tonight!"

At his invitation to come forward for healing, over two-thirds of the congregation leave their low, rickety benches to file up to the front. Still speaking into the microphone, the pastor asks the first *hermana* what she needs. Although her voice is barely audible, she has both hands uplifted into the air,

FIGURE 9.2.  Inside view of a pentecostal church in Nuevo Progreso, Bogotá, Colombia (1993). Courtesy Rebecca Pierce Bomann.

ready to receive the pastor's prayer. The requests come from the believers, one by one, for a job, for healing a sick child, for safety, for divine provision, for healing from back pain, for comfort following the death of a loved one, and for God to save an unbelieving spouse. The pastor lays his hand on each forehead, affirming God's power and desire to meet each need, petitioning God earnestly "in the name of Jesus of Nazareth" to heal, provide, save, and comfort. Believers stand waiting while he prays. They murmur softly, hands raised, and the musician plays slowly on the keyboard. Tears flow down the face of a young woman. "Oh, thank you, Lord," she whispers. "You are powerful, wonderful, loving." "Jesus is here tonight, hallelujah," affirms the pastor. "He is here and will touch you and make you whole tonight, praise his name." Outside, the dark muddy streets are emptying as barrio residents arrive at their homes to prepare for the next day's early rising. Into the dimly lit night, the pentecostal church boldly broadcasts its message of salvation, hope, and healing. It is not an imported, unsympathetic invitation given by foreign ministers.[2] Those with the microphone and accordion rode the bus home too, and they know well the pains that they are praying for God to heal.

This essay assesses the powerful role of healing in the lives of lower-working-class pentecostal believers in Bogotá, Colombia. The scholarship is based on 800 pages of field notes, which include 50 transcribed interviews with barrio believers, and notes and recordings from over 100 pentecostal worship services. I gathered the research while living as a full-time resident of the barrio for eight months in 1995, experiencing many of the hardships of life much as the believers did and witnessing their intense faith firsthand. This study occurred after three months of preliminary research, living with and studying the lives and faith of *evangélicos* in Salta, Argentina.[3] Drawing extensively on the words and experiences of barrio pentecostals, I will argue that divine healing practices provide a pivotal strategy for coping with a social context of poverty, insecurity, and violence, and that healing is the engine that fuels the growth and sustenance of pentecostal churches among Colombia's urban poor. I will show how the broad range of practical and emotional purposes met by divine healing practices and barrio believers' uniquely unrestricted access to this healing strategy make divine healing a pillar in the faith of marginalized, working-class, pentecostal Bogotános.


Social Context


In the mid-1990s, life in Nuevo Progreso was a visual testament to the strength of human determination. Only 10 years had passed since the barrio was empty acres of green hillside. Shortly thereafter, it was divided into small lots and sold to lower-working-class Colombians who wanted a better life for their families. Single makeshift shacks were built on the lots as the families struggled to save for the purchase of bricks, mortar, cement, and rebar. They held work parties on the weekends to pour slabs and build additional rooms. Development of the barrio was rapid, but it was made with great sacrifice, endless community projects, and noticeably absent government assistance. By the time of this study, the hillside of Nuevo Progreso was full of thousands of homes, but the barrio residents had done all the work with their own hands and pesos—creating utilities, bus routes, day care centers, parks, and schools.

Life in the barrio was a taxing journey. It was emotionally and physically exhausting, intensely insecure, drawing its inhabitants frequently to the limits of the human capacity for hardship. The heavy burden of normal daily living was exacerbated by Colombia's extreme violence and destitution. Bogotá was in the 1990s and is still considered one of the most dangerous cities in the world.[4] Tremendous tenacity was required of the barrio residents to get through each day. To do the laundry was a four-hour ordeal, leaving arms fatigued and hands raw from the rough cement washbasin. To bathe was a long process of heating rainwater and pouring it over oneself in a chilly stall. The commute to work was a cattle ride, daily wages a pittance. Family members doubled and tripled up in bed to combat the chilly nights with no heat. The infrastructure of the barrio was tenuous at best, and water and electricity were frequently cut. Just walking through the unpaved streets to one of the tiny *supermercados* was a major chore, as one had to weave around ditches and garbage, past hungry dogs, through slippery mud, and down steep streets. Violence was a constant threat, and residents were often assaulted, stabbed, raped, robbed, or murdered—with little hope of justice for the victim. Social cleansing, the heinous serial killings of marginalized Colombians by police, was a known occurrence in Nuevo Progreso. Law enforcement to protect barrio residents was almost nonexistent.

When setbacks came, as they often did, the only safety net for barrio residents was the social network of friends and family—who were also hard-pressed for resources. Government social programs had marginal effect. Employment benefits were rare. Residents hung precariously at the edge of what they were able to endure in order to *seguir adelante*, or continue forward, in life. The following examples are common to barrio families. When Esperanza[5] was told to work a three-day weekend, she had to leave her three young boys alone in their rented bedroom for over 14 hours each day. Her alternative was to lose her job and face eviction into the streets. Luisa, in full labor to give birth, had to walk a half-mile in the middle of the night to find transportation to the hospital. There was no ambulance or taxi. Her baby girl was born immediately after her arrival at the hospital. She was fortunate; many women bear their babies at home with the help of female family members or friends. Marta's home was broken into one night shortly before Christmas. The intruder held a gun to her head while his accomplice emptied her home of everything valuable, including her TV and appliances. There was nowhere to turn for help to recover the losses. When

Julio lost his job, he and his wife spent their last pesos on ingredients to roast peanuts on their stove. They sold them in tiny packages on the buses during commuter hours. The alternative was to starve. There were no food banks or food stamps to sustain their family when the groceries ran out. Loida's neighbor ingested rat poison and was found retching on the ground. He needed immediate care. The only hope was to find a sympathetic bus driver to take them to a hospital in downtown Bogotá. If the bus driver had refused their pleas, the man would have simply died. When Ximena and Luis heard teenagers being murdered in the street outside their home, they could only lock their doors and sit anxiously while the terrible violence was taking place a few meters away. The police would not have come. These marginalized Bogotános did not have the luxury of social justice. They were the sole guardians of their safety.

Accustomed to living with constant challenges like these, the barrio residents took for granted that their survival required long, hard workdays, regular sacrifices, and an almost paranoid vigilance for safety. They grew to expect that survival would be hard-fought. But hardship does take its toll, especially when there is an overwhelming sense of powerlessness against the constant battering of life. In Nuevo Progreso, it manifested in widespread domestic violence and child abuse, alcoholism, anxiety, and depression.

Within this context of life, it would not be surprising if many people looked to religious sources to find tangible help for crises large and small. However, seeking divine assistance was not a common practice in the barrio. The nominal Catholicism typically found in barrio families was more about decades-old rituals—such as keeping a religious candle lit continuously, or putting a baby Jesus figure in the bedroom—than finding help for daily life in one's faith. Residents relied on extended family, their will to survive, and the strength of their backs to get through rough times. For supernatural intervention in a special situation, some residents openly sought the powers and advice of *brujería*, or witchcraft. In practices that can be traced to indigenous customs and the influence of African slave culture in Colombia, spells were cast, visions seen and interpreted, potions mixed and slipped into drinks, and special rituals performed.[6] Divine help was rarely spoken of, and there was no evidence that the weekly mass was a place to seek God's comfort, healing, or provision. Most residents went to mass once during Holy Week and a few other times during the year, for a 40-minute standing service of prayers, rituals, and a short homily. They took their safety, well-being, and future prospects into their own hands, and from their perspective, God had little to do with the outcome of their lives.

Appeal of the Pentecostal Worldview

The dominant worldview shared by most barrio residents contrasted starkly with that of the pentecostal believers.[7] Pentecostals attended their church services between two and five times each week, and it was not uncommon to have two- to three-hour services. The preaching, teaching, worship, prayer, and Bible study consistently reinforced their belief that God was interested in each minute detail of their day and was their infinitely loving provider, protector, savior, healer, and friend. Jesus was not a helpless infant in the arms of the Virgin Mary, or a weak and suffering victim of crucifixion, as Colombian visual culture frequently portrayed him. Jesus was, instead, a strong and benevolent king who had defeated fear and evil and whose love for his followers moved him to act powerfully on their behalf.[8] The believers' faith was completely incorporated into daily life, such that every event and circumstance was understood through their pentecostal, Bible-based, spiritually focused worldview.[9]

Pentecostals held the same jobs, rode the same buses, and trudged through the same muddy streets as the Catholic barrio residents, yet their perception of their daily life struggles was radically different. The worldview of believers was remarkably positive compared to their non-pentecostal neighbors. The preconversion feeling of helplessness in the midst of constant hardship was replaced by a strong belief in divine purpose, high personal worth, hope in the outcome of trials, and ready, miraculous power from God to overcome obstacles. Although life continued to be a harsh journey, the burden of walking it alone seemed to have been lifted. This was the case for Loida:

> I was always concerned about my problems. But when I went to the second meeting, I knew the reason that I went. I surrendered myself, and gave all my burdens to God. All of the anguish that I carried disappeared, and I wasn't sad any more. . . . All began to change. The difficulties continue, but I have a faith in the Lord that he will provide the food, the job. I didn't feel so afflicted. I had a best friend.[10]

The striking contrast of worldviews suggested by Loida begs the question: How did barrio residents take the step of conversion to the pentecostal faith? Certainly, the common perception of pentecostals as *locos* would seemingly preclude any Catholic resident from being seen in the highly visible worship services of believers. Yet the pressing demands of daily survival and the need for immediate help and emotional relief provided the impetus for venturing into the pentecostal faith.

On the steep main road of Nuevo Progreso is one of the pentecostal churches of the barrio. It is a curious sight for all passersby. Several times a week, the high-volume sound system within the tiny chapel broadcasts the message of faith in Jesus to all—in music, preaching, prayer, and avowed miracles. Above the door, visible from the dirt street, is a banner that reads "Salvation and Healing." It is analogous to a store advertising its wares with signs in the window.

Salvation, the critical decision, according to Protestant theology, necessary for receiving eternal life and escaping the fires of hell, would perhaps seem to generate the greatest appeal. However, healing plays a pivotal role in drawing nonbelievers to church services—perhaps more than the idea of salvation, at least as this notion is commonly understood by North American and European interpreters of religion. Indeed, for barrio pentecostals, salvation *is* in large part a material transaction, much as the theologian Miroslav Volf has theorized.[11] For those who do not yet understand the pentecostal faith, to enter a service and receive divine healing is to meet a tangible, immediate need, with little risk or commitment involved.[12] On the other hand, to receive salvation and to convert to the strict pentecostal faith may seem more ethereal and less important to day-to-day survival. Divine healing, offered to whomever enters the church regardless of their religious affiliation, appears to display God's power to nonbelievers and is a catalyst for growing the new believer's faith in God. For this reason, healing is a powerful ritual that draws new converts to believe despite a widespread societal sentiment against pentecostalism. Consider Cristina's story:

> When I had recently separated from my husband, my daughter got sick. She was gravely ill. She was in the hospital 15 days. She came out of the hospital sicker than when she went in. We took her to different doctors, and they gave her drugs but nothing worked. They said, "It's not worth it, she's not living any more. Leave her to die." One day in my barrio I entered in the Christian church. I asked the pastor to give her to God. That if God wanted to take her, to do it, or to heal her, to do it, but don't let her suffer more. That God should do what he wants. So we gave her to God on Sunday, and on Monday, she was already showing signs of life. The Lord healed her. This was big for me. It made my faith grow a lot.[13]

As Cristina's account illustrates, the healing of a family member often induces relatives, and especially female caregivers, to affiliate with pentecostalism. Merarda also developed faith in God as a result of divine healing she believed herself to have experienced.

> One time I got sick, for three months with a terrible pain. I went to the doctor and spent 20,000 pesos on drugs. They didn't help. A pastor came to visit me, but I said, "No pastor, I don't feel well. There is no healing." He said pray and believe that the Lord can send out all sickness in the name of Jesus. I began to pray and ask for healing. I cried from the pain, it attacked me terribly. On the third day the pain disappeared. He does his work. I then began to draw myself closer to the Lord.[14]

For Merarda, like Cristina and many other barrio pentecostals, it was an experience of God as healer that provided the first attraction to the pentecostal faith.

In addition to drawing nonbelievers to pentecostalism, divine healing plays a paramount role in the lives of believers. This is true even after years or decades in the faith. Salvation, as the first "ware" on the church's sign, is the first step in the believers' long journey of faith.[15] Divine healing, however, is petitioned for, received, and administered consistently—even daily—throughout the journey. Consider the following example of the predominance of divine healing in the faith. In a typical church service, when the pastor offers salvation from the pulpit, perhaps 1–10 percent of those attending go forward to receive salvation. When he offers divine healing for the many ailments of life—sickness, disease, fatigue, pains, depression, anxiety—75–100 percent of his congregation often go forward to receive healing. Divine healing, to believers, is an oft-needed ritual of restoring wholeness to the entire person. Experienced in its many forms, healing is the anticipated ministry that anchors many believers in their steadfast commitment to the faith. In its practical, physical form, it promises a ready antidote for bodies worn and afflicted by daily life. In its emotional and spiritual purpose, it is the soothing remedy for hearts wearied by anxiety and helplessness. Pentecostal healing is the comforting salve upon which believers rely in their struggle to *seguir adelante* against all odds.

There are three primary elements of divine healing within pentecostalism that make it a pillar in the faith of lower-working-class believers in Bogotá: the ready accessibility of divine healing practices, the practical role that healing rituals play in daily survival, and the emotional wholeness that believers avowedly experience through divine healing.

## Accessibility of Divine Healing Practices

One of the strongest appeals of divine healing practices is their ready accessibility to those who desire them. It may be easier to understand this appeal by emphasizing how much is *inaccessible* to barrio residents. Higher education is almost impossible to attain. Quality health care is undeniably cost-prohibitive. Vehicle ownership is not an option for most. Safety, legal rights, representation, career choices, and exposure to fine arts are all out of reach. During my stay, mail still did not arrive in the barrio, which prevented access to important personal and business communication. To be denied so much, and then to discover a faith where visible demonstrations of power seem to be readily available through divine healing and other rituals, is a strong attraction for many. Imagine the reaction at a home Bible study when one of the *hermanos* shared this experience:

> At this point Omar, who had entered late, came in and said that a
> miracle had taken place in his life very recently. He was in the street

and witnessed an accident—two people on a motorcycle hit a truck head-on and were thrown. An accident with such force leaves people dead usually, and they were laying as dead. And Omar felt the Holy Spirit say to him to go pray over them—and he did, on his knees, and prayed for their bodies and lives. They got up, right in front of him, a little dazed, and didn't even have a broken bone. "Amen! Gloria a Dios!" said the *hermanos*. "We have words of life."[16]

The seeming accessibility of divine healing makes it appear very practical for believers. Pentecostals perceive that any ailment can be healed, in any physical location, at any hour. Healing may be administered with one person alone, or with dozens, hundreds, or thousands present. Those who mediate the healing can be children, young adults, or the elderly, anyone of any age who believes that God wants to and can heal the sick and afflicted. Healing can be administered by pastors to members of their congregation, and also without ordained or lay leaders present. Physical healing can presumably occur instantaneously or over a period of days or weeks. Those who receive healing can be believers, nonbelievers, atheists, or persons of any faith whom God has chosen to touch with healing power.

To define divine healing as a certain ritual, with specific participants, within a predetermined setting, would limit the way that it was practiced in this poor barrio of south Bogotá. As it was experienced and understood by believers, divine healing took place whenever there was a pain, sickness, or brokenness that God healed, whether physical, emotional, or spiritual. The believers' steadfast faith in the miraculous erased the limitations of how or who or where in divine healing. Believers drew upon the power of healing whenever they deemed it necessary. Here is Gilma's story:

> We once were with some children of a pastor. There was a window open in the kitchen—the house was big. There was a window through the dining room. I felt an explosion. I felt something, but nothing else. My stomach was inflated. And I said, "In the name of Jesus Christ, I am healed, in the promises of God." I got down and began to pray. They looked at me, and I was bleeding here and there. From where this bullet came, I don't know. And nothing, nothing happened. It didn't touch any organ, any intestine. . . . The Lord is my doctor.[17]

Gilma did not pause to diagnose her condition or to worry about the improbability that a bullet wound to her abdomen could possibly leave her unharmed. She simply turned to the one physician she knew would respond.

One of the great appeals of the pentecostal faith is that anyone can walk into a church service and request divine healing or participate in the rituals happening during the service. In a large church in downtown Bogotá, which some Nuevo Progreso residents attended, the pastor typically displayed the power of divine healing during the Sunday service.

> Then the pastor got up and greeted us. "How many have come for healing today?" "Amen!" [the congregation] shouted. He then asked those who were sick to raise their hands—and truly there were a couple hundred. He asked a woman to go to the front. "How many recognize her? No one, because she's only been going to this church for 10 days." He told us the story of how she was in a wheelchair 8 days ago. (She had walked up to the podium.) Applause. She had an operation and was in a wheelchair—and didn't think she'd walk again. Then she came to a service, in which he explained how one needs to have faith and what faith is. Then he made the prayer of faith and told her to get up and walk. And she did. In front of everyone he had her move her legs, lift her knees, and there was more applause. "And we all give glory to God," he said. More applause.[18]

In many similar examples, the recipient of divine healing publicly demonstrated an ability to perform simple tasks that had avowedly been impossible before. Such actions concretized and added to the persuasive power of the verbal testimonies.

Across the different denominations I observed, there were not significant variations in the pentecostals' practices of how to access divine healing. They all believed in praying and asking God for the healing, using the words "In the name of Jesus," and in some way touching the afflicted person. Some churches would send out the demons of sickness when praying for the afflicted, shouting, "Fuera! Fuera!" (Get out! Get out!). In large churches, pastors instructed the hundreds or thousands of believers present to lay hands on their own heads and receive divine healing. Even when touch could not be administered, healing was still available to the afflicted—even hundreds of miles away, or across radio or television waves. In typical fashion, one believer, Ana, accessed divine healing through the most basic means:

> I had a sickness, bronchitis. I couldn't breathe. I had something in my throat that would cut off my respiration. I was almost dying. I had already been baptized. I couldn't breathe through the nose or the mouth. I tried everything and nothing worked. So I put on the radio and the *hermano* Enrique was there preaching. So I put my hand on the radio—and I started improving little by little. And it hasn't come back to bother me.[19]

No matter who administered the healing or who received it, two things seemed very clear to participants: the power came from God, and it was available to whomever needed it whenever and wherever it was required.

Practical Role

To live in a barrio such as Nuevo Progreso meant that one's health and well-being were constantly at risk. Despite being 9,000 feet above sea level and drenched in the chilly Andes mountain air, there was no heat at night. Open sewer drains, piles of uncovered garbage, and foul-smelling meat markets were common sights in the barrio. Milk was sold in a plastic bag and hung on a nail in the kitchen. Hygiene was a luxury that only a minority could afford, and even fewer had access to quality medical care. In addition, with limited wages and hard labor, the barrio residents favored cheap, high-carbohydrate food, such as potatoes, fried yucca, and *plátanos*, and did not enjoy an abundance of fresh fruits and vegetables. The irony is that, while living in an environment with so many health challenges, the residents of Nuevo Progreso also needed a tremendous amount of strength, energy, and stamina to adequately meet the demands of daily life. They had fewer resources to maintain their health than did middle-class Bogotános, but needed twice the physical fortitude to survive. In practical terms, having access to healing for any kind of ailment was a critical part of the believers' survival. This did not preclude their use of medicine or doctors; many also used "science" for important procedures or situations of acute sickness. However, faith in God's healing power was their first recourse and, for some, their only solution.

During the interviews, believers were asked what they would do in the event that a child in their family were sick and the prescribed medicine cost two weeks' wages. Of the 44 believers who responded to the question, 73 percent said that they would simply pray to God and believe in the child's healing. Sixteen percent answered that they would trust God and then look for resources to pay for the medicine. Only 11 percent responded by saying they would find the money somehow to pay for the medicine, without mentioning God. This is not because the believers held that doctors or medicine were evil. Most often, they did not have the choice of medical care. Healing had become their *only* option. Rosa had a five-year-old son, Miguel Angel: "He's been sick, and I've prayed with all my heart that God would cure him. One night he was very sick, a fever, nothing to do. I got on my knees, laid hands on him that God would heal him, and the next day he was well. With God, all is possible."[20] Melisa had two sons and attended a small home group in the barrio. When asked what she would do in the situation of having a sick child, her answer was emphatic:

> I can answer all the questions with one answer, which I said before. The faith, simply. I know that if I am a daughter of God and I believe in him, and I have this faith, he's not going to leave me and I won't lack anything. In spite of circumstances and difficult situations, one feels like they don't have anything to hold onto, but I know that God

is going to provide a way. But we won't be left hungry or sick. No, I
know we won't, because I have testimonies of what God has done in
our lives since we were children.[21]

Pentecostal families in this study did pay for à la carte medical care—medicine,
small procedures, ointments, etc.—when the resources were available. However, with the subpar quality of care available to barrio residents, precious
resources were often spent on treatment that provided no results. Many pentecostals recounted stories of spending down to their last peso on medicine—
with no sign of healing.

Certainly, to have one's child denied critical medical care for lack of insurance or money could leave one feeling despondent and helpless. Parents who
felt overwhelmed by the enormity of their situations often prayed to God for
healing in urgent, fervent tones and demonstrated a willingness to go to any
lengths of fasting, prayer, and vigils to see their child get well. If healing seemed
evident, their faith in God grew, and as they began to depend on divine healing
more and more, they saw no practical purpose in paying for medical care in the
future. Elisabét was a teacher whose education had been funded by a global
child assistance fund. When asked what she would do if she were sick, she was
adamant about her experience:

> I would pray to the Lord, that He heal me or take me, but I'm not
> going to use money for the doctor. You can go to the doctor as a
> Christian, but for me, in the end, the doctor doesn't work for me. I
> was sick and I didn't eat. I had anemia, and the doctor gave me a
> drug and told me to eat. But I said, "No, this is a sickness from the
> devil, because I took the drug and it didn't work." So I have to buy
> this drug? No. I don't have money for other things, why would I
> spend on drugs? So I fasted for three days. And I got better! After
> this, I ate.[22]

Faced daily with decisions that weighed rent against food, bus fare against
electricity, medicine against school supplies, pentecostals chose to depend on
God for healing. Practically, divine healing seemed to meet a need that was
paramount in their lives: to have strength and health for the exertion needed
for daily survival.

Emotional Benefit

The attention given to divine healing in lower-class barrios cannot be interpreted solely through the lens of its practical physical use. The believers of
Nuevo Progreso did rely heavily upon their faith in God to heal when there was
no money for medical care, and experiences of healing from sickness and pain

are a welcome relief in any marginalized community. Believers' use of divine healing, however, amounted to much more than how patients use a community health center. The practice of divine healing was intimately wrapped around their core belief in a loving, generous, powerful healer: Jesus. Instead of the clinical image of a sick person receiving medication at a doctor's office, divine healing was, for believers, an emotional experience like sitting on a doting parent's knee and receiving healing ointment for the pain with a loving embrace. This pain did not have to be physical. It could be emotional pain, spiritual hunger, inner suffering, or any other unseen wound. The salve of divine healing seemed to be available for any hurt believers carried, and as they received it, it fortified their belief in a loving God.

This distinction between merely medical relief and *divine* healing is critical for several reasons. First, it explains the apparently illogical commitment that believers exhibited toward their faith and to service in their church.[23] With such a heavy workload and so few resources, why would a single working mother spend precious pesos on bus fare, expend valuable energy, and sacrifice already-scarce time with her children to engage in a two-hour church service at the end of a long day? She went for the renewal of her body and soul through the worship, prayer, teaching, and divine healing offered there. The emotional cleansing became a regular therapy that strengthened the believer to face the challenges that awaited her in the coming days and weeks.[24] Julio spoke of this in his interview: "The love and peace that one feels, being in the church. It attracts you. You miss it; you want Sunday school to come. You have to seek God. If I don't seek God, knowing all that he gives to one, providing life and health. . . . To not respond to him for all of this?"[25] Alberto also spoke of what he gained from attending the services in his small church: "It's a place where I can take all my problems, difficulties, and I have the security that when I come out, I come out calm, without problems, confident. I find the support that you can't find in people."[26]

Many "sicknesses" that are healed in pentecostal churches in Bogotá are afflictions of the heart and soul, anguish, depression, anxiety, fear, and despair, when those feelings are so deep and intense that they translate as real pain. This sensation of emotional healing was well described by a woman named Trinidad. Years ago, in a shack high up in the barrio, assembled with metal sheets for a roof and scrap-wood walls, Trinidad and her alcoholic husband were struggling.

> I never thought of myself, in the love one should feel. I lived sad, because he drank a lot. . . . I would think, "God, what am I going to do with this man?" . . . So on Tuesday she invited me and I loved it. And the reason I loved it is because lots of *hermanos* prayed for my home, for my husband. The pastor said, "Kneel here." They were rebuking the spirits of drunkenness. This really came and touched

my heart. I left with tranquility in my heart, a peace. I felt important, the only one that they prayed for.[27]

This was, for Trinidad, the turning point in her life, the moment when she began to join the faith. Similarly, Eduardo and his wife rented a small room from some believers when they were going through a rough time as newly-weds. He heard them having their prayer meetings and decided to join them:

> I went to the prayer, so did my wife. The Lord baptized me in the Holy Spirit. He did something extraordinary in my life, because I had felt a terrible weight on my shoulders, like stones. And I felt that a powerful hand took this off of me and I felt light. . . . And today though the problems are difficult, terrible, I don't carry them on my shoulders, on my back. The Lord takes the problem. That's one of the things that keep me in love with the Lord. This is what makes me stay faithful in the presence of the Lord, to serve him.[28]

For those who experienced these events of emotional or spiritual healing, the significance was comparable to a miraculous physical healing. It was a mile-stone in their faith, one that believers readily shared to show the reason for their commitment.

The second reason for making the distinction between clinical healing, or "cure," and the emotional experience of divine healing is that it sheds light on the common dual experience of receiving divine healing and subsequently converting to the faith.[29] No one "converts" to a medical clinic. However, many believers recounted receiving divine healing with intense emotional experi-ences of love and hope. These bound them firmly to their convictions that God was their true healer and friend. Often, a conversion would follow the healing experience, as with Mariela:

> I began to have a little sickness, on my face. My face was a terrible mess of blood, skin. It itched me. They took me to many doctors. They didn't know what it was. I was a monster. Every three days I needed an injection. My older brother knew the word of God. He talked to us. My mother wanted to take me to a witch to see if someone had put a spell on me. My brother said, "No, that's worse. I invite you to go to a meeting with me tonight. Go with me. The only one who can heal you is the Lord Jesus Christ." I went for curiosity, to see the pastor. They had to put a silk on my face. There were a lot of people. I saw many sick people. I sat with them. I saw a man at the pulpit—he had been converted, had on a gray suit. He began to tell his testimony. . . . I heard this and felt something terrible in my heart. It opened my eyes and I understood. He said, "Let the sick come forward." I was the first. When he put his hand over my face, I felt like I was flying. And I couldn't remember more. I woke up,

crying, on the bench. There I received the salvation of my soul and the healing of my body, 31 years ago. That night, I went home and slept—although I hadn't been able to for three months. I woke up at 9:00. My face felt soft, I could see well. I didn't have pus running down like before. So my grandma came in and was scared. "Chinita! What happened?" I looked at my face and said, "I'm healed. I was healed in the meeting last night by the Lord Jesus Christ." She called all the neighbors. From that miracle, so beautiful, I have been strong in the Lord.[30]

Emotional healing and the emotional experiences that accompany physical healing are common occurrences within the pentecostal church. They draw nonbelievers and believers to believe more strongly in the reality of God and his power. To many individuals, whether first-time visitor or decades-long believer, these experiences of divine healing provide inner hope, peace, wholeness, and the sense of being tenderly cared for by a loving God.

## Conclusion

Outside the pentecostal church in barrio Santa Librada, the sun is setting on a busy street. A vendor is selling fried meat, which crackles and spits on his grill; another has hot corn *arepas* for the moderate price of 300 pesos each. Just inside the sanctuary, a single mother stops near the doorway and reaches into a box where there are cushions. She selects one and finds an empty seat near the back. She lays the cushion on the hard cement floor and kneels on it, resting her elbows on her seat, facing the back of the church. Her hands are worn from years of labor. Her clothes are simple and unpretentious. She covers her face with her hands, and soft sounds of prayer are soon heard. Around her, other *hermanos* are arriving to the service. They, too, kneel to pray, and soon the room is a cacophony of voices, supplications, adoring words, cries for help, and prayers. "Señor, te alabamos, te adoramos, esta noche queremos levanter tu nombre" (Lord, we praise you, we adore you, tonight we want to lift up your name). "O Padre celestial, ayúdame hoy. Tú puedes ver las necesidades de tus hijos" (O heavenly Father, help me today. You are able to see the needs of your children). As the sanctuary fills, the volume of prayers rises, and one hears words of urgency, tones of anguish, tears, cries of pain, earnest supplication, adoring praise, and grateful devotion. It is an emotional river, with an intense current. No one seems indifferent or apathetic here. Their needs are raw, open, and vulnerable. As the musicians start to play in front, signaling the beginning of worship, the believers rise from their knees and join the singing. The atmosphere is charged with spiritual fervency. Healing has already begun for many.

Later that evening, after an hour of singing and an hour of preaching, the service is drawing to a close, and many of the chairs are empty. But no one has gone home. The open area near the pulpit is packed full of people, some kneeling, some standing, with hands raised in the air or clasped in front of them. Leaders of the church are stepping here and there, laying their hands on those with needs, praying for them, while the musicians continue to worship God on the stage behind them. Every kind of ailment and need is being prayed for. No one is turned away. No problem is too great. In the front, a *hermana* stands, as two deaconesses of the church lay their hands on her shoulders. They anoint her forehead with a finger stroke of oil. They pray for her strength, her heart, her spirit, her weary body, her stomach pains, her broken marriage, her financial needs, all in one continuous stream of requests to God, female voices raised and crying out simultaneously. They believe that physical and emotional healing are taking place right as they speak, that God will move mountains just for them, and that he is attentively listening and responding to them from his throne in heaven. Their conviction is fierce and emotive.

It matters not that these women are poor maids who must return to make-shift homes and shiver in cold cement rooms tonight, nor that their future prospects are decades more of backbreaking work, meager pay, humble living, and tenuous survival. In that moment, they see themselves as daughters of a great king, whose infinite love is available as a powerful salve to heal and comfort. In their poverty, they provide this salve generously and lavishly to one another. As the praying ends, and they wipe their tears and embrace, with expressions of "Amén" and "Qué lindo" (How beautiful), they are ready to *seguir adelante* another day.

NOTES

1 Charles W. Bergquist, Ricardo Peñaranda, and G. Gonzalo Sánchez, *Violence in Colombia, 1990–2000: Waging War and Negotiating Peace* (Wilmington, Del.: SR, 2001); Frank Safford and Marco Palacios, *Colombia: Fragmented Land, Divided Society* (New York: Oxford University Press, 2002).

2 For a consideration of pentecostal healing as a Latinizing tendency against the foreign influences of Anglo-Saxon Protestantism, see F. Laplantine, "Illness, Healing and Religion in Contemporary Latin American Pentecostal Movements," *Anthropologie et Sociétés* 23.2 (1999): 101–115.

3 See also Rebecca Pierce Bomann, *Faith in the Barrios: The Pentecostal Poor in Bogotá* (Boulder, Colo.: Lynne Rienner, 1999).

4 Rodrigo Guerrero, "Violencia y Exclusion: Las Experiencias de Cali y Bogotá, Colombia," in *Tercer Curso de Gestión Urbana Latinoamérica* (Lima, Peru: International Bank for Reconstruction and Development/World Bank, 2003), http://www.bvsde. paho.org/bvsacd/cd65/GuerreroViolencia.pdf (accessed 6 July 2009); Etienne G. Krug, James A. Mercy, Linda L. Dahlberg, and Anthony B. Zwi, "The World Report on Violence and Health," *Lancet* 360.9339 (2002): 1083–1088; Jorge A. Restrepo, Michael

Spagat, and Juan F. Vargas, "The Dynamics of the Colombian Civil Conflict: A New Data Set" (Nov. 2003), CEPR Discussion Paper no. 4108, http://ssrn.com/abstract=480247 (accessed 6 July 2009).

5 All names used in this study are pseudonyms chosen by the subjects.

6 On folk healing practices and pentecostalism, see Harvey Cox, *Fire from Heaven: The Rise of Pentecostal Spirituality and the Reshaping of Religion in the Twenty-First Century* (Reading, Mass.: Addison-Wesley, 1995), 147; Gastón Espinosa, "'God Made a Miracle in My Life': Latino Pentecostal Healing in the Borderlands," in *Religion and Healing in America*, ed. Linda L. Barnes and Susan S. Sered (New York: Oxford University Press, 2005), 10; André Corten, *Pentecostalism in Brazil: Emotion of the Poor and Theological Romanticism* (New York: St. Martin's, 1999), 35.

7 At the time of this study, perhaps a million people, or 4 percent of the Colombian population, were pentecostals; David Martin, *Tongues of Fire: The Explosion of Protestantism in Latin America* (Cambridge, Mass.: Blackwell, 1990), 51; the numbers have grown moderately since the mid-1990s, although remaining well below 10 percent of the population; Paul Freston, "Contours of Latin American Pentecostalism," in *Christianity Reborn: The Global Expansion of Evangelicalism in the Twentieth Century*, ed. Donald M. Lewis (Grand Rapids, Mich.: Eerdmans, 2004), 229.

8 On the visual culture of religion in Colombia, see Germán Rey, "Identities, Religion and Melodrama: A View from the Cultural Dimension of the Latin American *Telenovela*," in *Belief in Media: Cultural Perspectives on Media and Christianity*, ed. Peter Horsfield, Mary E. Hess, and Adán M. Medrano (Burlington, Vt.: Ashgate, 2004), 81–90.

9 For more on worldviews, see John Lofland and Rodney Stark, "Becoming a World-Saver: A Theory of Conversion to a Deviant Perspective," in *Religion in Sociological Perspective: Essays in the Empirical Study of Religion*, ed. Charles Y. Glock (Belmont, Calif.: Wadsworth, 1973), 28; Thomas Luckmann, *The Invisible Religion: The Problem of Religion in Modern Society* (London: Macmillan, 1967), 51; Michael Kearney, *World View* (Novato, Calif.: Chandler and Sharp, 1984), 41; Richard Shaull and Waldo A. Cesar, *Pentecostalism and the Future of the Christian Churches: Promises, Limitations, Challenges* (Grand Rapids, Mich.: Eerdmans, 2000), 168–169.

10 Interview (Feb. 1996).

11 Miroslav Volf, "Materiality of Salvation: An Investigation in the Soteriologies of Liberation and Pentecostal Theologics," *Journal of Ecumenical Studies* 26.3 (1989): 447–467.

12 R. Andrew Chesnut, *Born Again in Brazil: The Pentecostal Boom and the Pathogens of Poverty* (New Brunswick, N.J.: Rutgers University Press, 1997), 82, argues that Latin Americans seeking healing, who are accustomed to the idea of a Catholic *promessa*, or payment of a vow when healing is received, envision pentecostal healing as demanding not simply a one-time payment, but as requiring the "patient to convert, to be born again and become a *nova criatura* (new creature)."

13 Interview (Mar. 1996).

14 Interview (Mar. 1996).

15 Drawing on Emile Durkheim's distinction between "religion" (which creates a community) and "magic" (which merely creates a clientele), Freston, "Contours of Latin American Pentecostalism," 236, emphasizes that divine healing (when successful) is merely a first step in building a stable community.

16  Field notes (Nov. 1995).

17  Interview (Mar. 1996)

18  Field notes (Feb. 1996).

19  Interview (Apr. 1996).

20  Interview (Feb. 1996).

21  Interview (Mar. 1996).

22  Interview (Apr. 1996).

23  For a discussion of rational choice theory—that apparently irrational religious behaviors are based on the rational weighing of perceived costs and benefits—see Lawrence A. Young, *Rational Choice Theory and Religion: Summary and Assessment* (New York: Routledge, 1997).

24  There are also practical economic benefits to participation in pentecostal networks. Elizabeth Brusco, in her study of Colombian evangelicals, *The Reformation of Machismo: Evangelical Conversion and Gender in Colombia* (Austin: University of Texas Press, 1995), found that the conversion of a heavy-drinking husband could save 20–40 percent of household income, with further savings resulting when male converts ceased smoking, gambling, visiting prostitutes, and supporting other women. Similar also to the findings of Chesnut, *Born Again in Brazil*, 105, Colombian pentecostal churches function as mutual aid societies, providing help in finding jobs and administering relief in times of crisis. Susana Borda Carulla, "Resocialization of 'Desplazados' in Small Pentecostal Congregations in Bogotá, Colombia," *Refugee Survey Quarterly* 26.2 (2007): 36–46, argues that pentecostal churches in Bogotá's slum areas effectively reconstruct social networks and the identities of forcibly displaced populations.

25  Interview (Feb. 1996).

26  Interview (Feb. 1996).

27  Interview (Feb. 1996).

28  Interview (Apr. 1996).

29  For the distinction between "healing" and "cure," see Susan S. Sered and Linda L. Barnes, introduction to *Religion and Healing in America*, ed. Barnes and Sered, 10.

30  Interview (Mar. 1996).

# 10

# Learning from the Master: Carlos Annacondia and the Standardization of Pentecostal Practices in and beyond Argentina

*Matthew Marostica*

Argentine evangelical Protestants summarize their faith through the alliterative catchphrase "Jesus sana, salva, santifica, y vuelve como Rey" (Jesus heals, saves, sanctifies, and returns as King).[1] This saying captures the centrality of divine healing in the Argentine evangelical experience. Jesus is envisioned as actively intervening in the lives of his followers by first healing them. That which follows—saving, sanctifying, and returning as king—is future-oriented. Healing takes place here and now. Healing experiences typically launch new believers on the path toward being "saved" and affiliating with pentecostal churches.[2]

Divine healing became part of the pentecostal and the broader evangelical Protestant experience temporally very late in Argentina. Its practice did not become accepted and standardized until the late 1980s. As practiced in Argentina in the 1990s, the gift of healing seemed vested in a select few of God's chosen: Carlos Annacondia, Omar Cabrera, Hector Giménez, Claudio Freidzon, and, at the local level, the pastor in his or her church. Divine healing is now far and away the primary tool for evangelizing and church growth. This chapter traces the emergence of divine healing as a central practice of Argentina's evangelicals; the consolidation of specific healing practices in pentecostal services; and the effects of divine healing within the evangelical community once it was embraced as the first, and most public, experience on the path to Jesus.

The Argentine evangelical movement's appropriation and transformation of divine healing occurred in a compressed time frame between roughly 1985 and 1990 under the leadership of Carlos Annacondia. By embracing and popularizing *liberación*, liberation or deliverance from demons, and divine healing, and by insisting that local churches across denominations band together to sponsor his crusades, Annacondia created a community unified in accepting God's active intervention in their daily lives and, most particularly, their bodies. Crusade participants understood themselves as part of a larger community of Argentine and, to a significant extent, global pentecostal Christians.


The Historical Development of Evangelicalism in Argentina

The tremendous impact of the Annacondia crusades can only be understood when seen against the backdrop of the historical trajectory of Argentina's evangelical churches, which were established by North American missionaries, many of whom were Pentecostals, who came to Argentina and stayed. This generation of missionaries arrived in force beginning in the 1940s and generally did not relinquish church control to local leaders until the 1960s (a few missionaries administered churches into the 1980s).[3] Missionary founders brought with them social, cultural, and political prejudices, and, crucially, denominational antagonisms peculiar to marginalized conservative Protestants in the mid-twentieth-century United States.

The collective beliefs, practices, and personas of the missionaries—the missionary gospel—fused to create the rigid denominational identities that dominated Argentine evangelicalism into the 1980s. Missionary churches were stamped with a particular identity—the identity common to North American Protestants of the 1930s–1950s. Marfa Cabrera, who, into the 1990s, was the most influential woman evangelist in Argentina, described the endurance of the missionary legacy in this way:

> There were missionaries that taught things which later evolved in the
> United States. However, the organizations which they created here
> held onto those teachings. They remained stuck in time, to say it that
> way—Hair, forms of dress, make-up, whether or not you could read a
> newspaper or watch television, things like that. The same denomina-
> tions in the U.S. became "open" while the ones here remained very
> "closed."[4]

Indeed, the entire package of American Pentecostal beliefs from the mid-twentieth century became "stuck in time" within Argentine Pentecostal churches. Beliefs concerning the precise effects of Spirit baptism, whether or not women could wear makeup, and a deep-seated revulsion toward politics were held together in a web of belief linked to the memory of the revered founding missionaries. Importantly, this constellation of missionary beliefs also included a very restrictive (for pentecostals) view of divine healing—in part the reaction of U.S. denominational Pentecostals against independent healing evangelists.[5] Although it was acknowledged as a legitimate gift of the Holy Spirit, Pentecostal mission churches were uniformly suspicious of the practice of divine healing and did not make healing a regular part of their ministries.

This suspicion of divine healing was reinforced by the U.S. independent healing evangelist Tommy Hicks's 1954 crusade. Hicks capitalized on President Juan Perón's break with the Catholic Church to obtain permission to use a large Buenos Aires soccer stadium and to gain access to radio advertising. For three months, the Hicks crusade built into a truly massive event that culminated in a final day in which 400,000 people converged in and around the stadium to be blessed by Hicks. Rather than emulating Hicks, Pentecostal mission churches (other than the Union of the Assemblies of God, which organized the event), perhaps jealous of Hicks's success, treated him with contempt and veered even further away from "faith healing," which they associated with charlatans and magicians, not Christians.

Unlike Hicks, the missionaries were never very successful in reaching large numbers of Argentines, possibly because they fixated on trying to change the culture of those they had come to teach. The rigidity of the missionaries' teachings only permitted a limited repertoire of practices, and these practices did not resonate in the target culture. Despite this lack of success in what they came to do—church growth—the missionaries' doctrines, practices, and methods were enshrined as an inviolable whole and outlasted their period of leadership by an entire generation. Marfa Cabrera likened her own church's intermittently successful efforts to attract young people to the efforts of the missionaries: "Perhaps we are not reaching them as well as we would like because we are too insistent on changing the way they are. We want to change the youth of today just like the missionaries wanted to change our culture when they came here from the U.S."[6]

## Carlos Annacondia and the Creation of the Argentine Evangelical Movement

The contemporary Argentine evangelical movement, which has had a significant impact on global pentecostalism, formed in the mid-1980s during the massive crusades of Carlos Annacondia, who served as the charismatic (in a Weberian as well as a pentecostal sense) leader upon whom a new Argentine evangelical identity became patterned.[7] In addition to inspiring a new identity, Annacondia supplanted the old missionary gospel with a new, culturally resonant repertoire of practices appropriate to the Argentine popular sector. He further attacked and undermined the missionary model by demanding that local churches cooperate in organizing his crusades (or else he refused to conduct a crusade in the area), thus replacing the missionaries' strict denominationalism with a new spirit of evangelical unity. Crucially, Annacondia shattered the restrictions of the missionary by bringing divine healing to the forefront of pentecostal practices and extending the practice beyond the Pentecostal base to include, first, non-Pentecostal evangelical Christians, and then he recruited new converts from the country's historically Protestant and Catholic populations.

Annacondia, a successful small businessman and a Catholic, underwent a personal conversion to a decidedly pentecostal form of Christianity in 1979 at age 39.[8] His evangelistic enterprise, Mensaje de Salvación, or Message of Salvation, began as an independent church formed by Annacondia, his family, and his 30 employees who converted following his conversion. Within a year of his conversion, Annacondia began to see visions of himself preaching in a squatter settlement. In August 1981, he started preaching in such a settlement in Bernal (in greater Buenos Aires). Of that experience, he says:

> God showed me that *villa de miseria* for an entire year, but I didn't want to go. Finally I said, "I give up" and I went. I went into mud up to my knees but I didn't feel a thing. . . . I felt love for those people that had so many problems. God protected me; He gave me authority over that place—I cast the demons out of those people and out of that place and then one day God took me out of there and put me in a residential neighborhood. And I used the same message to convert the rich as I had used to convert the poor.[9]

Beginning in Bernal, Annacondia became known for his direct, confrontational style and his apparent power to cast out demons and heal the sick. His ministry quickly expanded beyond the initial group of converts in the squatter settlement.[10] By the end of 1983, he claimed that approximately 6,000 people had converted. At this point, Annacondia caught the attention of a group of pastors in the city of La Plata with whom he planned a crusade that both established his position within Argentine evangelicalism and dramatically altered the character of the evangelical community.

Annacondia and Unity

Annacondia presents himself as naive to denominationalism at the time of his conversion.

> When I was converted . . . I was converted without a pastor. Those of us in my business were converted and we started to pray. We invited

several pastors to come pray with us. We were looking for someone with experience to be our pastor. We said, well there can only be one church of Jesus Christ; we could not comprehend that serious divisions could exist. So I said, we are part of the church of Jesus. We'll take a name [Message of Salvation] to identify ourselves, but the name means nothing.[11]

Annacondia adopted for his church a nondenominational identity. He believed, as did many non-evangelical Argentines, that evangelicals were all the same: "I was unfamiliar with the politics of the Church before I began to preach. If I had known about them, perhaps I would not have had the same impact on unity."[12] Annacondia's quick conversion and the nondenominational character of the original Message of Salvation group kept them unexposed to the nuances of Argentine evangelical culture and to the missionary gospel that undergirded it. The intensity of the group's first year—they were praying, reading the Bible, or working together most of the time—kept them distant from the sharp cleavages within Argentine evangelicalism.

Soon, however, Annacondia began to understand "that the Pentecostals and the Baptists could not stand each other [*no se podían ni ver*]. I knew that it was a human defect; that the Devil had insinuated himself into the Church. So," Annacondia explained the rationale behind his distinctive crusade strategy, "when I started to attract attention I made one rule regarding my participation in crusades: I always invited all of the churches in the area to join the campaign. If the pastors had a problem with that, I would not preach in that area until they could resolve their differences."[13] Annacondia's rule, that all the local churches be invited to participate in his crusades, broke with the long history of missionary-inspired denominationalism.

The first campaign where Annacondia imposed this rule was in La Plata, capital of the province of Buenos Aires, in 1984. All the city's churches received an invitation from the organizing committee, but only eight decided to join— representing perhaps 10 percent of the city's Protestants.[14] The La Plata crusade, which was held in several open-air sites, lasted eight months. Annacondia preached seven nights a week, while still running his business during the day. The Message of Salvation reported 50,000 "decisions for Christ" in those eight months. The La Plata crusade was the last Annacondia crusade not to be widely supported by local churches. Unity became the rule for all subsequent crusades.

How are we to understand Annacondia's ability to demand unity from churches that were historically and doctrinally committed to strict denominationalism? Annacondia offers a practical explanation: "Since my ministry worked in their interest, the churches were forced to comply. The Pentecostals had no choice other than to invite the Baptists."[15] What interested the churches were the "fruits" left behind by Annacondia's campaigns—beginning with the 50,000 decision cards in La Plata. Coverage in *El Puente* of Annacondia's first crusade in Rosario (October–November 1985) similarly reports: "*There were 55,000 Decisions for Christ.* One of the most positive aspects of this crusade was the unity of the 77 churches belonging to different denominations that participated in this common effort, in a climate of companionship and Christian community that eliminated the walls of 'names,' 'customs,' and 'denominations.'" Echoing Annacondia's explanation, the article continues: "Someone said that 'when the wheat increases the fences disappear'; and someone else added 'the fences disappear when the fields all belong to one owner. One vineyard, one harvest, many workers and an immense work, all for the owner of the same, Jesus.'"[16] The evangelical community saw that Annacondia was delivering the goods. The "increase in the wheat" Annacondia was producing motivated denominations and pastors to put aside their differences in order to increase the harvest in their individual congregations.

The initial move toward cooperation in organizing crusades had occurred quickly. *El Puente* reported on the preparations for Annacondia's first crusade in the city of Buenos Aires:

*Auspicious Meeting in the Astral*

> The meeting held on July 22 in the Astral theater constitutes one of the most important and auspicious events in recent years. That ACIERA[Christian Alliance of Evangelical Churches of the Republic of Argentina] was the unit which convened the meeting and that over five hundred pastors and leaders from nearly all of the denominations operating in Buenos Aires were in attendance, is, without a doubt, an occurrence with few antecedents. . . . As we said, nearly all of the evangelical denominations were represented. Among them we can mention: Baptists, Free Brethren, Church of God, Holiness Church, Salvation Army, Nazarenes, Union of the Assemblies of God, Assemblies of God, Christian Alliance, Mennonites, Missionary Pentecostal, Christian Community, Independent Church of Christ, Christian Assembly and many independent churches.

Talking about the results of Annacondia's crusade in Haedo (the western sector of greater Buenos Aires) in August–September 1985, the crusade's president, Pastor Albert De Luca, said: "In addition to the 26,584 decision cards for Christ, the crusade left many other positive things. Among them: the huge number of churches that were involved, 109 total, from many denominations. Another positive aspect was the great unity of spirit that existed during the entire crusade."[17] Annacondia believed that the act of working together taught evangelical churches that "they had the same doctrine, the same love. That's where unity really started." The face-to-face interactions of pastors and lay workers from separate denominations produced a "unity of spirit."

Annacondia's Message

Carlos Annacondia's message was, and is, simple: God and the devil exist and are in permanent battle with each other. By accepting Christ, individuals gain access to divine power in order to overcome Satan. As Annacondia put it, "The mission of the Devil is to rob, murder, and destroy. Christ's mission is to save and give life. My mission is to confront Satan." With his direct, confrontational message, reiterated in every crusade, Annacondia gave the evangelical community a potent new grammar that connected the problems of everyday life to Satan and his demons and offered the power of Christ as a solution. This way of articulating the role of Christ in the lives of believers appealed to a fundamental concern in the Argentine popular sector. For many poor Argentines, evil spirits are both terrifying and commonplace; they are part of everyday life. Seeking Christ's power for life and against Satan has been a regular theme in Argentine popular religiosity. Sociologist Alejandro Frigerio argues that pentecostalism's message resonates in Argentine culture because it draws on the popular Catholic belief in Jesus as "a producer of miracles due to His own divine character or His power as an intermediary with God the Father."[18] In teaching that Jesus offers power to overcome Satan's destructive influence, Annacondia proposed a solution that accorded well with popular Catholicism.

The appeal of Annacondia's message was reinforced and invigorated by making good, night after night, on his promise to do battle with Satan and the infirmities he inflicts on God's children. Nonbelievers, believers, and pastors all came to accept Annacondia as a powerful man of God who combats Satan.

New Repertoire of Evangelistic Practices Spread to the Churches

Annacondia introduced a new set of practices to the evangelical community that provided a model for confronting Satan. These included (1) his specific method for casting out demons; (2) his regular use of divine healing; and (3) his use of music with popular appeal. These new evangelistic methods soon exerted a profound impact on the churches that participated in Annacondia's crusades. *El Puente* records an interview with "the pastor that gathered the greatest number of fruits" from the Annacondia campaign in La Plata in 1984. The pastor, Alberto Scataglini, saw his church of 300 members grow to approximately 5,000 one year after the crusade. Commenting on his model for retaining new believers, Scataglini warns other pastors, "Your churches are not going to be the same. If you make them the same, the people will leave you. If you allow the revival of the crusade to enter your church, the people will stay."[19] Scataglini's warning to his fellow pastors should be understood as more than a specific recommendation on how to benefit from Annacondia's crusades. It is a commentary on the changes that Annacondia quickly produced within Argentine evangelicalism. Scataglini's claim that "[y]our churches are not going to be the same," based on his experience in his own church, was clearly prescient. Annacondia's ministry altered the way evangelicals acted in their own churches and how churches and pastors interacted with each other.

Annacondia did much more than simply create an opportunity for pastors and workers from different churches to interact; he directly challenged the old missionary models. Argentine churches that had become stuck in time were forced to choose either to enter a new and unprecedented movement or to close themselves off completely from other Protestant churches and retain their missionary identities. The old evangelistic models were denominationally centered. They used street corner preaching, pamphleteering, and U.S. Sunday school music to attract new faces. From all accounts, they were boring. They did not have a message or style with wide appeal in the Argentine popular sector.

The Crusade

Annacondia explains the dramatic effects his crusades produced in their target neighborhood or city: "There are battles in the air. My crusades are long because it is through these battles that barriers are broken; chains break. . . . If you want to invade a new place, the devil is going to defend himself. The church has to be aggressive. When the church invades a city, society changes, homes change, people change."[20] Annacondia's crusades *are* long; his first mass crusade, in La Plata, lasted eight months. The next four mass campaigns lasted an average of 60 days. Into the mid-1990s, after he had evangelized nearly all the big and medium-size cities in Argentina, many of his crusades lasted weeks.[21]

In addition to being long, Annacondia's crusades are intense. As he says, when he enters a place he goes there to do "battle," and he expects the same aggressiveness by participating churches. Besides the pastors who generally organize crusades and work there nightly, churches contribute many workers, who seek out those who will commit to Christ by filling out decision cards; they carry off and minister to those overcome during their liberation from demons; and they gather testimonies from those who experience healing. All of the pastors and workers become involved in a battle with the devil.

Annacondia's crusades have a regular format: (1) music/praise (conducted by his team's worship leader); (2) the offering: passing baskets to collect money for the crusade (conducted by one of Annacondia's team or sometimes a local pastor); (3) preaching by Annacondia; (4) an invitation to accept Christ as savior; (5) liberation (rebuking demons); (6) healing; (7) testimonies from those who claim healing; (8) laying on of hands (Annacondia and several pastors pray directly for those who come to the front of the platform). The crusade, which generally begins each night around 8:00 p.m., lasts anywhere from three to five hours. However, those being liberated continue to receive prayer and counseling well after the crusade is officially over. This liberation portion often lasts until 5:00 or 6:00 a.m. This goes on for 30 or 40 consecutive nights with additional daytime meetings on the weekends.

The two practices in the crusades that have the greatest impact on those present are spiritual liberation, or deliverance ministry, and the divine healing of physical bodies. When Annacondia liberates those oppressed by demons, he paces the stage, naming different demons, his voice rising to add emphasis to the battle he is fighting: "Out, out, out! Every demon of Macumba, of black magic, of red magic, of spiritualism, of Judo, of Karate, of the New Age! Let go of them, let go of them, let go of them! Out, Out! Every demon of Umbanda, Out! All unholy spirits, Out!"[22] As he continues to reproach the demons, people begin to fall to the ground, some as if fainting, others writhing and shaking. Teams of two men carry those who fall to the "deliverance tent" where they are ministered to by pastors and other workers who have been trained by Annacondia's team in the techniques of spiritual liberation. Annacondia's Director of Deliverance Ministry, Pablo Bottari, moreover, through speaking at international conferences and publication of a how-to book, *Libres en Cristo: La Importancia del Ministerio de Liberación*, translated into English and marketed as *Free in Christ: Your Complete Handbook on the Ministry of Deliverance* (2000), has reshaped the deliverance practices of pentecostals globally.[23]

Fabian, a young man converted in an Annacondia crusade, relates his personal experience of liberation:

> When I was sixteen, I began playing around with some friends, one of whom practiced Macumba. One night my friend got me to drink a bit of unholy blood. After that I began to feel terribly sick in my heart—rebellious. I started to fight with my mother all the time. I had thoughts of killing her. She started going to Annacondia's crusade in San Martín [May–June 1985] and she became converted. She told me I should go and that made me furious. One night my friends and I decided to go, just to make fun of all the crazy people. When I stepped onto the field where they were holding the crusade, I fell down. I was completely overcome. When I woke up, it was six hours later—3:00 a.m. They explained to me that I had been possessed by an evil spirit and they wanted to know what type of spirit it could be so that they could help me more. I told them about the blood. . . . Since then my mother and I never fight. My brother is now a believer. I haven't left the way of the Lord since.[24]

Fabian's testimony is typical of the mass of new believers who entered churches through Annacondia's crusades in the mid-1980s. Night after night, as Annacondia rebuked demons, people fell by the hundreds and claimed to receive liberation. Beyond individual conversions, the impact this experience of liberation had on pastors and crusade workers cannot be exaggerated.

Not surprisingly, when those who had worked in the crusades returned to their churches, the churches were, as Scataglini suggested, "not the same." This was the case for two reasons. First, those who converted in the crusades and integrated into regular evangelical congregations expected to find something akin to the crusade in the church. But just as important, pastors and workers also had converted to Annacondia's way of doing things. So, for example, instead of avoiding the topic of demonization, which is of vital interest within the popular sector, churches began to devote a regular part of each meeting to casting out demons, divine healing, and testimonies of healing and deliverance. In so doing, pastors imitated Annacondia's method: shouting out the names of specific demons and telling them to leave (Out! Out! Out! all demons of black magic, of Macumba, etc.). This practice of exorcising demons through Annacondia's method continues to be widespread within Argentine evangelicalism.[25]

In much the same way, divine healing also became a regular practice in local churches as a result of Annacondia's crusades. Healing was and continues to be one of his primary attractions. The testimonies of people who feel physically healed in crusades rival those who claim spiritual liberation. One of the most common of these testimonies is the recurring claim that people's dental cavities become filled with "heavenly material" in the shape of a cross or a dove. When he prays for healing, Annacondia asks those who wish to be healed to place their hands on the place that needs healing. He then proceeds to cast out the demons that produce illnesses in different parts of the body. He also names various diseases (up to 100 on a good night). One other method he uses is to ask those with categories of sicknesses: cancer, arthritis, blood diseases, bad eyesight, back trouble, etc., to step forward as a group to be healed. Annacondia's innovative model of divine healing has become nearly ubiquitous in local churches.

In his crusades, Annacondia's healing is reinforced by the nightly testimony hour that immediately follows the healings. Most testimonies are given by people who attended the crusade on an earlier night, felt that they had experienced healing, and returned to the crusade to testify. In Annacondia's crusades, I have heard testimonies ranging from 70-year-old women who feel that their eyes have been healed so that they "no longer have to wear glasses to read the Bible" to people of all ages claiming cures of cancer. On any given night, there are 15–20 testimonies. Testimonies serve as a nightly affirmation that God acts through Carlos Annacondia to improve people's lives in immediate, tangible, material ways. For salvation to be real in popular Argentine culture, it must include a material as well as a spiritual component.[26]

In the Argentine popular sector, evil spirits are considered regularly to afflict people's lives—by making them physically ill. The possibility of overcoming those afflictions, through Christ and without visiting an expensive *curandero* or traditional healer (or after failing to receive help from such a healer), creates a powerful incentive to visit Annacondia's crusades. Bad health is, not surprisingly, a regular feature of the lives of the Argentine poor. The once well-regarded public health system has been in steady decline since the 1960s, so the possibility of an instant cure for long-standing and ill-attended health problems is appealing. There is a long history in Argentina of appeals to saints and other popular religious icons (such as La Difunta Correa) for the blessing of health. The transfer of the expectation of an immediate health blessing from a saint to a flesh-and-blood faith healer appears to have been easy.

## Annacondia's Crusades Transformed Non-Pentecostal Churches

The intensity of Annacondia's crusades for pastors, workers, and new believers produced a sudden and dramatic change in the practices of the evangelical community. Annacondia converted evangelicals to participation in a global pentecostal movement. He described this effect of his crusades:

> At first the Baptists and the Free Brethren would say that the Pentecostals were all possessed. The Pentecostals said that the Free Brethren were spiritually dead. Now in my crusades there are Baptists that are the president of the crusade, even though the style of my crusades—casting out demons, speaking in tongues, healing the sick—goes against everything they used to claim they believed.[27]

This conversion to pentecostal practices extends to nearly all the churches that have participated in Annacondia's crusades. Edgardo Surenian, a pastor from the fundamentalist and formerly non-pentecostal Armenian church, explained:

> Can you really imagine how we all feel about Annacondia and his effect in our churches? Look at me. I'm from the serious, quiet Armenian church. Here I am, vice-president of this crusade. I have thirty people from my church working here every night and look at what's going on here. People falling down, speaking in tongues, shaking all over from demons. This is the extreme end of the Pentecostal spectrum and here we are supporting it.[28]

Surenian went on to comment on the fact that currently Annacondia's crusades are attended by pastors, workers, and nonbelievers who are "seeking Jesus." When Annacondia first appeared, he attracted many believers, who came to his crusades looking for the "new gifts of the spirit that Annacondia was offering. Now," claimed Surenian, "they can get those things in their own churches, so they don't have to come to the crusades." This illustrates a fundamental shift undergone by the churches that participated in Annacondia's crusades. By the late 1980s, many local churches had adopted a uniform style of Annacondia-inspired practices: demonic liberation, divine healing, testimonies, and music that resonated in the Argentine popular sector.

Evangelists after Annacondia

In 1987, Annacondia made an important break from the routine his ministry had established since 1984: "In '87, God told me 'Get out of Buenos Aires!' So I went to the interior and out of the country because people had begun to follow me as their spiritual leader. I had to leave so that people could become accustomed to going to church. The correct thing is for them to go to the churches. I am not a pastor; they needed a pastor."[29] Annacondia's absence created space for the emergence of new charismatic leaders within the evangelical movement.

Horacio Salazar, a pastor whose church, part of the Union of the Assemblies of God, experienced significant growth in the early 1990s, summarized that period:

> First Annacondia's ministry appeared. Then came Giménez. Then came . . . well Omar Cabrera was around before, but he wasn't accepted by the evangelicals. He used a clerical collar, the form of his services was not the traditional form of the evangelicals, so he was not accepted. He put lots of emphasis on healing and, well, the evangelicals didn't like that back then. Today it is accepted. It's the same with Giménez, he used to not be accepted and now he is accepted. This seems to happen when something new appears, there is always the fear that it's not within the doctrine. The way of doing things is new, so there is resistance.[30]

Salazar's tentative summary of the careers of Hector Giménez and Omar Cabrera is understandable. Both of these pastors had churches, large churches, when Annacondia's crusades were just beginning.[31] Cabrera, in fact, was the first Argentine to organize mass meetings that emphasized healing. Neither Giménez nor Cabrera was, however, accepted by most evangelicals until after Annacondia's successful transformation of Argentine evangelicalism.

Commenting on the changes that enabled their ministry to become integrated into the evangelical movement, Marfa Cabrera explained:

> That was part of the spiritual opening. Our minds are more open now. We are not so closed in our concepts. . . . It's not so much that previously the Church was opposed directly to us. But anything new was extremely suspect. Nobody wanted to try something that had not

already been proven. Now I can say with fear and trembling before the Lord, that Omar is considered a wise person; pastors come to consult him; things have changed.[32]

The dominance of the missionary model had effectively closed off tactical innovation as well as changes in the collective identity of evangelical churches for more than 40 years. Annacondia's new model and the new evangelical identity that emerged out of his crusades opened the minds of evangelicals to innovative forms of evangelizing and to new charismatic leaders who would enhance that emerging collective identity.

Following Annacondia's departure from Buenos Aires in 1987, a more stable model of church building was necessary to accomplish precisely what Annacondia had suggested: people had to become accustomed to going to church. In addition, the evangelical movement needed charismatic leaders who could fill the void created by Annacondia's abrupt departure—maintaining and enhancing the collective identity created in Annacondia's crusades. Horacio Salazar suggested the creative ways in which Hector Giménez and Omar Cabrera fulfilled those tasks. They demonstrated to the Argentine church that "we could do it better than the missionaries. Why did we need them to show us how to go about building churches in Argentina, when we Argentines were doing it better than they ever had? Did you know that Cabrera has the second largest church in the world and Giménez the third largest?"[33] Salazar's statement exemplifies the shift away from the myth of the missionary that had begun with Annacondia. Giménez and Cabrera demonstrated conclusively, by building extremely large churches, that Argentine evangelicals could accomplish the central goal of evangelicalism—mass growth—better than the missionaries had ever been able to do. Their successes cemented the collective identity of Argentine evangelicals as a national movement with powerful leaders who were accomplishing God's purposes in Argentina.

## Claudio Freidzon's Crusade of Miracles

Following Annacondia, Giménez, and Cabrera, the shape of the movement, its themes and practices, and its collective identity became increasingly uniform. As the vestiges of the old missionary model were thrust aside, different ministries and denominations within the movement came to resemble one another more and more. Believers, moreover, came to respond in remarkably similar ways to the preaching and practices of the movement's popular figures. The most compelling evidence of this has been the ministry of the fourth movement-wide charismatic leader, Claudio Freidzon.

Freidzon's Crusade of Miracles (since renamed Ministry to the Nations) is based on the experience of what he calls "the new anointing" or the "fresh anointing" of the Holy Spirit, which reputedly expands and renovates believers' experience of God's power in their lives. Those who receive this anointing develop a heightened sensitivity to and awareness of the influence of the Holy Spirit. The outward manifestations accompanying this gift include falling in the Spirit, "drunkenness" in the Spirit, uncontrollable laughter, and crying with joy. Freidzon claimed to have received the new anointing through prayers from the Palestinian Canadian American evangelist Benny Hinn, but in Freidzon's hands, the anointing took on a life of its own.

I was present when this blessing was far from routinized and certainly before all of the modes of interaction between Freidzon and those seeking the spiritual blessing he offered had been defined. The result was unpredictability. Once the word spread that the Holy Spirit was manifesting in new and powerful ways, any meeting that Freidzon attended was overwhelmed by those seeking his blessing. So, for example, when Freidzon announced a meeting to be held in Luna Park (an indoor arena in Buenos Aires with a capacity of approximately 12,000), more than 40,000 people showed up. Such meetings, whether in his own church or in larger venues, were nearly interminable. Perhaps because there were no firm cues between leader and followers and because everyone was having so much fun (including Freidzon), meetings that were set for two hours would last six. Evening meetings often lasted nearly until dawn.

I attended a meeting led by Freidzon in the Obras Sanitarias arena (filled to capacity with 6,600 pastors and church workers) that began at 1:00 p.m. and was scheduled to end at 3:00 p.m. Freidzon spent the entire afternoon inviting pastors and other church leaders onto the platform where he would blow into the microphone, throw his suit jacket, lay his hands on heads, or simply wave his arms in the direction of an individual or group of individuals. The result was always the same: people fell to the ground laughing and praising God. Those who struggled to their feet would be smitten by another wave of Freidzon's arms or a thrown jacket and fall to the ground again. The only punctuation to the falling and laughing were interruptions so that everyone could sing the music of the popular German Mexican worship evangelist Marcos Witt.[34] The meeting finally ended at 9:00 p.m. with everyone simply too exhausted to laugh, sing, or, perhaps ironically, fall down any more.

Claudio Freidzon's new anointing created a moment of spiritual ecstasy within the Argentine evangelical community in 1992–1993. It also represents an important moment in the globalization of pentecostal practices as Freidzon's fresh experience of the Holy Spirit spread from Argentina outward and back to North America. The events in Obras Sanitarias described above (which took place in November 1992) capture this particular moment in the globalization of spiritual practices. The meetings in Obras Sanitarias were organized by a group of influential pastors as a training exercise for local pastors in the practice of geographical liberation/spiritual warfare—focusing on a single place with the goal of overwhelming Satan and his forces through spiritual warfare. Many of the conference speakers were spiritual warfare experts from the United States and Canada. They were invited according to the then-familiar pattern: teachings and techniques developed in North America were to be taught to local pastors on the periphery. In addition to the visiting instructors, some of the conference's speakers were local luminaries, including Annacondia and Giménez. However, in a remarkable turn of events, the conference was taken over by Freidzon and his fresh anointing. On the second afternoon of the three-day conference, the event's organizers announced that they were postponing a segment of the conference in order to give Freidzon a moment to discuss the movement of the Spirit that he and his congregation were experiencing. The two hours given over to Freidzon turned into an eight-hour overflowing experience of the fresh anointing. Pastors from the United States, Canada, and Argentina were invited to join Freidzon on the stage where he proceeded to bless them with the fresh anointing: a combination of trances, laughter, and moments of apparent sheer spiritual joy. Thus, an event held with the intention of sharing practices of spiritual warfare (from center to periphery) was transformed into an instance of communal spiritual exuberance driven by a middle-class Argentine pastor and flowing from periphery to center.

Before Freidzon burst onto the scene with his fresh anointing, a broad coalition of Argentine churches had invited the well-known German healing evangelist Reinhard Bonnke, who devotes most of his time to holding mass crusades throughout Africa, to conduct a six-night crusade in Buenos Aires in November 1992. The Bonnke crusade, held in the United Nations plaza, next to the Fine Arts Museum in the heart of the richest neighborhood of Buenos Aires, represented the movement's first major attempt to evangelize Argentina's middle and upper classes. Every night, thousands of people from the outer suburbs of Buenos Aires and other provinces descended on this neighborhood in rented buses; it is possible that not a single resident of the targeted neighborhood attended.

The Bonnke crusade nevertheless represented a statement of the pentecostal movement's unity and of its arrival in Argentine society, as summarized by the crusade prayer of Victor Lorenzo, a pastor and co-sponsor of the event:

> Oh God, we are holding this meeting in a neighborhood that is associated historically with those that have oppressed our country economically; with those that have provoked the kind of horrible things that are happening in Caracas [an attempted military coup]. We the people of God will not be oppressed any longer. . . . we are sending a message to those in office that we will not stand for their corruption and their oppression.

The invitation to Bonnke to preach to (and perhaps change the hearts of) Argentina's elite is telling. Annacondia, despite his transformation of the local evangelical community and growing international stature, was never invited to undertake this task. Annacondia has explained that other evangelical leaders thought of him as *un negro*, or a person of low social status.[35] He did not have the right look; he was not white enough; his speech did not exude education. For this, the churches turned to the tall, humorous, self-confident, German evangelist.

Despite Bonnke's unique credentials, what generated the greatest excitement in the crowd during his crusade was Claudio and Betty Freidzon's appearance onstage. However, the Freidzons, apparently recognizing that it would be bad form to upstage their movement's guest, disappointed the crowd by merely saying hello and sitting down to hear the visiting evangelist's message. Yet, in another way, Freidzon did upstage Bonnke, whose six-day crusade failed to produce observable shifts in local church practices; nor did local pastors refer to blessings they received from Bonnke. By the time of Bonnke's arrival, Freidzon's new anointing had already captured the attention of Argentina's evangelicals, and a visit from a foreign evangelist (even one of Bonnke's stature) could not eclipse popular enthusiasm to participate in the new anointing.

Freidzon's popularity and the fervor of the believers who wished to receive the new anointing resulted in an exciting, tumultuous year (August 1992–July 1993) within the evangelical community. Thousands of believers thronged Freidzon's own church in the Belgrano neighborhood in Buenos Aires. He also held meetings every Tuesday night in the Obras Sanitarias arena and began to travel to the other principal cities of Argentina, plus Uruguay, Paraguay, and Chile. Even with that, believers demanded more access to Freidzon and the new anointing. This practice, like the other pentecostal practices we have already seen, soon became widespread in nearly all the churches in the evangelical movement. Pastors visited Freidzon's crusades and returned to their own churches full of the fresh anointing and ready to share the same blessing with their congregations.

In April 1993, Freidzon staged a mass meeting in the Vélez Sarsfield soccer stadium, which he filled to overflowing (capacity 76,000). That five-hour evangelical celebration was, perhaps, the culmination of Freidzon's meteoric rise to prominence in the evangelical movement. While remaining extraordinarily popular in Argentina, Freidzon (like Cabrera, Annacondia, and Bottari) went on to become a star on the international pentecostal circuit, traveling throughout Latin America, Spain, and to both Spanish-speaking and, with the help of translators, English-speaking communities of the United States. Also in 1993, Benny Hinn invited Freidzon to join him on the platform in U.S. crusades, as the anointing exceeded and spread back to its North American origins. A widely noted moment of spiritual renewal in Toronto, Canada, in 1994 is attributed to a Canadian pastor's visit to Freidzon's church in Buenos Aires the previous year. (See Candy Gunther Brown's chapter, "Global Awakenings," in this volume.)

## Freidzon's Place in the Development of the Argentine Evangelical Movement

Claudio Freidzon arose as a popular figure well into the transformation of the evangelical movement commenced by Annacondia in 1984. The new collective beliefs and the new evangelical identity had become, by the time Freidzon appeared, increasingly well-defined. As the components of the old missionary gospel were overthrown, new and generally uniform beliefs and practices had begun to take shape.

Freidzon, a pastor and the regional administrative director of the Union of the Assemblies of God in the federal capital, understood the new constraints and capitalized on them. Annacondia, Giménez, and Cabrera were all outsiders to Pentecostalism who came to prominence through their demonstrated ability to reach nonbelievers. Freidzon was the first insider to establish a mass ministry; he did it by, in effect, preaching to the choir. Unlike any of his predecessors, his ministry was not directed, in any way, toward the unconverted. The new anointing was directed exclusively at believers: receiving a new anointing presupposes, of course, a first anointing. In order for Freidzon to succeed on the mass level, it was essential that a large group of believers with a well-formed collective identity already exist. Freidzon is well aware of the process that made his ministry possible. Regarding the changes that made this pool of believers available and open to embracing the new anointing, he said:

> Over the course of the last 15 years there has been a period of growth regarding the supernatural. With the arrival of Carlos Annacondia, it was as if the Argentine people was awakened to what God can do outside of a religious liturgy, outside of the normal life of a church. Carlos Annacondia came and threw down some of the preconceptions that we had regarding God's actions and the people began to realize that God was showing us a power that we had not been seeing before. For God this power is not new, but, rather, our experience of it is new.[36]

Freidzon's account of the changes in the evangelical community that began with Annacondia should be familiar. He is describing—as I have above—Annacondia's replacement of the missionary model with pentecostal practices: demonic liberation, divine healing, and culturally resonant music. Freidzon's Crusade of Miracles both took advantage of and expanded the openness to the new movements of the Spirit that Annacondia had initiated. Freidzon appreciated that Annacondia "threw down some of the preconceptions" that made his ministry impossible. By overturning the missionary model, Annacondia began a new cycle of innovation upon which Giménez, Cabrera, and Freidzon were able to capitalize.

Unlike his predecessors, Claudio Freidzon was the first popular evangelist to become widely accepted based on a ministry directed at believers, rather than attracting new adherents to the movement. Freidzon offered a message that reconfirmed to believers the importance of their existing beliefs. Freidzon reflected to his followers the pentecostal identity that they had developed in association with Annacondia, Cabrera, and Giménez over the preceding decade. In Freidzon's crusades, the community of believers discovered that they talked the same, worshiped the same, and responded to the same men of God.

## Extending Pentecostal Practices to New Segments of the Christian Community

Given that Freidzon's ministry functioned as a reaffirmation of the new evangelical identity, believers from all sectors of the movement thronged to his crusades, seeking what Freidzon calls "more" of God's power. The concept of the fresh anointing gave the community a new term with which to express its newly unified identity and pentecostal practices. Tactically, the new anointing was not a tool of recruitment; its target was those who already believe. The new forms in which the Holy Spirit was avowedly passed from spiritual leaders to followers—blowing on the microphone, throwing the suit jacket, and waving the arms—are unlikely, in themselves, to resonate with nonbelievers.[37] In fact, the fervor with which believers sought the new anointing severely limited Freidzon's ability to preach or to channel the phenomenon toward evangelistic ends. In any meeting he attended, believers demanded—by laughing, crying, falling down—immediate access to the gift that they believed Freidzon possessed.

Freidzon did extend the collective identity of the pentecostal movement, but he did this by bringing pentecostal practices to sectors of the historically Protestant churches that had previously not participated in the movement. In a meeting that I attended in Freidzon's church in Belgrano, an Anglican bishop was among the primary targets of the new anointing. Laughing and falling, the bishop assured Freidzon that he would carry the anointing back to his church. Other pastors from previously non-pentecostal churches invited Freidzon to come to their meetings and to share this new gift of the Spirit with their traditionally staid congregations.[38] This incorporation of a portion of the historic churches into the pentecostal practices of the new evangelical movement was unexpected by both sides and highlights the degree to which a movement toward unity had been operating within the entire Protestant community in Argentina. The spread of pentecostal practices promises, moreover, to break down traditionally hard barriers between Protestants and Catholics as the ecumenical Charismatic movement makes substantial inroads into the Roman Catholic Church, with the support of the Catholic hierarchy.

An effervescent spiritual movement began in Argentina in the mid-1980s in Annacondia's crusades. In those crusades, pentecostal practices, primarily demonic liberation and divine healing, spread across a broad swath of evangelical churches. The shared practices and sense of identity that Annacondia generated created fertile ground for further innovation. Freidzon capitalized by creating a new set of practices that energized the Argentine evangelical movement while, at the same time, generating further experimentation globally.

NOTES

1 Pablo Seman and Hilario Wynarzyk, two long-time observers of Argentina's evangelicals, use this phrase as a shorthand for capturing the core characteristics of Argentina's pentecostal movement.

2 The fieldwork on which this chapter is based was conducted from October 1992 to July 1993, and involved the ethnographic approaches of participant-observation, oral interviews, and written surveys, as well as archival research. For a more extended treatment, see Matthew Marostica, "Pentecostals and Politics: The Creation of the Evangelical Movement in Argentina, 1983–1993" (Ph.D. diss., University of California, Berkeley, 1997). Certainly, by now, some of the observations will be dated. However, serendipitously, the original research was done at a critical juncture in the development of the evangelical movement in Argentina. Claudio Freidzon took his Crusade of Miracles out of his own church to a broader audience for the first time in the second half of 1992, when I began my fieldwork. In that same year, Reinhard Bonnke came to Argentina to lead a massive six-day outdoor crusade in the heart of Buenos Aires (joined by Claudio Freidzon, Carlos Annacondia, and Omar Cabrera). In 1993, Freidzon (in conjunction with Annacondia) conducted a mass event in the outdoor soccer stadium at Velez Sarsfield. I was there to witness each event.

3 The bulk of the historical material concerning the various mission programs comes from Norberto Saracco's well-researched dissertation, "Argentine Pentecostalism: Its History and Theology" (Ph.D. diss., University of Birmingham, 1989). Saracco is a second-generation Argentine Pentecostal pastor and one of a handful of university-trained Argentine theologians.

4 Interview (23 May 1993).

5 David Edwin Harrell, *All Things Are Possible: The Healing and Charismatic Revivals in Modern America* (Bloomington: Indiana University Press, 1975), 7.

6 Interview (23 May 1993).

7 See Brown's introduction to this volume.

8 He was converted during a small crusade by a Panamanian evangelist named Ortiz.

9 Interview (21 June 1993).

10 The official claim of Mensaje de Salvación is that 100 people were converted in Bernal during the approximately eight months that Annacondia preached there.

11 Interview (21 June 1993).

12 Ibid.

13 Ibid.

14  This figure is taken from an article on Annacondia that appeared in the first issue (May 1985) of *El Puente*. This monthly publication, directed at the Argentine evangelical community, was started by a journalist and former pastor, Marcelo LaFitte, and served as an important source of information and as a symbol of the movement's turn from denominationalism. *El Puente* is still being published and can be found at www.elpuenteonline.com (accessed 19 Aug. 2009).

15  Interview (21 June 1993).

16  *El Puente* (Dec. 1985): 4.

17  Qtd. in *El Puente* (Oct. 1985): 8.

18  Personal communication to author (1995); see also Alejandro Frigerio, *Cultura Negra en el Cono Sur: Representaciones en Conflicto* [Black Culture in the Southern Cone: Representations in Conflict] (Buenos Aires, Argentina: Facultad de Ciencias Sociales y Económicas de la Universidad Católica Argentina, 2000).

19  *El Puente* (Oct. 1985): 8.

20  Interview (21 June 1993).

21  In 1993, I attended an Annacondia crusade in Castelar, outside Buenos Aires, that lasted 35 days. As of 2009, Annacondia posts his itinerary, which more often includes 1- to 5-day conferences, on Message of Salvation International, a Spanish-English website: http://www.reachingsouls.com/index2.htm (accessed 18 Aug. 2009). The website's home page looks beyond Argentina to announce: "Our mission is to serve the church of Jesus Christ, and our vision is to evangelize the world." An Annacondia crusade in Philadelphia, Pennsylvania, in 2003 attracted 10,000 attendees.

22  Transcribed from Annacondia's crusade in the western zone of greater Buenos Aires, 25 Jan. 1993.

23  Pablo Bottari, *Free in Christ: Your Complete Handbook on the Ministry of Deliverance* [Paolo Bottari, Libres en Cristo: La Importancia del Ministerio de Liberación] (Lake Mary, Fla.: Creation House, 2000).

24  Interview (19 Jan. 1993).

25  I witnessed approximately 40 pastors casting out demons, and they uniformly used Annacondia's precise wording and tactics. The ubiquity of the practice is testimony to the impact that Annacondia's ministry has had on Argentine evangelicalism.

26  Miroslav Volf, "Materiality of Salvation: An Investigation in the Soteriologies of Liberation and Pentecostal Theologies," *Journal of Ecumenical Studies* 26.3 (1989): 447–467.

27  Personal communication to the author (21 June 1993).

28  Interview at 3:00 a.m. after an Annacondia crusade in Ciudadela (a suburb of Buenos Aires). Incidentally, Surenian rescued me from a group of a half-dozen crusade workers who felt compelled to try to liberate me from demons. Their conclusion regarding my demonized state most likely stemmed from the fact that they had seen me jotting down notes instead of seeking a blessing from Annacondia. They also offered to cure the sickness that I have in my eyes—I wear glasses. When I refused these offers, they sought out the pastor since I was proving to be a tough case. Surenian and I had a fascinating conversation and a couple of sausages from his church's stand.

29  Interview (21 June 1993). According to crusade itineraries published in *El Puente*, Annacondia led only one crusade in greater Buenos Aires from 1987 to 1989.

30  Interview (29 Jan. 1993).

31  The name of Giménez' church was Ondas de Amor y Paz (Waves of Love and Peace). Cabrera's church is still called Visión del Futuro (Vision of the Future).

32  Interview (27 May 1993).

33  Interview (19 Feb. 1993); this claim, though certainly bearing the characteristic ring of Argentine self-importance, was regularly made around the same time by church growth specialist C. Peter Wagner (e.g., 12 Nov. 1992, Harvest Evangelism leadership seminar). Both churches claimed to have somewhere near 100,000 members in 1993 when the interview was conducted.

34  Marcos Witt's was the most popular music used in churches at the end of 1992. The popularity of his music appeared linked to its use in Freidzon's ministry.

35  Interview (21 June 1993).

36  Interview (29 Jan. 1993).

37  The tactics were even occasionally confusing to believers or at least resulted in interesting ad hoc explanations for what they were experiencing. One pastor, for example, carefully explained to his congregation (25 June 1993, San Miguel, Buenos Aires) that he had just returned from a Freidzon crusade and that he was full of the new anointing. He went on to explain that the anointing sticks to clothes, so that when he threw his jacket at them, the anointing passed from the jacket to them.

38  One of the most prominent pastors to have Freidzon in his church was the pastor of the Central Baptist Church of Buenos Aires, Pablo Deiros.

# PART III

# Africa and Asia

# 11

# New Wine in an Old Wine Bottle? Charismatic Healing in the Mainline Churches in Ghana

*Cephas N. Omenyo*

A common song used in pentecostal churches of the dominant Akan ethnic linguistic group in Ghana runs as follows:

> Oduyefo kese, fa wo nsa boto mo do. Besa me yare ma me
> na menya ahoodzen dze asom wo o. Yare nketse nketse
> rehaw me wo sumsum mu; nsem nketse nketse rehaw me
> wo sunsum mu. Mekyinkyin, ekyin, ekyin me nnya boafo
> biara, Egya e, besa me yare mame na menya ahodzen
> na m'asom wo o.[1]

Meaning:

> Great Healer, come and touch me. Heal my ailments that my
> strength may be renewed for your service. Lord I am deeply
> troubled; deeply troubled by spiritual sicknesses, anxieties,
> and worries. To many places have I been in search of
> healing; but none has been of help. Come Lord, release me
> from these spiritual ailments and troubles; that I may enjoy
> the health, strength, and vitality needed to serve you.

The song is a prayer asking God to heal the singer because he or she has tried many sources in search of healing without success. The practice among most Akans is that, financial resources permitting, when one is sick one goes around to a number of hospitals, traditional healers, Muslim spiritualists, and churches until one finds healing. The presupposition of the song is that the Christian God is the only one who can offer adequate assistance. There are numerous Akan and, more generally, African choruses that people sing as they seek healing from God the Father of Jesus Christ through the power of the Holy Spirit. In the ecclesiology of such believers, the church is a major source of divine healing.


Introduction

This chapter focuses on how the Charismatic phenomenon that began in the margins has become a central element of all the traditionally mainline/ historic churches in Ghana.[2] In the past, the African Independent/Instituted Churches and, later, Pentecostal and neo-pentecostal churches were noted for emphasizing the charismata, which invariably had divine healing as a major thrust. Currently, the phenomenon has found its way into the mainline churches, thus blurring the sharp distinction between mainline churches and pentecostals.

The mainline churches were established through the missionary efforts of Western-founded missionary societies aided by African assistants since the early nineteenth century. The theology, ethos, and practices of these churches were originally non-pentecostal. However, these churches are increasingly integrating the Charismatic phenomenon in their liturgies and practices. Initially, this trend began with Charismatic renewal movements that emerged within the framework of the mainline churches beginning in the late 1930s, becoming more prominent in the 1990s.

Right from its inception, Christianity was received and adapted by Africans. There were a variety of African responses to the New Testament gospel during the era of the various Western missionary societies in the eighteenth and nineteenth centuries. For the purpose of this chapter, I will isolate a two-fold African response to Western missionary Christianity particularly at the turn of the twentieth century. Africans either accepted the gospel and appropriated it within the African context, thus leading to the emergence of African Independent Churches, or they remained within Western-founded churches and later sought to renew those churches along the lines of pneumatic and African traditional spirituality. Abraham Akrong, a Ghanaian theologian, is right in asserting:

> The result is a different understanding of Christianity that has made
> it possible for African Christians to appropriate Christianity as a
> liberating, life-transforming religion of salvation which can help
> many desperate people in Africa to deal with the existential raptures
> and structural violence that continue to define their lives. At the
> centre of this liberated Christianity is a radical paradigm shift

nurtured by African traditional spirituality, which has given a place for the questions and concerns shaped by African culture and worldview.[3]

Invariably, prior to the 1970s, the mainline churches in Africa ruthlessly resisted movements that sought to renew Christianity along pneumatic lines because the doctrinal emphases of such movements were perceived as extraneous to time-tested Western theological traditions. Ghana is not an exception. Pneumatic phenomena such as speaking in tongues, prophecy, visions, and divine healing were disallowed in such churches. Members of the mainline churches who sought to manifest these gifts were compelled to leave their churches to form their own independent churches free from the control of the Western-founded churches, hence the name African Independent Churches (AICs).[4] This fact can be exemplified by a casual look at the origins of the leadership of the African Initiated Churches.

Initially, the mainline churches adopted a rather negative and contemptuous disposition toward the AICs and later pentecostal churches that followed in the trail of renewal movements. This attitude cost the mainline churches dearly, as it led to a mass exodus of their members to the various AICs due to a perceived lack of sensitivity of the churches to the spiritual needs of their members. With hindsight, one can understand the reaction of the mainline churches as a case of being unsure of how best to confront the challenge posed by the recently emerging churches. As pointed out by the Ghanaian theologian Kwame Bediako, the inability of the mainline churches to meet the needs of their members was not so much a case of "an unwillingness to relate to these realities, as of not having learned to do so."[5] It is significant to note that, while mainline churches were unsure about the way to confront the challenges posed by the AICs, movements appeared on the scene to address those very needs. These movements have from their inception been concerned about the lack of pneumatic dimensions in the life of the church. They have consistently sought

| Church | Background of Founder |
| --- | --- |
| Accra Congregational | Methodist |
| Apostles' Revelation Society | Presbyterian |
| Christ Apostolic Church | Presbyterian |
| Church of the Lord | Anglican |
| Divine Healers' Temple | Anglican |
| Eternal Order of Cherubim and Seraphim | Methodist |
| First Century Gospel Church | Anglican |
| La Christ African Tabernacle | Methodist |
| Musama Disco Christo Church | Methodist |
| Nazarite Healing Home | Methodist |
| St. Michael's Healing Mission | Methodist |
| Twelve Apostles' Church | Methodist |

*Source:* Ione Acquah, *Accra Survey* (London: University of London Press, 1958), 150.

to reclaim this tradition since they believe it is a lost heritage (either of the church universal/catholic or of their particular denomination) that needs to be restored by the contemporary church.

This essay traces the development of Charismatic renewal with its concomitant practice of divine healing among mainline churches in Ghana, particularly among predominantly Akan ethnic churches. Due to space limits, examples are drawn primarily from three mainline churches: the Roman Catholic Church in Ghana, the Presbyterian Church of Ghana, and the Methodist Church Ghana. These are the largest and oldest mainline denominations in Ghana, and developments within them are quite representative of what has obtained in all the other denominations.[6]

### Akan/African Traditional Worldview, Causality, and Salvation

The Akan view of the universe is that of an arena of both benevolent and malevolent spirits that are able to influence the course of human life for good or ill, respectively. For the Akan, who typifies most Africans in this respect, Rudolf Otto's idea of the *mysterium tremendum et fascinosum* (awe-filled and fascinating mystery) makes a lot of sense.[7] In light of this observation, the empirical and the meta-empirical are viewed as inseparable. John S. Pobee, a Ghanaian theologian, rightly asserts that "the sphere of the supernatural is much broader in the African culture than in any European context. This is why Africans have been castigated as given to superstition."[8] Max Assimeng, a Ghanaian sociologist, corroborates this position when he contends that "until the sphere of the African's conception of spiritual 'darkness' is reckoned with, one cannot claim that one is studying the religious consciousness of the traditional peoples of West Africa."[9]

These contentions by both Pobee and Assimeng perfectly pertain to Africans in general and the Akan in particular. For both Pobee and Assimeng, causality among Africans leans heavily on the spiritual. For the traditional Akan/African, nothing happens by chance. For instance, besides purely organic causes of sickness, no interpretation of causality that does not include elements like preordained destiny, punishment by angered ancestors, or witchcraft is adequate. When calamity strikes in an Akan society, a common phrase one hears from members of the community is *ennye kwa*, meaning "it is not an ordinary occurrence," a phrase that captures the dominant idea of the supernatural causation of evil.[10] John D. K. Ekem, a Ghanaian theologian, has summarized the view of the causation of evil among Akans:

> Each evil is closely associated with supernatural forces that are
> regarded as being either essentially good or evil. Much as there is
> room for human responsibility, events usually make sense only in

relation to supernatural causative factors. Illness may, for instance, be due to the displeasure of benevolent *abosom* [lesser divinities or deities] and *nsamanfo* [ancestors] or to the evil machinations of *abayifo* [witches and wizards]. It becomes necessary then, to take definite measures either to invoke the blessing, guidance and protection of good spirit powers, or to nullify the harmful designs of malicious ones.[11]

Therefore, uppermost in the mind of the Akan is to seek a harmonious relationship with all human beings and particularly with the mystical powers that control life and bestow it with vitality. Akans believe that obtaining favor from the mystical beings is "realized through various sacrificial rites for propitiation, expiatory and reconciliatory purposes."[12] Another scholar has observed, "[T]his orientation of the Akan makes the role of the diviners and traditional priests in Akan society crucial. The diviner is reputed to have the ability to diagnose diseases, misfortunes and other maladies that are believed to be caused by the wrath of several categories of spirits."[13] Akans believe that the traditional priest has knowledge of herbs, can create charms against witchcraft, attends to the gods, and serves as their medium and mouthpiece in order to assist people in need. These roles of the diviner and the traditional priest particularly with reference to sickness and healing have deep implications for the role of Christian priests/pastors and the church among Akans: Christian religious leaders are expected to play roles similar to those of the traditional experts.

For most Akans/Africans, moreover, "salvation" is not conceived in a limited sense, reducing it to a spiritual category which touches only on the inner being of a person. It must include the bodily human existence, what Miroslav Volf calls the "materiality of salvation."[14] Salvation is achieved by reinforcing life-affirming aspects of experience in the here and now. Salvation must ensure the preservation, protection, and enhancement of life. It must necessarily touch all dimensions of life, including the physical, psychological, spiritual, and social, which are intrinsically linked together as a whole. To this end, salvation includes healing and good health; the ability to ward off evil; protection against evil spirits and witches; financial and material prosperity; peace of mind; peace with God, the gods, ancestors, and fellow human beings; human and animal fertility; harmonious relationships with others and success in one's occupation; and abundant life.

## The African Christian and the African Worldview

When Africans convert to Christianity, they do not abandon their traditional worldview.[15] This worldview is ever present, but African Christians seek to

appropriate biblical resources to respond to the problems their worldview
raises. A careful observer would notice that, in Western-influenced African
Christianity, "local discourse on emotions, and conceptions concerning witchcraft, misfortune, illness and possession became muted and downgraded but
never fully disappeared as they were part of the basic structures of society."[16]
This is the aspect of the ethos of Western missionary-founded churches that is
unsatisfactory to most Africans. For all intents and purposes, this aspect of
African religiosity was seriously undermined by Western missionaries, thus
denigrating African spirituality and healing systems.[17]

What the pentecostal movements have done is essentially to expand the
soteriological appeal of the Christian message for African Christians.[18] As a
result, their understanding of salvation incorporates the traditional African
concept of salvation. The traditional concept of salvation of the Akan of Ghana
described above typifies the generic African concept of salvation.

## Healing in African Churches

Prominent among the issues that are emphasized overtly or covertly in most
African churches is healing. Specifically, healing is understood as liberation
from conditions that inhibit people's attainment of full humanity and the restoration of life. Furthermore, Africans view health as wholeness, the unity of
the natural and the supernatural. Jacques Mattey's summary of a consultation
organized by the World Council of Churches in Accra, Ghana, perfectly captures the understanding of healing among most African Christians: "To experience healing isn't just to experience freedom from sickness and illness, or
problems and suffering. Healing is a sign of what the Old Testament calls 'Shalom' (peace, salvation) as the establishment or restoration of right and reconciled relationships, now and at the end of time."[19]

Early scholars in the field of African Christianity and anthropology pointed
out that a major reason that many Africans join the AICs and indeed all the
pentecostal churches is the search for divine healing.[20] What's more, other
studies on contemporary pentecostalism underscore the fact that healing is
prominent in African churches. In his studies, Ogbu Kalu corroborates this
point by portraying healing as the "heartbeat" of the life of the church, which is
not in any way an overstatement. Kalu writes:

> The issue of health and healing is a very important aspect of religious life
> in Africa, and the explanation of the growth of both AICs and Pentecostal-
> ism in the continent. Healing is the heartbeat of the liturgy and the entire
> religious life. It brings the community of suffering together; it ushers
> supernatural power into the gathered community and enables all to
> bask together in its warmth. It releases the energy for participatory

worship that integrates the body, spirit and soul. I watched the
healing of a deaf and dumb boy in a Pentecostal gathering that met
in a schoolhouse in Monrovia, Liberia. Apparently, most of the
congregation knew the boy. Dancing and praise took over the rest of
the service. The din was so loud that the neighbourhood gathered
and, instead of complaining about the ruined peace on a Sunday
afternoon, joined in the celebration.[21]

Adherents of pentecostal churches in Africa believe strongly in healing
by faith in God through the Bible and prayer due to the robust conviction
that some sicknesses are either caused or worsened by Satan and demons.
For them, prayer for healing is invariably prayer to God, who is present at
their worship, to deliver the victim from the bondage of the devil and
demons that caused the sickness or that render orthodox medicine impo-
tent—hence, the inseparable relationship between healing and deliverance
from demons.[22]

African traditional priests deal with both the natural and the supernatural
dimensions in their administration of healing. An integral part of the task of
healing and restoration to wholeness of African traditional priests is the diagnosis of all kinds of ailments and the prescription of remedies. A particular
kind of disease may require divination and exorcism in order to restore a dis-
turbed person to wholeness. It is unacceptable and indeed a contradiction in
terms for a traditional priest to be unable to perform such functions. Members
of Western mission-founded churches in Africa judge their priests by the same
litmus test.[23] This explains the common complaints by mainline/historic
churches about the religious infidelity of their members, some of whom
remain in their respective churches but seek restoration to wholeness from all
kinds of ills elsewhere.

Pentecostal churches in Africa have replicated the traditional African religious practice of seeking healing through religious means.[24] The AICs were
the first Christians to correlate biblical texts with the African concern for healing. Akrong has noted:

The AICs movement was quick to point out, on biblical grounds, the
continuities between Christianity and African culture . . . and a
credible and legitimate vehicle for mediating the salvation message
of Christianity for the African society. . . . the AICs were able to
demonstrate that African concerns hitherto marginalized by missionary Christianity were legitimate questions for which the Gospel
has answers. The appropriation and re-interpretation of the Christianity from the perspectives of African spirituality and on biblical
grounds constituted the point of departure for the theology of the
AICs.[25]

Pentecostal movements in Africa have developed a contextualized Christology that presents Jesus as the one who redeems, rescues, and delivers believers from all forms of mishaps in life and from whatever robs people of the good elements of life. Christ is thus the *Agyenkwa* (Akan for the one who saves, protects, and preserves life). Mercy Amba Oduyoye, a Ghanaian theologian, captures this belief in the following words: "The *Agyenkwa* means the one who rescues, who holds your life in safety, takes you out of a life-denying situation and places you in a life-affirming one. The Rescuer plucks you from a dehumanizing ambience and places you in a position where you can grow toward authentic humanity. The *Agyenkwa* gives you back your life in all its fullness."[26] Spiritual explanations of causation and healing are so vibrant, entrenched, and central in the Akan/African worldview that any caring African church has no choice but to address it.

## Response of Mainline Churches

Christian Baëta, the Ghanaian theologian who conducted the earliest study of the AICs in Ghana (which he called the "Spiritual Churches"), highlighted the major prayer requests for which members often sought assistance. Consistently, the requests included prayer for health and healing, which, according to him, was the greatest and most pressing demand.[27] My own research and that of others among the mainline churches in Ghana indicate that, fundamentally, the prayer concerns, particularly those of health and healing, of members of the mainline churches are indistinguishable from those of AIC members. In essence, they are all responding to the same needs within their sociocultural milieu by using resources from the Bible. The problem that adherents of the mainline churches have is a lack of avenues to express their felt needs, as obtained in the pentecostal churches, a style of ministry which has not traditionally been part of their ethos.[28]

In arriving at the above realization, leaders of mainline churches felt compelled to address the need for the incorporation of divine healing in their practices. The Roman Catholic Church raised this concern in a major publication issued from a consultation on the state of the church in Ghana in the 1990s.[29] The Presbyterian Church of Ghana organized a special consultation, 9–12 August 1963, at Abetifi Kwahu to study the World Council of Churches' New Delhi and Ibadan report, "The Holy Spirit and the Christian Community."[30] On the role of the Holy Spirit and spiritual gifts, particularly spiritual healing, the consultation recommended the appointment of a competent committee to study charismata in the church, particularly the gift of healing, and produce an outline to be used in teaching church members.[31] Among other things, the Presbyterian meeting recommended the following:

a. The consultation wishes to see the New Testament ministry of healing through prayer restored within the congregations of the Church.
b. The ministry of healing through prayer should never be isolated from other healing ministries, especially medical treatment, but also the visits and care of other Christians. God can use all these means to give healing.[32]

In a study that was conducted among 44 Roman Catholic churches in the Tamale municipality of Ghana to find out why baptized Catholics visit the AICs and pentecostal churches, the report reads in part:

> 78% of the respondents maintained that in going to these churches they did not consider that they were "leaving" or being unfaithful to the Catholic Church. Rather, they were showing that in certain aspects of their faith experience the Catholic Church had become unfaithful to them. . . . It is a sign of their faith in Christ as Saviour in all aspects of their life that when in an area like "healing" they fail to experience it in the Catholic Church, they go to that Church or Christian sect where they can make this experience. If this is true, their presence should represent a great challenge to the Catholic Church.[33]

The Methodist Church Ghana conducted a similar study in 1999. It is interesting to note that the findings were similar to those of the Catholic Church and the Presbyterian Church of Ghana. Among other things, the report notes:

> It had been observed that for many years, especially during the 1970s and 1980s, the "Christian community" in many circuits and societies was either stagnant or actually declining. It was noted also that large numbers of Methodists, especially the youth and women, were leaving the Church, while others maintained a dual membership; they retained their membership in the Church but associated with other churches (notably, the new Charismatic churches, ministries, and fellowships) to satisfy their spiritual hunger. The exodus and lukewarm attitude was due to several factors including the poor prayer life, lack of adequate relevant biblical teaching and exposition, insufficient teaching on the manifestation of the gifts of the Holy Spirit, and what some regarded as dull worship.[34]

The concerns raised by the Presbyterian Church of Ghana, the Roman Catholic Church in Ghana, and the Methodist Church Ghana reflect the general situation in all the mainline churches in the country: members leaving these churches or maintaining dual membership as a sign of dissatisfaction with the styles of ministry of their respective churches. The churches were not oblivious to the lack of the pneumatic dimension in their ministries; they were able to diagnose the challenges facing them but did not know how to confront them.[35] The committee that was appointed by the Presbyterian Church of Ghana to examine the emergence of Charismatic groups brought this apparent inability of the mainline churches to confront the issue to the fore. The committee decided that members were "hungry" for something that the church was not providing and therefore challenged the synod to critically examine its own theology, liturgy, practices, and ethos to make room for the charismata, without which Presbyterians are unduly attracted to pentecostal movements.[36]

The solution demanded a complete departure of the mainline churches from a heritage that was largely influenced by the worldview of the Enlightenment developed in non-African cultures, which led toward the spontaneous emergence of Charismatic renewal movements within the mainline churches.

## Emergence of Charismatic Renewal Movements within the Mainline Churches and Their Response to the Challenge of the Pneumatic Dimension

Charismatic renewal movements emerged unexpectedly within the mainline churches in Ghana particularly in the 1970s. The movements were convinced that the mainline churches could be revitalized on pneumatic lines to be able to face the challenges that confronted them and to stem the exodus of their members to the AICs and the pentecostal churches. The renewal movements initially were formed and led by lay members of their respective churches. The leaders were people who were committed to the mother churches and at the same time had been exposed to the Charismatic phenomenon outside their church or through the reading of literature on it. They were convinced that one does not have to leave the mainline churches in order to experience the power and the gift of the Holy Spirit. In other words, the Holy Spirit is not the sole preserve of pentecostal churches or the AICs. They thus decided to remain in their mother churches to revitalize them through the infusion of the pneumatic dimension which they felt had been neglected.

These movements had a strong conviction that the renewal they sought was not an external phenomenon; rather, it had been part of the history and development of their respective traditions that had been forgotten. A concerned member of the Methodist Church Ghana captured this sentiment in an article in the *Methodist Times*:

> Today as we celebrate the 250th anniversary of John Wesley's conversion, let us pause to reflect soberly. . . . Methodism has lost its savour and we do not see the power there[i]n. Our pulpits are filled with

preachers who preach "Fairy tales." Class meetings are led by leaders who are not spirit-filled. The causes of such a divergence are to be found in the neglect of the old-time religion. . . . We say John Wesley was an evangelical and Pentecostal, but what do we see here, a cold and lack-lustre Church . . . sustained by the faithful few who are filled by the Holy Spirit. To bring the religion of the old times, then, there is the need to allow the fullest Holy Spirit operation in our Church. The time has come for us to uproot any witchcraft spirit, principalities and syncretism (lodges) assigned to rule over our Church [and] . . . stand in readiness for combat and resist every strategy of the fallen enemy, Satan.[37]

Participants in the renewal movements thus had three major motivations. First, they sought to revitalize their churches by going back to roots that emphasized the pneumatic, but which no longer seemed central in the ethos of their respective churches. Second, there were pressing issues such as healing and deliverance that members needed to experience in their lives, which were not being addressed despite the fact that the Bible is replete with resources to adequately deal with them as found in the AICs. Third, the only way to stem the drift of their fellow members to the newer pentecostal churches was to reinvigorate the churches and provide solutions to the pressing needs of their members.

Against the backdrop of this searching for alternative and more effective ways of ministering to their members, the mainline churches felt compelled to come to terms with the Charismatic eruptions within their respective frameworks. The earliest recorded emergence of such a movement was the Bible Study and Prayer Group of the Presbyterian Church of Ghana, which began in 1938 and was subsequently recognized by the church as a group within its framework in 1966. Later, similar movements started in the other mainline churches. For instance, the Roman Catholic Charismatic renewal movement started in the early 1970s, while in the 1980s various prayer fellowships emerged in the Methodist Church Ghana that later spread throughout the church.[38] These movements have served as major conduits for Charismatic spirituality, teachings, and practices to be introduced in the mainline churches to such an extent that various mainline churches in Ghana are becoming pentecostalized.[39]

## The Place of Healing in the Charismatic Movements and Mainline Churches in Ghana

Invariably, healing features prominently in the major teachings and practices of all the Charismatic renewal movements in mainline churches in Ghana.

This trend is consistent with the concerns and practices of the AICs and the pentecostal churches. They all have introduced new perspectives about Christianity by deconstructing the traditional images and paradigms they inherited from their founding Western missionary societies. This new approach to Christianity has resulted in the appropriation of the gospel by emphasizing its liberating and life-transforming dimension in addressing the existential concerns of church members. Thus, healing, which has always been part of the religious concerns of Africans, found a prominent place in the definition of salvation within the framework of the church. In a sustained study on Akan priesthood, John D. K. Ekem discerned:

> A relevant priesthood in the Ghanaian Christian context also depends
> on the promotion of an all-embracing healing/caring ministry. On
> the question of healing, Western Mission–founded churches have
> much to learn from African Independent Churches. The latter have
> succeeded, to a large extent, in linking psychosomatic wholeness with
> a proper disposition to the supernatural world (the vertical
> dimension), and the promotion of mutual solidarity among the faith
> community (the horizontal dimension). This is an important
> principle in the traditional African religious set-up.[40]

It has been generally noticed that members of the mission-founded churches stage mass exoduses to pentecostal churches due to the emphasis on "we feeling," where members support one another in times of crises. Sometimes, the entire membership of these churches declares a fast to pray for their members who find themselves in certain crises. Particularly, there is a well-developed, dynamic, prophetic healing ministry in these newer churches.[41]

Mainline churches seem to be taking a cue from the pentecostal churches by increasingly involving gifted lay members and teams of prophetic healers who work in concert with their priests/pastors administering healing and deliverance at all levels of their organizations. A brief history of this development may help our discussion. The mainline churches in Ghana have not been oblivious to the quest of their memberships for divine healing and the desire to encourage the manifestation of this gift in their respective congregations and parishes since the 1940s. During the late 1940s, the Presbyterian Church of Ghana encouraged the Reverend J. J. Manteaw, a catechist who organized prayer meetings during which he supposedly received the gifts of healing and the working of miracles. In recognition of his apparent gifts, the Presbyterian Church of Ghana stationed him at the church's hospital in Agogo as a lay chaplain. It is believed that he instantly healed a number of people who had been declared terminally ill. Consequently, the Presbyterian Church ordained him in 1959 and encouraged him to pursue his healing ministry.[42] Subsequently, other ordained Presbyterian ministers, such as

T. A. Kumi, Ankrah Badu, and Anim Nyantakyi, who similarly were perceived as having demonstrated gifts of healing, were recognized by the church and given the space to operate in the early 1960s, late 1960s, and 1980s, respectively.[43] In the Methodist Church Ghana, one classic example is the healing ministry of the late Very Reverend Samuel B. Essamuah, the former president (presiding bishop) of the Conference of the Methodist Church Ghana. Essamuah undertook a countrywide "olive-oil-aided" healing tour of Methodist churches in the 1970s, a phenomenon which at the time was uncharacteristic of the Methodist Church Ghana. This led to him composing the song cited at the beginning of this chapter.[44]

The official acceptance of these ordained ministers and numerous other lay leaders during the past half-century speaks volumes about how divine healing has become normalized in mainline Christianity in Ghana. There are certainly variations of emphasis in the teachings of newer pentecostal movements—some of which can fairly be characterized as promoting healing in the context of a broader concern for "victorious living," as Paul Gifford argues in this volume. Yet, it should be emphasized that such churches invariably stress divine healing—usually concerning themselves much more with healing than with financial prosperity—as a gift within the church and argue for the need for it to be part of the ecclesiologies of their respective traditions due to its biblical precedents and the expressed clamor for it by their memberships.

At the congregational level, there are various prayer meetings that are organized during which members who are physically unwell receive prayer specifically to be healed. Regular Friday prayer meetings start around nine o'clock in the morning and end around one o'clock. Other occasions for healing sessions are (usually monthly) prayer vigils, commonly called "all-night prayer meetings," during which space is created for individuals to receive prayer for healing from various ailments. Furthermore, congregations declare what are popularly known as "revival weeks," occasions when known Charismatic leaders (lay or ordained) are invited to preach and minister healing and deliverance to members.

It is quite striking that, at the regional and national levels of the mainline churches, prayer for healing with the consent of bishops, presiding bishops, moderators, etc. (and sometimes under the supervision of official heads or leaders of the churches) has become the order of the day in mainline churches. For instance, in the twenty-first century, the Methodist Church and the Presbyterian Church of Ghana have organized national crusades in Accra, the capital, under the auspices of their leaders (the presiding bishop and the moderator of the General Assembly, respectively). Key among the advertisements and handbills that the Methodist Church sent out inviting people to its crusade from 27 November to 1 December 2001 was the appeal: "Bring the sick for healing." Indeed, healing featured prominently in the crusade and in the reports on it.

The following excerpt from an official report on the 2001 crusade may throw more light on this point:

> There were many demonstrations of supernatural healing during healing sessions. Ministers present were all around to lay hands and effect healings. The dumb spoke, the deaf heard, those who had no sense of smell had their senses restored to them. One miraculous incident that needs special mention was the healing of a daughter of Rev'd Nana Apau Gyekye. After receiving her healing, Dr. Tetteh realized that one leg was shorter than the other by about four inches. She was put on the stage, prayed for and in the sight of everybody on the platform, the shorter leg was stretched, by God's Grace, like "plastic" to come at par with the longer one. Immediately, she was asked to jump and walk about. She did that to the amazement of everybody; she responded on several occasions that she was not tired of walking and jumping![45]

Apart from the national programs organized by the churches, there are individual Charismatic leaders (both lay and ordained) who are involved in healing and deliverance whose activities are recognized and given much prominence by their respective churches. For instance, Evangelist Abboah Offei, a lay healing and deliverance minister, runs a center that is officially recognized by the Presbyterian Church of Ghana as one of its official ministries. In 2001, Offei organized a retreat on healing and deliverance for the entire council of the General Assembly of the Presbyterian Church of Ghana. Furthermore, the moderator of the General Assembly officially sends Offei to the church's branches overseas, particularly to the United States and Europe, and to the tertiary institutions in Ghana to organize revival meetings that include healing and deliverance sessions. In addition, an ordained minister of the Presbyterian Church of Ghana, the late Reverend Antwi Boasiako, together with some of his ministerial colleagues, used to organize special prayer and healing retreats that involved four days of travel in the Atwea mountains in the Ashanti region of Ghana. Upon his death, the church's director of mission and evangelism, Rev. Godfried Bamfo, officially sent a circular announcing that another Presbyterian minister, Rev. K. Prah, had officially been appointed to take over that program. In addition, Bamfo sends circulars to all Presbyterian congregations in Ghana to officially announce the programs in the Atwea mountains, and as a result participants come from all over Ghana.

The Methodist Church Ghana officially reports on the activities of its recognized healing and deliverance ministers at its annual meetings. The following example of some of the activities of Rev. Joseph Bright Quarshie, a Methodist minister who is noted for his gift for healing and deliverance, having ministered to a total of 74,049 in 1996 alone, is typical of this kind of reporting:

Patronage of the Counselling Session is appreciably high, for at least 400 people see Rev. Quarshie each Monday, Tuesday and Saturday, while an average of 150 people see him on days other than the days specified above. Problems of clients range from marital, psychiatric, societal to spiritual harassment and impediments. Observations carried out reveal that 25 percent of clients complain of various diseases while about 18 percent of them come with trading or business inconveniences. Marriage problems cover about 40 percent. Some of the problems demand immediate deliverance from the hands of the evil assailant. . . . Some men have testified to having been healed of their impotency and many women who were barren have now given birth to children. Rev. Joseph Bright Quarshie is grateful to God for using him for His own glory.[46]

The Methodist Church Ghana has ordained a number of such Charismatic leaders as evangelists who are licensed to move among the congregations of the church to minister healing and deliverance.

The mainline churches in Ghana seek to root their spirituality and practices in the African maps of the universe. They have joined the pentecostal churches in interpreting the gospel from their meaning system.[47] In Africa, there is no unconsecrated medicine. Every medicine or healing system needs to be consecrated in order to be potent enough to deal with both the physiological and the spiritual dimensions of the sickness. Invariably, this worldview is shared by all Africans irrespective of their religious affiliation. Hence, Kalu's observation that "it is the pneumatic factor in Christianity that resonates with the vibrancy of primal African spirituality" is very apt in explaining the whole phenomenon.[48]

## Conclusions

For most Akan/African Christians, theology does not come to the fore; rather, religion, including Christianity, must serve existential needs. Therefore, what comes uppermost in their minds is salvation, which includes healing and well-being. Healing is sought vigorously through religious means as it was, and is, manifested in African indigenous religions. It is interesting to observe that, while debates rage on in academia, the most significant development in African Christianity—which has put African Christianity in the theological spotlight—is coming from the spiritualities, theologies, and practices of pentecostal movements (including those in the mainline churches) that are essentially marked by the quest to appropriate Christianity within the context of African spirituality. There is a major paradigmatic shift in the spirituality, practices, and programs of mainline churches in Ghana, making healing and deliverance central to their activities.

The AICs set the pace by expanding the scope of the soteriological appeal of the Christian message for African Christians; they gave direction for how Christianity might seek to address the pressing issues in life, such as healing, protection against evil and witches, and abundant life, which are of paramount concern for African Christians. Practices of healing found in the contemporary mainline churches are consistent with their discoveries of the need to incorporate healing practices in their respective churches since the 1960s. The fact that practices of divine healing similar to what obtains in pentecostal churches have been accepted in mainline churches is a clear indication that leaders of the mainline churches are listening, they are contextualizing, and they are seeking to do relevant theology. They are ceasing to unduly romanticize their Western missionary heritage in order to be more pragmatic and responsive to the cravings of their membership without which they would be perceived as insensitive and irrelevant. The reality is that the mainline churches are increasingly giving opportunities to their members to benefit from healing and deliverance ministries within the framework of their churches, thus increasingly blurring the hitherto sharp distinction between mainline churches and pentecostals.

Fundamentally, there is no difference between the members of mainline churches and of churches of the pentecostal genre in people's search for healing and deliverance. They all operate within the same worldview, which does not radically change when an African converts to another religion. They all see healing as "liberation from all that dehumanizes; it is the restoration of life."[49] Africans therefore expect any caring church, irrespective of its history or ethos, to meet the existential concerns of its members.

NOTES

1 This was the theme song composed and used by the Very Reverend Samuel B. Essamuah, former president of the Conference of the Methodist Church Ghana, when he undertook a nationwide "olive-oil-aided" healing tour of Methodist churches in Ghana in the 1970s. See J. Kwabena Asamoah-Gyadu, *African Charismatics: Current Developments within Independent Indigenous Pentecostalism in Ghana* (Leiden: Brill, 2005), 63.

2 In this essay, the terms "Western mission–founded churches," "mainline churches," and "historic churches" are used interchangeably to represent churches in Africa that were founded through the endeavors of Western missionary societies that operated in Ghana beginning in the early 1820s. Some of the churches that emerged out of their efforts in Ghana are the Roman Catholic Church, the Presbyterian Church of Ghana, the Anglican Church, the Methodist Church Ghana, the Evangelical Presbyterian Church, and the Baptist Church.

3 Abraham Akrong, "Deconstructing Colonial Mission: New Missiological Perspectives in African Christianity," in *Christianity in Africa and the African Diaspora: The Appropriation of a Scattered Heritage*, ed. Afe Adogame et al. (London: Continuum, 2008), 63–64.

4 The initialism AIC variously refers to African Instituted Churches; African Indigenous Churches; African Independent Churches; and African Initiatives in Christianity. These terms seek to mark the distinctiveness of typically African churches, as opposed to mainline churches, due to their emphasis on the pneumatic dimension of the life of the church. According to Turner, they are churches that are founded by Africans primarily for Africans; see H. W. Turner, "A Typology of African Religious Movements," *Journal of Religion in Africa* 1 (1967): 1.

5 Kwame Bediako, *Christianity in Africa: The Renewal of a Non-Western Religion* (Maryknoll, N.Y.: Orbis, 1995), 69.

6 I have discussed the Charismatic renewal movements in three other mainline churches in Ghana, namely, the Anglican Church, the Evangelical Presbyterian Church, and the Baptist Church in Ghana, in Omenyo, *Pentecost outside Pentecostalism: A Study of the Development of Charismatic Renewal in the Mainline Churches in Ghana* (Zoetermeer, Netherlands: Boekencentrum, 2002).

7 See J. S. Pobee, *Skenosis: Christian Faith in an African Context* (Gweru, Zimbabwe: Mombo, 1992), 64.

8 Ibid., 65; he refers to J. G. Wood, *The Natural History of Man* (London: Routledge, 1984), 617–618.

9 Max Assimeng, *Religion and Social Change in West Africa* (Accra: Ghana Universities Press, 1989), 64–65.

10 It must, however, be pointed out that Akans are not blindly fatalistic. Common sense and, for that matter, human responsibility are considered. J. N. Kudadjie has discussed this issue very well in his article "Does Religion Determine Morality in African Societies? A Viewpoint," in *Religion in a Pluralistic Society*, ed. J. S. Pobee (Leiden: Brill, 1976), 62ff.

11 John D. K. Ekem, *Priesthood in Context: A Study of Priesthood in Some Christian and Primal Communities of Ghana and Its Relevance for Mother-Tongue Biblical Interpretation* (Accra: SonLife, 2008), 39–40.

12 Kwame Bediako, *Jesus in African Culture: A Ghanaian Perspective* (Accra: Asempa, 1990), 25.

13 Assimeng, *Religion and Social Change*, 64.

14 Miroslav Volf, "Materiality of Salvation: An Investigation in the Soteriologies of Liberation and Pentecostal Theologies," *Journal of Ecumenical Studies* 26.3 (1989): 447–467.

15 Cephas N. Omenyo, "Charismatic Churches in Ghana and Contextualization," *Exchange: Journal of Missiological and Ecumenical Research* 31.3 (2002): 252–277.

16 Richard Van Djik, "Young Born Again Preachers in Post Independence Malawi: The Significance of an Extraneous Identity," in *New Dimensions in African Christianity*, ed. Paul Gifford (Nairobi, Kenya: AACC, 1992), 57.

17 See Ogbu Kalu, "Preserving a World View: Pentecostalism in the African Map of the Universe," *Pneuma* 24.2 (2002): 115.

18 The term "pentecostal" refers to the whole sweep of churches and movements in African Christianity that emphasize the pneumatic dimension, such as speaking in tongues, prophecy, visions, healing and deliverance, and ecstatic worship. It includes the AICs, Pentecostal churches, Charismatic renewal movements within the mainline/historic churches, nondenominational Charismatic movements and ministries, and independent Charismatic churches and ministries.

19 Jacques Mattey, "Faith, Healing and Mission," *International Review of Mission* 93.370–371 (July–Oct. 2004): 408.

20 See George Shepperson, *The Politics of African Church Separatist Movements in Central Africa, 1892–1916* (Edinburgh: Edinburgh University Press, 1960); Harold W. Turner, *Profile through Preaching: A Study of the Sermon Texts Used in a West African Independent Church* (Edinburgh: Edinburgh House Press, 1965); George Balandier, *The Sociology of Black Africa* (London: Praeger, 1970); Kofi Appiah-Kubi, *Man Cures, God Heals: Religious and Medical Practice among the Akans of Ghana* (Totowa, N.J.: Allanheld Osmun, 1981).

21 Ogbu Kalu, *African Pentecostalism: An Introduction* (New York: Oxford University Press, 2008), 263, emphasis mine.

22 Asamoah-Gyadu, *African Charismatics*, 164–200.

23 Emmanuel Y. Lartey, "Healing: Tradition and Pentecostalism in Africa Today," *International Review of Mission* 70 (1986): 75.

24 Cf. Ekenneh J. Anyanwu, "The Church's Healing Ministry in the Light of African Understanding of Health and Healing," in *Evangelization in Africa in the Third Millennium: Challenges and Prospects*, ed. Justin S. Ukpong et al. (Port Harcourt, Nigeria: CIWA, 1992), 73–75.

25 Akrong, "Deconstructing Colonial Mission," 68.

26 Mercy Amba Oduyoye, *Hearing and Knowing* (Maryknoll, N.Y.: Orbis, 1986), 98.

27 See C. G. Baëta, *Prophetism in Ghana: A Study of Some Spiritual Churches* (London: SCM, 1962), 136–141.

28 Cf. Bediako, *Christianity in Africa*, 65.

29 See concerns raised by the Catholic Church in J. Osei Bonsu, ed., *Ecclesia in Ghana: On the Church and Its Evangelizing Mission in the Third Millennium* (Accra: Catholic Bishops' Conference of Ghana, 1997), 133.

30 Rev. Paton was the convener of the committee. Other members were Rev. T. A. Kumi, Rev. H. A. Boateng, Rev. E. A. Ansah, Rev. G. Ankra-Badu (the acting synod clerk), Mrs. Ablorh Odjidja, and Mr. Frank Kotei. The moderator of the synod, Rt. Rev. E.M.L. Odjidja, also attended the last part of the meeting.

31 See the report on congregational prayer meetings, "What Has Happened to Our Prayer Services?" *Report to the Synod of the Presbyterian Church of Ghana* (Accra, Ghana: Presbyterian Church of Ghana, 1963), 1.

32 Ibid.

33 Bonsu, *Ecclesia in Ghana*, 133.

34 Joshua N. Kudadjie, "The Relevance of the Methodist Prayer and Renewal Programme," paper presented at the Accra District–Methodist Church–Ghana Evangelism Consultation, Accra, 28–30 Jan. 1999. The same paper was included in the report of the Methodist Church, Ghana Connexional Evangelism, Mission and Renewal Co-ordinators' Meetings held at Kumasi, 8–11 Dec. 1998, which was presented to the then-president of the Methodist Conference by the Reverend Michael P. Sackey, acting director, Evangelism, Mission and Renewal, 56.

35 All mainline churches studied made this same observation; for lack of space, these two examples must suffice; for more information, see Omenyo, *Pentecost outside Pentecostalism*, 101–198.

36 Ibid., 12.

37  *Methodist Times* (2 Oct. 1988): 4, quoted in Omenyo, *Pentecost Outside Pentecostalism*, 155.

38  See Omenyo, *Pentecost outside Pentecostalism*, 101–198, where the beginnings of the Charismatic movements in the Roman Catholic Church, the Anglican Church, the Presbyterian Church of Ghana, the Methodist Church Ghana, the Evangelical Presbyterian Church, and the Baptist Church in Ghana are discussed.

39  See Cephas Omenyo, "From the Fringes to the Centre: Pentecostalization of the Mainline Churches in Ghana," *Exchange* 34.1 (2005): 39–60.

40  Ekem, *Priesthood in Context*, 187–188.

41  Ibid.

42  See Omenyo, *Pentecost outside Pentecostalism*, 132.

43  See Ibid., 127–149.

44  Asamoah-Gyadu, *African Charismatics*, 63.

45  See "2001 Independence Square Crusade and How the Spirit of the Renewal Can Be Carried Forward," presented at the All Ministers' Retreat and Fellowship of the Kingdom at Swedru Secondary School, 7–11 Jan. 2002, by the Board of Ministries.

46  Methodist Church Ghana, *Report to the 36th Annual Synod* (Kumasi, Ghana: Kumasi Diocese of the Methodist Church Ghana, 1997), M. 34.

47  Kalu, "Preserving a World View," 115.

48  Ibid.

49  Kalu, African Pentecostalism, 265.

# 12

# Healing in African Pentecostalism: The "Victorious Living" of David Oyedepo

*Paul Gifford*

## African Pentecostalism

There is enormous variety in African pentecostalism, so much that it often seems impossible to generalize. I do not think either healing, deliverance, or prosperity is of itself the defining characteristic of African pentecostalism, though of course one can point to individual churches that can be defined by one or another of these. I am coming to the conclusion that, to the extent there is one defining characteristic, it is a stress on what can be called "victorious living." This victory is wide-ranging, embracing all areas of life, and at least six distinct avenues to this victory or success are discernible. First, through motivation. A church can inculcate drive and determination, creating success through a positive mental attitude. Second, through entrepreneurship. At an increasing number of churches, at least once every service one must turn to one's neighbor and ask: "Have you started your own business yet?" Third, through practical life skills— like hard work, budgeting, saving, investing, organizing time, avoiding drink. Fourth, through the "Faith gospel," by exercising faith, usually "seed faith" from the biblical metaphor of sowing and reaping, so having faith and giving tithes and offerings to the church become instruments of one's advancement. Fifth, and increasingly, success and prosperity come through the anointing of the "man of God"; pastors increasingly claim the ability to enhance the prosperity of their followers, and often make themselves indispensable. Sixth and related to this last point, the pastor can deliver followers from the evil spirits that impede the progress that is one's due as a Christian. These six ways in which Christianity is understood to lead to success and wealth are obviously not incompatible, and many churches seamlessly mix them together so that it requires effort to separate out the different strands. Other churches are more associated with one way, less with others.

I use the term "victorious living" rather than "prosperity." There are many African pentecostal churches—including many of the biggest—that could properly be labeled "prosperity churches," promising substantial wealth, most through faith. Indeed, it would be hard to find an African pentecostal church that is entirely untouched by the global Word of Faith movement. Nor is healing the defining characteristic of most churches, although likewise it is possible to find many churches with this as the central and defining focus. For most churches, in my opinion, healing is generally seen as one element (often an extremely important one) in a victorious life. Because a life of victory can hardly be characterized by sickness, a stress on healing is never far from the center nor far below the surface, but I would maintain that it is misleading to privilege healing as the one determining feature. Victorious living, including health, is frequently narrowly linked to a worldview that sees spiritual forces as responsible for all deficiencies and illnesses. Thus, many churches highlight deliverance from evil spirits, some exclusively and notoriously. This spiritual worldview is likewise probably seldom far below the surface even in churches where the practice of deliverance is less prominent.[1]

It is life in this world where the victory is evident. In fact, although the issue is seldom addressed, I think that in most African pentecostal churches there is not much idea of any subsequent life at all. This stress on "material salvation" I trace back not to any particular interpretation of biblical or Christian tradition, but to the African religious imagination.[2] In his classic work on the religion of the Nuer of the Sudan, the anthropologist E. E. Evans-Pritchard noted "their almost total lack of eschatology. Theirs is a this-worldly religion, a religion of abundant life and the fullness of days, and they neither pretend to know, nor, I think, do they care, what happens to them after death."[3] Though one cannot generalize over the entire continent, that verdict does not seem out of place for many African peoples.[4] African religion has been traditionally about this-worldly realities: flocks, crops, fertility, spouses, children, animals. Rituals have been geared to ensure their success. It is this religious worldview that has persisted into contemporary African pentecostalism.[5]

## Winners' Chapel

To address the place of healing in African pentecostalism, I will focus in this chapter on the particular rather than the general; I will discuss one church,

Living Faith Church Worldwide, better known as Winners' Chapel. It was founded in Lagos in 1983 by David Oyedepo. By 2000, it had 400 branches in Nigeria and was in 38 African countries. Winners' boasts in Lagos the biggest church auditorium in the world, seating 50,400, and in Nairobi where services draw up to 9,000 on Sundays, the organization is constructing what it claims will be the biggest church in East and Central Africa. Winners' policy is to have only one church in any one city or town, to which the church provides free or subsidized buses. This provision of transportation means that Winners' clientele is far more heterogeneous than that of most churches; besides the SUVs and Mercedes sedans evident in the parking lot, a large proportion of the congregation is bussed in from slums. The senior pastors, at least in the continent's major cities, tend to be Nigerians, well schooled in founder Oyedepo's teachings and fiercely loyal. They recommend Oyedepo's books (he always has four "books of the month") and promote the pilgrimage to the annual conference (Shiloh) at headquarters (Canaan Land, outside Lagos, where the Covenant University is situated as well). It is not claimed in this chapter that Winners' is representative of African pentecostalism. It is nevertheless one of the biggest and most successful examples.

In this chapter, I will try to give an understanding of what Oyedepo's Christianity is. Since the late 1980s, I have attended services in various African countries, seen a good many more on television, and read a good deal of Oyedepo's material. I will draw on all this information, but a prime source will be Oyedepo's 2006 649-page book, *Signs and Wonders Today: A Catalogue of the Amazing Acts of God among Men*.[6] This book gives his understanding of his ministry, and since it consists mainly of testimonies, it also gives a good insight into how his followers understand and experience it. Even if the testimonies have been doctored for public circulation, this strengthens the point that this is how Oyedepo wishes to be experienced and understood. Not least, he gives some dates for the innovations and new directions in his ministry (like the revelation of prophetic power in 1977), which provides a sense of its development. The examples and excerpts I have chosen from this book are representative; with the exception mentioned at the end of this chapter, they accurately reflect the whole and, indeed, they reflect my experience of the church across the continent over 20 years.[7] In this chapter, numbers in parentheses in the text are references to the pages of *Signs and Wonders*.

Obviously and unashamedly, Oyedepo's Christianity is about victory, triumph, blessing, dominion. Christians should be "gloriously distinguished in all spheres of life" (14). A Christian should "enjoy victory unlimited and on all sides" (42) because faith "overcomes all forces of darkness, economic problems, sickness, disease, family disintegration, untimely death, and every obstacle you can possibly imagine on earth" (42). "Everyone that is saved is saved to shine, not to suffer frustration. As a matter of fact, the believer can be said to be a celebrity, someone the world should celebrate" (403). "There is a land of plenty in the Kingdom of God . . . a land where there is no lack of any kind, and where you eat bread without scarceness. . . . It's a land full of treasures (Deut. 8:7–10)" (165).

## Features of Oyedepo's Ministry

Oyedepo claims to have introduced genuine innovations into Christianity. He lists the following as his special "biblical power instruments" (53). First and most particularly oil; anointing is a key feature of Winners' services (see, e.g., Exodus 29:21; James 5:4). Second, foot washing, arising from Jesus' action at the Last Supper (John 13:1–20, but also, as we shall see, Joshua 14:9). Third, "the blood" (e.g., Exodus 12:7; Luke 22:20). Fourth, the "mantle," something tracing its origins to Elijah, Aaron, the story of the woman being healed by touching Jesus' garment, and Paul. Oyedepo makes much of his special understanding of Christianity's central ritual, the Eucharist, too.

All of his claimed special contributions to Christianity reinforce his vision of Christianity as victory. The oil will "give a man or any object on which it is poured, immunity against any form of evil. . . . it is able to raise up any dying business, resurrect any collapsing career, and reverse any ancestral family curse. It makes a way for the plan of God for your life to find fulfillment" (101–102). It is an "all-purpose drug for any ailment of life" (113), bringing "honour and respect" (104). Oil "destroys all the discomforts of life" (98). So, too, foot washing:

> Jesus, by this mystery, was restoring to the redeemed the dominion
> that was lost in the first Adam. Jesus washed His disciples' feet so
> that they too could enter the realm where the father had put him.
> Something was being transferred to Jesus' disciples as He washed
> their feet. Evidently dominion was passed unto them through this
> mystery of divine transference, such that when Jesus left, His
> disciples represented Him spirit, soul and body. Everything bowed to
> them. As your feet are dipped into the water you are empowered to
> walk in the realm of dominion. (147)

"It provides access into our enviable inheritance. And what is this inheritance all about? Mysterious dominion for mysterious triumphs" (149). Among its benefits, it "empowers for access into realms of supernatural fortunes" (149). I have attended Winners' foot washings where the stress has been explicitly placed on Joshua 14:9: "Whatsoever your feet tread upon shall be given unto you for a possession." In such cases, this ritual, performed by the representative of God, becomes one more assurance of owning property.

Similarly, invoking the blood purges the inside of humans and will free believers from all forms of leprosy. "Through His blood, we are presented holy, unblamable, and unreprovable in His sight. And by that placement, all things come under our authority. All things that are under His authority automatically come under us" (125). "Man was made to have dominion over every other creation of God. He was also designed for blessings. This is the original inheritance of man that was lost to sin, but which the blood of Jesus has re-purchased for us" (128).

> Power is available to you by the blood, so you do not have to be a weakling anymore. . . . Pharaoh surrendered power after the Passover blood came on the scene. Then God gave Israel favour, and they spoiled the Egyptians. The Israelites were decked with riches at the expense of the Egyptians. . . . by the blood, the wisdom of God is available for us in every conflict of life. . . . the blood is able to give you instant, on-the-spot deliverance from any form of sickness and disease. . . . the blood of Jesus has justified you, so you can live a glorious life. . . . You have been restored back to blessing, which makes rich with no sorrow added to it. . . . We have access to greatness through the blood of Jesus. (131–132)

"The blood of Jesus is the seal of our victory in every conflict in life" (141). Merely by proclamation, one can turn one's bathwater (266), even breast milk (273), into the blood of Jesus with miraculous effects.

Even the central ritual of Christianity, the Eucharist, is interpreted to fit this message of abundance, success, prosperity, health. In Oyedepo's understanding, the Eucharist "is designed for strength, health and longevity. . . . It swallows up everything that is tying down your system or ravaging your body" (63–64). Given a social context through much of the African continent in which the constant threat of epidemic diseases inspires fear, assurances that Jesus is victorious over satanic diseases alongside promises of immunity from contagion must certainly be appealing. "After an encounter with the blood of Jesus in the miracle meal, none of the diseases ravaging the world will ever be able to follow you. . . . It is the seal of our covenant exemption from all satanic assaults" (71). "Every zero sperm count, dead womb, dead ovaries, whatever is called dead will be quickened back to life by the power in the blood contained in this miracle meal" (73). "The miracle meal is one of the Great Physician's covenant provisions for ensuring that you be in health and prosper in your spirit, soul and body" (80). "When you partake of the communion . . . expect every benefit of redemption to be brought your way" (92).

This is a good illustration of the way in which Oyedepo uses classical Christian concepts while transposing them onto a material plane (here, predominantly that of physical health). In another book specifically on the Eucharist, Oyedepo insists it is "designed to actualize the flow of eternal life in your system. It is designed to renew the flow of that life that is immune to all forms of sickness and disease."[8] In reference to the blood smeared on doorposts before the Exodus (Exodus 12:7): "Whenever the angel of death saw the blood he passed over. In that situation, the blood of the lamb was for the exemption of God's people from the evil befalling others around them."[9] Another Old Testament text reinforces this: "by the blood of thy covenant . . . I declare that I will render double unto thee" (Zechariah 9:9–12).[10] When Jesus died on the cross, "the earth quaked, the rocks rent, graves were opened and many dead—the saints which slept—arose (Matt. 27:50–52). Similarly, as that blood gets into your body, everything holding you down will quake, everything trying to pull you to the grave will be destroyed, anything dead in your system will be fully restored to life by the power of the blood."[11] "The communion is not some form of religious snack, it is what grafts you to the eternal dimension of life where the challenges of this world have no more power over you, where the enemy can reach you no more," so the believer should not die of sickness or disease.[12] "The miracle meal is one of the Great Physician's covenant provisions for ensuring that you be in health and prosper in your spirit, soul and body."[13] A believer can use any materials for a private Eucharist and can receive it on any occasion, even at home.

The Eucharist in Christianity is traditionally identified with the suffering and death of Jesus: in Catholic thinking, a reenactment, in Protestant, a memorial. But for Oyedepo, this is replaced with a pure substitution; Jesus suffered so believers do not have to. Jesus "hung on the cross so you can experience sweet things in your own life."[14] If asked, Oyedepo would likely say he means the afterlife too, but in practice at Winners' the reference is purely this-worldly. Here is a reworking of a major institution of Christianity to fit into his abundance, success, victory message.[15] I understand the this-worldly focus less as a rebalancing of a Christianity given to excessive emphasis on the next life than as evidence of the persistence of the pre-Christian African religious imagination.

Oyedepo's innovation with the mantle functions similarly. He cites Elijah (2 Kings 2), Aaron (Psalm 133:1–2), the woman with the issue of blood (Matthew 9:20–22), and Paul (Acts 19:11–12) to show that "any material that has come in contact with the anointed of God carries with it the unction" for dominion (155). God has not changed in his way of working:

> He is working through men sent for the deliverance of mankind. . . .
> these men carry transferable unction. . . . God gave me this mantle
> ministry for the liberation of mankind. . . . It is a ministry of trans-
> mission of unction. . . . It is a mantle for exploits. It is the end-time
> prophetic mystery in the hand of the carrier, for amazing results,
> signs and wonders. It is a carrier of divine energy and heavenly
> virtue. (158–159)

So a handkerchief, say, touched by Oyedepo can effect wonders.

Although, as just outlined, Oyedepo makes claims to substantial originality, his Christianity has considerable similarities with others', and indeed he often acknowledges his borrowings. He openly admits his debt to the Faith gospel of Kenneth and Gloria Copeland (199, 538, 565) and of Kenneth Hagin, even referring to Hagin's understanding of Mark 11:23, which is said to be the origin of the Word of Faith movement (32). Oyedepo cheerfully admits: "[My] commission is clearly a Word of Faith ministry" (25).[16] He acknowledges his debts to Oswald J. Smith, Smith Wigglesworth, and T. L. Osborn. He hosts at headquarters preachers like Mike Murdock and the Bahamian Myles Munroe, of whose gospel he obviously approves. In their testimonies, some of the church's members (with his evident support) link him to Joyce Meyer (399), John Avanzini (331), Ben Carson (417), and the London-based Nigerian Matthew Ashimolowo (539). As I noted at the outset, virtually no African pentecostal church has remained untouched by the Word of Faith movement, and the global influence of other (mainly North American) pentecostal luminaries is often not just acknowledged but trumpeted.

Pentecostalism is a global phenomenon, and in Africa its global character is accentuated. Globalizing processes have tended to bypass Africa; Africa is one part of the world which has experienced globalization as marginalization. Pentecostalism is one of the few global phenomena in which Africa can participate as an equal. Oyedepo proudly takes his place at crusades, conferences, and conventions with his peers from other continents, and he has no difficulty in bringing them to his celebrations. His media productions are screened with theirs. Oyedepo is one of the African pentecostal superstars who can demand a place on the global stage.

## Victorious Living Comes Mainly through Giving

Although the victory, success, and achievement promised at Winners' encompasses all areas of life, it is material success that is paramount.[17] Oyedepo's preoccupation with material success is evident from the account he gives of his calling by God. His experience is obviously modeled on the call of Moses, but whereas Moses in Midian was commanded: "Go and set my people free," Oyedepo in the United States was simply told: "Get down home quick and make my people rich."[18] It is equally clear from his literature and services that one achieves victory overwhelmingly through giving. The emphasis on giving is relentless. Oyedepo is quite clear: "Riches is God's will for you. . . . the covenant is your access to it. . . . What is the guiding law of the covenant, and how do we access it? . . . There is a law that connects you to the source of covenant wealth. . . . It is the law of seedtime and harvest" (166–167).

This is the logic of the overwhelming majority of testimonies. The following are representative. "I joined this commission [a term frequently used by members to refer to Winners'] in 1996, and in that same year the Bishop called for a sacrifice offering for 20-years covenant rest. . . . I brought my colour TV, video and sound system. Those were the only things I had then. . . . Two weeks after I gave the sacrifice, the Lord gave me another shop" (173). Another: "I paid my tithe, redeemed my pledge, and paid my foreign missions and Canaan Land subscriptions, and the heavens opened again" (191). Another records that the bishop "told us to give the most precious thing we had." He and his wife took their 21-inch color TV to the front during the service. "Between January and now, I've not only replaced that TV set with another beautiful one, I've paid a six figure amount as tithe! I used to pay a four figure amount last year . . . but this year I increased it to a five-figure amount, and have paid till April. I've also acquired a vehicle worth half a million naira" (187).[19] Another: "In July . . . the Bishop taught on sacrificial giving. . . . I sowed all my dollars and naira into the building projects. It may not be very much but I gave all! I even had to borrow some money to feed my family that month. Thereafter it started raining, and harvest time began! Within two and a half months, I made about one million naira net!" (200). Another reports that at Shiloh 2004, "there was a call for sacrificial offering, and we were enjoined to give our best. I had just finished a small building then that I wanted to put tenants in. But right in the church my wife and I gave it to God. I want to appreciate God that this year 2005, we have two houses!" (208). Another had read Oyedepo's 1995 book *Breaking Financial Hardship* (which stresses seed faith). As a result, "[I gave] all that I earned that month to God despite all the enormous bills I had to pay. Immediately after I dropped that money I got an invitation to be interviewed for a Chief Executive job" (212). Another reports that "the first day I came to church, the Bishop preached on sacrificial giving. After the service I asked my wife the meaning of sacrificial offering, and what we could give. . . . My wife then advised that we give our television and video set . . . and I willingly agreed . . . and dropped them in church as our sacrificial offering. And from then, my situation turned around!" (326). Similarly:

> When the Bishop made a call for the aircraft seed [to buy Oyedepo's private jet], I looked around for what to give as a sacrificial offering, as almost everything in the house had packed up [i.e., broken]; the radio and television had to be knocked on the head before they started working. I decided to give the video player that was at least in a fair condition. It was after that offering that things started to change. (329)

Another member reports that, after calling for a sacrifice for the Covenant University, "the Bishop said, 'if you want to see God in an unusual way, then sow an unusual seed.' Therefore I decided to sow my annual housing allowance for the year 2004 instead. That same year, God brought me from obscurity into limelight" (347). Another joined the church in 1996. Soon, he reports, "I had heard teachings on giving, so I decided not to sell the brand new photocopy machine but to give it to the Lord. The machine was worth 200,000 naira. I brought it to the church as a seed, and from then on, there was a turn-around!

First I got a four million naira contract in June 1998. Then in November of the same year, I got another contract worth 18 million naira" (350).

Given the debates about what this pentecostalism is contributing to development in the global South, it is striking just how little or seldom work contributes to the success envisaged by Oyedepo.[20] Indeed "sweatless success" is a refrain indicating precisely that success is not a product of human effort. Success or victory arises from a totally different dynamic. As we have seen, most victory stems from giving, but testimonies also attest to how important Oyedepo's specifics are. Victory comes from the use of oil, blood, or impartation (the latter is a ritual to access the bishop's anointing). Consider the case of oil. The bishop insists that "when the oil touches just the mirror of your car, it becomes immune to accidents and scratches. When you anoint the gates of your house, no devil, burglar or armed robber will dare come near it" (112). Testimonies make the same point. One person awoke to find his video player gone. "He anointed the space where the video player used to be with the anointing oil, and called back his video player. It was restored, along with the thief, in a matter of weeks" (106). Another anointed his TV set that had long been broken: "He turned it on, and the television showed clear pictures and produced a clear sound!" (107). Another applied anointing oil to her farm instead of fertilizer. "To the glory of God, that same year, she harvested the biggest tubers of yam ever, bigger than those of her colleagues" (108). A man "whose business was slow in yielding profit anointed his signpost, and thereafter people started flooding into his office" (111). Another, realizing that though God was blessing him, he was still borrowing,

> got angry, grabbed my bottle of anointing oil, poured out a handful
> and made some dangerous scriptural pronouncements [i.e.,
> dangerous to enemy forces]. I then splashed the anointing oil where
> we normally kept our money in anger, casting out whatever the devil
> had placed there. From that day on, we began enjoying a ceaseless
> flow of abundance! We have paid up all our debts, bought some new
> household items, and are living in supernatural abundance. (331)[21]

It is also striking how often success comes from miraculous provision on the part of others whom God brings to one's aid. (This is a fairly common motif in African pentecostalism, and although I have not heard this in Winners', some churches link this to God's bringing the Magi to Jesus, bearing gifts [Matthew 1:12].) One testifies: "I took the anointing oil one fine morning and anointed my pocket, in obedience to the counsel of God's servant, Bishop Oyedepo. At the close of work that day, someone called me and gave me a fat sum of money. Again, on the Saturday of that week, we went somewhere, and as we were leaving someone handed me a fat envelope, loaded with a fat sum of money" (105). Another, after Oyedepo's teaching on "covenant responsibility to parents," made up with his father:

> [My father] immediately stood up, went to his room and brought out
> packets of 50 naira notes, and gave them to me. He prayed for me to
> go and start my business (which I had been trying to start for the past
> five years). When I counted the money, it was 20,000 naira. I was
> dazed, because my father had never given me that kind of amount of
> money before. He always said he didn't have money. The covenant
> really works! (177–178)

Another's business was suffering from "devourers." But after a teaching at a
Winners' business fellowship, "I learnt that tithes and offerings should not be
mixed up or interchanged with one another. So I went back to God, asking for
money, and He opened the way for me again. Three weeks ago, I was led
to sow a seed . . . and a week later, a brother gave me a car!" (216). Another
"victim of inconsistency in business" received a "powerful miracle through the
blood of sprinkling" at a "breakthrough seminar." "Today I have a reputable
business, and a God-blessed family with no want at all, for the scripture says
that those who seek the Lord shall lack nothing (Ps. 34:9–10). In July 1996,
God blessed me with an eight figure favour from a relation, just by the sprinkling of the blood of Jesus" (322). A former Muslim gave a sacrificial offering,
and "from then, my situation turned around! . . . God has also miraculously
completed a building project I had abandoned for six years. People just started
blessing me with building materials, and before I knew what was happening,
the house was completed. . . . God also used a friend of mine to give me a car
free of charge . . . a Volvo 740" (327). Another testified that the bishop had
invited the congregation to ask God for whatever virtue they prized in Oyedepo's
life. "I had always heard the Bishop say, 'I can never be poor.' So I asked God
to remove the spirit of poverty and failure from my life. I knew I was free as
soon as the Bishop laid his hands on me! The following day, my younger sister
gave me some money with which to start a little business" (330).[22]


Oyedepo's Role

Oyedepo is not just a teacher and exemplar. He is the quintessential prophet,
claiming crucial significance in the victorious living of his followers. His ministry actually brings this about. He is explicit:

> The Holy Ghost has sent me to open a new chapter to this genera-
> tion. He has sent me with the powerful Word of Faith, and has also
> delivered into my hands mysterious instruments that have been used
> over the years to raise the dead, destroy HIV/AIDS, dissolve cancers,
> establish liberty, provoke success, and command favour, all for the
> uplift of Zion! We are grateful to God for counting us privileged to
> know these things which hitherto had been hidden, but which are

now revealed to us by His Spirit. God has delivered into our hands divine instruments for victory. Through their use, the lame have walked, withered limbs have been cured, the mad have been restored back to sanity, and the barren have become joyful mothers of children. It's been signs and wonders galore! [These] biblical instruments of power . . . were delivered [to me] purely by revelation. (58)

God has spoken to him clearly (152). What God has revealed, Oyedepo can pronounce and actually bring about. The implications of such a claim cannot be exaggerated:

Prophetic verdicts are divine verdicts; they are heavenly verdicts. They are God's commands given expression through mortal lips. . . . Every time the prophet says, "Thus saith the Lord," it is actually the Lord Himself speaking. He is only using the prophet's vocal system as a microphone. . . . Prophetic verdicts will cause your daystar to rise. It will always bring a change of position, as mountains and hopeless situations bow to it. It gives life to any dead situation, and turns worthlessness to exceeding greatness. (153)[23]

Oyedepo also claims to have "creative breath." "The Father has creative life in His breath, so does the Son. And because the Son says He has sent us as the Father sent Him, therefore, I have creative life in my breath also. And because the Son quickens whomsoever He wills (John 5:21), I too can quicken whomsoever I will by that same breath of life" (161). He immediately recounts that he breathed on a child with polio, and "instantly, the legs straightened out" (161). He claims to have healed many of HIV/AIDS this way (161). Testimonies tell of this miraculous breath, too: "At the November 'Breakthrough Night,' the Bishop called some people out for special ministration. I went out and he breathed into my mouth. On getting back to my seat, I started feeling the power of God inside me. My body was chilled" and the cure (from severe constipation) effected (303). A woman unable to conceive testifies: "As the Bishop breathed into me, something cleansed me, and I became pregnant" (527).

Such testimonies demonstrate that Oyedepo's Christianity undoubtedly extends to health, but his "creative breath" also affects all other areas. He has declared that there will arise five women shipping magnates in his congregation. One testifies to how the bishop miraculously brought this about (344). He has declared that everyone wanting to marry in the course of a particular year will do so (467). He has prophesied that no family member will die in a particular year (297); also "this year is your year of laughter; no sorrow is permitted in your lives. Nothing will die in your hands this year" (589, similarly 591). He has proclaimed: "Within seven weeks, you will get whatever you are asking for" (472). At the dedication of Faith Tabernacle, he declared: "You will not go home with any problem you came here with" (302). He can overrule doctors' reports

(535), because doctors deal in facts, not truth (521). In that sense, he calls science "an enemy of faith" (518) and has prophesied that on drinking "a shot of the anointing oil . . . every affliction in our bodies would vanish" (304). As he speaks, people are miraculously healed (301). A dream of the bishop is sufficient (349); even just touching his pulpit (175) and placing the bishop's picture on the picture of a missing loved one brings him home (375). Just looking at Oyedepo can heal one of a brain tumor (271). A man suffering memory loss, when asked by the bishop how he was, responded, "Fine, thank you," and found himself instantly healed (431). Oyedepo's words, promises, mantle, books, and tapes all bring about the health and victory he proclaims. He feels he must provide a disclaimer that he is a mere mortal, and that the power is God's, not his (647–648), but the testimonies are overwhelmingly to his power; only a few are to God himself, often the "God of David Oyedepo" (269, 596), or to what "God does through his servant, Bishop David Oyedepo" (383). "Nothing is impossible for the God of Bishop David Oyedepo" (518).[24]

There is the occasional element of do-it-yourself, of effecting prophecies without the agency of the bishop. In theory, anyone can use the oil, invoke the blood of Jesus (70, 83), consecrate the Eucharist at home (90–91), with all their miraculous consequences. A few testimonies reveal this. "The Bishop had instructed that those of us going for interviews should take off our shoes and claim our victory. In obedience to his command, when I got to the NNPC, I took off my shoes and prophesied. To God be the glory, I got the job" (454). One woman, desiring marriage, read a church bulletin that "talked about the creative wisdom of God"; she was led to collect some sand and say: "'God, you who made Adam and Eve from sand are going to create my husband today.' I started prophesying to that sand." The very next day, she met her future husband (475–476). At Winners', despite these few examples, testimonies are overwhelmingly to what Oyedepo does; there are a couple to what other pastors do, but just as often other pastors refer people to Oyedepo.

## An African Christianity?

What particularly African elements are evident in this Christianity? Obviously, shame, reproach, and status are major considerations in the testimonies, in a way that is not commonly found in the West. It is also important that enemies "suffer unparalleled devastation" (14). More significantly, there are touches which reveal the "enchanted" religious worldview, including family curses (102, 342, 559) and spells (460), but the word "witchcraft" seems studiously avoided. Nevertheless, Oyedepo reverses curses, a procedure in which the curse intended for a victim is turned back on the curser. One woman's "legs became swollen as though I had elephantiasis. . . . there was no medical solution to it; no name for it. The enemy wanted to paralyse my legs." The woman came to

Oyedepo's foot-washing ritual and was immediately cured. "The daughter of the person that charmed me is now paralysed in one hand; she can't hold anything with it. I thank the God of this commission who has been especially faithful to me" (253). One couple who had flourished individually before their marriage, afterward immediately experienced problems: "I killed a snake in the room where we kept our wedding gifts. And that was how our problems started." Oyedepo had "placed a curse on anyone who steals other people's things from the Shiloh ground, declaring that they would carry whatever curse the owner of the stolen property came to Shiloh with." This couple came to Shiloh, where they had their cell phone stolen. The wife "then began to dance, rejoicing that our problems were all over, as they had been transferred to the thief"—and indeed her good fortune returned immediately. The husband, however, continued to suffer all manner of ills. They returned to the Shiloh gathering the following year, where before going to bed, the husband prayed:

> "God make me to fly, make me to work again." And lo, I woke up the
> following morning to find a dead bird under my pillow. We shared
> the testimony in church that day, after which the Bishop called us
> back and decreed, saying, "Exactly a month from now, whoever is
> responsible for this will go down [die]." . . . And just as he had said,
> exactly a month later we got the news that the person behind all our
> problems was dead! And two weeks after his death, I got a job, and
> was started off with a very good package. Also I was called to come
> for my visa to Europe. . . . God used this church and His Word to
> restore us. (318–321)

Although testimonies like these are encountered at services and are referred to in *Signs and Wonders*, the significant point is just how peripheral they are, both for Oyedepo and those testifying. This is not an enchanted Christianity in which witchcraft and evil spirits are pervasive, as distinct from other Christianities of Lagos, like prophet T. B. Joshua's Synagogue Church of All Nations and D. K. Olukoya's Mountain of Fire and Miracles Ministry, or the pentecostalism of the Koreans and South Indians described by Kim and Bergunder in this volume. Satan, the Western construct, is far more prominent in Oyedepo's Christianity than are the spirits of Africa's (or Asia's) pre-Christian religions.

Conclusion

This essay has argued that Oyedepo's Christianity centers on victorious living, with victory understood to embrace all aspects of life. Health, extending to fertility in marriage, is among the most important, and the cures attested range from relatively minor ailments to incurable AIDS. Nevertheless, testimonies indicate that there is probably more emphasis on employment, promotion, remuneration, business success, and business expansion. At the beginning of this chapter, I outlined six ways in which African pentecostalism is associated with success: motivation, entrepreneurship, acquisition of skills, sowing in faith, prophetic declaration, and exorcism. Winners' exemplifies all six, but its primary emphasis is on sowing in faith and prophetic declaration. The sowing and reaping, I have argued, is relentless and unashamed.[25] It is probably the biggest single reason given for the victory, breakthrough, and healing.

The prophetic ministry of Oyedepo has become more salient in recent years. Nevertheless, the motivational element is still prominent. Oyedepo's stress on achievement, victory, and success is a strong motivating force. To be told that you belong at the top, that you should have a senior position or a successful business, that you should be well-off and well-married must encourage many to persevere in circumstances where it is all too easy to give up. The constant emphasis on the future, a glorious future, often involves a corresponding insistence on forgetting the past, however traumatic—even transcending debilitating memories of rape (399–400). Incentives to intellectual excellence are reported in many testimonies (403–431). In line with this emphasis on intellectual achievement, Oyedepo in 2003 opened Dominion University, situated at his Lagos headquarters and by some accounts among the best private universities in Nigeria. Such social involvement, however, is not yet a prominent feature of the ministry.

The relentless stress on victory raises in acute form the question: How can this success Christianity appeal in circumstances where so many obviously do not, indeed cannot, succeed? Obviously, a sufficient number must experience success in some measure (trumpeted in the testimonies) for the movement not to be discredited. Nevertheless, there is real tension here, even if largely unaddressed and unresolved. The tension undoubtedly contributes to the numbers who migrate from one church to another.[26]

I began by stating that African pentecostalism is an enormously varied phenomenon. It is not claimed that the Christianity outlined in this chapter is representative. However, Winners' Chapel is one of the most significant pentecostal churches on the continent, and at Winners' Christianity means victory, and of course a life of victory encompasses health. Oyedepo has been enormously successful, as attested in the size and spread of the church. Moreover, his influence extends far beyond his own church through his media productions, including books and television programs. His success has also made him a paradigm, a model to be imitated by others.

NOTES

1 For the variety within African pentecostalism, see Paul Gifford, *Ghana's New Christianity: Pentecostalism in a Globalising African Economy* (London: Hurst; Bloomington:

Indiana University Press, 2004); Gifford, *Christianity, Politics and Public Life in Kenya* (London: Hurst; New York: Columbia University Press, 2009).

2 Miroslav Volf, "Materiality of Salvation: An Investigation in the Soteriologies of Liberation and Pentecostal Theologies," *Journal of Ecumenical Studies* 26.3 (1989): 447–467.

3 E. E. Evans-Pritchard, *Nuer Religion* (Oxford: Clarendon, 1956), 154.

4 "To Africans this is the only world, and it is neither inferior to any other, nor 'illusory'"; Okot p'Bitek, *African Religions in Western Scholarship* (Kampala, Uganda: East African Literature Review, 1971), 110.

5 Paul Gifford, "African Christianity and the Eclipse of the Afterlife," in *The Church, the Afterlife and the Fate of the Soul,* ed. Peter Clarke and Tony Claydon (Rochester, N.Y.: Boydell Press for the Ecclesiastical History Society, 2009), 413–429.

6 David Oyedepo, *Signs and Wonders Today: A Catalogue of the Amazing Acts of God among* Men (Lagos, Nigeria: Dominion, 2006).

7 I have written of Winners' Chapel before, most notably in Gifford, *Ghana's New Christianity*; and Gifford, *Christianity, Politics.* I will not repeat previous material, but it supports everything I have written here.

8 David O. Oyedepo, *The Miracle Meal* (Lagos, Nigeria: Dominion, 2002), 16.

9 Ibid., 29.

10 Ibid., 30–31.

11 Ibid., 32.

12 Ibid., 50.

13 Ibid., 53.

14 Ibid., 79.

15 At a communion service in September 2006, Winners' Nairobi pastor explained the Eucharist as "a mystery to swallow every misfortune in your life. . . . Let it eradicate all sickness and affliction." The congregation was reminded that "mediocrity is a sickness," and was assured that "if your business is sick, it can be healed." Immediately after receiving communion, all received communion a second time, as an immunization: "Jesus was never sick once. By this second communion you will never be sick again. . . . Go and sack all your doctors. Tell your doctors, 'I will not come to your clinic again.' You will not contribute to buy their houses and cars; you will buy your own houses and cars."

16 Oyedepo also acknowledges his debt to Hagin and Copeland in *Riding on Prophetic Wings* (Lagos, Nigeria: Dominion, 2000), 103, 121, 124; and *Winners World* (May 2006): 11.

17 Oyedepo's books relentlessly advocate material success. In Winners' Nairobi bookshop in mid-2007, his books (all published by his Dominion Publishing House, Lagos) included *You Shall Not Be Barren, Winning the War against Poverty, Understanding Financial Prosperity, Creating a New Beginning, All You Need to Have All Your Needs Met, Walking in the Miraculous, The Release of Power, The Wisdom That Works, Maximise Destiny, Success Systems, Understanding the Anointing, Possessing Your Possession, Covenant Wealth, The Hidden Covenants of Blessings, Breaking Financial Hardship.*

18 David O. Oyedepo, *Breaking Financial Hardship* (Lagos, Nigeria: Dominion, 1995), 51.

19 One naira was equivalent to 0.01 U.S. dollars as of July 2010.

20  See Sandy Johnston, *Under the Radar: Pentecostalism in South Africa and Its Potential Social and Economic Role* (Johannesburg, South Africa: Centre for Development and Enterprise, 2008). Pentecostalism is understood to include features like intense spirituality, centering on the rebirth experience and the supernatural (divine healing, speaking in tongues); a relatively nonhierarchical and decentralized organization, reflecting a high level of local and even individual initiative and strongly entrepreneurial motivations; and a relative accessibility and informality in terms of ordination and leadership. Johnston's report is so convinced of the prominence of the entrepreneurial element that it actually recommends that the state promote pentecostalism (34).

21  Sometimes, victory comes from the power of proclamation, a key element of the Faith gospel. One believer testified that the bishop had preached on the significance of names for Christians. He changed the name of his business to "Higher Altitudes Ventures Enterprises. Today, barely a month after, I have more properties than I can ever sell, and many beautiful offers are still pouring in!" (324).

22  See also Oyedepo, *Signs and Wonders*, 176, 199, 203, 204, 250, 277–279, 576.

23  It can be disastrous for your blessing if you neglect a prophet. Thus, David Adeoye of Nairobi Winners' Chapel argues: "God is saying believe Him and you will be established, but your prosperity, success and breaking forth on the right and the left is tied to a prophet. . . . Any trace of disregard for their role in your life is a showcase of unprofitability for you." *Miracle Magazine* (Mar. 2006): 19.

24  One attested that the devil "could not resist my bishop" (285).

25  Among the opportunities referred to in Oyedepo, *Signs and Wonders*, are sacrificial offering, covenant seed, kingdom investment, prophetic offering, violent offering, chair offering, and unlimited favor sacrifice.

26  Gifford, *Ghana's New Christianity*, 51–53; and Gifford, *Christianity, Politics*, 124–125.

# 13

# Reenchanted: Divine Healing in Korean Protestantism

*Sean C. Kim*

South Korea is one of the most vibrant centers of global pentecostalism. Since the 1960s, there has been an explosive growth of the Pentecostal and Charismatic movement in the country, and its emergence has come to be symbolized by the Yoido Full Gospel Church, which claims over 800,000 members and is recognized as the single largest Christian congregation in the world. The Reverend David Yonggi Cho (1936–), the church's founder and senior pastor until his official retirement in 2008, has served as chair of the World Assemblies of God Fellowship and has reached millions around the world through his sermon broadcasts and bestselling books.[1]

Pentecostalism is a relative newcomer to the Korean religious scene, having only established itself in the last half of the twentieth century. The history of Korean Protestantism stretches back over 100 years and that of Roman Catholicism over 200 years. Estimates put the number of Protestants at anywhere from 20 to 40 percent of the total population. And Korean Protestantism has aggressively expanded beyond its national boundaries. Korea is second only to the United States in the number of missionaries dispatched abroad. Moreover, overseas emigration has led to the establishment of thousands of ethnic Korean churches in the United States and in other countries throughout the world. In spite of the shorter presence of pentecostalism in Korea compared to other Christian groups, it has nonetheless had an enormous impact. Numerically, pentecostals now make up the second largest Protestant group, after the Presbyterians. And they have brought a new theological emphasis, celebrating the gifts of the Holy Spirit. They have also introduced new models of church growth and organization, such as Cho's use of "cell groups" based on members' areas of residence. Since the 1980s, the pentecostal influence has manifested itself more broadly in the Charismatic movement that has swept both Protestant and Catholic congregations alike. As a result, divine healing, speaking in tongues, prophecy, and other pentecostal practices have spread far beyond traditional denominational boundaries.

While pentecostalism represents much that is new to Korea, it also forms a powerful continuum with many older beliefs and practices. Indeed, divine healing, a hallmark of the pentecostal movement, has deep roots in the history of earlier Protestant groups and in the indigenous religious culture. Part of the reason for the success of pentecostalism in Korea has been precisely its ability to build on the rich tradition of healing that preceded it. In a country torn by global wars, imperial occupation, and rampant poverty for much of the twentieth century, the climate was ripe for the rapid expansion of a religion that promised—and seemed to deliver—healing for bodies as well as souls. Perceived as more efficacious than other religious alternatives, pentecostal divine healing has converged with earlier healing practices and contributed to the ongoing indigenization of Christianity in Korea.


Missionaries in the Land of Spirits

Divine healing in Protestantism is usually associated with the Holiness and Pentecostal movements. The Holiness Church began its missions in Korea in 1907, but divine healing was not a major part of its missionary efforts. The Pentecostals did not establish a presence until 1928 and remained a small group until its growth began in the 1950s. Divine healing in Korean Protestantism thus first emerged in other Christian circles, primarily Presbyterian, despite the processes of "disenchantment" that had sanitized the world of Western missionaries.[2]

Ironically, the first Presbyterian missionaries in Korea, who arrived in the late nineteenth century, held to the Calvinist doctrine of cessationism and believed that the period of miracles had ended with the apostolic age. Yet from the outset of missionary activity, divine healing was widely practiced and was an integral part of spreading the new faith. One of the main reasons for this discrepancy was that the missionaries in Korea emphasized native initiative in the propagation of Christianity. Because of this policy, the Koreans quickly took over the work of converting and church building. And they began to challenge the doctrine of cessationism. When Korean evangelists began to heal the sick through prayer and exorcism, the missionary response was mixed and ambivalent. At one end of the spectrum were those who rejected divine healing outright and explained it away in naturalistic terms. At the other end were those who abandoned the doctrine of cessationism and came to believe that divine healing was valid. Some even came to participate in it. Between the two poles were many who did not know what to make of the phenomenon. Yet, whatever the individual views of the missionaries may have been, divine healing emerged as a prominent feature of Protestantism in Korea. In the hands of the Korean evangelists, it became a powerful instrument of conversion and played a major role in spreading and shaping the new faith.

The healings took place through Christian prayer and were validated in terms of the Bible. The healers saw themselves as following the example of Jesus and the apostles in healing the sick and casting out demons. The healings derived their meaning and power not only from biblical faith but also from traditional Korean cosmology. Korea in the late nineteenth and early twentieth centuries was a world ruled by spirits and ghosts. Missionary writings on Korean religions are filled with observations of the spirit world. E. B. Landis, an Anglican missionary, listed 36 categories of spirits, divided into three general groupings:

*Spirits high in rank.*
1. Spirits of the Heavens.
2. Spirits of the Earth.
3. Spirits of the Mountains and Hills.
4. Spirits of the Dragons.
5. Guardian Spirits of the District.
6. Spirits of the Buddhist Faith.

*Spirits of the House.*
7. Spirit of the ridge pole.
8. Spirit of goods and furniture.
9. Spirit demon of the Yi family [ruling royal house].
10. Spirits of the Kitchen.
11. Attendant spirits of No. 9 above.
12. Spirits which serve one's ancestors.
13. The guards and servants of No. 9.
14. The Spirits which aid jugglers.
15. Spirits of goods and chattels, like No. 8, but inferior in rank.
16. Spirits of small-pox.
17. Spirits which take the forms of animals.
18. Spirits which take possession of young girls and change them into exorcists.
19. Spirits of the seven stars, which form the Dipper.
20. Spirits of the house site.

*Various kinds of Spirits.*

21. Spirits which make men brave.
22. Spirits which reside in trees.
23. Spirits which cause tigers to eat men.
24. Spirits which cause men to die on the road.
25. Spirits which roam about the house causing all sorts of calamities.
26. Spirits which cause a man to die away from home.
27. Spirits which cause men to die as substitutes for others.
28. Spirits which cause men to die by strangulation.
29. Spirits which cause men to die by drowning.
30. Spirits which cause women to die in childbirth.
31. Spirits which cause men to die by suicide.
32. Spirits which cause men to die by fire.
33. Spirits which cause men to die by being beaten.
34. Spirits which cause men to die by falls.
35. Spirits which cause men to die of pestilence.
36. Spirits which cause men to die of cholera.[3]

The spirits, both benevolent and malevolent, were omnipresent. Inhabiting every part of the universe and beyond, the spirits were constant companions of the Koreans from birth to death to the afterlife. Early Korean converts to Christianity continued to believe in the world of spirits and the supernatural. But a transformation did take place. All the old spirits became "demons" and "devils." No distinctions were made between benevolent and malevolent beings. The Christian God was the only good spirit as well as the most powerful one.

Missionaries differed in opinion concerning the world of spirits, ranging from absolute denial to firm belief. Homer Hulbert, a Methodist missionary scholar, believed the spirits to be figments of the imagination.[4] But Hulbert was in the minority. Most missionaries seem to have believed in the world of spirits, especially in light of their experiences in Korea.[5] Charles Clark is a typical example of conversion to belief in the world of spirits. As a seminary student, he believed the phenomenon of "demon possession" could be explained scientifically as "insanity or nervousness or an injudicious lack of discipline in childhood." As a Presbyterian missionary in Korea, he had read about a missionary in China "casting out devils," and he dismissed the practice as having a rational explanation. But he changed his mind after a personal experience. Clark was helping to lead a revival when a man began to cause a commotion. He began banging on his Bible and raving. Clark and the Korean pastor had to take him to a back room, and Clark was totally unprepared for what came next:

When here to there he began to rage like a wild beast. He smashed his own hat and ripped off his coat, tore open his leggings, and then started to demolish the room. He fell on his face on the floor. . . . Just then he saw a box in the room shaped somewhat like the ancestral worship boxes for tablets and he prostrated himself before it. . . . The veins of his neck swelled till it seemed they must burst.[6]

At this point, Clark turned from skeptic to believer. Firsthand experience led him to believe in demon possession as well as the power to drive demons out:

Finally I became convinced that it was a devil's manifestation . . . so I went to him, took firm hold of his shaking hands, and ordered him in Jesus' name to be still. . . . Then I prayed and almost at once he became quiet. I prayed again and he subsided. After lying quietly for about 10 minutes while we prayed beside him he seemed suddenly to wake up and I will testify that he was as sane as any Korean I know. He gave us his name. Said he had been believing seven weeks. He did not have a very clear idea of what he had done but when he saw his head [hat] smashed and his clothes all torn he felt terribly. After prayer again we let him out a back way and he went home.[7]

Clark went on to validate the experience in terms of biblical precedent:

The Holy Spirit was doing so great a work that I finally believe the devil entered into that man to make him break up the meeting. As sure as I believe there is a Holy Spirit who can "convince men of sin and righteousness and judgment" I am convinced that the devil can work now in opposition to Him exactly as he did 1900 years ago.[8]

Clark later recounted several instances of such cures, including one involving an "explosive devil":

The leading man of Toikeiouel town has now believed. He got sick shortly after believing and his family wanted to call in *mutangs* [shamans]; but the Christians met at his house and prayed nearly all night; and they tell a wonderful story of how at last the devil went out of the man with such force that he knocked over three men standing out in the yard. Those men were so scared that they too now believe. There are about 70 attendants there. At Soipuni there were also several cases of wonderful cures of sickness in answer to the Christians' prayers.[9]

Horace G. Underwood, the first official Presbyterian missionary to Korea, was also a believer in divine healing. He recounted an experience of healing through prayer while he was out in the field. After sending away the shaman who had been unsuccessful in healing a dying patient, Underwood and two other believers prayed and fasted for three days and three nights, and the life was saved. The entire family converted as a result, and the shamanistic ritual objects around the house were destroyed. Underwood reported that afterward there were "many instances where the power of the Spirit and Word has freed the poor people from demon worship."[10]

In another account, Underwood described a typical healing by Korean Christians. In a village in northern Korea, a young girl, who had just been married, became possessed and was sent back to her mother. The shamans failed to exorcise the spirit, and the neighbors told her, "The Jesus they worship over the hills drives out devils." The mother took the daughter to the Christians, who initially failed even though they prayed two or three times a day, and the neighbors began to taunt the Christians: "Your Jesus God can't do what you claim." The Christians turned to the Bible and realized that the case would involve more prayer as well as fasting. Then, finally, in a dramatic midnight showdown at the village shrine, the Christians got on their knees to pray, and the girl fell on the ground and later got up, free from the possessing spirit.[11]

Almost all of the reported cures were carried out by Koreans who, like Clark, validated the experience in terms of Jesus being the model of the divine healer.[12] But on occasion missionaries themselves also became healers. Presbyterian missionary Annie Laurie Baird recalled an instance of reluctantly joining in a cure. A young woman of about 18 years of age, the mother of a six-month-old baby, was possessed by two spirits, one female and one male. The possession led her to spend most of her time with her head bowed and eyes closed. In spite of the attempts of the shaman, the spirits could not be exorcised. Then, some neighbors suggested going to a Christian village, whispering lest the spirits hear: "They say the devils don't stay where Jesus is." When she was taken to some Christian women, they succeeded in exorcising the male demon but not the female. Hence, they took her to Baird, who put the finishing touches on the process of healing:

> I had never expected to play the role of exorcist of evil spirits, but my mind was made up in an instant that if I had any power, be it no more than mere animal magnetism, this poor creature should get the benefit of it. I drew her close to my side, stroked her shoulders and arms and held her hands in a close clasp. She looked at me dully, without the least change of countenance. The next Sunday the little scene was enacted as before, but on the third Sunday when I put my arm around her, her face relaxed into a smile. On the fourth Sunday she failed to appear, and when I asked after her I was told she had gone home cured.[13]

Divine healing was common in the early years of the Korea mission and was crucial to church growth. Richard Baird, the son of Annie Laurie Baird and also a missionary, wrote: "In the days when Christianity was in the 'cutting edge' stage of its penetration of Korean society, exorcism was an important church activity. Instances almost identical with New Testament casting out of demons accompanied the starting of many—perhaps most churches in the early days."[14]

Whatever the personal views of the missionaries may have been on the issue of divine healing, they recognized its power as an instrument of conversion. In spite of the official doctrine of cessationism, few were the voices that protested the phenomenon.

Revivalism and Divine Healing

Divine healing in early Korean Protestantism reached its peak under a dynamic revivalist Presbyterian preacher named Kim Ik-tu.[15] Part of a group of Korean ministers who fanned the flames of revival in the 1920s and 1930s, Kim established his fame based on "praying for the sick and demon-possessed."[16] As he traveled throughout the country and to Korean communities in Manchuria and Russia, large numbers of people gathered to be healed of all sorts of diseases and illnesses. Kim was perhaps the most popular preacher of early Korean Protestantism, drawing more people to his revival meetings than anyone else. One hagiography lists his accomplishments as follows: "He led 776 revival meetings, preached 28,000 times, and healed 10,000 persons. Under the influence of Kim's preaching about 288,000 persons became Christians, 185,000 Korean Won was offered, and 200 became ministers. He built 150 new churches and 120 preschools while he enlarged 140 churches and 100 schools."[17] Kim's name was a household word in the Protestant community, known to Western missionaries and Korean believers alike.

Kim's battle against the spirits began from the moment he converted to Christianity. Before the conversion, his family had worshiped many spirits, in particular a "gentleman" spirit and his servant. On the day that Kim confessed his faith as a Christian, his mother had a dream in which the two spirits were expelled by Kim. Interpreting the dream to be a divine message, Kim's mother, wife, and younger sister all converted. Kim, however, immediately experienced a lapse after confessing his new faith; he returned to his old vice of drinking. The missionary biographer Victor Wellington Peters interpreted the lapse as the revenge of the spirits that had been previously expelled from this household: "The evil spirits saw how it turned out and determined not to lose without a struggle."[18] But Kim persevered, and he not only overcame his drinking problem but also embarked on the path to ministry. Kim's newfound faith did not, however, bring an end to the world of spirits. On the contrary, his ministry was one of struggling against the "demons" that stood in the way of spreading the Christian faith. In one instance, Kim exorcised an evil spirit out of a "sorceress," or shaman, but the spirit was so strong that it refused to give up and possessed her father-in-law. Kim then had to perform another exorcism.[19]

From the outset of his Christian ministry, Kim developed a reputation for healing. A few years after his conversion, while working as a preacher and Sunday school teacher in a small village, he had his first avowed miracle. Kim reputedly healed a sick boy through prayer, fasting, and the burning of a shamanistic object of worship in the household. Miraculous healing also seemed to occur in Kim's own family. His wife, Kim Ik-chin, had a sore on her neck, which refused to go away even after three years of treatment at a mission hospital. Kim and his wife decided to pray for healing, and the sore went away.[20] But he also encountered disappointment. Shortly after graduating from seminary and beginning his career as a Presbyterian minister, he tried to heal a crippled man but failed.[21] Subsequently, while leading a Bible class, Kim and a fellow clergyman, who also practiced divine healing, discussed a biblical passage describing the supernatural powers available to believers.[22] Inspired, Kim prayed for the gift of healing. A month later, he claimed to have healed a woman in his church.[23]

Kim's first public healing followed a few months later during a Bible class meeting. With several hundred people present, he reportedly cured a man with a dislocated jaw; again, the method was prayer and fasting over several days. Word spread of his healing powers, and soon thousands were flocking to his meetings to be healed. He soon added a new method of laying his hands on the sick, in addition to praying. His first case using the new method was a girl "with a great swelling in her stomach." Kim was reputed to heal all manner of diseases and illness. At his revival meetings, he was said to make the mute speak and the crippled walk. News of his healings also included curing blindness, paralysis, and hemophilia.[24]

The healing ministry of Kim Ik-tu is noteworthy not only for its role in spreading the Christian faith in Korea; it also had a doctrinal impact. At the height of his popularity, a group calling itself the Miracle Verification Association launched an investigation into the healings and concluded that the miracles were authentic.[25] Subsequently, it submitted a report to the presbytery, leading to debate over the provision on cessationism in the church constitution. In 1923, the Korean Presbyterian Church officially abandoned the doctrine—which is today still privileged by most non-Korean North American Presbyterians. Cessationism could not hold up against the overwhelming presence of the spirits and the supernatural, which dominated the Korean religious landscape. Nor could the doctrine stand up against the New Testament stories of Jesus healing the sick and chasing out demons. Divine healing represented a powerful common ground between the old and the new for the Korean converts, and the age-old promise of saving body and soul became key to the successful propagation of the new religion.

Pentecostal Healing

The tradition of healing in revival services that Kim helped to establish has continued in Korean Protestantism. Following the Korean War (1950–1953), Christianity was virtually eradicated in Communist North Korea, but in the South, it began a new period of growth and development. Numerous revivalist healers attracted large followings. One of the most popular was a Presbyterian elder named Pak T'ae-son, who eventually broke away from the Presbyterian Church to begin his own movement, the Chŏndogwan (Hall of Evangelism).[26] The postwar decades provided fertile ground for the growth of Christianity and new religions. It was in this context that Pentecostalism also started to take off in Korea.

The first Pentecostal missionary to Korea was Mary Rumsey, a product of the Azusa Street revival, who arrived in 1928 when Korea was under Japanese colonial occupation (1910–1945). Rumsey introduced speaking in tongues and other "gifts of the Spirit," and helped to found the first Pentecostal church in the country. Soon, a handful of other congregations began to form. But the outbreak of World War II disrupted the growth and development of the fledgling Pentecostal movement. The Japanese expelled Western missionaries and cracked down on the Christian churches in Korea. The end of World War II and the departure of the Japanese brought little relief as the country became torn apart by the Korean War that soon followed.[27]

Not until the 1960s was Pentecostalism finally able to gain a significant following, and its growth in Korea has become almost synonymous with David Yonggi Cho and his Yoido Full Gospel Church (figure 13.1). Cho was born to a Buddhist family, but he converted to Christianity in his youth while battling tuberculosis and facing death.[28] He experienced healing shortly after his conversion. Subsequently, he worked with Assemblies of God missionaries Kenneth Tice and Lou Richards, translating their sermons and learning the Bible from Richards. Cho had acquired English from American soldiers stationed at a military base near his school. During a period of praying and fasting, Cho avowedly experienced a vision of Jesus, who called him to preach the gospel. After studying at the Full Gospel Bible College, run by the Assemblies of God, he and a former classmate, Jashil Choi, began a church in a tent in a slum area of Seoul in 1958, with the only others in attendance being Choi's three children.[29] This humble tent church eventually developed into the largest church in the world, and divine healing was one of the major reasons for the dramatic growth. Through services at the church and revivals that attracted people from far beyond the confines of the church, claims of cures from various diseases and illnesses spread throughout the city. By 1961, the church had already increased to 600. And the years that followed continued the rapid

FIGURE 13.1. Yoido Full Gospel Church, Seoul, Korea (2010). Courtesy Sean Kim.

growth. The congregation relocated a couple of times to accommodate the increase in numbers, eventually settling in its present location on Yoido island in the heart of Seoul.

Divine healing constitutes an integral part of the worship experience for members of Yoido Church and for Korean pentecostals in general. In a typical Sunday service at a pentecostal church, the minister leads the congregation in praying aloud over individual requests for healing. The prayers are usually highly emotional and often involve weeping and flailing of arms. The cacophony of voices is punctuated by the minister's repeated shouts of "Hallelujah!" or "O Lord!" The minister and deacons may approach and pray with individual members. As they do so, they may perform a laying on of hands or clap one hand on the back or shoulder of the person for whom they are praying. At times, they may also directly address the spirits of disease and illness and command them to leave the afflicted. The services often produce immediate claims of healing (figure 13.2). The ranks of healers are not restricted to the clergy but are open to anyone who has received the gift of healing. Such persons are often invited into private homes to pray for the sick and carry out healing.

In addition to churches and homes, divine healing is also practiced in secluded mountain prayer retreats designed for extended periods of prayer and fasting. Scattered throughout the country and interdenominational in

FIGURE 13.2.  Woman claiming cure of spina bifida in a Korean
divine healing service (2004). Courtesy Brian S. Yeo, M.D. (a) Before prayer.

character, the retreats are often advertised with personal testimonials of healing that have occurred on the premises. At the Osanri Choi Ja-Sil Memorial
Fasting Prayer Mountain, established by the Yoido Full Gospel Church, the
facilities include several chapels for public worship and "prayer grottoes" for
individual prayer.[30]

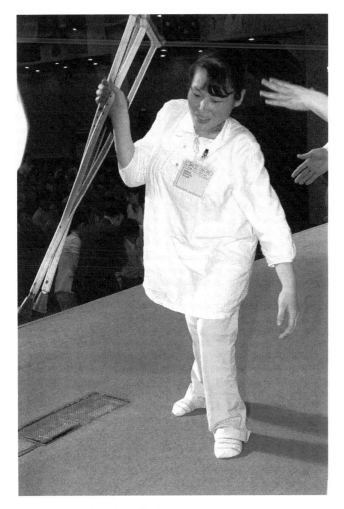

FIGURE 13.2. *(continued)*  (b) During prayer.

## Shamanization?

Although divine healing is a universal feature of pentecostalism, the ways in which it is practiced in Korea have become a source of controversy. Both Korean and Western scholars and clergy, some even within the pentecostal camp, have laid the charge of "shamanism." Critics point to three main features: the trance-like nature of pentecostal experience, the theology of health and prosperity, and the belief in spirit possession and exorcism. Korean pentecostals are accused of having gone too far in their accommodation to native shamanism and thus compromised the integrity of the Christian faith. One prominent Korean scholar, Yoo Boo Woong, points out the similar "structure and worldview" between pentecostalism and shamanism, using Cho as his example: "The only

FIGURE 13.2. *(continued)* (c) After prayer.

difference is that a shaman performs his wonders in the name of spirits while Rev. Cho exorcises evil spirits and heals the sick in the name of Jesus."[31] Yoo is correct in noting the phenomenological parallels between pentecostalism and shamanism, as well as the shared cosmology of spirits.

But beyond these basic, largely surface similarities, the association of pentecostalism with shamanism poses several theoretical problems. To begin with, the term "shamanism" itself is extremely difficult to pin down. By its very nature open and fluid, shamanism displays few boundaries. It has no canon of sacred texts nor ecclesiastical institutions, and it coexists with other religions in a state of mutual interaction, each absorbing the other's beliefs and practices while also exerting its own influence. Hence, the lines between shamanism and other religions are often blurred. What is often labeled shamanism may actually have origins elsewhere. For instance, many of the deities in the shamanistic pantheon derive from Buddhism or Daoism.

Further complicating any attempts at a neat and tidy definition is the extraordinary diversity of shamanism. On one hand, it is highly localized and displays a wide range of regional variations; there are many different types of Korean shamanism in different parts of the country. On the other hand, shamanism is a religious phenomenon found not only in Korea but spread throughout the world. Although it is usually associated with northern and central Asia, it also appears in North America, Africa, Australia, and a host of other places. Korean shamanism has many aspects that distinguish it from other forms, such as the fact that most Korean shamans are women.[32] Some Korean scholars believe that Korean shamanism is so unique that they have stopped using the term "shamanism" altogether and have opted for *mugyo*, or "the religion of *mu*" (the word for a Korean shaman).

In spite of the diversity of shamanism, the many different forms do share one basic feature: the shaman. The classic definition of shamanism was formulated by Mircea Eliade based on the Siberian and central Asian model: a "technique of ecstasy" in which "the shaman specializes in a trance during which his soul is believed to leave his body and ascend to the sky or descend to the underworld."[33] It is this specific skill for "magical flight" that gives the shaman his or her identity. Eliade explains that not all forms of ecstatic experience are shamanic; they must involve magical flight in order to be considered as such. Although some Korean pentecostals may claim visions of heaven in their ecstatic states, "baptism by the Holy Spirit" generally does not entail magical flight above or below. Rather, for the pentecostal, it is God in the form of the Holy Spirit "descending" on the believer.

Another problem with identifying shamanic ecstasy with the pentecostal experience is that in shamanism it is only the shaman, the highly trained ritual expert, who enters into the trance, encounters the spirits, and acquires supernatural powers. Everyone else is a spectator; shamanic ceremonies require little or no audience participation. Hence, while there have been some cases of shamans who converted to Christianity in Korea, the vast majority of Koreans have had no personal experience with the kind of trance that can be properly termed shamanic. In spite of the surface resemblance between shamanic and pentecostal forms of ecstatic experience, it is quite a stretch to argue that there is a carryover from one to the other.

Korean pentecostalism has also been criticized for preaching a gospel of health and wealth, and Cho is at the center of this controversy. According to his theology of the "threefold blessing," Christian faith is about not only saving the soul but also enjoying physical health and material prosperity. The key is to unleash the power of God within the believer: "You can tap that power for your tuition, your clothes, your books, your health, your business, everything! When you go out to preach the gospel you are not preaching a vague objective, a theory, philosophy, or human religion. You are actually teaching people how to tap endless resources!"[34] Shamanism is also oriented toward the physical and material, tapping into the power of the spirits to confer health and prosperity. But to identify Korean pentecostalism with shamanism in this regard loses sight of two broader contexts. First, the focus on material blessings in this world is an aspect not only of Cho's theology or Korean pentecostalism but of global pentecostalism. Whether it is American television evangelists or African preachers, many pentecostals believe that Christian salvation is, as theologian Miroslav Volf puts it, not only spiritual but also material in nature.[35] Cho represents part of this larger current in pentecostalism. Second, although the emphasis on health and prosperity is indeed integral to shamanism, it is not exclusive to shamanism. Rather, it is more accurately an aspect of the broader Korean religious culture, of which shamanism is but one expression. Confucianism has a clear this-worldly orientation. Its ethics deal with how to live life in the here and now, and it also has as its goal the flourishing of one's family across generations. Daoism has a long tradition of cultivating techniques for maintaining health and achieving longevity. And although Buddhism, like Christianity, is a religion of other-worldly salvation, it also has many practices geared toward obtaining the blessings of health and wealth for devotees. Thus, the fact that pentecostalism preaches the availability of health and prosperity makes it part of this general religious and cultural orientation. In a social context, moreover, in which widespread poverty has often threatened survival, a "God who cannot provide the basic needs for survival is not," in the words of the scholar Wonsuk Ma, "a true God, especially when, before conversion, their ancestor spirits were able to 'bless' them."[36] Indeed, pentecostalism has spread in Korea because it has been seen as more, rather than less, effective than other religions in responding to basic human needs in the present life.

Another area in which shamanism receives far more credit than it deserves concerns belief in the spirit world. The diagnosis of illness and disease as spirit possession in Korean pentecostalism has been labeled shamanistic. Indeed, on the surface, there is a direct parallel, for Korean pentecostals—unlike pentecostals in some other cultural contexts—believe that the source of the possession can be not only the devil and his demons but also the troubled spirits of dead relatives and ancestors. In shamanism, the possessing spirit is often a family member who bears a grudge toward the living. To the list of possible grievances, pentecostalism has added the state of having died without becoming Christian. Spirit possession is an essential feature of shamanism, but again, as in the case of health and wealth, it is not exclusive to shamanism. The belief that the spirits of the dead interact with the living is common to Korean religious culture more broadly. The time-honored ritual of ancestor veneration, with roots in the Confucian value of filial piety and also in Chinese folk religion, is based on the principle of offering sacrifices to the spirits of deceased relatives and ancestors to ensure their well-being and to prevent misfortune from falling on their posterity. Buddhism also has numerous rituals for consoling the spirits of the dead. Before the arrival of Christianity in Korea, Buddhism was the main source of funerary rites, and it also had its own tradition of exorcism.[37] Hence, the pentecostal belief in spirit possession and the practice of exorcism can be seen as yet another form of responding to this shared cosmology of spirits.

In addition to the threefold blessing, Cho has also come under fire for his idea of a "fourth dimension," a spiritual sphere that has the power to control and transform the physical world. The fourth dimension resides in the hearts of all human beings and can be accessed through "the development of concentrated visions and dreams in their imaginations."[38] It can then be used for divine healing and other miracles that defy the natural order. Cho's concept of the fourth dimension has been labeled occultism and magic. What has been especially troubling to critics is the idea that the power is available not only to Christians but to anyone who develops the skills to tap into it—for good or evil. But while the fourth dimension is presented in the language of modern science, in particular geometry and psychology, it can also be seen as a twist on the old Korean cosmology of the spirit world. The traditional realm of spirits also has control over the human and natural world, and is accessible to anyone who has the ability and power to tap into it.

Cho's pentecostalism thus represents an adaptation of Christianity to two general currents and patterns in Korean religious culture, namely, the cosmology of spirits and a this-worldly orientation that values the material conditions of life. It cannot simply be reduced to shamanization. Rather, it is part of a broader process of indigenization.

## Divine Healing and Indigenization

Controversy is nothing new to the process of Christian indigenization in Korea. It goes all the way back to the first Western missionaries and the early Korean converts, who debated cessationism in the face of insistence on the reality and immediacy of the supernatural. Kim Ik-tu, the revivalist healer, like David Yonggi Cho, was also accused of being a shaman in Christian guise.[39] The adaptation of Christianity to the Korean cultural and religious landscape has pushed the boundaries of orthodoxy. Critics point to deviations from established models of contemporary belief and practice. For Korean practitioners of divine healing, there is no question about the authenticity of their Christian identity. They deny the association with shamanism and instead turn to the Bible as their ultimate source of validation.

The contested nature of indigenization actually stretches back to the beginning of Christianity itself. As the religion spread from its Jewish origins to the Mediterranean world and beyond, it encountered many different cultures and religions, ranging from Hellenism to paganism.[40] The interactions produced debates and controversies over orthodoxy as well as the formation and rupture of boundaries delineating the nature of the religion. But through this process, Christianity was transformed and took on diverse forms. And it is still evolving today as its global center shifts from Europe and North America to Asia and Africa. Korean pentecostalism represents, in this regard, an important new chapter in the continuing growth and dynamism of Christianity as a global religion.

NOTES

1 Cho initially had the first name Paul, but he later changed it to David. Hence, some of his earlier publications still have "Paul Yonggi Cho."

2 For the "disenchantment of religion," see Max Weber's classic *The Protestant Ethic and "The Spirit of Capitalism,"* trans. Peter Baehr and Gordon C. Wells (1905; reprint, New York: Penguin, 2002).

3 E. B. Landis, "Notes on the Exorcism of Spirits in Korea," *Journal of the Anthropological Institute* (1899), reprinted in Tan'guk Taehakkyo Tongyanghak Yŏn'guso, *Kaehwagi Han'guk kwallyŏn kumi so ch'aekcha mit nonmun charyojip* [Sourcebook of Western Pamphlets and Articles Related to Enlightenment Period Korea] (Seoul: Kukhak Charyowŏn, 2003), 187–188.

4 Homer Hulbert, *The Passing of Korea* (Seoul: Yonsei University Press, 1969), 413.

5 Martha Huntley, *Caring, Growing, Changing: A History of the Protestant Mission in Korea* (New York: Friendship Press, 1984), 124.

6 Donald N. Clark, *Living Dangerously in Korea: The Western Experience, 1900–1950* (Norwalk, Conn.: Eastbridge, 2003), 39–40.

7 Ibid., 140.

8 Ibid.

9 C. A. Clark, "An Explosive Devil," *Korea Mission Field* 4.1 (Jan. 1908): 8.

10 Horace G. Underwood, "Prayer Cure," *Korea Mission Field* 3.5 (May 1907): 68–69.

11 Horace G. Underwood, *The Call of Korea, Political-Social-Religious* (New York: Revell, 1908), 90.

12 Horace G. Underwood, *Within the Gate* (Seoul: YMCA Press, 1934), 69, qtd. in Huntley, *Caring*, 124.

13 Annie Baird, *Inside Views of Mission Life* (Philadelphia: Westminster, 1913), 129–131, qtd. in Huntley, *Caring*, 124–125.

14 Huntley, *Caring*, 123–124.

15 The convention for Korean names is to place the surname first followed by the given name. But in the case of many Koreans who are well known abroad, such as David Yonggi Cho, the order follows that of Western names, with the surname placed last.

16 Harry A. Rhodes, ed., *History of the Korea Mission, Presbyterian Church, U.S.A.* (Seoul: Chosen Mission Presbyterian Church, U.S.A., 1934), 1:289, 235, 290.

17 Moontak Oh, "The Impact of Korean Revival Movement on Church Growth of Korean Evangelical Christianity in 1903–1963" (Ph.D. diss., Southwestern Baptist Theological Seminary, 2000), 126–127.

18 Victor Wellington Peters, "Gold, Good Measure Running Over, Being an Account of Korea's Great Evangelist, Kim Ik Doo [Kim Ik-tu]," part 1, *Korea Mission Field* 21.1 (Jan. 1933): 11.

19 Peters, "Gold," part 2 (Feb. 1933): 37–38.

20 Ibid.

21 Peters, "Gold," part 3 (Mar. 1933): 54–55.

22 Peters, "Gold," part 2, 38. The passage was Mark 16:17–18: "And these signs will accompany those who believe: by using my name they will cast out demons; they will speak in new tongues; they will pick up snakes in their hands, and if they drink any deadly thing, it will not hurt them; they will lay their hands on the sick, and they will recover."

23 Peters, "Gold," part 3, 55. The source does not specify what her condition was.

24 Ibid., 55–57; Min Kyŏng-bae, *Han'guk Kidokkyohoesa* [History of the Christian Church in Korea] (Seoul: Taehan Kidokkyo Ch'ulp'ansa, 1991), 354. Peters also reported an instance when Kim prayed for a paralyzed woman without effect; Kim interpreted this failure as occurring because her husband, though a Christian, had not given up tobacco and ancestral rites.

25 Min, *Han'guk*, 354.

26 Kim In-su, *Han'guk Kidokkyohoe ui yoksa* [History of the Korean Christian Church] (Seoul: Changnohoe Sinhak Taehakkyo Ch'ulp'anbu, 1997), 616–619. For a brief summary of the movement in English, see James Huntley Grayson, *Korea: A Religious History* (New York: Oxford University Press, 1989), 245–247.

27 Donald N. Clark, *Christianity in Modern Korea* (Lanham, Md.: University Press of America, 1986), 12–17.

28 The biographical information on Cho is based on Young-hoon Lee, "The Life and Ministry of David Yonggi Cho and the Yoido Full Gospel Church," *Asian Journal of Pentecostal Studies* 7.1 (2004): 4–5. Lee has been named Cho's successor at the Yoido Church and is also one of the leading scholars of Korean pentecostalism.

29 Cho later married Choi's daughter, Kim Sung-hye. Jashil Choi's name would be spelled Ch'oe Cha-sil according to the conventional McCune-Reischauer romanization system, but many Koreans well known in the West use their own personal spelling.

30 The prayer mountain has an official website: http://www.fgtv.org/n_english/prayer/p._index.asp (accessed 16 Nov. 2009).

31 Yoo Boo Woong, "Response to Korean Shamanism by the Pentecostal Church," *International Review of Mission* 75.297 (1986): 70–74. The first scholarly study of Korean pentecostalism was Yoo's *Korean Pentecostalism: Its History and Theology* (New York: Lang, 1988). Cho has also been attacked by U.S. Christians for engaging in "occultism." See, for example, Hank Hanegraaff, *Christianity in Crisis: The 21st Century* (Nashville, Tenn.: Nelson, 2009), 110–111. The most comprehensive critique of Cho is presented by the Rick A. Ross Institute, an organization that maintains an online database for the study of "destructive cults, controversial groups and movements": http://www.rickross.com (accessed 5 Aug. 2009).

32 Korea is not altogether unique in the predominance of women shamans; for instance, women also outnumber men among Japanese shamans. See also Susan J. Rasmussen's study of women healers in Niger and Mali, *Those Who Touch: Tuareg Medicine Women in Anthropological Perspective* (DeKalb: Northern Illinois University Press, 2006).

33  Mircea Eliade, *Shamanism: Archaic Techniques of Ecstasy*, trans. Willard R. Trask (Princeton, N.J.: Princeton University Press, 1964), 4–5.

34  Paul [David] Yonggi Cho, *The Fourth Dimension* (Plainfield, N.J.: Logos International, 1979), 186.

35  Miroslav Volf, "Materiality of Salvation: An Investigation in the Soteriologies of Liberation and Pentecostal Theologies," *Journal of Ecumenical Studies* 26.3 (1989): 447–467.

36  Wonsuk Ma, "Asian (Classical) Pentecostal Theology in Context," in *Asian and Pentecostal: The Charismatic Face of Christianity in Asia*, ed. Allan Anderson and Edmond Tang (Costa Mesa, Calif.: Regnum, 2005), 66.

37  Roger L. Janelli and Dawnhee Yim Janelli, *Ancestor Worship and Korean Society* (Stanford, Calif.: Stanford University Press, 1982), 58.

38  Cho, *Fourth Dimension*, 38–40.

39  Min Kyŏng-bae, *Ilcheha Han'guk Kidokkyo* [Korean Christianity under Japanese Imperialism] (Seoul: Christian Literature Society of Korea, 1991), 325.

40  For a historical survey of Christianity across the centuries from its origins to the present, see Martin Marty, *The Christian World: A Global History* (New York: Modern Library, 2007).

# 14

# Miracle Healing and Exorcism in South Indian Pentecostalism

*Michael Bergunder*

In a country dominantly shaped by the different traditions of Hinduism, Indian Christians account for just 2 percent of the population. Nevertheless, in South India, where nearly two-thirds of India's 24 million Christians (17 million of whom are Roman Catholic) live, Christianity represents a relatively strong minority.[1] The percentage of Protestant pentecostals (as well as Catholic Charismatics; see Thomas Csordas's essay in this volume) is relatively high with a growing trend; my conservative estimate is that more than 20 percent of South Indian Protestants are now pentecostals. In this chapter, I will argue that the South Indian pentecostal movement owes a great part of its appeal to claims of miracle healing and exorcism, and that certain of these practices exhibit phenomenological parallels to popular Hinduism. It is here where one can most convincingly show that the South Indian pentecostal movement is a quite contextualized version of Indian Christianity. Multicontextuality must also be kept in mind, however, since in most cases, parallels to popular Hinduism are not one-to-one, but are simultaneously found in Indian Christian popular religiosity and elsewhere in the global pentecostal movement.[2]

## Causes of Disease and Misfortune

The demonology of Hindu and Indian Christian folk religiosity largely determines Indian pentecostal views of the etiology of sickness and misfortune. Modern biomedical diagnostics and treatments are not generally rejected as contrary to "faith," but neither are they widely utilized or viewed as unquestionably authoritative.[3] Belief in the existence and activities of evil spirits, as well as the possibility of recourse to black magic through their agency, is widespread in South India among Christians of all confessions. But such ideas are hardly ever expressed by pastors and theologians of established Protestant churches who were educated in Western-influenced theological colleges. Similarly, among Hindus of higher social levels such ideas seem less pronounced or are rejected.

Within the South Indian pentecostal movement, the existence of evil spirits is uncontested, and exorcism is an essential part of pastoral and evangelistic practices.[4] But it is noteworthy that one rarely hears independent statements about the nature of evil spirits; rather, it becomes clear from usual practices that pentecostals have taken over the demonology of Hindu popular religiosity.[5] It is not the case that the whole of Hindu religion is taken as demonic by pentecostals, but exorcism is practically confined to the evil spirits of popular Hinduism (Tamil: *picācu* or *pēy*).[6] In the commonly used Tamil Bible translation, *picācu* (occasionally, *pēy*) is used for "demon" (Greek: *daimonion*) and also for "devil" (Greek: *diábolos*), but "Satan" is a loan word.[7] Translators have theologically anchored the evil spirits of popular Hinduism in the Christian conception of the devil, since *pēy* and *picācu* have become underlings to Satan.[8] In their views on the origin of evil spirits, many pentecostals agree with the conceptions of popular Hinduism that they are the spirits of deceased persons who experienced premature or unlucky deaths. Only a few interviewees viewed demons as fallen angels.[9] In such a conceptual framework, bodily illnesses are one among many types of misfortune in which evil spirits can be involved. For example, demonization can be the cause of marital problems, as in the following testimony from an evangelical rally of the pentecostal ministry Jesus Calls (figure 14.1), a group founded in 1973 by the prominent Indian evangelist D. G. S. Dhinakaran (1935–2008): "I was convulsed very much in the clutches of the devil for the past four months. I used to beat and drive my husband out of the house. Today my elder brother brought me here. During Brother Dhinakaran's prayer, the devil departed from me. I am now very happy."[10]

Illnesses, interpersonal conflict, personal misfortune, failure in family life or in one's profession all fall into the same category insofar as they are attributed to evil spirits or "black magic." A pastor from Madras related a case of a Hindu family attacked by black magic:

> The owner of this house is a Hindu man. He was affected by
> witchcraft. He lost his third daughter. . . . So, two sons. One son is
> insane. . . . one doctor, who used to attend our worship, he said:
> "Pastor, there is a family who is coming [in my practice] for

FIGURE 14.1. Entrance to the prayer tower of Jesus Calls ministry, Chennai, India (2004). Courtesy Michael Bergunder.

treatment. I gave a lot of treatment; nothing has happened. Why don't you go and visit?" At the time they had kept their house locked up for seven years because there was some devil, witchcraft going on. So, they were staying far away, around forty miles away from the city. . . . they were in the hands of a Hindu magician, a Mantiravāti. . . . Totally, they were committed to him, and they were well off. So, the Mantiravāti was getting a lot of money to help them. The Mantiravāti said that he will make them free.[11]

Religious specialists like *mantiravātis* are twilight figures who perform exorcisms but also may offer black magic for payment. This double role of *mantiravātis* is recognized by pentecostals, who often report that *mantiravātis* caused illness or misfortune by black magic.

Within the South Indian pentecostal movement, illness is not, however, only attributed to the possession of evil spirits and black magic, but is also viewed as the result of sin.[12] As one instructional publication explains, "Sickness is in the world because God has allowed sickness to enter the world as a curse on the disobedient human race."[13] This presumed causal connection between sin and illness is not abstract theological speculation but is understood concretely: "Most of the sicknesses seen among people are the direct result of sin."[14] This conception stands in close connection with folk Hindu demonology, where the work of evil spirits and the notion of sin can become connected. An early scholar of popular Hinduism, Bartholomaeus Ziegenbalg, enumerated 69 distinct *pēys* and concluded that, "in summa, there are specifically just as many devils as there are sins."[15] The assumption of such a close relationship among evil spirits, sins, and sicknesses or accidents is consonant with pentecostal thinking and, indeed, pentecostals make lists that relate evil spirits to particular sins.[16]

The sins of ancestors are viewed as bearing upon their descendants, as the following example shows. D. G. S. Dhinakaran recalled a Christian woman telling him: "Sir, our home is a veritable place. All who see us say that we are very much blessed. But we do not get a square meal every day. However much the income may be, it vanishes without a trace." Upon hearing this description, Dhinakaran made "enquiries about her forefathers," which led him to explain the woman's problems as having resulted because her ancestors "had acquired all that wealth unlawfully by ruining many others."[17] Generational curses thus passed through the family line; sins committed by one's ancestors had to be confessed and renounced, and the resulting curses had to be broken before evil spirits could be expelled.

Alongside seeking to identify and counter spiritual trains of causality, pentecostals also recognize natural causes for the onset of disease without necessarily drawing theological conclusions. Dhinakaran gave the following explanation of disease etiology:

> There are countless such microscopic beings which are beneficial to us. There are again microscopic beings in their teeming, millions which are injurious and produce disease. These bacteria and viruses bring harm to our bodies. When infection spreads due to the infestation of these harmful bacteria, physicians inject healing drugs into our system to destroy them, and our bodies are restored to health. At this point some may naturally raise a doubt. The Bible says: "God is Love" (I John 4:8, 16). Why then did He create these harmful bacteria? . . . Can we plumb the depths of His great wisdom? . . . (Romans 11:33–36).[18]

Such an interpretation prevents the notion that every illness must be caused by some specific sin; in its vagueness, the statement is typical for its low speculative interest in such questions. It is not so much the causation of sickness that arouses interest but rather the promise that Jesus, the healer, can cure all diseases. In particular cases, it often remains unclear whether illness and misfortune derive from natural causes, evil spirits, or black magic. There is likewise in popular Hinduism the conception that evil spirits can visit people without any practice of black magic.[19] The determination of each case of sickness or misfortune is a matter of judgment, and often there are different diagnoses of the same case.

## Divine Punishment through Sickness

In many testimonies, pastors and evangelists report that their devotion to full-time ministry resulted through an illness and miraculous recovery. "Divine punishment" is an established motive, but it comes primarily from oral tradition with the exception of one group, which has also published on this topic.[20] Two types of testimony may be distinguished. In one type, the sick person promises God that, if he is healed, he will go into full-time ministry, as did one prominent Tamil evangelist: "In the year 1968, I had a sickness called micro-stenosis in the heart. . . . The doctor said . . . I am going to live just four hours. . . . I said: 'Lord, if You heal me, I will resign my job, and I will step out for the ministry.'" Soon after, the man's doctor pronounced him healed "through the God whom you are worshipping," and he consecrated his life to evangelism.[21] On the other hand, one respected pastor from Bangalore reported becoming ill after refusing a call from God to resign his job and enter full-time ministry:

> At the beginning of 1979 the Lord started to speak to me about my
> calling. Many times and strongly came the call: "Resign the job!" But,
> I did not because the family had a lot of financial problems. . . . But,
> anyhow, by September, God's dealing became heavier and heavier.
> And, [by] September end I was in hospital, October sixth, being on
> the threshold of death, I made a decision, a covenant with the Lord:
> "I know that You call me, and I am running away from Your call like
> Jonah, but I will surrender my life now, and, I will not go back in any
> kind of trade or business, making money. I will serve You full time."
> When I made that decision on October sixth, the Lord healed me.[22]

In this example, God did not "will" sickness but health, but first he required obedience and used sickness as a means to motivate the called person to respond to a call that he had, while healthy, ignored repeatedly.

It can be a great advantage for someone in the healing ministry to have experienced healing himself, as is suggested by a Tamil healing evangelist's interpretation of his experience: "in 1969, I had a terrible sickness with my lungs. . . . one day, Jesus appeared, and said: 'I love you. I want you to know . . . unless you go through sickness yourself, you will never know the agony of My people. Then only, you can really pray with compassion. So, this is the truth, you should know. Now, rise up. And you will carry My love and compassion.'"[23] As soon as the evangelist learned from his sickness, God provided healing.

The theme of divine punishment is extensive. As an explanation for sickness and bad luck, it often goes along with the general view that sickness is a consequence of sin. An outstanding example of this combination was reported by Dhinakaran:

On the 1st day of April 1961, I lost my first child. My parents and all
our relatives wept bitterly. I myself cried bitterly: "O Lord I am
serving Thee. I am preaching Thy Gospel to hundreds. Why have You
dealt with me thus?" The Lord spoke to me in the depths of my
being. . . . I had mistaken impressions about God's anointed servants. I confessed this sin to God. He absolved me. In the years that
followed He blessed me with two other children.[24]

This death of a child presumably resulted from the father's unconfessed sin—
reflecting the idea that blessings and curses can affect not only the individual
but can pass through generational lines. The pastoral consequences of such
views are sometimes hair-raising. In one pentecostal family whose youngest
daughter died very young, relatives blamed the father for causing her death
through his alleged sins.

## Miracle Healing and Exorcism

Miracle healing and exorcism are central to the practice of South Indian pentecostalism.[25] Because South Indian pentecostal etiology does not basically
distinguish between sickness and unfortunate accidents, and because there
is no clarity concerning the place and extent of the activities of evil spirits,
miracle healing and exorcism must be treated together. For our purposes in
this chapter, "miracle healing" often involves exorcism, while "exorcism"
refers specifically to casting out evil spirits. Strictly speaking, miracle healing
should not happen to born-again Christians, since for them the promise of
"divine healing" stands: they are supposed to live a life overcoming sin and,
with it, sickness. But in practice, the distinction is not clear, since born-again
Christians often seek prayers from those with recognized gifts of healing.
The practice of miracle healing as a rule consists of a prayer—often no more
than the short sentence "In the name of Jesus, be healed!"—with the laying
on of hands and anointing with oil. In big rallies, but less often in ordinary
worship, the healing is announced through prophetic gifts. In all this, the
practices associated with prayer for healing are not spectacular.

The case of exorcism is more complicated, and here elements from popular
Hinduism are more influential. Pentecostal exorcists and Hindu specialists
like *mantiravātis* claim the same professional competence, as in the following
Jesus Calls testimony: "My husband drank too much and was breaking up the
family. I used all my money on a Mantiravāti to bring him to his senses. . . .
With this wish I came to the rally. As brother Paul Dhinakaran prayed for
me . . . I had a good feeling in my heart."[26] Between Hindu specialists and
pentecostal exorcists, there are striking phenomenological parallels. The
former seek to affect the world of evil spirits by means of an incantation, called

a mantra; the force exerted can be greater or lesser according to their level of ability. Calling on Jesus—for instance, "In the name of Jesus, come out!"—has definite but external similarities to a mantra. Other pentecostal practices resonate more clearly with Hindu traditions. One recognized exorcist, a well-known Tamil pentecostal leader's wife, says that she requests a visible sign from the evil spirit that it has really gone out. Such a sign could be, for instance, that the branch of a tree breaks off of its own accord.[27] In popular Hinduism, when spirits are driven out, they often pass into trees.[28] Furthermore, a person from whom an evil spirit has been expelled by calling on the name of Jesus with the laying on of hands often falls immediately to the ground in a kind of faint and then revives after a little while.[29]

When pentecostals trace sickness or misfortune to black magic performed by *mantiravātis*, special exorcising rituals include the visible elimination of the presumed tools of sorcery—whether by directly removing physically introduced cursed objects from an inanimate object or by inducing a person who has been attacked by black magic to spit out ritual objects that were presumably introduced through spiritual means. South Indian pentecostals occasionally report exorcising evil spirits from haunted houses. A prominent Tamil healing evangelist was called to pray over a beautifully whitewashed house that its owners had been trying to sell for five years: "With a glass of water, I prayed over it, I started sprinkling. When I came to the four corners, you won't believe, there were four [limes] on four corners which were covered in a white paper, and it was stuck over there. From outside, even the man who whitewashed it did not notice it. So, once that was removed, the house was sold."[30] The evangelist's practice of sprinkling holy water and assuming that the limes were ritually cursed objects reflect a worldview shared by Hindu exorcists.

The exorcism of evil spirits from individuals similarly may involve the expulsion of cursed objects. The prominent leader of a pentecostal Yesunamam church in Kerala attested that black magic had caused a "nervous problem" that caused him to perform poorly in school: "Do you know why I believe it was witchcraft? As the pastor was praying for me, I felt something coming out of my stomach. It was a lemon, a big lemon. While he prayed, I felt I ought to vomit it out. As they prayed, it came out."[31] Similarly, reports circulate of Tamil pentecostal pastors, in the course of exorcisms, discovering little metal tablets (Tamil: *takaṭu*) on which curses had been written, although many pentecostals suspect fraud in such cases.[32]

Even in cases where most pentecostals are convinced of the verity of claims, there is no lack of impressive phenomena associated with exorcism. The following example related by a Tamil pastor in Bangalore illustrates how dramatic an exorcism can appear:

One lady's husband had spent ten thousand rupees to kill her by witchcraft. This was revealed to me [by the Lord]. I said: "Who is that lady here? Your husband has spent ten thousand rupees to kill you. Come forward." So, nobody came. I called three times and then I left it. Then, this lady got up and she came. [She said:] "I am the one. . . . that is the first time, I am meeting pastor T. and he told everything about me." From that distance I looked at her and said: "In the name of Jesus!" She fell flat by the power of God. . . . And, then, she got up. She was having this demon and evil spirits. Three times, she had planned to kill herself. From all those powers of the enemy, she was released completely, with the anointing of God. And her husband was totally shocked. Three months [and] she was still alive. So, again he went to that witchcraft fellow, because he had promised that she would die. When the man came back to him, he said: "I am chanting the maximum evil on her, but something powerful is stopping it."[33]

In a similar context, one well-known pentecostal healing evangelist claimed with some plausibility that he had received threatening letters from an angry *mantiravāti* with the request to refrain from interfering with particular cases of black magic.

In general, it can be said that, in the practice of exorcism, a whole range of phenomenological parallels can be discerned between popular Hinduism and the South Indian pentecostal movement. Nevertheless, the basic particularity of the pentecostal exorcism should not be overlooked. An important fact is that, unlike in the case of Hindu specialists, no payment is taken. In pentecostal exorcism, the evil spirit is identified only in rare cases, and the ritual is comparatively simpler than in Hinduism. But the essential difference lies in that, while the Hindu specialists make use of small divinities or spirits for exorcisms, pentecostal exorcists envision themselves as calling upon the direct power of the one God or issuing commands in the name of Jesus, whose supreme authority no evil spirit can withstand. Thus, in pentecostal exorcism, the traditional Hindu system of references is decisively broken and recentered on the Christian God.

The persons who pray for healing and perform exorcisms play a special role in pentecostal communities, although they always emphasize that it is God who heals. Yet, since God has granted them gifts of healing, they enjoy an exalted status as the ones God has chosen to receive these gifts. Some abuses are inevitable, but it should be noted that within pentecostalism there is an emphasis on God as the one true healer and thus there is a sharp critique of any kind of personality cult. A brochure of the Apostolic Christian Assembly relates an instance in which a woman testified to receiving healing, concluding her remarks: "I gave all the glory to God, who healed me." Rather than encourage the congregation to join the woman in praising God, her pastor insisted that the woman "give the witness more clearly," and publicly asked her probing questions until she "confess[ed] that it was the pastor's prayers which were responsible for the healing she received. This attitude," the brochure lamented, "is yet another reason for discord and strife in the Christian church."[34] This sharp critique implies that religious leaders do sometimes call attention to their own gifting.

For evangelists as much as pastors, a successful ministry is closely connected with recognition of an extraordinary gift of healing. One Tamil evangelist not atypically claimed that his voluntary celibacy had heightened his authority to cast out evil spirits.[35] Recounting an encounter with a possessed person, the evil spirit avowedly spoke through the person, saying: "have you come to torture us? . . . Yes, yes, I know, you are a chap who is not married, no woman has touched your body, that's why you are able to stand before me. No one else yet has been able to do it."[36] Such accounts typically include details that, not coincidentally, affirm the speaker's spiritual authority. Sometimes, pentecostal leaders are more explicit in advertising their particular gifting. Dhinakaran distributed prayer oil, with a label in Tamil saying: "This is oil which Brother Dhinakaran has blessed with his prayer."[37] A drop of this oil was to be applied to the body of a sick person while praying to Jesus for help. Special healing power thus was attributed to oil blessed not just by the name of Jesus or the anointing of the Holy Spirit but by a particular pentecostal wonder worker.

Successful pentecostal healers and exorcists have their counterparts not only in Hindu specialists like the *mantiravātis*, but also in popular Hindu gurus who are believed to perform similar healing miracles and who are often venerated by their followers as *avatāras*, or "divine incarnations." The guru Ramsurat Kumar in Tamil Nadu is credited with healing those given up even by Western doctors with the "Grace" of his presence and a touch of his "Holy Hands."[38] International visitors from as far away as Australia visit Bangalore to receive miracle healing and exorcism through the ministrations of gurus like the well-known Sai Baba.[39] Not surprisingly, then, Dhinakaran, by far the most successful pentecostal healing evangelist, was viewed by Hindus, among whom he had a great following—and quite possibly by some Christians—as an *avatāra*. This attribution does not reflect a mere misunderstanding, as the case of another famous healer-prophet illustrates. During the 1960s, Paulaseer Lawrie acted as an extremely successful pentecostal healing evangelist. He broke with the pentecostals in the 1970s and was thereafter venerated as a Hindu guru and *avatāra*.[40] In both popular Hinduism and South Indian pentecostalism, healing and exorcism practices center on the personality of the miracle worker, who might occasionally move between religious communities.

Of great importance in assessing pentecostal healing and exorcism practices is the question of their effects on congregational practices and on the lives of individual believers. Evangelistic rallies and conventions, with their spectacular healing events, play a distinctive role here. Without any kind of qualification, participants are often promised that "all," "here and now," can experience healing. Given the numerous testimonies published in pentecostal periodicals, there is little doubt that at such events several visitors experience some healing. I have the impression that, in essence, these are quite authentic accounts. This means that, as a rule, healings that are not falsified or fantasized are interpreted and described by both healer and healed as miracles. However, there are also enormous exaggerations and even false reports, and unfortunately, there is a lack of critical research into the reliability and veracity of healing testimonies. Such an investigation would be extremely difficult in the Indian situation. Many cases would doubtless be assessed by scholars as within the range of psychosomatic illnesses or spontaneous cures, and would be explained in that way. But healings do seem to occur that are difficult to explain by the scientific means available to us.[41]

One problem the South Indian pentecostal movement does not seem to recognize is that of only apparent cures. In the extraordinarily stressed situation of the thaumaturgic drama and the apodictic affirmation of the healer, an emotional tension is produced that gives some sick people the feeling that they are healed. But in many such cases, no real healing has taken place. This false belief of being cured by God leads these people, presuming full health, to put medicines aside all too easily. Even if this choice only occasionally leads to such serious consequences, it was distressing for me to observe how, in a big rally, an elderly, disabled man received prayer. Through the suggestive power of the event, the old man was brought onto the stage, walked a few steps without crutches, and testified to his cure at the microphone. Later, I saw how, after the supposed cure, the man was carried from backstage by two strong men and, overtired by the whole effort, finally could no longer move at all. There was no cure to observe—and this was not an isolated case.

Critics of pentecostal healing complain that, at large rallies, all the sick people are promised healing but many go home unhealed. The charge is that expectations of the unattainable are aroused, which leads to disappointment.[42] Such criticism is only partly justified, since there is much to indicate that visitors to these rallies are quite clear that not all will be cured. One visitor to a Jesus Calls rally testified that she had brought her sister "from far away and with much labor and difficulty." The girl had for three years been

> bound by black magic [pillicūṇiyam] and she did not know who she was. There was no place we would not go, no gods [teyvaṅkaḷ] we would not implore to make her well. They all let her down. Out of the belief that she would be cured if she came here, we brought her with great difficulty. When it was time for prayer, . . . a power came down on her. Now she knows who she is and she has a complete cure.[43]

From this typical testimony, it is clear that, even before visiting the rally, many other ways had been tried to obtain a cure. This rather sober and pragmatic approach is often overlooked. People who hope for a miracle healing are at the same time acting experimentally. If they are not healed at this rally, they will, as a rule, try other events and other healers. Although frustrated, they will not give up hope in spite of the disappointment in once again finding no cure. In my estimate, real frustration occurs only in isolated cases.

The big rallies that most people associate with faith healing, although important, are not the only or even the most significant forums where healing prayer occurs. It also has its place in the daily life of the congregation. After each worship service, the pastor lays hands on all who ask for it and prays for their concerns, often with the assistance of recognized elders. When healings seem to result, these are presented as testimonies at the following Sunday's worship. An extremely popular event is weekly fasting prayer, which is organized within local congregations. In general, the power to reinforce the gift of healing is attributed to fasting. Sick people come to the church's fast days and prayer is offered for their healing. Many of the sick also go straight to the pastor—on any day of the week—and he prays for them individually. I can scarcely remember one interview period with a pastor that was not interrupted by a member of the congregation coming to seek prayer for healing or blessing. An important part of the personal care that a pastor exercises in a congregation consists of prayer for healing. Moreover, a large proportion of both male and female lay church members also pray for the healing of family members, other church members, and non-Christian neighbors and friends. The big rallies divert our attention from the fact that a great part of healing prayer goes on rather unspectacularly in the daily practice of the congregation and in the neighborhood.

If an Indian attributes his healing to the prayers of a particular pastor or evangelist, he often joins the corresponding congregation. Perceived miracle healings contribute to a considerable extent to the numerical growth of the pentecostal movement. It is noteworthy how readily healing is attributed to a specific prayer, as the case of 25-year-old student A. shows. He suffered from slight pains that occurred during urination. By chance, he attended a pentecostal rally, where the following words were spoken: "A., you will be cured of an abscess." The next morning, he perceived that the pain had ceased. He concluded that the healing had taken place the day before through prayer at the rally. On the basis of this insight, he left the Catholic Church and became a member of the pentecostal church that had led the rally.

The readiness of Indians to attribute healing to a particular prayer leads to many church plantings. A successful Tamil pastor from Bangalore related how he gathered his first church members through a successful healing. Believing himself called by God to ministry, he printed notices that read: "If the doctors have given up, contact Pastor T." A man soon came asking help for his mother, who had cancer. When Pastor T. went to pray for the woman, he asked the people gathered: "'How many of you believe that Jesus Christ can heal this lady? And, all those who don't believe,'" I said, 'go out of this room.' And, I closed my eyes [to pray]. When I opened my eyes, nobody was there.'" Pastor T.

prayed for the woman and, within a few days, when she began to recover, some of those who knew her joined his church.[44] Similarly, a leading pentecostal pastor from Madras gave a striking description of the role played by healing in founding his independent church. For months, he had no one attending his services except his own family. Then, on New Year's Eve at the midnight service, a family of three living in the same quarter attended the service because they could not get an autorickshaw to go to their non-pentecostal, but Protestant, home congregation. The pastor—despite his apprehensions about how the gesture would be perceived—felt led to lay hands on the man and prophesy: "The Lord is doing a new thing in your life. . . . Receive it now!" Nothing obvious to the pastor occurred at the time, and he felt disappointed when the family slipped out while his eyes were shut for the closing prayer—before he could get their address. But the following day, the family returned, reporting that the man had received healing of a nervous breakdown that had kept him from working for four and a half years. During the prayer, he had experienced heat and his constant shaking had stopped, and the next day his doctor cleared him to return to work. When friends asked what had happened, the man answered, according to the pastor: "'This church.' That's all he said. So, that Sunday morning, we had about thirty-five people for the first time."[45] The only thing that had changed since the previous week was this one man's healing testimony.

Without doubt, miracle healings and exorcisms are one of the main attractions of the pentecostal movement, but they are not the basis on which pentecostal congregations are built. They just represent the contact point for winning church members and, through healing testimonies, they are understood to demonstrate God's power in the life of the congregation. Although healings effectively draw new members, such experiences are insufficient by themselves to retain members over time. One Madras pastor lamented that "some people, they just come for healing. After the healing is over they again are back in their own temples."[46] This pastor admitted that he had baptized 250 people, but only 70 still attended his church. Another Madras pastor explained that if people "experience a healing they stay a while in the congregation but if there is no system [to hold them] they go away again. . . . They come just to be healed and then they go. Once they have come to church they must really see the presence of God. That is our strong point."[47] Successful pastors accordingly devote considerable attention not only to praying for the sick and exorcising evil spirits, but also to building institutions and cultivating an atmosphere in which members perceive themselves to experience the presence of God on a regular basis.

## Divine Healing for Born-Again Christians

In the pentecostal movement, there is generally a promise of healing for born-again Christians that should be distinguished from the miracle healing of which we have been speaking.[48] In South India, the Ceylon Pentecostal Mission (now The Pentecostal Mission [TPM]) expresses the teaching on divine healing with great emphasis: "Jesus came to abolish all causes of death. . . . a Christian can continue to live overcoming sin, sickness, death through Christ, and to serve Him until he is called Home like some of the saints in the Bible. . . . God has promised to grant us length of life preserving us from sickness and death."[49] These general and cautious formulations would probably find agreement among most South Indian pentecostals. But they are complemented in the CPM by a radical oral tradition. True believers are given the promise that they will be healed solely through faith in Christ and that consequently they need take no medicine. Hence, the CPM strongly discourages its members from undergoing any medical treatment. Often, this has led and still leads to fatal cases or to lasting harm that could easily have been avoided. The CPM's founding father, P. Paul, died from an untreated carbuncle on his back, likely aggravated by diabetes. Similarly, a well-known Tamil healing evangelist suffers from a lame foot that was caused by an illness contracted in childhood and not treated because his parents were devoted CPM followers.

Underlying this radical rejection of medical treatment is the view that medical healing is not real healing: "Medical and surgical healings cannot cure the mind and soul, while divine healing heals not only the body, but also the mind and soul."[50] A problematic consequence of this viewpoint is the tendency to explain persistent sickness by saying that one's faith is not strong enough: "That was the reason why he continued to be sick. He always believed that Jesus could heal anyone, *only if it was the will of God*. . . . We must claim our healing against all doubts, fears and symptoms."[51] Typical CPM publications urge the necessity of "claiming" healing by "faith":

> Confess that Jesus has already borne your sickness and carried
> your pain, and therefore provision is already made for your
> healing. It is up to you to claim it by faith. . . . You are sure to be
> healed. Although your symptoms may say that you are still sick,
> stand on the word of God firmly, without wavering, and praise God
> for healing you. God's word says, "With his stripes you are
> healed." What His word says, God will surely confirm. Keep
> praising God for your healing, until He accomplishes what He has
> promised you.[52]

It is noteworthy that almost all other pentecostal churches in South India sharply criticize the CPM for its radical rejection of medical treatment. The pentecostal evangelist Zac Poonen writes:

> There are believers who do not take any medicine when they are
> sick. They do not have any Scripture to base their so-called "faith"
> on. But they imagine that they are "trusting" God. That is exactly like

jumping down from the temple, expecting the angels to provide supernatural protection! [Luke 4:9–10]. Many of them finally die of their sickness—and the Name of Jesus Christ is dishonoured among the heathen, who get the idea that Christianity is the religion of foolish fanaticism.[53]

Of special paradigmatic interest is a detailed critique prepared by E. J. C. Job, a medical doctor who is affiliated with the Assemblies of God.[54] He formerly belonged to the CPM and renounced medical treatment for himself and his family, although practicing as a doctor. After his wife fell ill and no divine healing was available for her, her condition became life threatening, and he decided, in a quandary, to put her in the hospital. There, she successfully underwent surgery and regained her health. On the basis of this key experience, he came to the following conclusion: "[E]ven though the promise of divine healing is available for every child of God . . . the comfort of medical science need not be withheld from them when they are sick and seeking divine healing. God will provide divine healing even when a person is taking medical treatment. They need not fear any judgment from God for using medical treatment."[55] This standpoint, that belief in divine healing can be combined with medical treatment, is today, with the exception of the CPM and churches close to it in teaching, the general and official understanding in the South Indian pentecostal movement.

It should not, however, be concluded that most South Indian pentecostals unreservedly embrace Western medicine. In interviews I conducted, most informants asserted the compatibility of divine healing and medical treatment, while suggesting the superiority of the former. Explanations like the following were common: "If you have strong faith, God can heal you. If you have little faith, go to a doctor, no problem."[56] Similarly, "If there is no faith, and you are not taking medicine, what will happen? Understand? You need faith. If you have faith, you don't need to take any medicine. Without faith not taking medicine is meaningless."[57] Informants most often admitted candidly that they themselves used medical treatment. A minority of pastors and evangelists interviewed asserted that they personally did not need medical treatment. As one prominent evangelist declared: "I believe God keeps disease away from me. So, I am not against people who take medicine, but for me no need. . . . That's all a matter of faith. And according to the faith I have, I take [or don't take]. So, I won't judge anybody."[58] Similarly, another pastor interviewed insisted: "I haven't taken any treatment for the past 24 years [since the time of his conversion]. I believe in divine healing. But, people who are taking medicine, I am not condemning them. It is up to their level of faith."[59] It is not only in the CPM that medical healing is viewed as inferior to divine health, but generally in the South Indian pentecostal movement a similar theological view is widely shared.[60]

Even in CPM churches, many laypersons and pastors—despite official proscriptions—admitted to accepting medical treatment when they became seriously ill or injured. This pragmatic approach seems to be the rule. Tellingly, when there was a tragic accident on a CPM Sunday school excursion in May 1994, the congregation prayed for God's help without attempting to transport the seriously injured to the hospital. In the Tamil weekly that commented in detail on the accident, it was noted that first aid is unknown in India and that, even after those injured reached a state hospital after accepting the generous offer of help from bystanders, in the end no emergency medical help was available.[61] Such events point to a further aspect worth consideration. As a rule, no medical treatment that deserves the name is available to the poorest levels of Indian society, and state hospitals are often in a catastrophic condition. Consequently, the rejection of medicine for poor people is only a theoretical affair without practical effect. Indeed, the rejection of medical treatment, which was formerly widespread in non-CPM pentecostal churches, was given up by a large proportion of the pentecostals who have risen into the more prosperous levels of society and for whom medical treatment in expensive private clinics has suddenly become a genuine alternative.

Sometimes, even the combination of conventional medical treatment and prayers for divine healing fail to produce a cure, yet South Indian pentecostals steadfastly affirm their belief that the Christian God is the Great Physician. The moving witness of a woman from Kerala, who died of cancer and believed to the end in divine healing, is an example. Her husband published a book describing his wife, Grace's, suffering:[62]

> Grace read many books on "healing"[;] she held the view that God would heal her completely in spite of the medical verdict. One of the first things she mentioned to me, as soon as the diagnosis of cancer was conveyed to her, was that we pray only positively for healing and not negatively at all. At times when friends prayed for her in a doubting manner by saying "if it is God's will, let her be healed completely," she took objections to such prayers and told me to inform such friends to change their attitude to pray only in a positive way. . . . It became a fact that her physical condition deteriorated very rapidly; we had to stop further chemotherapy; she was unable to take solid food, even liquid food only in very small quantities and that too not very frequent, unable to sit up. For all intent[s] and purpose[s] one finds it difficult to see complete physical healing.[63]

Out of Grace's faith in divine healing arose an unshakeable will to live. Although she received treatment at the best hospital in South India in vain, she hoped to the end that God would heal her. As she approached death, it became clear that her faith in divine healing was the consequence of an iron-hard confidence in God. Her husband wrote:

Therefore it became necessary to prepare Grace for a change of
attitude towards the whole question of complete physical healing. . . .
On the night of March 8th, Grace raised the question of her complete
healing again. I took the opportunity to lead her to a change of
attitude by explaining once more what I had told her a few times
before, the three levels of healing—physical, mental, spiritual. She
agreed with me that she had already obtained complete spiritual
healing as she had reconciled completely with God and with man
thus establishing a perfect vertical and horizontal relationship. . . . At
this stage Grace said: "Yes, Lord, whether we live or whether we die,
we belong to the Lord. I don't make any demands on you. I obey you
completely. I completely surrender to you, Lord. Use me as you like. I
am just clay and you are the potter. Mould me as a potter would
mould the clay. Let your will be done on me."[64]

Grace's experience illustrates how faith in divine healing can be preserved even
in the face of sickness and death. Seen from a medical point of view, Grace's
unshakeable will to live was certainly not a negative factor that would have hin-
dered a successful biomedical treatment, rather the opposite. Viewed theologically, because of her conviction Grace was able to accept her death with
composure and to clarify the basis of her faith in the God she trusted to heal her.

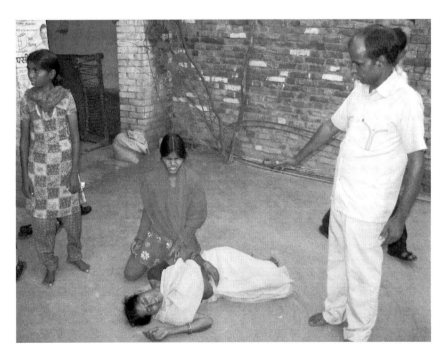

FIGURE 14.2. Pentecostal exorcism, rural India (2010). Courtesy John Samuel.

## Perspective

Questions of religious healing are a central part of the South Indian pentecostal movement. Miracle healing and exorcism play a prominent role in congregational life (figure 14.2). Many such healing practices exhibit phenomenological parallels to popular Hinduism indicative of the contextualization of Christianity in South India. However, much missionary activity takes place on a personal level in families, in neighborhoods, or among workmates or fellow students, usually without the direct intervention of pastors. For pastors, important opportunities for mission occur during house visitations. The spectacular nature of miracle healing and exorcism must not overshadow the fact that the missionary success of the pentecostal movement in South India is also very much based on individual communication and intensive pastoral care.

### NOTES

This essay was adapted, and significantly modified for the present volume, from Michael Bergunder, *The South Indian Pentecostal Movement in the Twentieth Century* © 2008, Wm. B. Eerdmans Publishing Company, Grand Rapids, Michigan. Reprinted by permission of the publisher, all rights reserved. My fieldwork was done during the years 1993–1995.

1 "Census of India," Office of the Registrar General and Census Commissioner, India (2001), http://censusindia.gov.in (accessed 8 Sept. 2009).

2 Bergunder, *South Indian Pentecostal Movement*, 123–129.

3 For the cultural dependency of diagnoses, see D. Sich, H. J. Diesfeld, A. Deigner, and M. Habermann, eds., *Medizin und Kultur* [Medicine and Culture] (Frankfurt am Main, Germany: Lang, 1993).

4 This chapter uses the term "exorcism" to describe the general practice of casting out evil spirits. Related terms like "deliverance" often confer more specific meanings in the Indian context.

5 For pentecostal appropriations from popular Hinduism, see the British anthropologist Lionel Caplan's *Religion and Power: Essays on the Christian Community in Madras* (Madras, India: Christian Literature Society, 1989), 32–71.

6 Ibid., 65, indicates that many pentecostal healers admit the possibility that one of the higher gods, e.g., Murugan or Ganesh, could on occasion possess people like evil spirits. But, as far as I know, in the overwhelming majority of cases, exorcism is concerned with evil spirits.

7 R. N. Asirvatham, *Paricutta Vētākama Ottavākkiya Viḷakkavurai (Paḷaiya Tirupputal)* [Concordance to the Tamil Bible (O.V.)] (1961; reprint, Madras, India: Evangelical Literature Service, 1994), 467–468, 505–506. In the Revised Version, *picācu* is almost everywhere replaced by *pēy*. Also see the Catholic Tamil Bible, 3rd ed. (Tindivanam, India: Tamilnadu Biblical Catechetical and Liturgical Centre, 1986), which has *pēy* throughout. See Michael Bergunder, "The 'Pure Tamil Movement' and Bible Translation: The Ecumenical Thiruviviliam of 1995," in *Christians, Cultural Interactions, and India's Religious Traditions*, ed. Judith M.

Brown and Eric Robert Frykenberg (Grand Rapids, Mich.: Eerdmans, 2002), 212–231.

8  E.g., Mark 3:22–27, and synoptic parallels.

9  Caplan, *Religion and Power*, 54–55.

10  *Jesus Calls* (Apr. 1995): 30.

11  Interview. Names and dates of interviews are omitted to protect the identities of informants.

12  See Pentecostal Mission (CPM), *Divine Healing Messages* (Madras, India: Pentecost Press Trust, 1986); CPM, *Divine Healing* (1980; reprint, Madras, India: Pentecost Press Trust, 1994); Apostolic Christian Assembly, *Spiritual Questions* (Madras, India: Divine Deliverance Publication, n.d.); D. G. S. Dhinakaran, *Healing Stripes* (Madras, India: Jesus Calls, 1979); E. J. Chandran Job, *Guide to Divine Healing* (Bombay, India: Job, 1989).

13  Job, *Guide to Divine Healing*, 37.

14  Ibid., 36.

15  Bartholomaeus Ziegenbalg, *Genealogie der Malabarischen Götter* [Genealogy of the Malabarian Gods] (Madras, India: Christian Knowledge Society's Press, 1867), 186.

16  E.g., Ebenezer Gnaniah, *Deliverance from Darkness to Light* (Madras, India: Eleventh Hour, 1994), 50–57.

17  Dhinakaran, *Healing Stripes*, 16.

18  Ibid., 5.

19  Caplan, *Religion and Power*, 44.

20  CPM, *Divine Healing*, 20–30, does cite specific biblical precedents, e.g., Numbers 12:1–15; 2 Samuel 12:15–19; 2 Kings 5:27; 2 Chronicles 16:12–13, 21:4, 13–20, 26:16–21; Daniel 4:30–37; Revelation 5:1–10, 12:20–23, 13:6–12; 1 Corinthians 5:5.

21  Interview.

22  Interview.

23  Interview.

24  Dhinakaran, *Healing Stripes*, 18–19.

25  See Miroslav Volf, "Materiality of Salvation: An Investigation in the Soteriologies of Liberation and Pentecostal Theologies," *Journal of Ecumenical Studies* 26.3 (1989): 447–467, for an interpretation of the prominence of healing practices in pentecostal churches as reflecting the concept that salvation encompasses a material as well as a spiritual dimension.

26  *Iyēcu aḻaikkiṟār* [Jesus Calls] (Mar. 1995): 34.

27  Interview.

28  Michael Moffatt, *An Untouchable Community in South India: Structure and Consensus* (Princeton, N.J.: Princeton University Press, 1979), 244–245.

29  Robert Caldwell, *The Tinnevelly Shanars* (1849), abridged version in Bartholomaeus Ziegenbalg, *Genealogy of the South-Indian Gods: A Manual of the Mythology and Religion of the People of Southern India, Including a Description of Popular Hinduism* (Madras, 1869), 165; Moffatt, *Untouchable Community*, 242.

30  Interview.

31  Interview.

32  This form of black magic is mentioned also by Richard Froelich, *Tamulische Volksreligion: Ein Beitrag zu ihrer Darstellung und Kritik* [Tamil Popular Religion: A Contribution to Its Representation and Criticism] (Leipzig, 1915), 15.

33  Interview.

34  Apostolic Christian Assembly, *Spiritual Questions*, appendix, 6–7.

35  The specific idea that spiritual power can be increased by celibacy is widespread in the South Indian pentecostal movement, although celibacy is only obligatory in CPM and a few small churches.

36  Interview.

37  "Āttuma, Carīra, Piṇi Nīkkum Jepa Eṇṇey" [Prayer Oil That Takes Away Disease of Body and Soul] (Madras, India: Jesus Calls Ministry, n.d.).

38  Ranganayaki Srinivasan, *Bhagwan Sri Yogi Ramsuratkumar: His Divine Life and Message* (Nagercoil, Tamilnadu: Yogi Ramsuratkumar Manthralayam Trust, 1991), 24.

39  K. R. Paul and Lydia Paul, *Eṅkaḷ Cātciyum Capaiyiṇ Ūliyamum* [Our Witness and Our Congregational Work] (Bangalore, India: Gospel Prayer Hall, 1977), 29–30; Vinayak Krishna Gokak, *Bhagavan Sri Sathya Sai Baba: The Man and the Avatar, an Interpretation*, 3rd ed. (New Delhi: Abhinav, 1989); Joel D. Mlecko, "The Guru in Hindu Tradition," *Numen* 29 (July 1982): 50–56.

40  Michael Bergunder, "From Pentecostal Healing Evangelist to Kalki Avatar: The Remarkable Life of Paulaseer Lawrie alias Shree Lahari Krishna (1921–1989)," in *Christians and Missionaries in India: Cross-Cultural Communication since 1500*, ed. Robert Eric Frykenberg (Grand Rapids, Mich.: Eerdmans, 2003), 357–375.

41  See the cases described by Werner Hoerschelmann, *Christliche Gurus* [Christian Gurus] (Frankfurt am Main, Germany: Lang, 1977), 244, 268, 270, 349.

42  Klaus Schäfer, "'Demonstration of the Spirit and of Power': A Necessary Critical Note on the Recent Mass 'Healing Festival' in Hyderabad," *Bangalore Theological Forum* 25.2–3 (June-September 1993): 40.

43  *Iyēcu aḷaikkiṟār* [Jesus Calls] (July 1995): 32.

44  Interview.

45  Interview.

46  Interview.

47  Interview.

48  Vernon L. Purdy, "Divine Healing," in *Systematic Theology*, rev. ed., ed. Stanley M. Horton (Springfield, Mo.: Logion, 1995), 489–525.

49  CPM, *Divine Healing Messages*, 61, 64–65.

50  CPM, *Divine Healing*, 40.

51  Ibid., 86.

52  CPM, *Divine Healing Messages*, 82; the verse referenced is Isaiah 53:5.

53  Zac Poonen, *Know Your Enemy: A Guide for Young People to Overcome Satan* (Katunayake, Sri Lanka: New Life Literature, 1994), 26.

54  Job, *Guide to Divine Healing*.

55  Ibid., 115.

56  Interview.

57  Interview.

58  Interview.

59 Interview.

60 See the similar arguments made by African American Word of Faith inform-ants in Bowler's essay in this volume.

61 *Jūṇiyar* [Junior] [Madras] (11 May 1994); *Nakkiraṇ* [Critical Enquirer] [Madras] (14 May 1994).

62 The couple belonged to the Church of South India and were influenced by a Charismatic circle of St. Andrew's Cathedral in Sydney, Australia; K. M. George, *Grace through Gate of Cancer* (Punnaveli, Kerala: George, 1991), 36.

63 Ibid.

64 Ibid., 36–37.

# 15

# Divine Healing and the Growth of Practical Christianity in China

*Gotthard Oblau*

I will never forget my talk with Dr. Wang. As a young medical researcher, he studied in my German-language class at a university in eastern China in the late 1980s. He was a typical intellectual who, after decades of cultural isolation, class struggle, and ideological indoctrination in Marxist and Maoist thought, had embraced the opportunities occasioned by China's new policy of openness and reform. One day, during a break between classes, Wang took me aside and, using his newly acquired language, pointedly asked me: "Mr. Oblau, you are a Christian. I am not, and I know nothing about religion. But please tell me, what difference does your religion make? What is the difference between your life as a Christian and my life as an atheist?" When I started to talk about my religious observation, including Sunday worship and Bible reading, he responded impatiently: "This is all about religion, which I do not understand. But what difference does it make in your normal, everyday life?" I am afraid that I did not give Dr. Wang a satisfying answer. As a Lutheran Christian from Germany, who was accustomed to understanding religious faith as the cultivation of one's inner being, I was being confronted with a Chinese man who took it for granted that any meaningful religion has practical effects for people's everyday lives.

In subsequent years, my employment from 1985 to 1997 with a Chinese Christian aid agency, the Amity Foundation, gave me ample opportunity to travel the country far and wide, to meet with Christians and non-Christians, with church leaders and congregations, with local officials and professionals of various kinds in urban and rural areas. I did this in a country in which Christianity had never had a strong tradition and Christian believers accounted for 3–5 percent of the overall population, and I did it at a time when Protestant communities were growing so rapidly that the majority of all Protestants were first-generation Christians. With Dr. Wang's question in mind, I now asked why Chinese people decided to become Christians and what the practical effects were for their individual lives and communities. When I asked social elites—church leaders, state officials, urban intellectuals—who, like most Chinese intellectuals, shared an implicit Confucian mindset, they emphasized the moral and ethical fruits of Christian religion: Christians pay their taxes, are diligent workers, refrain from gambling and drinking, etc. When, in contrast, I talked to people at the grassroots level, I heard countless stories about healing experiences, prayers for the sick, and the physical blessings enjoyed by the faithful.[1] My impressions corresponded with those of many other international observers and Chinese colleagues.

Testimonies about divine healing experiences are a regular and widespread phenomenon among Protestant Christians in China. Strikingly, they are not limited to particular denominations or specific Christian traditions. In China, one need not be a Pentecostal or Charismatic to believe in or experience divine healing. It permeates Protestant Christianity as a whole and appears to be a mainline phenomenon in official and unofficial churches, in registered and unregistered congregations, in rural and urban communities. Equally striking is the fact that, among China's Protestant Christians, prayers for the sick tend to be a democratic practice. All in all, no special healing gifts are perceived as needed, no particular healing ministries relied upon. Healing crusades are unheard of, and special church services for the sick appear to be uncommon. The Chinese understanding of the classic Protestant principle of the priesthood of all believers is that any Christian can say a simple prayer for somebody else's recovery, while the actual miracle is expected from God's supernatural power and the corresponding faith of patients or their entire fellowship.

This chapter explores conditions in the Chinese context that may explain why Chinese Protestant Christianity and divine healing testimonies are so broadly and solidly linked together. It must be admitted, however, that this essay is based mainly on anecdotal evidence. As of 2010, almost no religious field studies by international researchers have been possible in China. There are a few exceptions, undertaken without official permission from China's authorities and restricting themselves to urban areas.[2] In China's towns and villages, however, any structured religious research would attract much attention and hence not be possible without government approval. For Chinese researchers of religion, employed by state-run academies, institutes, and universities, the empirical and descriptive approach of field studies is a new method of research. The few studies there are have been done in big cities, be it for reasons of political restriction, convenience, or both.[3] Hence, the following conclusion reached in 2008 by British China-watcher Edmond Tang holds true: "Access to field research is restricted, and reports on the religions are heavily 'packaged' by both the government and the churches themselves, both inside and outside of China. Consequently, our knowledge of the contemporary development of Chinese Christianity remains fragmentary and anecdotal. This is especially true of the situation of Chinese Protestantism."[4] This chapter draws on nine years of field experience to help explain how divine healing practices have contributed to the dramatic growth of Chinese Christianity.

## Divine Healing in a Post-Denominational Context

The fact that, in China, divine healing experiences are not restricted to Pentecostal churches but appear to be a general Protestant phenomenon has first of all to do with China's post-denominational situation. Before the Western mission era in China came to an end in connection with the Communist revolution in 1949, foreign missionaries had imported their denominations into China, and Pentecostals, many of them from Scandinavia, had been among them. While foreign missions were still building their own ecclesial institutions in China, indigenous denominations came into being in the early twentieth century. At the end of the 1940s, of the approximately 700,000 non-Catholic Christians, over 100,000 belonged to the indigenous pentecostal Zhen Yesu Hui (True Jesus Church); in the mid-1990s, it claimed over a million adherents in China and had established churches in Southeast Asia and North America.[5] Even more influential were indigenous movements and independent Chinese evangelists who were not explicitly pentecostal but who spread a pentecostal-style fervor and spirit throughout the country. A Holiness movement manifested itself in 1931 in Shandong Province, emphasizing visions, dreams, exorcisms, divine healing, and glossolalia.[6] John Sung (1901–1944), an independent preacher, toured all of China and Southeast Asia, and his daughter Song Tianying played a formative role in the independent house church movement in the 1970s–1980s.[7] They and others, including Leland Wang and Wang Mingdao, were popular speakers at meetings and rallies that extended beyond denominational divisions. By 1949, indigenous churches accounted for about one-quarter of all Protestant Christians in China. As theologian Philip Wickeri observes, these churches typically claimed to have "recovered true biblical teachings based upon apostolic principles which were untainted by modern perversions of the gospel. . . . [Their leaders] jumped back two thousand years to biblical times, discarding much of what happened in between with the singular exception of the Protestant Reformation."[8]

Soon after the Communist revolution in 1949, most foreign missionaries had to leave the country, and overseas mission boards had to stop their financial support to mission-established churches in China. Institutional denominational structures, both Western and indigenous, were forcibly disbanded and by the late 1950s were no longer in existence. About 3 million Chinese Christians nurtured their faith despite persecution during the Cultural Revolution (1966–1976), with many of them meeting in informal, private, or even clandestine gatherings. Since then, China's Protestant Christianity has undergone tremendous growth. Today's estimates vary between 20 and over 100 million believers, with the most credible figures lying within the range of 30–40 million Protestants and perhaps 14 million Catholics.[9] Protestant Christians gather in local churches, at meeting points,[10] and in private homes (figure 15.1). All those local establishments are more or less independent, supporting themselves and managing their own affairs. They are not isolated from each other, though. Formal and informal, official and unofficial networks of Christian communities have evolved, providing translocal support and regional representation.

The most established, formal, official, and state-sanctioned of all those networks is the one governed and nurtured by the China Christian Council (CCC), which was founded in 1980 and has since organized itself from the national level through provincial and municipal levels down to most counties. Yet even the CCC is by no means an institutionalized church, but still a network of more or less independent Christian churches, without even a formal membership. The Christian councils at all levels serve the churches by providing Bibles,

FIGURE 15.1. Chinese village church meeting in a warehouse (2008). Courtesy Kim Bennett.

hymnals, and Christian literature; organizing Bible classes and theological training; giving advice in all matters of church life; and liaising between churches and government authorities. A great number of Christian groups keep their distance from the CCC. They are usually called "house churches," but the term is misleading since within the CCC network there are countless congregations meeting in private facilities, whereas more and more Christian groups not affiliated with the CCC have erected church buildings. Some of these non-CCC-affiliated churches have registered directly with the government, while presumably the majority have not.

In contrast to the assumptions of many international observers, the divide between Christian communities which are affiliated with the CCC and those which are not should not be overestimated. There is no such thing as the "state-sanctioned church" over against the "underground church" or the "house church movement." There are more continuities than schism. The two sides do not differ much in spiritual orientation, liturgical style, or political behavior, with most groups following a low-church, Bible-centered pattern of worship, and most Christians nurturing an apolitical, pietistic, and family-centered faith life. Charismatic and Pentecostal elements, too, are to be found both in CCC-affiliated and non-affiliated circles, and likely among Catholics as well as Protestants. Emotional worship with weeping, wailing, and a "prayerful noise" is widespread in China, as is the belief that faith in Jesus and an active prayer life have an empowering and transforming effect on people's lives here and now as well as in the afterlife (figure 15.2). Also, a fierce sense of independence, which is so typical for pentecostal groups and individuals, is to be found among many Christian groups in China, making the attempt by the CCC to build up a unifying national church an arduous task. All in all, it may be fair to claim that China's Christianity as a whole carries a strong pentecostal flavor. In this context, divine healing is neither a sectarian nor a denominational but rather a mainline phenomenon.


## Divine Healing as Part of the Priesthood of All Believers

A visitor to a Sunday service in a Protestant church in China, be it in Shanghai or in a rural town, can observe typical scenes taking place after the final hymn is sung and as the crowd of worshipers gradually disbands. Little groups remain in the sanctuary, kneeling at the steps before the altar or sitting in the pews, lost in prayers murmured under their breath. Others stand in the aisle conferring with an elder or usher, or line up to speak to the pastor and to receive his or her personal blessing. Worshipers unload their personal burdens, and volunteers offer their prayers.

Sick people go to church to have someone pray for them. The laying on of hands during such prayers is rarely seen. Gestures learned and practiced by

FIGURE 15.2. Church service in a Chinese city (2008). Courtesy Kim Bennett.

non-ordained Christians are usually restricted to kneeling, lowering the head, and folding the hands, while the laying on of hands appears to be reserved for ordained evangelists and ministers. Prayers for the sick, present or absent, are also common in midweek Christian meetings and in prayer and Bible groups, whether they convene in churches or in private homes. Church members pay visits to fellow believers who are sick at home or in the hospital. Many congregations organize rosters of people responsible for such visits. It is clear that Christians in China who fall ill will seldom have to suffer in isolation but will become the center of loving attention from their congregation. Healing prayers for non-Christians are not uncommon either. Individual Christians may pray for sick family members, neighbors, colleagues, or people who share their hospital ward. In praying for those unfamiliar with Christianity, Chinese Christians commonly disavow their own gifting and emphasize God's agency in healing. Thus, Zhang Guangming, an almost illiterate peasant evangelist in Yunnan Province, tells non-Christians requesting his healing prayer: "I will gladly pray for you to my God. But if you don't recover, you must not blame me. And if you recover, you should not thank me but give thanks to my God."[11]

Among Christians in China, there appears to be a common conviction that any single believer can pray for the sick and expect healing, as countless testimonies like the following reflect: "When my son started to get worse, I became more and more desperate . . . but there was an old woman in the hospital who believed in Jesus. Pretty soon she kept coming and praying with me for the child. And then he started to get better."[12] As international observer Claudia Währisch-Oblau concludes:

> It cannot be stressed enough that prayers for the sick in China take place "democratically," i.e., without any one person specifically assigned to this role and with virtually no fixed ritual applied. Illiterate peasant women as well as university professors and pastors ordained decades ago, as well as newly converted Christians, all pray for those who are sick, without any sense that a special gift or training is needed for this. This is possible because of the extreme simplicity of procedures: There is rarely any laying on of hands, no anointing with oil, no ecstatic prayers, no falling and "resting in the Spirit," no holy water, no specific place or situation for healing prayers.[13]

Such simplicity corresponds with the style of lay worship that became common during the times of religious persecution, when church buildings were closed and pastors sent away for manual labor. Simple hymn singing, praying, Bible reading, and some sharing of religious encouragement or admonition became the standard elements of worship, all performed by the laity and often by people with sketchy formal training.

This typically Chinese low-key approach to divine healing is also, at least in part, caused by the political climate. The little fanfare with which Christians practice their healing prayers may be seen as an act of self-protection of the church in a country whose constitution states that "no person is permitted to use religion to conduct counterrevolutionary activities or activities which disrupt social order [or] harm people's health" and where influential party theoreticians count the practice of "exorcising spirits to cure illnesses" among the "feudal superstitious activities" that are incompatible with socialism and China's modernization.[14] This concern presumably also accounts for the relative absence, or at least invisibility, of an emphasis on prayers for deliverance from demonic oppression.

## Divine Healing as an Entry Point into Christian Faith

Due to the tremendous growth of Chinese Christianity since the late 1980s, the overwhelming majority of China's Protestants are first-generation Christians. Based on estimates from the Chinese church, at least half of them became Christians because they were motivated by a healing experience, either a personal one or one observed in the family.[15] According to many local Chinese Christians and my own random observations, this figure may be as high as 80–90 percent.

Christian believers tell neighbors and friends who are ill that they should believe in Jesus for their recovery. Conversely, due to the numerous divine healing experiences reported, especially in the countryside, non-Christians who fall ill and do not find a cure in the established medical system often seek out Christians and ask them for prayers so that they can be healed. The following testimonies are typical:

> I used to be a party member. . . . So of course I was an atheist, I didn't believe in anything. But then my daughter contracted some kind of heart disease. . . . We were so poor; we didn't have much money for expensive treatments. At that time, someone introduced the Gospel to me. I started to pray and became a believer. . . . My daughter also believed. After ten days, she could leave the hospital because she was much better. After that, my whole family became Christian. . . . And the really miraculous thing is: Since then, none of us has ever been back to the hospital ever. We didn't have to spend one penny on health care![16]

Similarly:

> My neighbor fell seriously ill. She was hospitalized, but the doctors couldn't help her. . . . She tried what she could to regain her health. Finally she said, "I will try and become a Christian now, then the other Christians will come to pray for me. Perhaps that will help." The woman was indeed healed![17]

The connection between religious conversion and recovery from illness may not always be as utilitarian as the above testimonies suggest. Practiced in a natural, democratic way by laypeople, healing prayers are not so much conducted as an official, isolated ritual but are rather part and parcel of a loving, comforting, and supportive attention in general. More often than not, it is the apparent commitment and human warmth with which church representatives keep visiting their members in the hospital rather than any spectacular recovery that makes Christianity attractive for doctors and for other patients who observe this. Although, in China, loyalty and love within the family are still more common and intense than in the West (though the mobilizing forces of the free market economy have already changed that to a great extent), what makes Christianity so attractive in China is the expansion of traditional family values to the extended family of the church. That people help each other though they are not blood relatives causes astonishment and admiration from outsiders. Even when prayers do not seem to result in total, immediate cure, those receiving prayer are often observed to experience a betterment of life, in terms of social support, nurturing human relationships, and improved living conditions, which may also have positive effects on physical well-being. In this sense, a personally experienced health crisis, help received, and betterment felt mark the starting point for the majority of people who affiliate with China's Protestant churches.[18]

## Divine Healing in a Context of Poor Medical Care and Daoist-Inspired Self-Help

In China, religious preoccupation with matters of health and physical well-being is fueled by two specific factors: culture and economics. At the socioeconomic level, there is an obvious and scandalous absence or insufficiency of medical care for the majority of the population. Although medical science has a long history in China, medical care has long benefited a privileged elite only. This is partly true even today after 60 years of socialism. Medical care in China is not free, and often doctors must be bribed to gain their full attention. Health insurance systems are nonexistent in rural areas, and large segments of China's peasant population can simply not afford to seek sound treatment in the cities, while the cheaper doctors at the village and township levels are usually poorly trained. In the mid-1990s, a World Bank report cited severe or chronic illness as the number one cause of impoverishment in China, and impoverishment causes or exacerbates much disease.[19]

Countless Chinese healing testimonies reflect a real socioeconomic problem when they recount how doctors could not help or hospital treatments had exhausted all available resources before Christian believers were found who could help through their prayers. Unlike in other developing countries, traditional medicine is no alternative for the poor. Traditional Chinese medicine (TCM) has become a field of official scientific study, and today it is part and parcel of the established health care system, alongside Western medicine; although sometimes less expensive, TCM is still often unaffordable. Although anti-medical sentiments are occasionally expressed by non-CCC churches (official CCC publications exhort the sick to visit doctors rather than rely exclusively on prayer), often the primary factor pushing reliance on prayer alone is the economic and geographic inaccessibility of medical treatment.

In addition to the socioeconomic reality, there is also a cultural factor to be reckoned with. Chinese people have always put a strong focus on human health, diet, and physical energies. Most people in China act as their own health experts, ever eager to recommend to others their own personal remedies, readily sharing pills and concoctions. It should be no surprise that Daoism, the only truly indigenous Chinese religion, has a lot to say about the topic. Daoist alchemy forms the basis of TCM, and in all schools of Daoism physical well-being is seen as an outward sign of the believer's harmony with the Dao, whereas illness is understood as a symptom of religious imperfection. Perhaps the most prominent teaching in this respect can be found in the Daoist Five Pecks of Rice sect, which was very influential during the Song

Dynasty (960–1279) and almost exclusively dedicated to health issues. It developed sophisticated theories about the connection between sin and sickness, repentance and healing.[20] Spiritual purification, sometimes exercised in special chambers of silence, was viewed as going to the root of sickness as it enabled believers to combat the evil spirits responsible for maladies. If, however, the relationship between believer and deity was unmarred and harmonious, any illness could be cured through prayer without medical treatment. Ideas like this, though perhaps in diluted forms, appear to persist in rural Christian circles today. Christians do not typically reject TCM because of its Daoist foundations. Although little research has so far been done on the influence of Daoism on Christianity in China, it seems reasonable that Daoist and Christian folk religious elements may overlap and influence each other, forming a syncretistic folk religion in many parts of the countryside.

A fruit-selling peasant woman, Li Shuying, however, sharply distinguished between the spirits of Daoism and the Jesus of Christianity, emphasizing that the latter does not demand money or sacrifices, but simply responds to prayers and hymn singing:

> About ten years ago, I suffered from serious anemia. I fainted frequently; but in order to earn a living, I had to sell fruit every day on the streets. One day I overheard someone say that I was possessed by six demons. I was very frightened and asked the help of a sorceress. I spent a lot of money with her, but my health was not a bit improved.
>
> Another day, while selling fruit, I heard some strangers reciting unfamiliar words which I later learned were the Ten Commandments. These people claimed that Jesus was the greatest god and could heal the most stubborn illness. I hurried home to tell my husband what I had heard on the street, adding that I was determined to seek this greatest god. My husband, however, mistook the word Jesus for Zushi [founder of Daoism], because the two sound familiar in Hakka. But I knew it could not be Zushi, for I remember clearly that this god Jesus did not take chickens or ducklings as offerings.
>
> Then, months later, I came across a preacher named Jiang Yunying and I inquired about Jesus. She first taught me to sing a hymn of praise. I was so anxious to seek God, I memorized the whole hymn and it has stayed in my heart: "Opening the door we see the blue sky. Do not worry about firewood, or about money. Do not worry about rice, or about clothing. For all these are in the hands of the Lord." . . . Every Sunday I asked my husband to take me [to church] to Huacheng by bicycle, a journey of 17 miles one way. It was through [the preacher's] influence that I learned to be an honest person. Like all hawkers, I too often gained extra advantage at the expense of the customer. To be a Christian means that I must never

cheat again. In practical terms, I lost money in my business. This antagonized even my own mother, but I cared little about the derision and taunting of others. On the contrary, I felt enthusiastic and shared with them what I learned from the church.

Now, my anemia is gone, my whole family, including my mother, are Christians, and my business is good. With all these blessings, how could I ever forget to thank the Lord?[21]

This testimony displays a pragmatic, almost mercantile attitude toward religion. It is shaped along the lines of investment and return, not surprising given the context of daily struggle for survival. Interestingly, Li's journey toward Christianity began with memorizing a song expressing trust in the divine provision of daily necessities. It was through the singing of these lines that her healing began. Freedom from fear led to bodily recuperation but at the same time to moral improvement (no more cheating). Both factors eventually enhanced her success in business. Like her, countless poor and marginalized Chinese Christians are much less concerned with personal gain or with using health or wealth to "prove" faith than with advising their peers to seek help from God to meet desperate physical and financial needs. Such people simply cannot afford a religion that does not deliver practical benefits. It is against this socioeconomic background that the pragmatic and somewhat utilitarian flavor of all Chinese Christian faith needs to be understood. It is for the poor that religion must be effective, and truth is what works.

China's grassroots Christianity has certainly been influenced by its folk religious context with its polytheistic flexibility. Gods who can deliver are revered and deserve a place in the pantheon of the village temple. In this way, originally rather obscure local deities can ascend to fame, as is obvious, for instance, in the rise of Wong Tai Sin from a marginal figure in a Daoist legend to the most important and widely revered Daoist deity in contemporary Hong Kong.[22] Likewise, Deng Xiaoping's political slogan of "seeking truth from facts" may have struck a chord deeply rooted in the Chinese soul. The conclusion with regard to China's Protestant Christianity is simple: it grows because it is viewed as more effective than other religions. Its effectiveness is evident where the needs for the majority are most urgent: in health and physical well-being.

Divine Healing and the Urban-Rural Divide

But exactly this makes some Chinese church leaders worry. Theologians and administrators at the upper levels of the CCC are concerned that Christianity at

China's grassroots could degenerate to a folk religious sect. When they try to describe the situation in rural churches, they talk about backwardness and a lack of education. Typical phrases used are "low-quality faith," "superstition," "sects and heresies," "self-styled evangelists," "destabilization of the social order under the cloak of religion," and "exploitation of the sentiments of religious people." A too-materialistic and this-worldly faith orientation is frequently warned against in CCC-published sermons. In one of these, Nanjing Seminary theologian Kong Xiangjian castigates the rural Christian faith motivated by healing experiences as folk religious syncretism: "In their hearts they have replaced Jesus Christ with the boddhisattva [sic] Guanyin to protect them from harm, a Daoist god to exorcise evil spirits and the legendary healer Hua Tuo to restore health."[23]

Such appraisals, however, may say more about the deep-rooted cultural divide between China's urban intellectuals and the country's peasant population than reflect an accurate picture of grassroots realities. In addition, religion is still a sensitive issue, and the government is wary of sectarian and superstitious movements that could undermine social stability and public order. Church leaders, therefore, try to present Christian religion as a stabilizing force by downplaying healing and miracle testimonies and emphasizing the positive effect Christianity has on people's moral and ethical behavior. Careful observation, however, shows that healing prayers and testimonies of divine healing are in no way restricted to people with little formal education in remote rural areas but can be found among urban and academically trained Christians, too.

A retired physics professor turned preacher, who was ordained in a CCC-affiliated church in Jiujiang (Jiangxi Province), would not be the typical faith healer or believer in supernatural miracles anywhere in the world. Yet this informant reported that, while traveling to villages around his city, he was approached by a farmer who had a tumor the size of a soccer ball on his leg. This farmer had been to a hospital and was informed that his condition was too serious to be remedied by any other (Western or traditional) cure than an operation. Like most farmers in China, however, he lacked health insurance, and the necessary operation would have cost more than he earned in a year. He thus had few options besides asking prayer for healing. As a scientist who had worked in an ideological environment of enlightened materialism and as a church worker trained in a CCC-run course of study, the preacher was skeptical about divine healing. However, due to the farmer's urging and out of love for this poor, stricken man, the preacher gave in and said a prayer, since he could not help him financially. When he visited the village again a few weeks later, the farmer came running toward him, greeted him enthusiastically, then pulled up one trouser leg to show him that the tumor had all but disappeared.[24]

At a CCC-run seminary in a provincial capital, a young theological student fell ill with a severe kidney condition. Fellow students started praying and fasting for him. In prayer meetings convened on campus in the house of one of the younger teachers, students and other young Christians prayed for the patient with the laying on of hands. Those who participated in the meetings got the impression that his health improved. For instance, he started to eat again. The seminary leadership condemned the prayer meetings as superstition. However, as the prayerful sympathy for the ill student had pervaded great parts of the student body, the leaders felt forced to help in their own ways and provided RMB110,000, then the equivalent of a teacher's salary for 10 years, to cover the cost of a transplant and follow-up surgery.[25]

Although healing experiences are almost never reported in CCC publications, reports of healing in China occasionally can be found in international Christian journals. As an issue of *Areopagus*, a Norwegian-funded magazine of the Tao Fong Shan Christian Centre in Hong Kong, reported in 1993, an evangelist in charge of a local CCC-affiliated church had prayed for a little child who had already been pronounced dead by a hospital doctor. The child came back to life shortly afterward and then gradually recovered in the hospital. Fearing that people might misinterpret the situation and start bringing the dead to the church, the evangelist played down the experience but was quoted as saying: "Did not Jesus heal the sick and cast out demons? How can we deny these miracles?"[26]

The ambivalent attitude of this CCC-appointed evangelist appears to be typical. Healing experiences are talked about everywhere among China's Christians, but the CCC does not encourage preachers to speak about them from the pulpit. Sermons in front of large CCC congregations paint Jesus Christ in Confucian or Buddhist colors, presenting him as educator and teacher, as heavenly Lord and cosmic Christ, but hardly ever as healer or miracle worker.[27] Sermons before smaller audiences may be different, though, as I observed in a house church in Beijing, where a migrant laborer from Anhui Province spoke about the biblical story of Jesus healing 10 lepers and gave a tearful account of how she herself was healed of a serious illness that her doctor had suspected was caused by HIV/AIDS.[28]

## Divine Healing in a Context of Minimal Theological Training

China's world of Protestantism is marked by a relative absence of theologically trained personnel due to the difficult times the Chinese churches went through from the 1950s to the 1970s. At the same time, Bible distribution has been a top priority for the CCC since its inception in 1980. As of February 2009, over 60 million Bibles had been printed by the Amity Printing Company in Nanjing, which today is the largest Bible-producing facility in the world. Although Bible stories are read, listened to, and preached about wherever Chinese Christians meet and worship, catechism classes for ordinary believers or systematic Bible courses for lay preachers and evangelists can hardly keep pace with the rapid grassroots growth of Christianity.

In a context of endemic poverty, pervasive health problems, insufficient medical care, and a Daoist-inspired preoccupation with health, biblical stories of miraculous healing and food multiplication strike a chord with Chinese believers. In the absence of Western-style theological instruction, Chinese Christians tend to read the Bible literally and prescriptively. For them, there is no historical-critical or theological gap between the text and their present-day reality. They are definitely not cessationists. Biblical healing stories go hand in hand with reports circulated in villages today. Present-day experiences and the Bible interpret one another. As one church elder in eastern China confessed:

> In Christ, our Lord, we can see God's love. His love is the same
> yesterday, today and certainly in the future, too. Because his love does
> not change, we who believe and follow him can do what the Lord has
> allowed us to do: Ask, and it will be given to you; search, and you will
> find; knock, and the door will be opened for you. When the Lord Jesus
> Christ lived on earth almost 2000 years ago, he helped a lot of sick
> and wretched people. Our church today is in no other situation at all!
> There are still many suffering and miserable people in our midst.[29]

According to this Chinese interpreter, the benefits of God's material and spiritual salvation have not been fully realized—for there are still many suffering and miserable—but the marginalized and sick are earmarked for redemption, and it can happen at any time.

Lay training courses organized by the CCC at all levels try to balance the ordinary believers' focus on divine healing by emphasizing the spiritual and eternal benefits of Christian faith. Divine healing experiences are accepted by official CCC spokespersons as a way for novices and the spiritually immature to be drawn into the faith, but they then have to grow and mature beyond this initial, childish state. Such a provisional acceptance of physical healing as a lesser expression of eternal salvation is reflected in the following testimony by a CCC woman evangelist in Shaanxi Province:

> The healing of my daughter was just the beginning of my faith. But
> there is a lot of faith healing around here. In most cases, people first
> start asking about Christ when they are sick. They don't have any
> other way to go. To believe in Christ is their last resort, when nothing
> else is possible. When they have received Christ, they also realize the
> need for change and repentance. Of course, those who are ill and
> experience other obstacles on their life roads need to believe in
> Christ, but those who don't have these obstacles need to believe even
> more. . . . Because we don't just believe in Jesus for reasons of our
> flesh, our body. We need the salvation of our souls. Faith is not just
> for now, it is also for the future. . . . So, if you are healed, you should

believe, but if you are not healed, you should also believe. Because faith is not only for our life on earth.[30]

## Divine Healing in a Context of Limited Theological Reflection

According to my observation, divine healing is widely discussed by Chinese pastors, who are close to the people concerned, but hardly at all by Chinese theologians or church leaders. At the top level, the topic is more or less neglected, presumably because it is seen as backward and unenlightened as well as politically too sensitive. This is ironic because the CCC leadership has since the 1990s stressed the need for a contextual Chinese theology to be developed. Yet, here, an important area of contextual Christian practice is passed over in silence. A strategic opportunity is being missed to affirm the empowering and disarm the oppressive potential of grassroots practices.

Where the empowering potential is concerned, an open-minded analysis and discussion of divine healing testimonies may contribute more to the emergence of a genuinely Chinese liberation theology than any Marxist-Christian dialogue at the top of the social ladder could do. Li, the simple fruit-seller cited above, appears to have instinctively grasped the materiality of salvation, which, according to theologian Miroslav Volf, is an essential constituent not only of pentecostalism but also of liberation theology.[31] Volf sees a point of contact between pentecostals and liberation theologians insofar as both understand salvation in the strict theological sense to include the material aspect of human life. Both reject the claim that salvation is spiritual and inward only and emphasize instead the holistic effect of the gospel on both body and soul. Thus, a gospel message centering on divine healing has no need to postpone salvation to heaven but expects its saving power to become effective at any place and moment, in the here and now. Grassroots Chinese Christians take initiative and mobilize people to claim full health and humanity in a dehumanizing world. Their divine healing stories are stories of protest. They tell of people who do not resign themselves to the vicious circle of illness, hunger, and debt. Their message is: suffering does not have to be. In addition, divine healing testimonies talk about empowerment. As Währisch-Oblau observes: "Simple, poor, uneducated people gain access to the power of God through their prayers. In so doing, these people show themselves to be more powerful than those who are usually invested with power: more powerful than doctors with their university degrees, and more powerful than party officials who have not succeeded in providing a functional health care system."[32]

While both pentecostalism and liberation theology understand salvation in terms of material change, they disagree about where to look for it. For liberation theologians, salvation is first and foremost a matter of socioeconomic change, whereas pentecostals put their focus on individual believers and their potential for physical and material betterment. In this latter conception, salvation seems more circumscribed than in liberation theology. From the perspective of the individual believer, however, a divine healing experience is a much more immediate and effective liberation than seeking eventual socioeconomic change. Thus, while pentecostalism, like liberation theology, would never postpone salvation to the end times, it would neither—in contrast to liberation theology—postpone it to a later world revolution.

All in all, divine healing testimonies contain a liberating potential that should be acknowledged and analyzed. However, it should be conceded that they also have an oppressive potential. When healing experience becomes an expected norm and proof of religious faith, the liberation effect may dwindle away. People may then feel pressed to mold their biographies and religious experiences according to peer group standards, as is suggested by the following set of typical examples:

> "I was sick and repeatedly hospitalized. But in the hospital, they could not help me. Then I got to know a woman who told me about Jesus. I became a believer, and Jesus has healed me. God is good!" . . . "Thanks to God, I became a believer in 1985. I also was healed. I had stomach problems for over twenty years. But then the Spirit moved me, and I started to work for God. This is God's guidance." . . . "I used to have mental problems. But when I started to believe [in Jesus], I received eternal life. And my health has greatly improved."[33]

These testimonies, uttered by choir members at a reception held for a foreign Christian visitor in their CCC-affiliated church in a small town in a remote part of eastern China, are conspicuous for their abstraction and standardized narrative pattern. In all their brevity, each testimony contains the same five elements, albeit in different sequence: (a) a past health problem that is not necessarily specified is claimed; (b) its severity is underlined (hospitalization could not help, the suffering lasted for decades, the problems were not physical but mental); (c) an encounter with Christian religion (a believer, Jesus, the Spirit) is mentioned as the turning point; (d) healing or betterment is attested; (e) a Christian confession is expressed ("God is good," "This is God's guidance," "I received eternal life"). Here, individual biographies are pressed into standardized narrative patterns, thereby becoming abstract and de-individualized. Form reigns over content; the biographical material serves its testimonial interpretation. This happens if church members scrutinize their personal histories for material out of which socially accepted religious realities can be constructed. In such a context, relatively minor healings of everyday illnesses fulfill the same religious and social function as miraculous healings of cancer or other life-threatening illnesses.

Of course, fairly healthy people can always exaggerate former little maladies against which healing testimonies meeting the expectation of fellow believers can be constructed. But what about an enduring and obvious illness or disability that is not overcome in spite of all prayers, promises, and hopes? It then easily happens that the sick person is at least implicitly blamed for the assumed failure of all those countless healing prayers and, in addition to the burden of the illness, has to bear the frustrations of fellow believers. After visiting a church in remote Shaanxi Province in 1997, Währisch-Oblau reported:

> In one rural church, I met a young woman who had been paralyzed from the waist down through a bus accident. She was clearly a very important person in this congregation, being one of only a few members who could read and write. As she spends much time in reading and meditating on the Bible—for a paraplegic in a small Chinese county town, there are no employment opportunities—she is considered something of a spiritual authority by the other members. To enable her to participate in church activities, church members pick her up at her house and wheel her to the church building, where a ramp has been constructed for her access. The paralyzed woman, who was surrounded by so much loving care, herself radiated serenity and joy that was almost palpable. When I asked a church elder why this woman had not become their appointed preacher even though she was the best educated and qualified, I got an astonished reaction. They had prayed for her healing for 12 years. It had not happened, so there had to be something in her life that had not yet been forgiven. Therefore, even though she might be qualified in other ways, she could not hold an office in the church. The theological reasoning that kept this paralyzed woman from becoming a preacher is certainly appalling. On the other hand, the woman had obviously found a place, meaning, and plenty of love in the church. . . . Considering that most paraplegics in China are hidden at home by their families who are ashamed of them, this woman was in a much better situation than many others.[34]

This account is revealing not only in terms of the oppressive potential of divine healing practices, but also with regard to the role and image ascribed to church leaders. Chinese pentecostal congregations typically put their pastors on a spiritual pedestal, making them almost mediators between heaven and earth. In such a religious framework, spiritual blamelessness and, as its visible evidence, physical integrity may be required from anyone who would want to lead a congregation as pastor.

## Divine Healing and Holistic Transformation

Religion proves its value by being effective, and faith is a practical remedy for life's maladies. This concept, which I first encountered from the atheist

Dr. Wang, presented itself to me in China as an across-the-board phenomenon. It went across denominational traditions, the urban-rural divide, and different educational backgrounds and age groups. People did disagree, however, about where one would expect the effectiveness specifically to materialize. While for most Protestant Christians it was physical health, for others it was moral and ethical behavior, mental peace, or the social harmony of family, neighborhood, and society.

Although these different expectations with which religion is met in China seem to be competing, at a closer look they might instead complement and influence each other. A holistic understanding of health as consisting of more than individual physical well-being may, for instance, bridge the divide between liberation theologians and pentecostals, or between Daoist-inspired and Marxist-inspired Chinese Christians. Individual health depends to a great extent on socioeconomic conditions, and at the same time the living conditions of a community can be improved if its members are physically and mentally healthy. A holistic approach to healing may include physical and social health, making room for both the miraculous and scientific social analysis. Likewise, poverty and other dehumanizing forces lead to sickness, despair, and the subsequent breakdown of individual and public morality, while the interruption of this vicious circle serves the betterment of material and moral, individual and social conditions. In this way, Confucian-inspired Christians with their concern for moral perfection and the health of the community may find common ground with Daoist-inspired Christians.

Such an inclusive concept of health is reflected in the following narrative from Xiyang, an extremely poor village in the coastal mountains of Fujian Province.[35] Church history in Xiyang village covers scarcely 30 years. It originated through three experiences, one of sudden death and two of apparently divine healing. A young girl from Xiyang had been sold by her parents into marriage to a man from another province. When she arrived at her in-laws', her fiancé had suddenly died. But instead of blaming her for bringing bad luck, which would have been expected, the grieving parents received her in generous hospitality. They turned out to be Christians, and under their influence the young woman from Xiyang became a Christian herself. After some time, she moved home to Xiyang, where she openly confessed her faith but managed to win over only a few elderly women, until one day a nine-year-old boy fell into the village pond and almost drowned. He was pulled out of the water unconscious and carried home. Since the village had no real road connection and the next clinic was very far, his parents and their neighbors resigned themselves to his fate. The Christian believers, however, came and sat at the boy's bedside, asking God for the boy's life, until many hours later he awoke and recovered quickly and fully. As a result, many young people and entire families joined the Christian group. Later, a young woman called You Muhua married into Xiyang. She was a recent Christian convert. Prayers in her aunt's house church had reputedly cured her from chronic fatigue and turned her into a fervent Christian. Her personal healing testimony plus her record of nine years of schooling gave her sufficient credentials to be put in charge of preaching and pastoring in the emerging house church.

Meanwhile, the social situation of the area was unhealthy and disheartening. Some young men had been sentenced to death and executed for crimes, including piracy. Poverty and destitution had led them to seek their fortune by robbing and sometimes murdering people down the coast. You's husband, too, had been involved in criminal activities. The young Christian woman, however, managed to win him over, and told all who were willing to hear that the Lord Jesus wanted people to repent from their wrongdoings and in turn would provide for their sustenance. Xiyang's new converts developed an active social life. A visitation team looked regularly after all Christian families and cared for the sick, a production team organized assistance during times of sowing and harvesting for families with insufficient labor power, a know-how team of several young people was sent to the county town to attend courses in mushroom growing and the tending of orange trees. They shared their newly acquired knowledge with Christians and non-Christians alike, and the entire village population benefited from the Christian presence in numerous ways. When the Christian congregation had outgrown You's family courtyard, the local Communist cadres provided a piece of land for a special price and helped to build a church. They had become sympathetic to Christianity as they observed how it brought social and economic development and drastically lowered the crime rate. A simple brick structure was erected. As people leave the building now, they pass underneath an inscription above the door which reads "Peace to those who go out."

As in Xiyang, many Chinese people become attracted to Christianity because it is viewed as practically beneficial for individual and social health. Divine healing, understood as both the restoration of physical bodies and in a more holistic sense as the transformation of individuals and communities, may be the single most important factor explaining the extraordinary growth of Christianity in China.

NOTES

1 Until the mid-1990s, I rarely heard material prosperity mentioned as a benefit of Christianity, although the slogan "getting rich is glorious" had been officially proclaimed by party leaders since the 1980s.

2 See Katrin Fiedler, *Wirtschaftsethik in China am Fallbeispiel von Shanghaier Protestanten* [Economic Ethics in China: A Case Study among Protestants in Shanghai] (Hamburg, Germany: Institut für Asienkunde, 2000).

3 See Liu Qi, "Mingongjiaohui jin juli: Yige xianxiang de kaocha" [An Approach to a Church of Migrant Workers: A Study of a Phenomenon], *Dandai zongjiao yanjiu* [Contemporary Religious Studies]: *Journal of the Shanghai Academy of Social Sciences* 2

(2007): 1–10; German summary in *China Heute: Journal of the China-Zentrum* [St. Augustin, Germany] 27.1–2 (2008): 155–156.

4  Edmond Tang, "The Changing Landscape of Chinese Christianity," *China Study Journal: Journal of the China Desk of Churches Together of Britain and Ireland* [London] (Spring–Summer 2008): 34.

5  *Bridge: Church Life in China Today* [Hong Kong] 63 (Jan.–Feb. 1994): 2; 75 (Feb. 1996): 8–9; 80 (Dec. 1997): 17; Daniel H. Bays, "Indigenous Protestant Churches in China, 1900–1937: A Pentecostal Case Study," in *Indigenous Responses to Western Christianity*, ed. Steven Kaplan (New York: New York University Press, 1995), 124–143; Deng Zhaoming, "Indigenous Chinese Pentecostal Denominations," in *Asian and Pentecostal: The Charismatic Face of Christianity in Asia*, ed. Allan Anderson and Edmond Tang (Costa Mesa, Calif.: Regnum, 2005); Lian Xi, "A Messianic Deliverance for Post-Dynastic China: The Launch of the True Jesus Church in the Early Twentieth Century," *Modern China: An International Quarterly of History and Social Science* 34.4 (Oct. 2008): 408, 430. In some but not all regions of China, True Jesus Church congregations are CCC-affiliated.

6  Bob Whyte, *Unfinished Encounter: China and Christianity* (Glasgow: Collins, 1988), 176.

7  Tony Lambert, *The Resurrection of the Chinese Church* (London: Hodder and Stoughton, 1991), 253.

8  Philip Wickeri, *Seeking the Common Ground: Protestant Christianity, the Three-Self Movement, and China's United Front* (Maryknoll, N.Y.: Orbis, 1988), 157.

9  A fairly credible survey of Christians in China was done by China Partner, a U.S.-based Christian organization with strong links to both the CCC and the independent house church movement (www.chinapartner.org); it is summarized in *ASSIST News Service* [Lake Forest, Calif.] (8 Dec. 2008), http://www.assistnews.net/stories/2008/s08120056.htm (accessed 26 Aug. 2009); cf. *Amity News Service* [Hong Kong] 97.10 (1997): 27–28; Alan Hunter and Kim-Kwong Chan, *Protestantism in Contemporary China* (Cambridge: Cambridge University Press, 1993), 66–71.

10  "Meeting point" is a fixed term in China's religious policy, meaning a place for gatherings bigger and more formal than a private home and smaller and more informal than a church building. A meeting point could be a redecorated barn, an old cinema, the backyard of any commercial place or a simple building specially erected for the purpose of worship activities.

11  Gotthard Oblau, field notes, Zhaotong (Yunnan Province) (Mar. 1994).

12  Claudia Währisch-Oblau, interview, Zhejiang Province (Apr. 1991).

13  Claudia Währisch-Oblau, "God Can Make Us Healthy Through and Through: On Prayers for the Sick and the Interpretation of Healing Experiences in Christian Churches in China and African Immigrant Congregations in Germany," *International Review of Mission: Journal of the Conference on World Mission and Evangelism of the World Council of Churches* [Geneva] 90.356–357 (Jan.–Apr. 2001): 89.

14  Article 36, qtd. in Donald MacInnis, *Religion in China Today: Policy and Practice* (Maryknoll, N.Y.: Orbis, 1989), 35, 404.

15  Währisch-Oblau, "God Can Make Us Healthy," 93; Katrin Fiedler, "The Growth of the Protestant Church in Rural China," *China Study Journal* (Spring–Summer 2008): 49.

16  Währisch-Oblau, interview, Shaanxi Province (1997).

17  Währisch-Oblau, interview, Zhejiang Province (1991). These events took place during the Cultural Revolution, when all religious activities were officially banned.

18  This view was corroborated in a publication by my successor in the position of international communicator for the Amity Foundation, which gave her access to China's rural churches until not long ago: Fiedler, "Growth," 49.

19  Ibid.

20  M. Kobayashi, "The Celestial Masters under the Eastern Jin and Liu-Song Dynasties," *Taoist Resources* 3.2 (May 1992): 17–46.

21  *Areopagus: Magazine of the Tao Fong Shan Christian Centre* (Advent 1993): 28.

22  G. Lang and L. Ragvald, *The Rise of a Refugee God: Hong Kong's Wong Tai Sin* (New York: Oxford University Press, 1993).

23  *Tian Feng: The Magazine of Christianity in China* [Shanghai] 7 (1992); *Amity News Service* [Hong Kong] 93.1 (13 Feb. 1993); *Amity Newsletter* [Nanjing] 36 (Jan. 1996): 1–3.

24  Währisch-Oblau, field notes (Feb. 1993).

25  Oblau, field notes (Feb. 2002).

26  *Areopagus: Magazine of the Tao Fong Shan Christian Centre* [Hong Kong] (Advent 1993): 31.

27  Gotthard Oblau, "Heiler, Tröster, Lehrer, Weltenherr: Jesusbilder im chinesischen Protestantismuss" [Healer, Comforter, Teacher, Lord: Concepts of Jesus in Chinese Protestantism], in *The Chinese Face of Jesus Christ*, ed. Roman Malek (Nettetal, Germany: Steyler, 2007), 1431–1456.

28  Oblau, field notes, Beijing (2000).

29  Währisch-Oblau, field notes (May 1995).

30  Währisch-Oblau, field notes, Shaanxi Province (1997).

31  Miroslav Volf, "Materiality of Salvation: An Investigation in the Soteriologies of Liberation and Pentecostal Theologies," *Journal of Ecumenical Studies* 26.3 (1989): 447–467.

32  Währisch-Oblau, "God Can Make Us Healthy," 98.

33  Währisch-Oblau, interviews, Binhai, Jiangsu Province (May 1995).

34  Währisch-Oblau, "God Can Make Us Healthy," 94–95.

35  Oblau, field notes, Fujian Province (May 1997).

# PART IV

# Global Crossings

# 16

# Catholic Charismatic Healing in Global Perspective: The Cases of India, Brazil, and Nigeria

*Thomas J. Csordas*

The Catholic Charismatic renewal movement is a paradigm for an examination of the globalization of religion. Originating in the United States and centered in Rome, Italy, but spread throughout the world, it invites reconsideration of center-periphery and local-global dynamics in the contemporary world system. This chapter traces the international expansion of the movement and compares its local instantiations in India, Brazil, and Nigeria. The movement simultaneously invokes contrasting images of universal culture and cultural fragmentation, and raises a series of questions about religion and social class, bodily experience, and "reenchantment" of the world from a global perspective. Christianity in its earliest phase of globalization spread on the power of a church that was the dominant world institution of its time, and later on the power of the colonial empires that were the dominant institutions of their time. No such dominant institution supports the current wave of globalization of Christianity, which often takes the form of Pentecostal or Charismatic evangelization through divine healing and deliverance from demons. Christianity in the present era has spread rapidly and dramatically by means of movements, ministries, fellowships, and independent denominations taking advantage of all the available technologies of travel and communication to spread their gospel of full salvation as addressing material and spiritual concerns for the health of both the body and the soul.[1]

The Catholic Charismatic renewal began in the United States in 1967, synthesizing elements from the Catholic Cursillo movement that originated in Spain in 1944 and the indigenous American Charismatic movement that was then pentecostalizing many mainstream Protestants. In the midst of the 1960s cultural ferment, the ecumenical Charismatic movement promised a dramatic renewal of church life based on a born-again spirituality of a "personal relationship" with Jesus and direct access to divine power and inspiration through "spiritual gifts," or "charisms," including divine healing, discernment of spirits, words of knowledge, prophecy, and glossolalia. Catholic participants in the Charismatic movement associated into informal prayer groups or tightly disciplined covenant communities, with larger institutional structures taking the form of a National Service Committee in the United States in 1970 and an International Communications Office (ICO) in 1975. The latter began under the auspices of the Word of God covenant community in Ann Arbor, Michigan, subsequently moving to Brussels, Belgium, under the auspices of Cardinal Leon Joseph Suenens, and finally to the center of the Catholic world in Rome, where it was renamed the International Catholic Charismatic Renewal Services (ICCRS). Pope Paul VI took note of the movement's existence as early as 1971 and publicly addressed the movement's 1975 International Conference in Rome. Pope John Paul II continued to be generally supportive, apparently tolerating the movement's relatively radical theology for the sake of encouraging its markedly conservative politics, "traditional" values, encouragement of individual spirituality, and contributions to parish activities and finances.

The movement expanded internationally through two principal modes. Typically, the movement entered a two-thirds world region when a missionary priest visited the United States, was exposed to baptism of the Holy Spirit, organized a prayer group upon his return, and subsequently called on outside help for doctrinal instruction or healing services. A class of Catholic healer-evangelists can be called on for such purposes. The ICCRS has become an instrumental clearinghouse in this respect through the retreats, workshops, leadership training, and newsletter that it sponsors. The second mechanism is via the communitarian branch of the movement. From early on, some Charismatics wanted to live lives of greater commitment to the spiritual ideals of Christian community than they found in weekly prayer groups. They adopted formal written documents called covenants that established basic rules of life, and referred to the resulting groups as covenant communities. The Word of God, whose leaders founded the ICO/ICCRS, was among the earliest covenant communities. During the 1980s, these groups began to affiliate, creating two broad-based international communities of communities. The Word of God created a supercommunity called the Sword of the Spirit. Authoritarian and even apocalyptic tendencies within the Sword of the Spirit led to a split within the Word of God, with one of its two founding leaders remaining within the original community and founding an international Charismatic evangelistic ministry focused on countries in Eastern Europe and Africa, and the other becoming the president of the Sword of the Spirit.[2]

The second major network is called the Catholic Fraternity of Charismatic Covenant Communities and Fellowships.[3] The cultural distinction between the two major networks is that the Sword of the Spirit is "ecumenical," meaning that non-Catholics can be members of the constituent communities, while the Catholic Fraternity is restricted to Roman Catholic membership and is embraced by the Vatican as "an international private association of the faithful having juridical personality in accordance with Canon 322 of the Code of Canon Law."[4] These covenant community networks are powerful transnational religious entities alongside the ICCRS.

Given this formulation of the typical modes of the movement's transnational expansion, however, there is no consensus over whether the movement spread initially from a North American center and later from its official center in Rome or whether separate local movements eventually became co-opted by the Charismatic renewal and hence tied to its social center and ideological agenda. There is some evidence that in Costa Rica and Zaire non-Charismatic Catholic prayer groups began independently and were subsequently drafted into the international movement. In Zambia, the movement had two origins, one with missionary priests and one with former Archbishop Emmanuel Milingo. In Italy, independent groups appear to have existed outside formal movement sanction.[5]

The present essay draws on the work of ethnographers who have encountered the Catholic Charismatic renewal in India, Brazil, and Nigeria. Integrating the insights of these scholars with earlier research on the movement's development in the United States, Canada, France, Italy, Mexico, Chile, Brazil, Nigeria, Zambia, Zaire, Indonesia, Malaysia, and Japan, I will examine what the Catholic Charismatic renewal and, particularly, its emphasis on spiritual gifts, such as divine healing and deliverance, and its promotion of these gifts through modern technologies of communication and travel can teach us about religion and globalization.[6] I will argue that the Catholic Charismatic renewal contributes both universalizing and fracturing impulses to the construction and ongoing reinvention of global and local religious cultures.

India

The Catholic Charismatic renewal began in India in the 1970s. A 1976 national convention in Bombay attracted 1,500 registered delegates; a 1978 convention attracted 3,500, including Cardinal Lawrence Picachy of Calcutta, the archbishops of Bombay and Hyderabad, and the bishops of Quilon and Kottar. Adjunct to the convention were a leaders conference, two priests retreats, and a three-day leaders seminar on healing conducted by the renowned American Francis MacNutt, then a Dominican priest. A report in the movement's international newsletter in 1986 cited its spread into rural northwest India; a 1994 newsletter documented evangelization into tribal areas of northeast India bordering China.[7]

The movement is most prominent in the southwestern state of Kerala, where there is a concentration of Catholics of the Syro-Malabar, Syro-Malankara, and Latin rites. In 1987, a priest of the Vincentian congregation named Mathew Naickomparambil avowedly received a divine inspiration to transform his small prayer group at Potta into a healing ministry, which has since grown into a moral metropole within the movement, even bragging its own train station. Daylong healing services attract as many as 5,000–10,000 people, foreigners as well as people from across India, apparently including substantial numbers of non-Christians. The church/ashram's Divine Retreat Center hosts weeklong retreats for as many as 20,000 visitors in the summer season, with preaching from 6:30 a.m. until 10:00 p.m. simultaneously in six auditoriums: in the Malayalam, Tamil, Telugu, English, Konkani, Hindi, and Kannada languages.[8]

Anthropologist Murphy Halliburton visited Potta in 1997 and reported that during the weeklong retreat participants are not allowed to leave the grounds nor to drink or smoke. The facilities are impressive, with physicians, bookstores, snack bars, and pharmacies onsite, and auditoriums large enough to hold several thousand people. Halliburton described the atmosphere as "like that of a major rock concert in a big stadium, only with more facilities." In patient wards, including locked wards for alcoholics, television monitors constantly show what is transpiring onstage in the auditorium. An estimated 60 percent of participants are patients with a variety of medical troubles, including psychiatric and substance abuse problems; many others come for help with issues such as marital struggles, infertility, and other life situations; and about 10 percent come "just for prayer."[9] Of critical import for our discussion is not only that Potta is a destination for foreigners and non-Christians and that Father Naickomparambil and his colleagues conduct retreats and services throughout India, but that they also have an energetic presence in North America and Europe. For example, when I accessed it, the Potta website announced a five-week, nine-stop tour of the United States and a Bible conference in Germany, and it listed numerous contacts among past retreat participants from the United States, England, and Germany.[10] The result is that a distinctive, locally contextualized variation on pentecostal healing—one that ironically emphasizes the role of regulation and indeed coercion as necessary to freeing those bound by addictions—exerts an influence from periphery to center, thereby contributing to the heterogeneity as well as the homogeneity of global healing.

Heterogeneity of meaning is present as well in local contextualizations of renewal. Anthropologist Matthew Schmalz documented a series of striking postmodern dislocations and juxtapositions of Hindu and Catholic elements in North Indian healing practices. Representative of this cross-fertilization is the healing ministry of Jude, a lay Catholic South Indian living in a North Indian city sacred to Hindus, who attracts both Catholic Charismatic and Hindu supplicants. Jude was a repentant alcoholic and womanizer who relocated following a dishonorable discharge from the military and a failed business venture selling an Ayurvedic remedy for sexual impotence; he subsequently returned to the church and joined the Charismatic renewal on the advice of a confessor. The forms of empowerment Jude deploys include the readily recognizable Charismatic spiritual gift of word of knowledge, a form of divine inspiration which allows him to identify the problems of supplicants, often embodying their afflictions himself as cues to their nature. They also include an authenticating narrative of a miraculous birth in which, during a medical crisis, he was surgically removed and then replaced into his mother's womb, a theme paralleled in myths of the births of Krishna, Mahavira, Buddha, and Parikshit.[11]

On the level of disjunction in practice and interpretation is the case of a female patient who experienced disturbing visions of three men, who appeared to be Hindu *bhut* or *pret* spirits, who was brought to the Catholic healer by a Protestant lawyer convinced of the satanic identity of the traditional spirits. The Catholic healer attributed the problem instead to the effects of sin and troubled interpersonal relations, but this was understood by the patient's parents in terms of a Hindu paradigm of the body's response to purifying fluids when the patient was blessed with Catholic holy water. Homologies in ritual symbolism appear in the juxtapositions of the Christian Eucharist and the eating of *prasad*, or food left over from offerings to Hindu deities; of the Christian scapular and the *rakhi*, or wrist string worn as protection; of Christian holy water and the water or milk used to ritually cool Hindu deities; of prayerful repetition of the name of Jesus and the Hindu use of mantra; of the Charismatic blowing of a blessing in a supplicant's face and the parallel Hindu practice of *duha*. That such parallels can be found is predictable; what is of interest is how they are thematized in practice. For instance, the healer Jude strenuously objected to equation of repeating the name of Jesus with the "pagan" practice of uttering mantras, but quite un-self-consciously blew his blessings in a way that would not be recognized by Catholic Charismatics elsewhere. In several ways, Indian and non-Indian notions become inextricably conflated, as in the healer's implicit understanding of sin not necessarily as a matter of intent but as one of contamination by the acts of others, implying an Ayurvedic conception of the body in terms of vital fluids passing through channels, such that the effect of sin is that it "occludes the flow of grace as it ripens or hardens in the body."[12]

Such points of syncretism and contradiction are more than jarring anomalies; they are symptomatic of the simultaneous pull toward universal culture and postmodern cultural fragmentation that characterizes the global condition of religion. Further insight is provided by the anthropologist Corinne Dempsey's work on Christianity in Kerala with respect to competition between the indigenous Syrian Christianity purportedly introduced by Thomas the apostle in the first century and the Roman Christianity forcibly imposed by Portuguese colonialists in the sixteenth century. Dempsey recounts a conversation with a priest

whose denunciation of Western influences included everything from the Portuguese to contemporary culture (which he claimed was undermining the faith
of young people), but who felt optimistic in part because of the Charismatic
renewal. Ironically, this movement is itself an import from the United States,
yet Dempsey resolves the irony by suggesting that "the Charismatic movement
has been assimilated and transformed by the Kerala Catholic community. . . .
Domestic adoption of this 'Western' movement seems to have been so thor-
ough as to enable it to be wielded by and on behalf of Malayali Christians as a
means to combat what it used to be itself: 'Western' influence."[13] Dempsey
cites the Indian postcolonialist theorist Homi Bhabha's understanding of how
hybridity reverses the effects of "colonialist disavowal," that is, the rhetorical/
ideological assertion of sameness that masks domination. The hybrid assertion
of sameness—here, participation in a purportedly universal and homogeneous
international movement under allegiance to Rome—functions not only as a
strategy for autonomy, but has the potential to subtly transform the center. In
this sense, the empirical fascination of the Charismatic renewal is that there is
no bipolarity between colonist and colonizer but a multinational religious con-
glomerate that invites the layering of hybridity upon syncretism upon synthesis in a universal culture that is not polyglot but glossolalic.[14]

## Brazil

Brazil, unlike India, is a predominantly Catholic country, and therefore the cultural landscape in which the Charismatic renewal moves differs in precisely the
most significant way. The Charismatic renewal was introduced to Brazil in São
Paulo by Jesuit priests from the United States between 1969 and 1972. By
1992, the movement's international office reported 2 million Catholic Charismatics in Brazil. The estimated number of followers in 1994 was 3.8 million.
The renewal has largely been a phenomenon of the middle class. Among the
many Charismatic prayer groups and communities in Brazil, the Catholic Fraternity covenant community network claims three Brazilian affiliates, while the
Sword of the Spirit has none.[15]

Brazilian anthropologists uniformly situate their analyses in relation to
four cultural forces within the Brazilian religious landscape: popular Catholicism, with its devotion to Mary and the saints; liberation theology, with its base
communities; Protestant pentecostalism; and the dynamic between clerics and
laity; strikingly little is said about spiritism or African Brazilian religions.[16] A
common theme is that the Charismatic renewal has imposed itself on the religious scene in a striking and unavoidable fashion. Anthropologist Raymundo
Heraldo Maués attests that his initial interest was in popular Catholicism in
rural Pará state, but his attention was "powerfully diverted" by lay Charismatics
in the city of Belém.[17] The research of Carlos Steil—at the other end of the

country, in Porto Alegre—originally focused on contemporary apparitions of the Virgin Mary, but his attention was drawn to the involvement of Charismatics in activities of the faithful surrounding these apparitions.[18]

Anthropologist Maria Jose Alves De Abreu examines the manner in which Charismatic experience is understood as unmediated access to the divine not only in relation to the church as the traditional mediator of religious experience for its faithful but also, and especially, in relation to electronic media, in the manipulation of which the movement has exhibited virtuosity. The issue is the possibility of "transferring an idea concerning non-mediation to the very core of the media sphere" such that "the TV screen is not so much about images as about revelatory communication." Televangelism may be conceived in terms of transparency and immediacy or opacity and mediatization. The problem for Charismatics is how to maintain the "principle of subjectivity," or the fundamental experiential postulate that the imitation of Christ "is an inward process of imitation, a spiritual resemblance, which stems from *a presence* rather than a mere representation enacted on stage." De Abreu looks at two of the most visible Charismatic media presences in Brazil, the Canção Nova media system of communication and evangelistic healing priest Marcelo Rossi. Canção Nova is one of the original and best-known Brazilian Charismatic communities, with 12 branches throughout Brazil, 2 in Portugal, and 1 in Rome; facilities on campus for retreats, services, broadcasting, and publishing; 150 transmission antennas across the country; and the capacity for internet broadcasting. Rossi is a handsome priest in his late 30s, who has composed many devotional songs and is widely known for elaborate masses "of cure and liberation of bad energies, during which people participated in what he called the 'aerobics of Jesus,'" masses that are in effect Charismatic pageants performed in front of large audiences. De Abreu sees both phenomena as reflecting "the extent to which the Charismatic Renewal has gradually moved from the intimate space of the prayer group (*grupo de oração*) to the big stadiums and the global media space."[19] This movement has produced not only universalized templates for communal experiences, but also contradictions in the meanings of mediatization—as both presence and representation.

A key event—and a symbol of these contradictory impulses—in De Abreu's account is a gathering at which Rossi, regarded by some both within and outside the movement as a marginal loner who has become more a showman than a Charismatic leader, who consorts with celebrities and film stars, was recognized by the preeminent movement leader and founder of Canção Nova, Father Jonas Abib, as having been the victim of enemies of renewal. As Abib called on the crowd, including those watching on television, to collectively pray for and lay hands on Rossi, the latter fell on his knees, awash in tears, and Abib cried out that the movement belonged to the masses, who should not be afraid to say so. De Abreu accounts for this event by noting that, unlike both popular Catholicism and liberation theology, the Charismatic renewal is "compatible with the urban segmentation of identities and spatial fragmentation" and, further, that it holds the "idea that it is not the content per se, but the form and means of dealing with symbols and images that distinguish the movement." The movement is in part predicated on the fundamental need to transmit the word of God by testimony, prophecy, and healing, but "as a result of the mass media, the gift of transmission, which should be a sign of inward spirituality, becomes an outward token of popularity." Mediatization produces two contradictory effects: "jeopardizing the distinction between a living icon and an icon of idolatry," but also reaffirming the "notion of 'living icons' rather than that of religious representations." Thus, the famous healing priest, by falling on his knees and allowing himself to be prayed over in public, was saved for the movement from becoming a representation, a creature of the virtual reality of media stardom.[20]

Anthropologist Carlos Steil views the encounter between the Charismatic renewal and apparitions of the Virgin Mary in terms of multiple intersections or syncretism between pentecostalism and Catholicism, popular Catholicism and the Charismatic renewal, tradition and modernity; one might add the intersection between the local and the global in the precise sense in which Steil, while placing the Brazilian apparitions firmly in the Brazilian context, recognizes the Marian apparition of 1981 in the Croatian village of Medjugorje as the transnational prototype of a new mode of performativity in the historical genre of Marian apparitions.[21] Charismatics were involved from the outset with an apparition in Taquari in 1988 and in a phenomenon known as the Piedade dos Gerais, some moving to live near the apparitions, some deploying their access to media (in Taquari acquiring control of a local radio station; in Piedade dos Gerais assisting the original visionaries in travels to other cities and even to Europe) to transmit the message beyond the locality as one of universal significance. Yet, Charismatic involvement contributed to cultural disintegration as well as uniformity. As translocal Charismatics appropriated discourse from the local visionaries, they shifted the emphasis away from revelations externally received from the apparition by a select number of visionaries toward prophecies, or inner locutions, impressed by God upon any number of devotees, thereby contributing to the subjectivity and reflexivity characteristic of the Charismatic sacred self.

The Charismatic renewal, Steil notes, is not only a synthesis between Catholic and pentecostal ritual forms, but its activities provide a revolving door between Catholicism and pentecostalism for participants and thus form a threshold between the two forms of religious sociality.[22] In this process, aspiration to a universal culture (or in indigenous terms, to the task of bringing about the kingdom of God) exists in generative tension with the cultural prismatics of culturally distinct settings and syncretistic opportunities crisscrossed by the transnational media activities of healing and evangelization (or in indigenous terms, the movement of the Holy Spirit among the people).

Nigeria

Pentecostalism has exerted an influence on the religious scene in Nigeria since the early twentieth century, taking the form of the Aladura churches as well as the classical Pentecostal denominations.[23] Neo-pentecostal or Charismatic Christianity originated in the early 1970s among college students and university graduates of various denominations. As in many settings around the globe, a primary emphasis is divine healing, but in addition there is much attention to restitution "for one's past sins, mistakes, and every sort of unchristian act" (reflecting aspects of the traditional Yoruba concern for purification). Restitution often takes the form of returning stolen articles, which Matthews Ojo interprets as a reaction against the quest for material wealth following the Nigerian oil boom of the 1970s and which was duplicated during the mid-1990s among students at American Christian colleges in a wave of public confessionals quite likely in reaction against the quest for wealth during the yuppie "me generation" of the 1980s.[24] Restitution as an antidote to materialism presents a striking contrast to the emphasis of many scholars, including those who have studied Nigeria, on a "health and wealth" gospel that links a material concern for healing with the pursuit of financial prosperity.[25]

By 1976, the Catholic Charismatic renewal's first national leadership conference in Benin City attracted 110 participants with official support from the local bishop. In 1983, a National Advisory Council was formed to oversee the movement's activities. By the late 1980s, born-again neo-pentecostalism was widespread in southern Nigeria, and the notion of charisms, or spiritual gifts, was intriguing to many Protestants and Catholics; the number of adherents skyrocketed during the 1990s and the movement became highly mediatized by the 2000s. Particularly striking has been the popularity of "spiritual warfare" against Satan and his legion of evil spirits, which in Nigeria includes the seductive sea spirit Mami Wata (Queen of the Coast) and a variety of ancestral spirits, through the form of healing called "deliverance" as popularized by North American neo-pentecostals. In the early 2000s, Catholic Charismatic regional integration was manifested in events like the International Praise and Worship Workshop, which was organized by the Anglophone West African Co-ordinating Team Services and drew 85 participants from Nigeria and Ghana. The first joint Francophone-Anglophone Charismatic event was held in 2002, and in 2004 the Council of the Catholic Charismatic Renewal for Anglophone Africa had as part of its agenda the organization of a pan-African event that took place in 2006.[26]

The renewal gained momentum by building upon and transforming the meanings of indigenous practices. Francis MacNutt, the first and most widely known among American Catholic Charismatic healers, recounts a Charismatic retreat in Nigeria in which traditional deities were exorcised as demons, including the claimed deliverance of a man in Benin City:

An outstanding Catholic Layman, he was a convert who had been
brought up in the old religion. He discovered as a child that after
certain practices of dedication his toes were affected by a divining
spirit. If the day of his plans were to be propitious, one toe would
pinch him; if they were to be unlucky, a different toe would pinch.
Consequently, he came to plan his life around these omens, which he
said always came true, even if he tried to disregard them. When he
desired to pray out loud at our retreat, however, his unpropitious toe
began to act up; at this point, he decided that these strange manifestations must be from an evil spirit and had to be renounced.[27]

This incident is a variant of the time-honored Catholic strategy of ritual incorporation of indigenous practices, based on acceptance of their existential reality
but negation of their spiritual value, condemning them as inspired by the
demonic forces of Satan. On the communal level, the event fostered a shared
Charismatic identity, but it did this by fracturing an individual participant's
self-understanding, as he felt impelled to invalidate the embodiment of a major
component of his religious identity.

The anthropologist Misty Bastian encountered the Catholic Charismatic
renewal during the 1980s in the ethnically Igbo southeast of Nigeria, where
Catholicism is the dominant form of Christianity. Bastian describes a male
healer-visionary firmly ensconced in the official church networks and endorsed
by the hierarchy, and a female healer-visionary who was both explicitly criticized by her male counterpart and marginalized by the church hierarchy.[28]
Comparing the two healers, both of whom were most active from the mid-
1980s through the early 1990s, shows how the Charismatic renewal can be
interpreted as a discrete interactional milieu in which cultural tensions between
tradition and modernity, male and female, theological conservatism and experimentation, and cohesive and dislocating impulses are played out.

Father Edeh was a mainstream priest whose ministry was at least initially supported by his colleagues in the church hierarchy and appreciated as
an overt counterbalance against the appeal of Protestant pentecostalism. He
was academically trained at a U.S. university and had published a book titled
*Igbo Metaphysics*, based on ethnographic fieldwork, with Loyola University
Press. His ministry was highly mediatized, and he was building a cathedral
and prayer compound at his home parish to accommodate the press as well
as day-trippers and campers wanting to experience healing prayer; he also
traveled to conduct open-air rallies and healing masses throughout Igboland. His ministry was in decline by the late 1990s, according to Bastian, in
part because his followers did not see enough of the miracles they expected,
because his reputation was compromised by his involvement in commercial
activities, and because a variety of other spiritual options had emerged to
compete with him.

Sister Kate was a young woman who described herself as having three occupations: housewife, hospital worker, and prophet. She had experienced visions since her youth in the 1960s, beginning at her first communion. Alienated from her family in part because of her spiritual characteristics, her father disinherited her and she found a haven among Protestant pentecostals. Eventually, she became reinvolved in the Catholic Church and began exercising her spiritual gifts of healing and prophecy in the 1970s against the background of the Charismatic renewal. She carried out her ministry entirely from her home, remaining deferential to a disapproving pastor by attending mass but abstaining from the sacraments in order to avoid confrontation. During the Marian year of 1987, she heard increasingly from both Mary and the Holy Spirit, and was banned from her parish and eventually excommunicated from the Catholic Church.

The contrast between these two healers illuminates a variety of crisscrossing themes in the dynamics between tradition and modernity, male and female, orthodoxy and improvisation, cohesion and dislocation. The power manifest in Edeh's ministry could have a remote effect through notes submitted with prayer requests or holy water blessed by the priest to protect against theft, expose witchcraft, or tap the healer's power, whereas Kate's power was manifest only in direct personal contact with the healer, who granted individualized attention to each patient. Geographically, Edeh's activities and reputation extended throughout Igboland, whereas Kate's ministry was localized in her home and parish. Edeh's group disseminated items such as bumper stickers and preprinted prayers, engaging in a variety of commercial ventures, whereas Kate had no merchandise and charged a nominal fee for those who registered for her consultations. Edeh's activities invoked the power of literacy both through preprinted prayers and the practice of submitting written prayer requests, whereas Kate's communication with her followers was exclusively oral.

Edeh attributed his inspiration for the most part to the Holy Spirit, whereas Kate claimed inspiration from both the Holy Spirit and the Virgin Mary. Edeh's prayers and revelations were primarily directed toward healing, whereas Kate engaged in both healing and prophecy. Kate's prophetic messages often included quite precise predictions of personal tragedy—a feature that was likely perceived by religious authorities as a focus on the negative and hence spiritually suspect—and predictions of the dark political times under the regime of General Sani Abacha. Although Edeh emphasized the struggle against evil and countering witchcraft, Kate in addition focused on healing barrenness in her female clients. Finally, Father Edeh preached spiritual submissiveness, while the life, work, and demeanor of Sister Kate was a testimony to spiritual and personal independence.

Indeed, Sister Kate explicitly described herself as "modern," and Bastian not only describes her as a full-time career hospital worker but also describes her demure but contemporary attire, in contrast to the black clothing of the traditional Igbo visionary woman, who never bathes and is either sexually submissive or celibate. It was likewise striking that, during Bastian's interview with her, Sister Kate remained seated while a male follower stood in her presence, an explicit reversal of traditional gender dominance. In this context, it is noteworthy that Father Edeh in public made overt attacks on Sister Kate, saying that she was inspired by Satan and a manifestation of Mami Wata, the archetypal urban witch. Among the stories of Edeh's healings is one about a rich woman who obtained her money by witching and killing her husband and who repented when touched with holy water blessed by Edeh. Likewise, sick children who were enchanted *dada* twins when sprinkled with holy water turned into serpents, the moral of the incident being that bringing animal spirits into a patrilineage through bestial adultery is to be condemned. This Edeh story bears the anti-female message that multiple births are bad; for Sister Kate, multiple births were signs of blessing and double evidence of the healer's success in relieving barrenness.

These Nigerian examples outline the convergence of Igbo culture, in which it is more common to encounter male than female *dibia*, or diviners, and Catholic culture, which is characterized by an age-old tension between female visionary experience and male hierarchical control or suppression of such experience. Although males have never been excluded from such visionary experience, in the Charismatic renewal males as well as females have relatively equal access to the charisms, with the overall apparent result of strengthening the framework of patriarchal domination. Thus, while Edeh's healing ministry contributed to the cohesiveness of the Catholic Charismatic renewal, Kate's dislocations of tradition, gender norms, and doctrine proved too disruptive for her to retain a place within the movement.

## Charismatic Permutations of Transnational Transcendence

When I began to examine the international expansion of the Catholic Charismatic renewal in the mid-1970s, there was no scholarly language of globalization to support the discussion. What we had was the initial wave of world systems theory, which paid virtually no attention to the cultural dimension or to the existence of religion.[29] In this climate, I reverted to describing the movement as a "religious multinational" in analogy to multinational corporations, which were beginning to attract attention with respect to the interplay of local and global economic forces, and to the influential intentional communities that were the center of much Charismatic activity as "moral metropoles" in analogy to the center-periphery imagery of dependency theory.[30] The Charismatic renewal today still offers an opportunity to examine the nexus of local and global insofar as transnational influences within the movement, including highly mobile healing ministries and highly organized evangelism such as that associated with Ralph Martin's "FIRE Rallies,"[31] intersect with prayer groups and communities embedded in the religious life of distinct cultural settings. Likewise, the renewal offers the opportunity to examine the center-periphery relation with respect to its orientation toward Rome and its embeddedness in distinct local cultural milieus.

The three cases I have discussed represent three continents and, perhaps not coincidentally, are populous countries each of which is recognized as the most dynamic and diverse nation on its continent. Standing economically between the developed and developing worlds, these three crucibles of globalization may also be points of convergence between the fetishization of commodities and the fetishization of experience, and hence crucibles of religious ferment and reenchantment. Part of this is certainly related to the technological possibilities for the mediatization of spirituality in these nearly developed nations. At the same time, specificities of the cultural milieus in these countries offer intriguing grounds for further comparison of Charismatic permutations. Brazil is a predominantly Catholic nation where the renewal interacts with strong Marian traditions, Kardecist spiritism, and the gamut of African Brazilian religions. Nigeria is an ethnically diverse nation where Catholicism is strongest among the Igbo, and the renewal exists in relation to traditional religion in the local setting and within the Christian-Islamic dynamic on the national scene. India's Catholic population tends to be concentrated regionally in the southwest, and the renewal exists in relation to Hindu and Muslim traditions.

The dimensions of comparison multiply if one considers the varying contours of the movement around the globe. The relative roles of clergy and laity constitute one such dimension: the renewal in Canada emphasizes its distinctiveness from the U.S. branch by highlighting the prominent role of clergy. The degree of U.S. influence is varyingly acknowledged; for example, in France, the flavor of the movement was quickly nationalized toward French sensibilities. The relative roles of missionaries from various religious orders and of covenant communities from the United States and France also affect the tenor of transnational transcendence within the movement. Differing patterns of penetration to ethnic Catholics in multicultural societies such as the United States and to indigenous groups like the Mapuche in Chile or the Navajo in the United States can be traced. Some countries entertain more than one strand of what is ostensibly the same renewal: Italy has one strand associated with the international movement that includes both prayer groups and communities, and another composed of conservative and elderly people oriented toward experiencing and documenting charisms; Zambia has a branch started by Irish missionaries and a branch started by the indigenous Archbishop Milingo; Zaire has *charismatiques*, who participate in organized prayer groups with an identified leader and emphasis on charisms, and the *renouveaux*, composed of young educated urbanites whose practice emphasizes group prayer.[32]

Adherents in some countries can cite precedents for the renewal or for orientation toward the Holy Spirit. In the United States, it was the Cursillo movement; in the Congo, it was the Jamaa movement; Hungary had the Social Mission Society founded in 1908 and the Holy Spirit Society founded in the 1930s. Various patterns of transclass alliances in the name of helping the poor and in competition with social justice Catholicism can be identified in a number of countries, particularly in Latin America. There is variation in the relative importance of ritual healing, especially deliverance from evil spirits, in countries where the encounter with "paganism" in the form of indigenous religion or of "new age" spirituality is prominent. In some instances, the renewal may be part of a broader shift in the entire religious landscape; for example, in Indonesia it has been reported that the main distinction within the Christian community is no longer between Catholic and Protestant but between Charismatic/Pentecostal and non-pentecostal, or between "those who clap in Church and those who don't."[33]

Equally as interesting as examining relations within the Charismatic renewal between the global and the local, or center and periphery, is to recognize in this and perhaps other contemporary transnational religious phenomena a tension between the impulse toward a universal culture and the tendency for postmodern cultural fragmentation. I will identify the poles of this tension with two images, the first of which epitomizes uniformity and the second, disintegration.

In 2001, I was poised to reinitiate my study of the Charismatic renewal after a 10-year hiatus. I learned that the International Catholic Charismatic Renewal Services in Rome was planning to hold a seminar in the Mediterranean on the topic of deliverance from demons led by a leading expert on this form of healing, a Portuguese-surnamed priest from the west of India. This seminar, intended as advanced training for those from around the world who already had experience in the deliverance ministry, appeared to present an ideal opportunity for me to gain an initial sense of the cross-cultural variation in encounters with evil spirits and to develop a set of contacts that could be pursued with subsequent visits to the field. Mobilizing some of my old contacts among the movement leadership, I obtained the letter of sponsorship required to register for this seminar—a prerequisite intended to ensure the necessary level of spiritual maturity and legitimacy among participants who were to deal with the sensitive issue of casting out demons, and certainly necessary for a movement outsider such as myself. Then, just as the preparations were under way, I learned that the seminar had been canceled for lack of sufficient participants. The reason, however—and this is the point of the story—was not that there was insufficient interest nor that the likely candidates could not afford the expense of travel, but that the Portuguese Indian priest had already presented his experiences among so many Charismatics in so many settings around the world that those who might have participated appear to have judged the experience as redundant. The voice for a universal culture of healing had preempted itself from drawing into the center that which it had already sallied forth to touch in its indigenous settings. Perhaps such an encounter among healers with diverse experiences might have called into question rather than promoted the homogenizing goals of the event.

The contrasting image of cultural fragmentation is contained in the story of Archbishop Emmanuel Milingo of Lusaka, Zambia. Independent of any broader movement, Milingo began to practice divine healing in 1973.[34] In 1976, he established a relationship with the Word of God covenant community in the United States and founded his own Divine Providence Community. In 1979, the archbishop was a prominent participant in a Charismatic pilgrimage to Lourdes. His teachings exhibited a simultaneous indigenization of Charismatic ritual healing and a Charismatization of a distinctly African form of Christian healing. More remarkable, however, is that within four years, in 1983, his healing ministry had created such controversy that he was recalled to Rome. There, he was detained and interrogated, and he eventually relinquished his ecclesiastical post. In return, he was granted an appointment as a special delegate to the Pontifical Commission for Migration and Tourism, with the freedom to travel (except to Zambia), and was reassured by the pope that his healing ministry would be "safeguarded." Ironically, given that the overt goal of his recall was in part to protect Zambian Catholics from what must have appeared to church officials as a kind of neo-paganism, Milingo subsequently became immensely popular as a healer among Italian Catholic Charismatics. In 1987, with established followings in 10 Italian cities and already a figure on national television, he moved his public healing service from the Church of Argentini of Rome to a large room in the Ergife Hotel. Once again, in 1989, his controversial ministry was temporarily suspended by the Catholic Church, and later renewed outside Rome.[35] In 1994, the Bishop's Conference in Tuscany issued a pastoral note on demonology and witchcraft quite likely targeted at Milingo's ministry. The archbishop next reemerged into the public spotlight at the turn of the millennium as a new devotee of the Reverend Sun Myung Moon's Unification Church. As much of a scandal as his apparent defection from the Church—or perhaps from his own standpoint, a new level of ecumenism—was his ritual marriage to a young Korean follower of Moon in a ceremony central to the Unification doctrine. Only after a great deal of effort that doubtless included coaxing, negotiation, and threat did Milingo recant and return to the Catholic fold. The odyssey of Archbishop Milingo has contributed to a decentering of meaning and a diffusion of authority that cannot but take place in a global movement whose key symbol is, after all, speaking in tongues. The anthropologist Vittorio Lanternari describes the Milingo affair as a "religious short-circuit" between Africa and Europe. The case appears more representative than anomalous, however, if the Charismatic renewal is envisioned not as a modernist circuit diagram but as a global, postmodern montage of transposable spiritualities.[36]

Neither of these two images—of coherence and dislocation, respectively—allows us to conclude that the global Catholic Church has simply served as a kind of institutional trellis upon which the florescence of the Charismatic movement easily climbed. What is at stake is the fate of that particularly powerful master narrative called "salvation history" which, rather than being undermined by the decentering force of postmodernism, is now globally promulgated in a Charismatic, sensuous immediacy and in a multiplicity of idioms, not least of which is glossolalia. The differences between the early globalization of Catholicism and the globalization of the contemporary Catholic Charismatic renewal lie in the changed conditions for mass media and the ease of travel, both of which dramatically affect interactions between local adherents and the central leadership, and in the changed idioms of interaction with indigenous religions. A movement such as the Charismatic renewal weaves the cosmic time of salvation history into the fabric of everyday life, speeding it up and lending it a sense of urgency with the notion that the movement is part of a preparation for the end times before Christ's second coming. But it also provides the discipline of a carefully reconstructed habitus that organizes the rhythms of everyday life, particularly in the more highly elaborated Charismatic intentional communities.[37]

I am convinced that consideration of this movement will allow us to pose, if not yet to answer, some of the issues central to an understanding of religion as a global phenomenon in the twenty-first century. In my early analysis of the global implications of the movement, I proposed three hypotheses. The cultural hypothesis was that the Charismatic renewal was a potential vehicle of class consciousness for a transnational bourgeoisie insofar as it could be assumed that a world political/economic system must be accompanied by world religious and ideological systems. The structural hypothesis (especially relevant to Latin America) was that the appeal of the movement leapfrogs over the working classes to link the bourgeoisie with the very poor, with the excluded middle being the group with the greatest class antagonism to the bourgeoisie and to which the appeal of both classical Pentecostalism and socialism are strongest. It thus may be an ideological articulation of preexisting social relationships in terms of transcending class and cultural barriers in the name of Christianity, and also (as appears now to have been quite true) it may be an appeal to communitarian sentiment while advancing conservative values in opposition to liberation theology. Finally, the historical hypothesis was that the Charismatic renewal may play a role on a global scale analogous to that played by Methodism on a national scale in eighteenth-century England, insofar as it can be argued that both played a role in providing a moral framework and motivational language for the emergence of a new socioeconomic order.[38]

On another level—bodily experience—I will consider one theme with implications for the constitution of the self in global religious phenomena. Charismatics place a premium on bodily events and practices, including revelatory sensory imagery, the sacred swoon of being overcome by the Holy Spirit, and ritual gestures such as the laying on of hands and prostration in prayer.[39] To understand the central place of embodiment in the global Charismatic resacralization, it is useful to turn to the concept articulated by social theorists Philip Mellor and Chris Schilling of the "baroque modern body" that is characteristic of contemporary society. Baroque modern bodies are characterized by heightened sensuality and are, in addition, "internally differentiated, prone to all sorts of doubts and anxieties, and [prone] to be arenas of conflict."[40] Such a description fits the Charismatic body perfectly, and given examples such as those from India and Brazil, we can suggest that the Charismatic renewal, and perhaps other planetary religious forms, are promulgating this variant of embodiment in the global arena. Certainly, an analogy between the contemporary upsurge of sensuousness and that of the baroque cultures of Counter-Reformation Catholicism is telling, insofar as in the contemporary world Charismatic healing and other spiritual gifts are playing a role counter to the enthusiastic spirituality of Protestant pentecostalism.

Finally, the Charismatic renewal and other global religious phenomena lead us back to the question of whether we are witnessing an era of resacralization or reenchantment. In everyday social life, religious phenomena have already led to reformulated relations between local and global, center and periphery. As we have seen in the case of the Charismatic renewal, this has potential cultural and structural consequences and implications for our understanding of historical processes. Contrary impulses toward universal culture and toward cultural fragmentation have both become imbued with an aura of enchantment. Religious inflections of body and self combine with new modalities of alterity and subjectivity. At the least, such phenomena are of interest because they constitute the religious dimension of a global social system; at the most, they portend that religious consciousness will be seen to be a defining feature of contemporary global consciousness.

## NOTES

This essay, which has been revised for the present volume, is adapted by permission from Thomas Csordas, ed., *Transnational Transcendence: Essays on Religion and Globalization* (Berkeley: University of California Press, 2009).

1 Karla O. Poewe, ed., *Charismatic Christianity as a Global Culture* (Columbia: University of South Carolina Press, 1994); Simon Coleman, *The Globalisation of Charismatic Christianity: Spreading the Gospel of Prosperity* (Cambridge: Cambridge University Press, 2000); André Corten and Ruth Marshall-Fratani, eds., *Between Babel and Pentecost: Transnational Pentecostalism in Africa and Latin America* (Bloomington: Indiana University Press, 2001); Joel Robbins, "The Globalization of Pentecostal and Charismatic Christianity," *Annual Review of Anthropology* 33 (2004): 117–143; Alberto Melucci, *The Playing Self: Person and Meaning in the Planetary Society* (Cambridge: Cambridge University Press, 1996); Miroslav Volf, "Materiality of Salvation: An

Investigation in the Soteriologies of Liberation and Pentecostal Theologies," *Journal of Ecumenical Studies* 26.3 (1989): 447–467.

2  The Sword of the Spirit Worldwide Communities, http://www.swordofthespirit. net/sosmap508.pdf (accessed 4 Sept. 2009).

3  National Service Committee of the Catholic Charismatic Renewal: Resources, http://www.nsc-chariscenter.org/searchdb.asp (accessed 4 Sept. 2009).

4  Catholic Fraternity International, http://www.catholicfraternity.net/definition. html (accessed 1 Sept. 2009).

5  For Costa Rica: Setha Low, personal communication; for Zaire: Johannes Fabian, "Charisma: Global Movement and Local Survival," paper presented at the Global Culture: Pentecostal/Charismatic Movements Worldwide conference, Calgary Institute of the Humanities, 1991; for Zambia: Emmanuel Milingo, *The World in Between: Christian Healing and Struggle for Spiritual Survival* (Maryknoll, N.Y.: Orbis, 1984); for Italy: Enzo Pace, "Charismatics and the Political Presence of Catholics," *Social Compass* 25 (1978): 85–99.

6  Thomas J. Csordas, "Religion and the World System: The Pentecostal Ethic and the Spirit of Monopoly Capital," *Dialectical Anthropology* 17 (1992): 3–24; Csordas, "Oxymorons and Short-Circuits in the Re-enchantment of the World: The Case of the Catholic Charismatic Renewal," *Etnofoor* 8 (1995): 5–26; Csordas, *The Sacred Self: A Cultural Phenomenology of Charismatic Healing* (Berkeley: University of California Press, 1994); Csordas, *Language, Charisma, and Creativity: The Ritual Life of a Religious Movement* (Berkeley: University of California Press, 1997).

7  *ICCRS Newsletter* 11 (1986); *ICCRS Newsletter* 19 (1994).

8  "Potta Divine Retreat Center, Muringoor; Kerala, India," http://www.potta.com (accessed 16 Dec. 2009).

9  Murphy Halliburton, "Possession, Purgatives, or Prozac? Illness and the Process of Psychiatric Healing in Kerala, South India" (Ph.D. diss., City University of New York, 2000).

10  Divine Retreat Center, http://www.drcm.org (accessed 3 Sept. 2009).

11  Matthew N. Schmalz, "A Space for Redemption: Catholic Tactics in Hindu North India" (Ph.D. diss., University of Chicago, 1998); Schmalz, "Images of the Body in the Life and Death of a North Indian Catholic Catechist," *History of Religions* 39.2 (1999): 177–201; Schmalz, "The Silent Body of Audrey Santo," *History of Religions* 42.2 (2002): 116–142.

12  Schmalz, "Space for Redemption," 32.

13  Corinne Dempsey, *Kerala Christian Sainthood: Collisions of Culture and Worldview in South India* (New York: Oxford University Press, 2001), 32.

14  Homi Bhabha, *The Location of Culture* (New York: Routledge, 1994), 162.

15  Antonio Flavio Pierucci and Prandi Regeinaldo, "Religiões e Voto: A Eleição Presidencial de 1994 [Religions and the Vote: The Presidential Election of 1994]," *Opinião Publica Campinas* [Public Opinion Campinas] 3.1 (1995) 20–43; Pedro A. Ribeiro Oliveira, "Le Renouveau Charismatique au Brésil [The Charismatic Renewal in Brazil]," *Social Compass* 25 (1978): 37–42; Reginaldo Prandi, *Um Sopro do Spirito* [A Breath of the Spirit] (São Paulo, Brazil: EdUSP, 1997), 159–162.

16  Carlos Alberto Steil, "Renovação Carismática Catolica: Porta de Entrada ou de Saída do Catolicismo? Uma Etnografia do Grupo São José, em Porto Alegre [The

Catholic Charismatic Renewal: Port of Entrance or Exit from Catholicism? An Ethnography of the Group São José in Porto Alegre]," *Religião e Sociedade* [Religion and Society] 24 (2004): 11–36; Marjo de Theije, "A Caminhada do Louvor; ou, Como Carosmáticos e Católicos de Base vem se Relacionando na Pratica [The Walk of Praise; or, How Charismatics and Catholic Base Communities Relate in Practice]," *Religião e Sociedade* 24 (2004): 37–45; Eliane Martins de Oliveira, "O Mergulho no Espírito Santo: Interfaces Entre o Catolicismo Carismático e a Nova Era (O Caso da Communidade da Vida no Espirito Santo Canção Nova) [Diving in the Holy Spirit: Interfaces between Charismatic Catholicism and the New Age (The Case of the Community of the Life in the Holy Spirit New Song)," *Religião e Sociedade* 24 (2004): 85–112; Antonio Mendes da C. Braga, "TV Católica Canção Nova: Providência e Compromisso X Mercado e Consumismo [Catholic TV New Song: Providence and Commitment by Market and Consumerism]," *Religião e Sociedade* 24 (2004): 113–123.

17  Raymundo Heraldo Maués, "O Leigo Católico no Movimento Carismático em Belém do Pará [The Lay Catholic in the Charismatic Movement in Belém of Pará]" (Ph.D. diss., Universidade Federal do Pará, 1998).

18  Carlos Alberto Steil, "Aparições Marianas Contemporâneas e Carismatismo Católico [Contemporary Marian Apparitions and the Charismatic Catholic]," in *Fiéis e Cidadãos: Percusos de Sincretismo no Brasil* [Governors and Citizens: Impacts of Syncretism in Brazil], ed. Pierre Sanchis (Rio de Janeiro, Brazil: EDUER, 2000), 117–146; Carlos Alberto Steil, Cecília Loreto Mariz, and Mísia Lins Reesink, eds., *Maria Entre os Vivos: Reflexões Teóricas e Etnografias sobre Aparições Marianas no Brasil* [Mary among the Living: Theoretical and Ethnographic Reflections on Marian Apparitions in Brazil] (Rio Grande do Sul, Brazil: UFRGS, 2003).

19  Maria Jose Alves De Abreu, "On Charisma, Meditation and Broken Screens," *Etnofoor* 15.1–2 (2002): 240–258.

20  Ibid.

21  Steil, "Aparições Marianas Contemporâneas."

22  Steil, "Renovação Carismática Catolica."

23  Harold W. Turner, *History of an African Independent Church* (Oxford: Clarendon, 1967); J. D. Y. Peel, *Aladura: A Religious Movement among the Yoruba* (Oxford: Oxford University Press for International African Institute, 1968).

24  Matthews A. Ojo, "The Contextual Significance of the Charismatic Movements in Independent Nigeria," *Africa* 58 (1988): 184–185.

25  See Paul Gifford's essay in this volume.

26  Misty L. Bastian, "Take the Battle to the Enemies' Camp: Militarizing the Spirit in Nigerian Neo-Pentecostal Christianity," paper presented to the annual meeting of the American Anthropological Association, 2002.

27  Francis MacNutt, "Report from Nigeria," *New Covenant* 4 (1975): 9.

28  Misty L. Bastian, "A Tale of Two Visionaries: Father Edeh, Sister Kate, and Visions of the Everyday in Southeastern Nigeria," in *Religious Modernities in West Africa: New Moralities in Colonial and Post-Colonial Societies*, ed. Rijk van Dijk and John Hanson (Bloomington: Indiana University Press, forthcoming).

29  Immanuel Wallerstein, *The Modern World-System: Capitalist Agriculture and the Origins of the European World-Economy in the Sixteenth Century* (New York: Academic, 1974). For early recognition of the importance of culture and religion, see Maurice

Godelier, *Perspectives in Marxist Anthropology* (Cambridge: Cambridge University Press, 1977); Robert Wuthnow, "World Order and Religious Movements," in *Studies of the Modern World-System*, ed. Albert Bergeson (New York: Academic, 1980); Roland Robertson, "Globalization, Politics, and Religion," in *The Changing Face of Religion*, ed. James A. Beckford and Thomas Luckman (London. Sage, 1989), 10–23; Robertson, *Globalization: Social Theory and Global Culture* (London: Sage, 1992); Roland Robertson and JoAnn Chirico, "Humanity, Globalization, and Worldwide Religious Resurgence: A Theoretical Exploration," *Sociological Analysis* 46 (1985): 219–242; Daniel Chirot and Thomas D. Hall, "World-System Theory," *Annual Review of Sociology* 8 (1982): 81–106; Immanuel Wallerstein, "Crises: The World-Economy, the Movements, and the Ideologies," in *Crises in the World-System*, ed. Albert Bergeson (London: Sage, 1983), 21–36; and Wallerstein, "Culture as the Ideological Battleground of the Modern World-System," *Theory, Culture, and Society* 7 (1990): 31–55.

30  Since that time, Robertson in "Glocalization," in *Global Modernities*, ed. Mike Featherstone, Christopher Lash, and Roland Robertson (London: Sage, 1995), 25–44, has borrowed the international business jargon term "glocalization" and introduced it to social theory as a means of identifying the local-global problematic.

31  "FIRE" stands for Faith, Intercession, Repentance, and Evangelism.

32  Csordas, *Language, Charisma, and Creativity.*

33  Selly Errington, personal communication.

34  Milingo, *World in Between*, 137; Gerrie ter Haar, "Religion and Healing: The Case of Milingo," *Social Compass* 34 (1987): 475–493; and ter Haar, *Spirit of Africa: The Healing Ministry of Archbishop Milingo of Zambia* (London: Hurst, 1992).

35  Vittorio Lanternari, *Medicina, Magia, Religione, Valori* (Naples, Italy: Liguori, 1994).

36  Vittorio Lanternari, *Medicina, Magia, Religione: Dalla Cultura Populare alle Società Traditionali* (Rome: Libreria Internazionale Esedra, 1987), 165–182.

37  Csordas, *Language, Charisma, and Creativity.*

38  Csordas, "Religion and the World System."

39  Csordas, "Embodiment as a Paradigm for Anthropology," *Ethos* 18 (1990): 5–47; and Csordas, *Body/Meaning/Healing* (New York: Palgrave, 2002).

40  Philip A. Mellor and Chris Schilling, *Re-Forming the Body: Religion, Community, and Modernity* (London: Sage, 1997), 47.

# 17

# Global Awakenings: Divine Healing Networks and Global Community in North America, Brazil, Mozambique, and Beyond

*Candy Gunther Brown*

On a steamy, 90-degree evening in 2007 in the equatorial town of Imperatriz in northeastern Brazil, the Miracle Healing Crusade sponsored by 20 local churches and featuring North American evangelist Randy Clark and his Global Awakening team attracted 10,000 attendees, 5 percent of the town's population. The night before, a marching band waving a welcome banner lettered in English had greeted Clark and the 70 other North Americans who had volunteered to travel with him at their own expense. As the crusade began, Clark called a young Brazilian woman up to the platform to sing. Sylvia—a local television news anchor—electrified the audience with a popular Brazilian song: "Podoroso," or "Most Powerful God." Many of those present knew Sylvia and the story she retold that evening. Two years before, she had come to a Global Awakening crusade in Imperatriz. Doctors had sent her home to die from cancer of the thorax. Sylvia had arrived at the 2005 crusade weighing a mere 80 pounds, too weak to stand, and coughing up blood. Clark and some of his team had spent an hour praying for Sylvia as she felt the power and love of God coursing through her body. By the end of the prayer, Sylvia believed herself miraculously healed and felt strong enough to stand up to testify of her healing and to sing a song of praise to God. During the past two years, Sylvia had remained symptom-free, soon regaining a healthy weight and returning to her broadcasting job.[1]

After Sylvia sang and gave her testimony at the 2007 crusade, Clark announced that the power and love of God were present to heal tonight just like God had healed Sylvia two years before. Clark called up members of his team to deliver "words of knowledge"[2]—divine revelations about specific conditions that God wanted to heal immediately: pain in the right knee, kidney failure, lower back pain. Clark prayed over the entire congregation using a mixture of English, which an interpreter translated, and brief Portuguese phrases he had memorized. Clark began by welcoming the Holy Spirit and asking God to send angels to assist with the healings. He commanded each of the problems mentioned in the words of knowledge to be healed in Jesus' name and took authority over all sicknesses, pains, and demons present, commanding them to leave in Jesus' name. Clark then asked the audience to test their bodies to see what they were able to do now that they could not do before and to find out whether pains had disappeared. He asked those whose conditions were at least 80 percent improved to wave their arms so that others could have their faith encouraged. Scores of arms began to wave across the auditorium, and people filed up to the stage to testify to their healings. Clark gave an altar call, telling those who were not Christians but who had just witnessed the power and love of God that they now had an obligation to respond by placing their trust in Jesus and renouncing all other gods and spirits. Dozens streamed forward to pray, after which they were greeted by local pastors, who counseled them as new believers.

Clark then released his team to pray one-on-one with those who still needed healing. Lines formed behind each team member, as people eager for prayer came forward. With the help of Brazilian translators—mostly young adults who had learned English in school—team members conducted brief interviews: "What is your name? Why do you want prayer? Are you a Christian? What was going on in your life when the pain began? Is there anyone you need to forgive? Have you ever been involved in the occult?" Team members led those who needed healing through short prayers to forgive those who had wronged them and to renounce participation in "occult" practices. Then they prayed briefly for healing: "In the name of Jesus, demons leave now. Be healed in Jesus' name. Check your body. A little better? Let's keep praying. Check again. No pain left? Praise God!" Around midnight, Clark called his team back to the buses, promising more prayer at tomorrow night's crusade.

Global Awakening (GA), founded and directed by Randy Clark and currently headquartered in Mechanicsburg, Pennsylvania, is one of the most influential of a number of transnational, cross-cultural, relational and institutional networks whose divine healing practices are contributing to the global expansion of Christianity. This essay uses a discussion of GA international ministry trips to Brazil and the broader context of GA's transnational ministry networks to illumine three themes: first, the creation of new forms of community through the globalization of healing practices; second, the reciprocal impacts of cross-cultural divine healing networks; and third, how divine healing practices fuel church growth. In this chapter, I will argue that GA international trips exemplify a multidirectional pattern of exchange between North American missionaries and healing communities on other continents. By emphasizing the capacity of "ordinary" Christians as agents of healing, North American pentecostals facilitate the democratization of global healing practices. In turn, supernaturalizing trends return to North America through people's exposure to worldviews and rituals in such places as Brazil and Mozambique.

Global Awakening grew out of revivals dubbed the Toronto Blessing—nightly meetings at a midsize Toronto church that began in 1994 and continued for more than a decade.[3] The revivals reputedly began unexpectedly—shortly after local pastor John Arnott visited Argentina to receive prayer from Claudio Freidzon— during a visit by Missouri pastor Randy Clark, who had himself recently received prayer from a South African missionary to the United States, Rodney Howard-Browne. As participants in the Toronto meetings experienced unaccustomed manifestations that they attributed to the Holy Spirit, such as laughing, shaking, falling, and avowed miraculous healings, a planned four-day service series turned into the longest protracted meeting in North American history. An estimated 3 million people from many Christian denominations and countries undertook pilgrimages to Toronto, searching for physical healing or spiritual renewal, and many claimed that when they returned home they brought the revival fires with them.[4]

Heidi Baker was one such pilgrim, a self-described "burned-out" American missionary to Mozambique. After visiting Toronto in 1996, Baker reported that her organizational network, Iris Ministries, grew from two churches and a children's home to 7,000 churches and homes for 10,000 orphaned children—as miraculous healings, the supernatural multiplication of food, and resurrections of the dead fueled church growth in predominantly Muslim areas of one of the poorest countries in the world. Iris, which often works in partnership with GA, also opened bases in 24 additional countries, and Baker now spends 100 days per year speaking at international conferences.[5] As others traveled to Toronto, Clark founded GA as an "apostolic network of churches and ministries," and regularly took with him hundreds of volunteers to conduct meetings in 36 countries, prominently including Brazil, Mozambique, and India. Global Awakening has attracted crowds of 100,000 people at a time; divine healing claims often number in the thousands for a single event.[6]

Global Awakening's strategies have been shaped by and have also shaped global healing practices. Hearing reports of revivals in Argentina, Colombia, and Brazil, Clark traveled to observe the revivals and to find out why evangelistic events seemed more effective there than in North America—reportedly attracting 60,000 people to a typical crusade with retention rates for new converts of

85–90 percent, in contrast to the 6 percent average retention for smaller U.S. crusades.[7]

Clark has sought to combine Billy Graham's interdenominational networking and follow-up through local churches with the supernaturalist approaches of Latin Americans. Clark emulates the Argentine Omar Cabrera's strategies of evangelizing through healing crusades, asking God to send healing angels, explaining words of knowledge, and asking people to begin waving once they feel 80 percent better. Clark borrows from Argentine evangelist Carlos Annacondia and his Director of Deliverance Ministry, Pablo Bottari, in praying en masse against demonic oppression followed by one-on-one ministry in a designated deliverance tent to bring individuals *liberación* from demons.[8] (See Matthew Marostica's essay in this volume.) Clark's *Ministry Training Manual*, which is used by churches worldwide and has been translated into eight languages with several more translations under way, takes its section on exorcism directly from Bottari's book *Libres en Cristo*, which has been translated from Spanish into English as *Free in Christ*.[9] Cabrera, Annacondia, Bottari, and two Brazilian worship bands, Casa de Davi (House of David) and Nova Geração (New Generation), have conducted crusades and marketed their books, CDs, and DVDs in the United States and Canada.[10]

Clark became particularly interested in Brazil—spending 50–60 days there annually over a 10-year period—after hearing what he understood to be a prophetic word from God: that there would be a revival in Brazil 12 times greater than the one in Toronto, just as Argentina and Brazil's Iguazu Falls are 12 times larger than Niagara Falls, and that a missionary movement would go from Brazil to Mozambique, in both of which Portuguese is spoken.[11] Global Awakening works closely with networks of local Pentecostal, Baptist, and New Apostolic movement churches and ministries, such as Casa de Davi and Nova Geração in Brazil and Iris Ministries in Mozambique, seeking to build international bridges among the groups in its global network.

Global Awakening is not as high profile—or wealthy—as some pentecostal television ministries; names like Benny Hinn in the United States or the Igreja Universal do Reino de Deus (IURD), the Universal Church of the Kingdom of God, in Brazil might sound more familiar. Global Awakening—like many of its network affiliates, such as Iris in Mozambique—has intentionally steered away from prosperity teachings that emphasize that Christians can become wealthy by sowing money into the kingdom of God via contributions to the speaker's ministry—even though such teachings are effective in raising funds.[12] Yet few organizations have approached GA's effectiveness in networking leaders and members of diverse Christian traditions worldwide, including Word of Faith megachurches, classical Pentecostals, Catholics, Anglicans, Lutherans, Methodists, New Apostolic networks, and Baptists. Clark seeks to bring diverse "streams" of the church together. "[H]ealing streams come together to make a major healing river of God. My purpose," says Clark, "is not to put any stream down, but to say here is the stream, here is the teaching, here are the strengths and the weaknesses. This weakness can be handled by this stream over there that is strong in that area. We need all streams flowing together."[13] Because GA uses conferences and training materials to equip pastors and laity to return to their *own* churches with greater effectiveness rather than seceding to form a new denomination—in Clark's language, his role is "lighting fires"—it is diffi-cult to quantify the organization's influence.[14] Yet there is reason to believe that this influence is enormous and that the activities of GA are representative of a large number of similar transnational healing networks—such as those bro-kered by Mensa Otabil, Reinhard Bonnke, David Yonggi Cho, Sérgio Von Hel-der, Mahesh Chavda, Ché Ahn, David Hogan, Dennis Balcombe, Heidi Baker, Bill Johnson, and Leif Hetland—the last three of whom acknowledge major debts to Clark and GA.[15]

## Divine Healing Networks and the Creation of Global Community

Hundreds of North Americans each year participate in a GA international ministry trip; the most popular destination is Brazil. Traveling with GA can be viewed within the overlapping frameworks of short-term missions, Chris-tian tourism, and religious pilgrimage.[16] A Brazil trip is moderately expensive: $2,500 for two weeks, including transportation, the best hotels, and buffet breakfasts and meat-heavy lunches. By contrast, the $3,500 Mozambique trip fee does not include lodging or meals—but Iris provides these at no charge, asking only that visitors consider a donation. Participants sleep in hostel-style bunk rooms under mosquito nets, share simple co-ed bathrooms and showers, often go without running water or electricity, and eat the same rice and beans served to the base's resident children and pastors in training. Although the modal age of Mozambique trekkers is a bit younger than those bound for Brazil, most GA travelers are middle-class empty-nesters or retirees with time and money on their hands, who want more than a tourist experience. Many people on a given trip have traveled with GA before and know others from previous trips. Small church groups sometimes travel together, but more often individ-uals and couples come on their own, expecting and generally finding an imme-diate sense of community with others influenced by the same conference speakers and books.[17]

The leading reason people give for traveling with GA is that they are tired of listening to other people's stories of the miraculous and want stories of their own. Many—including leaders like Clark and Baker—point back to at least one time in their lives when they experienced God's love for them in a particularly intense way through healing, which whetted their appetites to experience more of the love of God and to express greater love for God and for other people, including those from other cultures.[18] Most team members, whether pastors or laity, also feel dissatisfied with their local church and want to participate in a community of like-minded believers and to receive personal attention from charismatic leaders.[19]

Participants always refer to GA network leaders like Randy Clark and Heidi Baker by their first names without titles; many insist that they decided to go on a trip because Randy extended a personal invitation to travel with him—although Clark would likely not remember most of these individuals since he typically extends a hundred such invitations in a single conference. The accessibility of leaders like Clark is nevertheless striking when compared with higher-profile figures like Benny Hinn—who also leads international trips, but keeps his distance from attendees who might at most hope to stand within a few feet of "Pastor Benny."[20] On a GA trip, it is possible to sit next to Randy at breakfast. Hinn, moreover, cultivates an aura of his own distinctive anointing, whereas Clark insists that, in the words of one his book's titles, *God Can Use Little Ole Me*—which refers to Clark and to every team member, whom Clark encourages to pray for the sick and to expect to see miracles through their own prayers.[21] Clark also assures people that they are not on their own to work up enough faith for their own or another's healing; he and other team members are available to pray repeatedly.[22]

The pace of most GA trips is intense. On a typical day in Brazil, the team rises in time to eat breakfast and travel by bus for up to an hour before a 9 a.m. meeting. The service breaks up by 1 p.m., after which the team eats lunch at a local restaurant—the last formal meal of the day. During the afternoon, there might be an hour or two back at the hotel, but some days this time is spent visiting an orphanage or rehabilitation center. Then, it is time to get back on the bus to go to the evening meeting—which might last from 6 p.m. until after midnight, when light snacks are provided by local churches. Bedtime is typically after 1 a.m., followed by an early start the next day. Rooming groups—GA assigns two team members per hotel room—take turns praying for one-hour shifts throughout the night. During a two-week trip, the team is given at least one afternoon to buy souvenirs and visit a single tourist site; during a trip to Rio de Janeiro in 2007, the trip coordinator pointed out the famous tourist beaches outside the bus window, noting that there was not time to stop. The intensity of the trip is part of the appeal. This type of travel is a pilgrimage experience in which participants enter into a liminal, transformative zone distinct from their everyday routines.[23] Although an expression of globalization, the trip provides a rare opportunity to escape the constant sensory input, work and family obligations, and communication demands of life in a globalized world. Long airplane and bus rides, hours spent singing and praying every day, the difficulty and expense of calling home or accessing the internet, and trip policies against watching television—all create an atmosphere in which the sacred is expected to intrude into the mundane world at every moment.[24]

Although volunteering as short-term missionaries, trip participants expect to get as much as they give. This shift from the older philosophies of Christian missions can be read as reversing patterns of colonialism and cultural imperialism by exhibiting greater sensitivity to the weaknesses of North American Christianity and the strengths of other cultures. A more troubling reading is also possible. North American missionaries can be interpreted as products of engrained patterns of imperialistic thought that function to reinforce rather than resist the problematic aspects of globalization. Short-term missionaries feel compelled to travel to other countries less by their desire to pray for the sick—who can be found in abundance at home—than by their desire to benefit from cultural others' experiences of pain and its relief. Local churches and ministries, such as Iris in Mozambique, do provide long-term relief and development aid; however, at the conclusion of mass crusades such as those commonly held in Brazil, short-term missionaries quickly leave without making any commitment to the individuals for whom they prayed and without working to transform the political, economic, and social structures that contribute to ongoing suffering by limiting access to nutrition and health care.[25] Indeed, participation in GA international trips seems to confirm the prior assumption of many North American pentecostals that the problems confronting the developing world are so severe that miracles offer the only viable solution. After returning home, North American pentecostals may be even less likely to engage in political or social activism addressing the systemic material causes of global political and economic oppression. These pentecostals may even be confirmed in self-satisfied complacency, since they have done their part by replacing an annual vacation in the Bahamas with a ministry trip to Brazil.

North American team members and Christians in host countries like Brazil nevertheless share many values, beliefs, and practices in common, and they usually identify as members of a single church universal (figure 17.1). During their first day after arriving in Brazil in September 2007, a team of 60 North Americans stepped off their tour bus and filtered into the pews of a large, unfinished concrete church building in Rio, from which they could view dilapidated housing through cut-outs in the walls that served as windows. Within 15 minutes, the visitors had blended almost seamlessly into the local congregation, as all participated in a common culture of singing songs to God—in Portuguese, with English translations projected overhead for the visitors' benefit.

Linguistic differences are viewed as superficial barriers to communication within the church universal. Since God—as well as angels and demons—presumably understand prayers in every language, participants expect that healing can take place even when communication is imperfect. Glossolalia, or speaking in tongues, is seen as a universal language that reaches God directly.[26] Brazilian churches do attempt to provide translators, but their abilities vary, and often there are more North Americans than translators (figure 17.2). Global Awakening provides team members with a CD of Portuguese phrases commonly

FIGURE 17.1. Brazilians welcoming the Global Awakening team upon their arrival at the airport in Rio de Janeiro, Brazil (2007). Courtesy Candy Gunther Brown.

used in prayer and urges their memorization. Yet most team members arrive without having learned much, if any, Portuguese. They simply plan to rely on the provided translators, a stance which might be criticized as reflecting North American cultural arrogance. Disregard for the cultural respect exhibited by learning someone else's language extends to most visible GA preachers—with the significant exceptions of Baker, who is fluent in Portuguese and conversant in several local Mozambican languages, and Clark, who uses as much Portuguese as he can while preaching and even when conversing with English-speaking Brazilian pastors. Other GA network preachers—even after as many as 18 trips to Brazil—continue to speak exclusively in English, even when repeating such a common refrain as "Praise God," which could easily be rendered as "Glória ao Deus."[27] Neither have most GA team members done any background research on Brazilian churches, yet at least some assume, condescendingly and inaccurately, that Brazilians know very little about Christian practice—as, for instance, when the U.S. leader of a joint intercessory prayer meeting in Rio instructed Brazilian co-leaders and participants in how to conduct intercessory prayer. There are almost always, in the larger meetings, a few Brazilians fluent in both Portuguese and English who can prevent such major miscommunications as giving public testimony to a healing that obviously has not occurred. It seems probable, however, that team members working with

FIGURE 17.2. Brazilian translators assisting the Global Awakening team during a stadium crusade, Belém, Pará, Brazil (2004). Courtesy Candy Gunther Brown.

less-proficient translators do make unsubstantiated claims, especially since those requesting prayer might not want to disappoint the person praying.

The ideal of a global Christian community, rather than obscuring cultural differences, values using differences to correct weaknesses in each cultural expression of Christianity. One reason Brazilian churches invite GA to visit—much as North American churches invite international visitors—is that they want an outsider's perspective. Sometimes, this leads to sharp criticisms, as when Clark directed a pointed sermon at pastors in Imperatriz, urging them to set aside their translations of old American hymns in preference for new Portuguese songs birthed in the Brazilian revivals, and to shed their climate-inappropriate, dark, two-piece suits and ties that they had modeled after U.S. missionaries.[28] Clark also urged the pastors to stop sitting onstage—joking that these were bad seats that gave them a view of the back of the preacher's head—and follow GA's democratized model of leaders mixing with the people.

Cross-cultural criticism goes in both directions, as when Brazilian leaders of Casa de Davi called on a U.S. team visiting the group's headquarters in Londrina to repent of national sins, which the Brazilians believed had caused 9/11 and Hurricane Katrina.[29] Writing a chapter for a book edited by Clark and marketed in the United States, Argentine Pablo Deiros argued that the need for deliverance ministry is greater in North America than in Latin America, and he estimated that 80 percent of U.S. church members are demonized.[30] When Pablo Bottari speaks in the United States, he criticizes practices accepted in North American churches that he sees as dangerous dabbling with the occult.[31]

Reciprocal Impacts of Cross-Cultural Interactions

North Americans take from cross-cultural interactions an expectancy that God performs miracles and that supra-human agents, such as angels and demons, help or hinder healing; these views push against a faith plus holiness equals healing formula that accuses those not healed of lack of faith or of holiness. Significantly, however, it is a decontextualized supernaturalism that North American pentecostals often borrow from pentecostals in Latin America and elsewhere. Most economically and politically marginalized Latin American pentecostals are poignantly aware that there is a material context for their experiences of bodily suffering; although they call upon supernatural aid, many also engage in political and social activism and pursue entrepreneurial economic activities, because they assume a dynamic interaction between the material and spiritual worlds. North American appropriators are more prone to rely solely upon spiritual rather than material solutions—at least when contemplating the seemingly overwhelming needs of the developing world. At the same time, GA exports healing models—including those originating in Latin America, but repackaged in democratized forms—to Latin American churches that have defined healing and deliverance as the special province of gifted evangelists or pastors.

Global Awakening team members are most likely to express discomfort not with supernatural healing claims—however implausible these may sound to outsiders—but rather with apparent demonic manifestations, which sometimes involve unseemly bodily expressions, such as vomiting, biting, screaming, clawing, or writhing, that sit uneasily with North American middle-class sensibilities of decorum.[32] Although Clark emulates Latin American evangelists in commanding demons to leave from the platform, he admittedly does not like to teach on deliverance nor handle one-on-one deliverance himself.[33] Every GA team member is expected to pray for healing, but only those who feel comfortable with deliverance are asked to place an identifying mark, such as an orange sticker, on their name badges so that other team members can find them if the need arises. Although most participants in GA conferences agree about the basics of divine healing, sometimes impassioned disagreements arise—among North American team members, between North Americans and Brazilians, and among Brazilians—over how deliverance should be conducted.[34]

As North Americans gain a heightened expectation of the supernatural, they disseminate a democratized model for how divine healing should be practiced.[35] Global Awakening's contribution is less theological—since Brazilian churches already commonly embrace a theology that God heals miraculously—than practical, teaching and showing by example that God will heal through the prayers of ordinary church members. Whenever Clark travels to Brazil, he takes with him a team of 60–180 self-described homemakers, business people, doctors, retirees, and teenagers whose prayers for healing are represented as being as effective as Clark's. One reason that Brazilian churches invite Clark—and invite him to return repeatedly—is that he does not emphasize his own unique gifting so much as he equips local churches to continue praying for healing after the conclusion of a crusade. A large proportion—by Andrew Chesnut's estimate, 86.4 percent—of Brazilian Christians claim to have received divine healing, but a much smaller proportion—an estimated 11.4 percent—claim to have been used by God to heal others.[36]

Global Awakening typically offers morning training sessions as well as evening healing crusades. In addition to teaching, team members model how to pray for healing—particularly mentoring the young translators, who by the end of a weeklong crusade are beginning to pray on their own. Global Awakening uses some training materials developed in North America, including a 5-step healing model and instructions on how to receive words of knowledge introduced by Vineyard USA founder John Wimber in the 1970s; this material is coupled with training materials developed by Latin Americans, such as a 10-step deliverance model created by Pablo Bottari in the 1980s.[37] During a typical morning training in Rio, Clark's associate Rodney Hague, in the characteristic drawl of a Southern Baptist from Texas that his interpreter had trouble translating, taught on deliverance. He emphasized the need to "close doors" to demonic activity by forgiving others, breaking soul ties established by sex outside of marriage, and renouncing occult involvement—using Bottari's model filtered through several layers of linguistic mediation, having been translated from Spanish to English to Portuguese. Some teachings—particularly on controversial topics such as deliverance—seem to be more acceptable to Brazilians when re-presented with the stamp of American approval, rather than being communicated more directly by other Latin Americans.[38]

As clearly as teaching, modeling, and imitation play roles in how GA transmits healing practices, Clark's central theological contribution is the concept of impartation.[39] Pointing to biblical precedents such as the apostle Paul's encouragement to his disciple Timothy that he not forget the gift given to him through the laying on of hands and prayer, Clark envisions healing as more contagious than disease, and the anointing, or oil-like spread, of the Holy Spirit as a tangible, transferable power, or love energy, that is caught rather than taught and imparted to others through human touch.[40] The emphasis on impartation encourages the democratization of healing practices—since anyone can become anointed by receiving impartation (and, indeed, new leaders within GA networks can emerge rapidly based upon a single, dramatic impartation experience)—but the emphasis also singles out certain leaders, like Clark, as particularly anointed.[41] Regardless of Clark's repeated insistence that people can be healed through the prayers of any team member—and that often the greatest miracles occur through someone else's prayers—there is always what insiders refer to as a long "Randy line" of those who will settle for prayer from no one else. Every international trip begins with an impartation service for the team during which Clark lays hands on each person. As one team member, Bill, a university-employed biomedical researcher who recounts that he was divinely healed of a brain tumor, described the experience, "Randy prayed for me to impart gifts of healing, and it was really powerful. My right hand was shaking for a long time after that. Then I had some other person pray over me, and it was powerful. . . . Later, I saw Randy standing by himself and asked for a second prayer of impartation, so he did. My hand was still shaking, so he just said something like 'I bless the power in that right hand.'" This team member went on to explain his apparent greediness for prayer: "I want as much anointing as I can carry, because there are many people who need healing. . . . The crusade that night was to be the most powerful yet for me."[42] Among those he believed healed through his prayers were two blind, orphaned brothers, 7 and 10 years old. An impartation service for Brazilians is always included in a multiday conference; team members who have received impartation help to pray for the Brazilians.

## Healing Practices and Church Growth

Prayer for healing and evangelism typically go hand in hand in GA conferences, as in the opening anecdote in which Clark gave an altar call for salvation from sin following testimonies of physical healing. Team members also evangelize as they pray for healing. Oblivious to scholars' explanations of healing claims as attributable to "misdiagnosis" or "placebo effect," believers relate intense subjective experiences of God expressing love through healing.[43] Indeed, salvation is, much as theologian Miroslav Volf articulated, envisioned in material as well as spiritual terms, providing health for body and soul.[44]

During a typical crusade interaction, a young man named Carlos requested prayer because he had pain caused by a lump on his foot. Carlos watched as several people in line before him claimed to experience healing. When Carlos's turn came, team member Bill asked Carlos whether he was a Christian. When Carlos said no, Bill told him that Jesus wanted to heal the whole person, not just his foot, and asked him whether he wanted to experience the love of God by becoming a Christian. Bill clarified that this would mean renouncing all other gods and spirits and trusting in Jesus only. Carlos said that he wanted to do this, so Bill, with the help of his translator, led Carlos through a prayer to accept Jesus as his only savior. Then Bill commanded the spirits of infirmity to leave

Carlos and commanded healing to his body in Jesus' name. Carlos soon reported that all pain was gone, and those around him attested to seeing the lump that had been on his foot disappear.[45] One of the local pastors then took over to counsel Carlos as a new Christian.

The distinctive epistemology shared by participants in GA events is that feeling, even more than seeing, is believing. Medical confirmation might be a plus, but it is viewed as inessential, even by team members who by profession belong to medical and scientific communities. Dan, a retired radiologist, prayed for a young man complaining of vision problems in his right eye, who appeared to have a white cataract; when Dan could no longer see a white spot in the man's eye and the man reported improved eyesight, a healing was declared. Bill, the biomedical researcher mentioned above, informally tested improvements in vision by asking those receiving prayer to count the number of fingers he held up from several feet away.[46] Similarly, Bill asked 18-year-old Sergio, presented by his father as having been deaf and mute since birth, to repeat words and sounds as he intoned them from behind his line of sight; Sergio did so in a hoarse, raspy voice that elicited applause from the gathering crowd.[47] Particular value is placed on experiences that can be felt by participants and witnessed by others, especially if there is a trophy seemingly proving that a problem once existed but does no longer. These conditions seemed to be met when 9-year-old Pedro showed that his right leg was two and a half inches shorter than his left leg. Within a few minutes of prayer, Pedro felt his leg grow out, those around could no longer detect a difference in length, and Pedro left carrying his shoe lift in his hands.[48] Often, people report experiencing heat or electricity, feeling pain move around before it disappears, or seeing a vision— for instance, of an angel performing surgery.

Global Awakening does not bring diagnostic equipment or medical personnel to conferences, nor is there any systematic effort to track whether people continue to claim healings the next day, let alone the next year. Internet-published trip "statistics"—the term used by GA for an unsystematic tally based upon a show of team members' fingers for how many people were saved, healed, and delivered each night through their prayers—are inherently unreliable for multiple reasons, including inconsistent standards for what counts as healing and an implicit pressure to inflate the number and severity of conditions healed. But the primary audience for trip statistics is not scientists but potential team members who want to travel where they, too, will experience the miraculous.[49] At the same time, GA neither preaches against the use of medicine as contrary to faith, nor does the group resist third-party scientific investigation of its healing claims. Indeed, GA granted permission for my team of researchers to use an audiometer and vision charts to test hearing and vision before and after prayer during healing conferences in Brazil and, co-sponsored with Iris Ministries, in Mozambique in 2009. Without attempting here to explain the results as a product either of psychosomatic or divine

processes—given space constraints that preclude such complex considerations—it must be noted that the post-prayer diagnostic tests did indicate significantly improved function for many, but not all, subjects who claimed
healing.[50]

North Americans who participate in GA's international ministry trips
believe that healing should be equally available at home, while confessing a
higher expectation of seeing miracles in places like Brazil, Mozambique, or
India, where faith in the supernatural seems more common and where there
is less opportunity to rely on doctors instead of God.[51] Global Awakening
leaders urge team members to use the faith boost gained from an international
trip to pray more expectantly once they return home. Global Awakening also
conducts healing schools and sells books, CDs, and DVDs in the United States
and Canada that attempt to demonstrate the accessibility of miracles—
especially in marketplace spaces sacralized by the performance of healing
rituals.[52] In 2009, GA began production of videotaped North American marketplace healing practices designed for broadcast on nonreligious networks as
reality TV.[53] The premise is that North American Christianity will be revitalized once people experience, not just read or hear about, the power and love
of God.

Notably absent in the valorization of marketplace healings is any sustained
critique of the social consequences of economic and political globalization. Healing advocates do envision their performances as counteracting selfish consumerism. Yet this same discourse can be read as contributing to the very commercial
processes that offers of free prayer purportedly destabilize. By harmonizing
prayer and commerce, sacralizing rituals seductively transform highly suspect
consumer-oriented spaces into sites of religiously legitimate activities. There is
nothing subversive here of white, patriarchal, capitalistic, U.S.–dominated structures that subsidize multinational corporations by paying inadequate wages
under substandard working conditions. The practice of marketplace healings
implies an acceptance of the existing economic and political structures as a
given, rather than subjecting them to critical scrutiny. By marketing healing
prayer—especially as North Americans borrow inspiration from pentecostals in
the two-thirds world—to supplement rather than critique marketplace practices,
North American pentecostals make opaque their own complicity in the problematic aspects of globalization.

In sum, Global Awakening brokers transnational divine healing networks
that make miracle cures appear more attainable. Yet, North American participants in multidirectional patterns of cultural exchange often overlook the material contexts and social, economic, and political implications of their
involvement in larger globalizing processes. Envisioning both the threat of
disease and the promise of healing in global terms, members of translocal
Christian communities contribute to and borrow from cross-cultural, health-
oriented interactions. North Americans may not expect to see many miracles at

home, but they do expect miracles in countries like Brazil. Lay Brazilians may expect miracles to occur, but perhaps not through their own prayers. At the conclusion of a GA conference, visiting and local participants may all express greater expectations of miraculous healing. Thus, the globalization of divine healing networks fuels the twin engines of supernaturalism and democratization, which together forcefully propel the global expansion of Christianity.

NOTES

1  Following an exploratory weeklong research visit to the Toronto Blessing in January 1995, I have been studying Global Awakening (GA) since 2003, using the ethnographic approaches of participant-observation, written surveys, and oral interviews; clinical measurements and statistical tests; and narrative analysis and archival research to study print and audiovisual materials. This study received Institutional Review Board approval before I began the ethnographic stage of research in 2005 (St. Louis University study no. 13946 and IU study no. 06-11383). I attended a large number of GA-related events in the United States (in California, Washington, Texas, Massachusetts, Pennsylvania, North Carolina, Florida, Missouri, Illinois, Indiana, Ohio) and Canada (Ontario), and conducted formal surveys and interviews at seven conferences: Toronto, Ontario, Canada (17–20 Aug. 2005); Harrisburg, Pennsylvania (2–5 Nov. 2005); St. Louis, Missouri (28 Feb.–3 Mar. 2006); Rio de Janeiro, Brazil (15–19 Sept. 2007); Imperatriz, Maranhão, Brazil (21–25 Sept. 2007); Londrina, Paraná, Brazil (10–15 June 2008); Pemba, Cabo Delgado, Mozambique (31 May–13 June 2009). The opening anecdote is based primarily on a single evening's meeting in Imperatriz, 24 Sept. 2007, although some details were borrowed from similar services. I have changed names, like Sylvia's, to protect the identities of informants, with the exception of public leaders.

2  Pentecostals cite 1 Corinthians 12:8 for the "word of knowledge" as one of the nine gifts of the Holy Spirit.

3  See David Hilborn, *"Toronto" in Perspective: Papers on the New Charismatic Wave of the Mid-1990s* (Waynesboro, Ga.: Acute, 2001), 7; Margaret Poloma, *Main Street Mystics: The Toronto Blessing and Reviving Pentecostalism* (New York: Rowman and Littlefield, 2003), 87.

4  For the claim that 3 million people visited Toronto, see Global Awakening, "About Us," http://www.globalawakening.com/Groups/1000014260/Global_Awakening/Global/Global.aspx (accessed 18 Mar. 2009).

5  Heidi Baker and her husband, Rolland, co-direct Iris Ministries, but Heidi is the more public figure. See Iris's website, http://www.irismin.org/p./home.php, and Rolland Baker and Heidi Baker, *There Is Always Enough: God's Miraculous Provision among the Poorest Children on Earth* (Grand Rapids, Mich.: Chosen Books, 2003); Heidi Baker and Rolland Baker, *Expecting Miracles: True Stories of God's Supernatural Power and How You Can Experience It* (Grand Rapids, Mich.: Chosen Books, 2007); Heidi Baker with Shara Pradhan, *Compelled by Love: How to Change the World through the Simple Power of Love in Action* (Lake Mary, Fla.: Charisma House, 2008).

6  See Global Awakening, "Trip Reports," http://www.globalawakening.com/Groups/1000013724/Global_Awakening/Global/International/Reports/Reports.aspx (accessed 19 Mar. 2009).

7  Randy Clark, ed., *Power, Holiness, and Evangelism: Rediscovering God's Purity, Power, and Passion for the Lost* (Shippensburg, Pa.: Destiny Image, 1999), xxiv.

8  Personal interview with Clark (23 Sept. 2007).

9  Randy Clark, *Ministry Training Manual* (Mechanicsburg, Pa.: Global Awakening, 2002), M1–42; Pablo Bottari, *Free in Christ: Your Complete Handbook on the Ministry of Deliverance* [Paolo Bottari, Libres en Cristo: La Importancia del Ministerio de Liberación] (Lake Mary, Fla.: Creation House, 2000).

10  Omar Cabrera, *Lo Positivo del "No"* [The Positive of "No"] (Miami, Fla.: Vida, 2002); Carlos Annacondia, *Listen to Me, Satan!* [Oíme Bien, Satanás] (Lake Mary, Fla.: Charisma House, 2008). The Casa de Davi band, for instance, flew to Harrisburg, Pennsylvania, to lead worship and speak at GA's 1,500-person Voice of the Apostles Conference, 5–8 Nov. 2003; the group maintains an English-language website at http://www.casadedavi.com.br/en (accessed 26 Jul. 2010).

11  Randy Clark, sermon, "Benefits of Partnership," delivered to GA team in Imperatriz, Brazil, 24 Sept. 2007; "prophetic words" circulate informally in GA networks via word of mouth, emails, newsletters, and sermons.

12  Prosperity theology has become a popular topic among researchers. See the essays by Bowler, Coleman, Sánchez Walsh, and Gifford in this volume.

13  Clark, "Benefits of Partnership."

14  Randy Clark, *Lighting Fires: Keeping the Spirit of Revival Alive in Your Heart and the Hearts of Others around You* (Lake Mary, Fla.: Creation House, 1998).

15  For a discussion of Mensa Otabil, pastor of Ghana's International Central Gospel Church, see Paul Gifford, "The Complex Provenance of Some Elements of African Pentecostal Theology," in *Between Babel and Pentecost: Transnational Pentecostalism in Africa and Latin America*, ed. André Corten and Ruth Marshall-Fratani (Bloomington: Indiana University Press, 2001), 73. For a treatment of Reinhard Bonnke, a German evangelist who itinerates across Africa, see Marko Kuhn, *Prophetic Christianity in Western Kenya: Political, Cultural and Theological Aspects of African Independent Churches* (Frankfurt am Main, Germany: Lang, 2008), 244; and Marostica's and Währisch-Oblau's essays in this collection. For treatments of David Yonggi Cho, pastor of South Korea's Yoido Full Gospel Church, see Wonsuk Ma, "Asian (Classical) Pentecostal Theology in Context," in *Asian and Pentecostal: The Charismatic Face of Christianity in Asia*, ed. Allan Anderson and Edmond Tang (Costa Mesa, Calif.: Regnum, 2005), 66; Allan Anderson, *An Introduction to Pentecostalism: Global Charismatic Christianity* (Cambridge: Cambridge University Press, 2004), 222; and Kim's essay in this volume. Brazil's Universal Church of the Kingdom of God, under the leadership of Sérgio Von Helder, is discussed by R. Andrew Chesnut, *Born Again in Brazil: The Pentecostal Boom and the Pathogens of Poverty* (New Brunswick, N.J.: Rutgers University Press, 1997), 45; and in Chesnut's essay in this volume. There has been relatively little academic research on Mahesh Chavda, an internationally prominent itinerant evangelist of Indian descent born in Kenya and currently based out of All Nations Church in Fort Mill, South Carolina; Ché Ahn, the Korean American director of Harvest International Ministry, based in Pasadena, California; or David Hogan, a North American who has planted hundreds of churches among indigenous peoples in rural Mexico. All three are discussed in a popular book by John Crowder, *Miracle Workers, Reformers and the New Mystics* (Shippensburg, Pa.: Destiny Image,

2006), 74, 143. For scholarship on Heidi Baker's Iris Ministries, see Donald R. Kantel, "The 'Toronto Blessing' Revival and Its Continuing Impact on Mission in Mozambique" (D.Min. diss., Regent University, 2007). Little has been written on Bill Johnson, a much-in-demand itinerant based out of Bethel Church in Redding, California; the Norwegian Leif Hetland, the founder of Global Mission Awareness, which is active in 22 countries, most influentially Pakistan; or Dennis Balcombe, a U.S. missionary to China and founder of the wide-reaching Revival Chinese Ministries International.

16  Although Protestants have frequently voiced suspicions of pilgrimages as superstitious, the practice has persisted throughout the history of Christianity, and has arguably become more prevalent in the past century; indeed, tourism and pilgrimage serve some of the same purposes, as described by John F. Sears, *Sacred Places: American Tourist Attractions in the Nineteenth Century* (New York: Oxford University Press, 1989), 5–6; David Chidester and Edward T. Linenthal, eds., *American Sacred Space* (Bloomington: Indiana University Press, 1995), 6.

17  See Benedict Anderson's classic *Imagined Communities: Reflections on the Origin and Spread of Nationalism* (London: Verso, 1983).

18  For a theoretical model of "godly love" as a perceived interaction between divine and human love that enlivens benevolence, see Matthew T. Lee and Margaret M. Poloma, *A Sociological Study of the Great Commandment in Pentecostalism: The Practice of Godly Love as Benevolent Service* (Lewiston, N.Y.: Mellen, 2009).

19  See Max Weber's classic essay "The Sociology of Charismatic Authority," in *Max Weber: Essays in Sociology*, ed. and trans. H. H. Gerth and C. Wright Mills (New York: Oxford University Press, 1946).

20  Catherine Bowler, "Searching for Faith on Benny Hinn's Holy Land Tour," paper presented at the American Society of Church History, New York, Jan. 2009.

21  Randy Clark, *God Can Use Little Ole Me: Remarkable Stories of Ordinary Christians* (Shippensburg, Pa.: Revival, 1998).

22  Cf. the greater emphasis on taking personal responsibility for one's own healing in the Word of Faith churches described by Bowler and Sánchez Walsh.

23  See Victor Turner and Edith Turner's classic *Image and Pilgrimage in Christian Culture* (New York: Columbia University Press, 1978); and Catherine Bell, *Ritual Theory, Ritual Practice* (New York: Oxford University Press, 1992).

24  For theories of how the sacred is perceived as intruding into the mundane world, see Mircea Eliade, *The Sacred and the Profane: The Nature of Religion*, trans. Willard R. Trask (San Diego, Calif.: Harcourt Brace, 1987), 20–65; and Chidester and Linenthal, *American Sacred Space*, 10.

25  Lamin Sanneh, "Mission and the Modern Imperative—Retrospect and Prospect: Charting a Course," 301, in *Earthen Vessels: American Evangelicals and Foreign Missions, 1880–1980*, ed. Joel A. Carpenter and Wilbert R. Shenk (Grand Rapids, Mich.: Eerdmans, 1990); John C. Rowe, ed., *Post-Nationalist American Studies* (Berkeley: University of California Press, 2000), 23; Michel Foucault, *The Birth of the Clinic: An Archaeology of Medical Perception*, trans. A. M. Sheridan Smith (New York: Pantheon, 1973), xi.

26  A. F. Droogers, "Globalization and Pentecostal Success," 55, in *Between Babel and Pentecost*, ed. Corten and Marshall-Fratani.

27  Postcolonial theorists have exposed how the imposition of the English language can reinforce relations of dominance, a pattern that can be resisted when

cross-cultural communication is conducted in local languages; Philip Jenkins, *The Next Christendom: the Coming of Global Christianity* (New York: Oxford University Press, 2002), 113.

28  Clark, sermon to Assemblies of God churches in Imperatriz, Brazil, 24 Sept. 2007.

29  Mike Shea, sermon to GAteam in Londrina, Brazil, 11 June 2008; two years later, on June 18, 2010, Shea, an expatriate American with Brazilian citizenship, similarly called members of the group he founded, Casa de Davi, to repentance, publishing a public retraction of claims made by one of his Brazilian co-leaders that were discovered to be false; Shea, "Announcement," http://casadedavi.wordpress.com/announcement/ (accessed June 21, 2010).

30  Pablo Deiros and Pablo Bottari, "Deliverance from Dark Strongholds," in *Power, Holiness, and Evangelism: Rediscovering God's Purity, Power, and Passion for the Lost*, ed. Randy Clark (Shippensburg, Pa.: Destiny Image, 1999), 111.

31  For example, speaking at a conference in St. Louis, Missouri, on 25 Sept. 2003, Bottari denounced U.S. residents' participation in alternative health care.

32  Margaret Poloma, *The Assemblies of God at the Crossroads: Charisma and Institutional Dilemmas* (Knoxville: University of Tennessee Press, 1989), 85, has found in her sociological research that even many U.S. Assemblies of God pastors have "played down the significance of 'deliverance.'" Harvey Cox, *Fire from Heaven: The Rise of Pentecostal Spirituality and the Reshaping of Religion in the Twenty-First Century* (Reading, Mass.: Addison-Wesley, 1995), 109–110, has argued, moreover, that many middle-class pentecostal churches in the United States "have begun to soft-pedal healing, as they become more 'respectable.'"

33  Personal interview with Clark (26 Sept. 2007).

34  Disputes among GAteam members (19 Sept. 2007) and between GAteam members and Brazilian pastors (25 Sept. 2007) over how deliverance should be practiced arose at least twice during a single two-week GAtrip. For the importance and controversial nature of deliverance among Brazilian pentecostals, see André Corten, *Pentecostalism in Brazil: Emotion of the Poor and Theological Romanticism* (New York: St. Martin's, 1999), 35; and Chesnut, *Born Again in Brazil*, 45.

35  Poloma, *Main Street Mystics*, 87, argues that the Toronto Blessing reflects a "democratization of healing practices."

36  Chesnut, *Born Again in Brazil*, 80, 98; see also Chesnut's essay in this volume.

37  John Wimber and Kevin Springer, *Power Healing* (San Francisco, Calif.: Harper and Row, 1987); Bottari, *Libres en Cristo*. To contextualize GA's dissemination of American-authored training materials translated into Portuguese, an estimated 70 percent of evangelical books published in Brazil in 1991 were translations; Paul Freston, "Contours of Latin American Pentecostalism," in *Christianity Reborn: The Global Expansion of Evangelicalism in the Twentieth Century*, ed. Donald M. Lewis (Grand Rapids, Mich.: Eerdmans, 2004), 249.

38  Brazil's IURD has generated particular controversy through its highly dramatized exorcism tactics; Chesnut, *Born Again in Brazil*, 46. See Gifford, "Complex Provenance," 69, for a similar observation that Ghanaian Christians have been more accepting of deliverance teachings when presented by Americans like Derek Prince

rather than by fellow Africans; as Ghanaian sociology professor Max Assimeng aptly put it in an interview with Gifford, 26 May 1995: "Things are Truer if Un-African, so we quote Americans."; see also Max Assimeng, *Salvation, Social Crisis and the Human Condition* (Accra: Ghana University Press, 1995).

39 Randy Clark, *There Is More! Reclaiming the Power of Impartation* (Mechanicsburg, Pa.: Global Awakening, 2006).

40 1 Timothy 4:14–15.

41 For example, two of Clark's associate crusade speakers began as ordinary GA team members, but they quickly became widely known in GA networks after they self-published books about their avowed impartation experiences (and Oates subsequently branched off to form his own ministry): Gary Oates, *Open My Eyes, Lord: A Practical Guide to Angelic Visitations and Heavenly Experiences* (Dallas, Tex.: Open Heaven, 2004); Lucas Sherraden, *When Heaven Opens: Discovering the Power of Divine Encounters* (Stafford, Tex.: Sherraden, 2006). An additional wrinkle to this story is that, by 2009, Sherraden had retired as a conference speaker and pastor and, as announced by a new website, had embarked on a career as a realtor.

42 Trip journal entry by Bill (12 Sept. 2004).

43 See, for example, Chesnut, *Born Again in Brazil*, 86–87; Sidney M. Greenfield, *Pilgrimage, Therapy, and the Relationship between Healing and Imagination*, Discussion Paper no. 82 (Milwaukee: Department of Anthropology, University of Wisconsin, 1989), 20; Corten, *Pentecostalism in Brazil*, 50.

44 Miroslav Volf, "Materiality of Salvation: An Investigation in the Soteriologies of Liberation and Pentecostal Theologies," *Journal of Ecumenical Studies* 26.3 (1989): 447–467.

45 Trip journal entry by Bill (12 Sept. 2004).

46 Personal interview with Dan (26 Sept. 2007).

47 Trip journal entry by Bill (4 June 2009).

48 Trip journal entry by Nick (18 Sept. 2007).

49 Global Awakening posts trip reports and testimonies from international trips at http://www.globalawakening.com/Groups/1000016876/Global_Awakening/Global/International/Testimonies/Testimonies.aspx (accessed 19 Mar. 2009).

50 Candy Gunther Brown, Ph.D., Stephen C. Mory, M.D., Rebecca Williams, MB. BChir., DTM&H, and Michael J. McClymond, Ph.D., "Study of the Therapeutic Effects of Proximal Intercessory Prayer (STEPP) on Auditory and Visual Impairments in Rural Mozambique," *Southern Medical Journal* 103.9 (Sept. 2010): 864–869.

51 See, for instance, Leif Hetland, lecture, Global Awakening School of Healing and Impartation, Toronto, Ontario, 20 Aug. 2005.

52 On the sacralization of space through ritual performances, see Claude Lévi-Strauss, *Structural Anthropology* (Garden City, N.Y.: Doubleday, 1967), 206; Chidester and Linenthal, *American Sacred Space*, 10; and Candy Gunther Brown, "From Tent Meetings and Store-front Healing Rooms to Walmarts and the Internet: Healing Spaces in the United States, the Americas, and the World, 1906–2006," *Church History* (Sept. 2006): 631–647.

53 "GodSquad," http://www.globalawakening.com/Groups/1000035814/Global_Awakening/Global/GFS/godsquadshow_com/godsquadshow_com.aspx (accessed 19 Mar. 2009).

# Afterword

*Candy Gunther Brown*

This volume began by advancing the argument that globalization characteristically heightens the threat of disease, which fuels the growth of religious movements such as pentecostalism that are centrally concerned with healing. Intriguingly, pentecostalism itself might be counted among the aspects of globalization that amplify the risk and perception of contagion by encouraging travel and close physical contact between bodies and by constructing divine healing as even more communicable than disease. The foregoing essays have illuminated local variations, hybridities, and tensions in healing practices, and have made a forceful case for the extent of human suffering and powerlessness experienced by people everywhere and the attractiveness to many of a global religious movement that promises material relief by invoking spiritual resources. This afterword contemplates the future trajectory of pentecostalism, healing practices, and globalization as well as scholarship about them.

The collected essays have both exemplified and qualified the utility of the volume's opening claim that divine healing practices are an essential marker of Pentecostal and Charismatic Christianity as a global phenomenon. The terms healing, pentecostalism, and global-ization are all open-ended, and the chapters have explored various dimensions of their meanings. If healing is to replace glossolalia or prosperity as a litmus test for defining pentecostalism, does the operative definition of healing inevitably become so expansive that it loses its distinctiveness? The essayists have, after all, defined divine healing holistically as embracing not only the cure of physical diseases, but also emotional support, racial reconciliation, economic betterment, and social integration on an individual and sometimes a communal level. Indeed, the historian Amanda Porterfield has elsewhere insightfully described Christianity in general as a "religion of healing."[1] Nor do all of the Christians treated in these essays privilege the terms Pentecostal or Charismatic, let alone embrace both labels, despite large numbers of Catholics and Protestants from a range of denominations sharing a pentecostal emphasis on the ongoing gifts of the Holy Spirit, especially healing. It is also the case that local variations in practice and identity markers such as race, ethnicity, class, language, and nationality often persist amid the homogenization of pentecostal cultures across geographic regions.

Political and economic, as well as religious and cultural, globalization have had both empowering and limiting implications, which have been experienced in multiple ways by diverse pentecostals. Different individuals and groups of pentecostals have, moreover, differently negotiated their stances toward proximate religious and healing traditions such as shamanism, *curanderismo*, hoodoo, spiritualism, Islam, Daoism, Buddhism, Hinduism, and biomedicine. Because of such dissimilarities, in editing this collection it did not make sense to impose total uniformity in the terminology employed by the authors treating divergent contexts; for instance, preferences for the terms deliverance, exorcism, or liberation evoke important differences in emphasis. It seems then that the central contribution of this volume is not to replace one litmus test with another, but rather to call attention to the importance of healing as a crucial category of analysis for investigating the pentecostalization of Christianity in a globalizing world.

Future Directions and Key Terms for Research

This book is not intended to be the final word on its wide-ranging subject matter, but to encourage and help set the agenda for a new program of scholarly inquiry into some of the largest forces of change at work in the world today—each of which is extremely powerful in itself and in combination are reshaping our world in vastly significant ways. Because this is the first book of its kind, it has seemed strategic for most of the essays to put thick descriptions before large theoretical claims. This has seemed particularly important given the emphasis of pentecostals on the specifics of how practices are enacted and narrated. Thus, the descriptive work here, in all of its local complexity and cross-regional variety, lays an essential foundation upon which scholars can build more powerful theoretical frameworks.

The total effect of this body of scholarship is greater than the sum of its parts. By juxtaposing essays focused on diverse regions and cultural groups and written from multiple disciplinary perspectives, the evidence and arguments presented in each chapter inform the others and can be used to develop and test hypotheses. The participation of local communities of pentecostals within global networks of practices and self-understanding heightens the potential applicability of findings for one region to those of another. Although the uniqueness of each local situation must be kept in view, no one regional expression of pentecostal healing can be fully understood without a sense of the larger historical and contemporary contexts in which it has developed. For this reason, the present volume is the first of four books that I am preparing on various aspects of spiritual healing, pentecostalism, and globalization. The other volumes will focus on global divine healing networks; U.S. divine healing and deliverance practices; and the intersections between pentecostal and metaphysical healing traditions.

It is my hope that this book will also provide a resource for other scholars as they, too, build upon this body of knowledge and consider the interconnected themes addressed here in relation to both historical and contemporary subjects, using multiple disciplinary methods. Other scholars might profitably continue to make transregional comparisons, as well as fill in the regional and cultural gaps left by this volume. More work might, for example, be done to illuminate variations in healing practices across the African continent. Even cultural groups that have elsewhere received a great deal of scholarly attention—such as U.S. televangelists and prosperity preachers—might be reread in light of the multidirectional cultural flows and sometimes strikingly different emphases of the pentecostals who populate this volume.

The interconnectedness of the themes of globalization, pentecostalism, and healing has resonated throughout these chapters. None of the three themes, however, is simply defined, and indeed, the regional sweep of these essays illuminates the flexibility with which people understand, confront, and create from their experiences of all three processes in their manifold forms. Indeed, *flexibility* might begin a list of key terms to guide future studies of global pentecostal healing. The flexibility of pentecostals in relating to their surrounding culture is sometimes misidentified with syncretism. The latter term has accreted so many negative, reductive connotations that alternatives such as *hybridity, synthesis, inculturation, contextualization,* and *indigenization* seem better able to capture pentecostals' flexible relationship with culture. As I have argued elsewhere, evangelicals have long sought to transform the world by balancing *presence*, or active engagement, with *purity* from the potentially corrupting influences of culture.[2] And pentecostals, as compared with other evangelicals, seem to have an even more flexible stance toward how this balance might be enacted.

There are several corollaries to the claim that globalization, pentecostalism, and healing are interrelated in powerful ways. First, this body of scholarship encourages researchers in a variety of fields to look for concern for healing—since they are more likely to find it where it exists if they understand healing as an important category of analysis. It is striking, given how much has been written about pentecostalism in recent years, how little of this scholarship goes into any depth about specific healing practices—in part because many scholars have absorbed caricatured images of "faith healing" and "exorcism" as being everywhere essentially similar, and often, moreover, distasteful, fraudulent, or trivial. Likewise, future studies of globalization need to take more seriously the role of religion in general and of pentecostalism in particular as an agent, not merely a by-product, of globalization. Scholars in disciplines outside religious studies could gain analytical traction by considering religious healing as a phenomenon not fully reducible to terms utterly foreign to its participants. The presence of pentecostal communities, moreover, needs to be recognized, not merely as anomalous subcultures, but as significant shapers of the cultural worlds of those outside their movement.

Future studies of pentecostalism might more fully account for the insight that pentecostals construct their identities in global terms. Pentecostals, even more than other evangelicals, envision themselves as members of a church universal that not only unites co-religionists across linguistic, cultural, and national barriers, but also transcends perceived boundaries between earth and heaven—as individuals speak with the "tongues of men and of angels" and envision themselves as pulling down the resources of heaven to heal earthly ills. Temporal, spatial, and ontological barriers dissolve as pentecostals cultivate an immediate, tangible relationship with a god whom they can touch and from whom they feel a personal touch right now. Past experiences (for instance, having once spoken in tongues as initial evidence of Spirit baptism) receive less emphasis for most pentecostals than feeling God's presence now in one's body. Indeed, pentecostals implicitly embrace an epistemology that *feeling is believing*. Not only is there no need to wait for mediation from saints, priests, or mediums, but neither does it seem necessary to await the dissolution of physical bodies as a precondition for an unmediated relationship with God.[3] Material salvation is available to material bodies, as well as souls and spirits. At the same time, pentecostal immediacy is counterbalanced by new, material forms of mediation; rather than seeking only personal intermediaries between humans and God, pentecostal communication with the divine is also mediated by the physicality of human speech, especially as it is amplified by print, radio, television, satellites, and the internet, and by material wealth envisioned as an outward marker—and measure of the increase—of inward faith.

The globalization and spiritualization of pentecostal identity do not utterly submerge other, more material markers of identity, such as race, ethnicity, nationality, language, class, and gender, although the salience of these other modes of self-identification is muted to varying degrees. The effect can sometimes be to minimize the economically, socially, and politically liberating potential of pentecostalism, by subordinating the material causes of oppression and by unduly individualizing systemic social problems and solutions. Yet because pentecostals envision salvation itself in material terms, there is also evidence that pentecostal healing can facilitate social protest, communal empowerment, and human benevolence, thereby accelerating holistic liberation in the here and now. Pentecostalism is very much about meeting the practical, everyday needs of humans living in a material world, rather than postponing the liberating potential of Christianity to an afterlife or to an eventual social and political revolution.

To say that pentecostalism is *practical* in orientation ought not to imply that it is merely utilitarian—any more than recognition of the materiality of pentecostal understandings of salvation should be misread as mere materialism. Such one-to-one correlations miss the central insight that, for pentecostals, the spatial and temporal boundaries between heaven and earth are permeable, and the present world is itself in motion toward a future world. In the enchanted worldview of pentecostalism, material problems such as sicknesses are envisioned as being, at least in part, caused and remedied by spiritual forces and agents. Yet pentecostalism also retains an eschatological expectation that today's partial successes in pulling down heavenly resources build toward a future reality in which, one day, God's ultimate redemptive purposes for all of creation will be totally fulfilled. Thus, material experiences of salvation in the present world do not replace but are thought to provide an anticipatory foretaste, and help to bring about, a *full* salvation that is both material and spiritual. Despite the tendency of theologians and historians of religion to draw sharp distinctions between premillennial and postmillennial visions of the present and future worlds (and of other evangelicals to charge pentecostals with having an "overrealized eschatology" that expects too much of heaven on earth), in pentecostalism the two visions often merge into hope both of a progressive transformation of the present world and of a radical rupture between an imperfect earthly order that is passing away and the apocalyptic coming of the perfected kingdom of God.

The centrality of healing to pentecostal experience, moreover, invites closer consideration of phenomenological, interpretive, and functional parallels and divergences between divine healing practices and other medical and spiritual healing techniques drawn upon by people in particular cultural contexts. I hope to see the development of more nuanced analytical frameworks that move beyond reductive concepts like syncretism or shamanism in exploring people's complex, sometimes simultaneous negotiations with multiple healing systems. Such frameworks might consider how unmet human needs fuel therapeutic experimentation, and also people's propensity for boundary setting or determining which means of meeting needs are or are not legitimate; the ways in which "science" is defined and functions as an authenticating strategy; how much history matters to present practices and the extent to which similar techniques are invested with diverse meanings; what specifically gets appropriated, rejected, or transformed and the degree to which borrowings are self-conscious or unreflective. Because healing is often about much more than the cure of discrete physical ailments, such studies can lead to larger insights about the relationship between religions and culture.

The study of pentecostalism is complicated by the fact that pentecostal cultures are by no means stationary, but mobile and growth-oriented. Because standing still is envisioned as moving backward, pentecostals are always seeking more numerical growth for their movement and more intense experiences of the divine. Although sharing with other evangelicals a concern for missionary expansion, *mobility* may be a more apt term than mission for explaining the distinctiveness of pentecostalism. Pentecostal evangelism characteristically involves more than the proclamation of a message. Pentecostals seek to mobilize the resources of heaven, invoking spiritual *power* to literally and metaphorically move people into experiences of full bodily and spiritual health. Pentecostal bodies are mobile bodies—shaking, falling, growing, and traveling literally and figuratively by means of transportation technologies and communications media. Mobility suggests a multidirectionality of translocal influences, rather than a unitary flow from cultural centers to peripheries. Indeed, more fully recognizing the creative, dynamic innovations and global influences exerted by physically and culturally mobilized pentecostals in the two-thirds world may help to nuance postcolonial theories of missionary legacies.

At the same time that pentecostals are constantly transcending geographic and temporal limitations, their practices and communities are spatially located. Indeed, since pentecostalism is, in a sense, a modern phenomenon, an analogy might be drawn to how the theory of quantum mechanics envisions mobility and spatialization as a wave-particle duality, or as two sides of the same coin. Like particles, individual pentecostals move across space, yet pentecostalizing influences also behave like waves, rippling across groups of pentecostals and their local surroundings. Pentecostals are constantly moving away from, moving toward, and entering into particular places to perform healing practices that in effect sacralize bodies, buildings, and landscapes.[4] Pentecostal healing practices might be understood differently, moreover, in contexts where they represent the only remedy available to impoverished communities in makeshift barrios on the outskirts of town or in rural villages, as compared to being one among many alternatives competing in industrialized cities. Because physical spaces are intrinsically material, the notion of space belongs to the pentecostal narrative of material salvation (and sometimes of "world conquering"). Healing practices can represent breaking free from the spatial constriction of illness, as well as claiming new spaces for pentecostalism. Even as globalizing processes facilitate more rapid conversion to pentecostalism and more translocal interactions among pentecostal communities in defiance of spatial limits, globalization also makes possible the preservation of local cultural islands within more diverse surrounding societies.

Future Directions for Pentecostalism, Healing, and Globalization

Drawing once more upon the language of quantum physics and the Heisenberg uncertainty principle, it seems impossible to pin down both the position and the momentum of pentecostalism simultaneously, and thus to predict exactly what the future holds for the movements assessed by this volume. Yet, the soundings taken by the collected essays provide insight into the probabilities of possible developments. First, there is every indication that globalizing processes will continue to expand exponentially. Both the threat of disease and the fear of disease will likely fuel ongoing interest in spiritual, as well as biomedical, healing, even in industrialized societies. Globalization, as we have seen, breeds both universalizing and fragmenting tendencies, and both trends can be expected to intensify as the potent combination of supernaturalism and democratization together fuel pentecostal expansion. Neither is there any clear indication that the growth of pentecostalism will slow or reverse itself, though other scholars have predicted that retraction will inevitably follow expansion. Although it is true that pentecostalism is expanding most rapidly per capita in much of Latin America, Africa, and Asia, it is also the case, as the analyst Philip Jenkins has elsewhere observed, that overall population growth is also proceeding most rapidly in these regions.[5] It seems correct to suggest that Christians in the global South will increasingly set the agenda for global Christianity. Jenkins has further predicted intensifying clashes between Christians and Muslims as both populations increase in roughly the same areas; although the present volume does not speak directly to this possibility, it does suggest that the nature of such cross-religious encounters may involve healing practices. Up until this point, the numerical growth of pentecostalism in some regions has depended nearly as much or more upon conversion as childbearing. It is yet to be seen whether the routinization of charisma is really inevitable even in contexts where domesticating tendencies are continually counterbalanced by ongoing needs for physical healing and social empowerment.[6]

Finally, it seems possible that this book, alongside future scholarly research, may—in unpredictable ways—play some role in shaping the very developments that it describes. This scholarship may, for instance, encourage global health analysts to reconceptualize the ways in which experiences of disease and healing practices play out in local contexts and across global networks, leading to world health policy changes. Both pentecostals and non-pentecostals may come, more than they have before, to understand pentecostalism as centrally concerned with healing. By contrasting contexts in which pentecostalism has been more or less successful as a strategy for social and political liberation, this

research may also suggest ways to maximize the liberating potential of pentecostal practices—given their pervasiveness, whether or not this seems a welcome fact—while minimizing oppressive tendencies. Although the future
always remains uncertain, what does seem clear is that pentecostalism, healing
practices, and globalization will all play important, indeed increasing, roles in
shaping the twenty-first-century world.

NOTES

1 Amanda Porterfield, *Healing in the History of Christianity* (New York: Oxford
University Press, 2005), 3.

2 Candy Gunther Brown, *The Word in the World: Evangelical Writing, Publishing,
and Reading in America, 1789–1880* (Chapel Hill: University of North Carolina Press,
2004), 1. Evangelicals, invoking the language of biblical passages such as John
17:14–15, have often framed their goal as to be "in the world, but not of the world." See
Mark A. Noll, *American Evangelical Christianity: An Introduction* (Malden, Mass.:
Blackwell, 2000), 2, for a useful definition of evangelicalism as "culturally adaptive
biblical experientialism."

3 Many Christian theologians, interpreting biblical passages such as 1 Corinthians 13 (which also references the "tongues of men and of angels") that "now we see
but a poor reflection as in a mirror; then we shall see face to face" in light of philosophies of mind-body dualism, have emphasized the necessity of "putting away" the old
body (i.e., through death) before an unmediated relationship with God can be realized.

4 This argument is developed more fully in Candy Gunther Brown, "From Tent
Meetings and Store-front Healing Rooms to Walmarts and the Internet: Healing
Spaces in the United States, the Americas, and the World, 1906–2006," *Church
History* (Sept. 2006): 633.

5 Philip Jenkins, *The Next Christendom: The Coming of Global Christianity* (New
York: Oxford University Press, 2002), 3, 13.

6 For the "routinization of charisma," see Max Weber, *The Theory of Social and
Economic Organizations*, trans. A. M. Henderson and Talcott Parsons (New York: Free
Press, 1947), 358–392.

# Index

4695297R00246

Printed in Germany
by Amazon Distribution
GmbH, Leipzig